CHRISTIAN MISSION

The *American Society of Missiology Series,* in collaboration with Orbis Books, seeks to publish scholarly works of high merit and wide interest on numerous aspects of Missiology—the study of mission. Able presentations on new and creative approaches to the practice and understanding of mission will receive close attention.

Previously published in
The American Society of Missiology Series

American Society of Missiology Series, No. 21

CHRISTIAN MISSION

A Case Study Approach

Alan Neely

ORBIS BOOKS

Maryknoll, New York 10545

Second Printing, October 1997

The Catholic Foreign Mission Society of America (Maryknoll) recruits and trains people for overseas missionary service. Through Orbis Books, Maryknoll aims to foster the international dialogue that is essential to mission. The books published, however, reflect the opinions of their authors and are not meant to represent the official position of the society.

Cataloging-in-Publication Data is available from the Library of Congress, Washington, D.C.

ORBIS/ISBN 0-57075-008-4

To Virginia

Sin ti,
no hubiera sido posible

CONTENTS

PART ONE
CONTEXTUALIZATION AND CASE STUDIES

PART TWO
CHRISTIANS AND OTHER FAITHS

PART THREE
CURRENT ISSUES IN CHRISTIAN MISSION

APPENDIXES

LIST OF MAPS

PREFACE TO THE SERIES

The purpose of the American Society of Missiology (ASM) Series is to publish—without regard for disciplinary, national, or denominational boundaries—scholarly works of high quality and wide interest on missiological themes from the entire spectrum of scholarly pursuits relevant to Christian Mission, which is always the focus of books in the Series.

By "mission" is meant the effort to effect passage over the boundary between faith in Jesus Christ and its absence. In this understanding of mission, the basic functions of Christian proclamation, dialogue, witness, service, worship, liberation, and nurture are of special concern. And in that context questions arise, including, How does the transition from one cultural context to another influence the shape and interaction between these dynamic functions, especially in regard to the cultural and religious plurality that comprise the global context of Christian mission?

The promotion of scholarly dialogue among missiologists and among missiologists and scholars in other fields of inquiry may involve the publication of views that some missiologists cannot accept, and with which members of the Editorial Committee do not agree. Manuscripts published in the Series reflect the opinions of their authors and are not understood to represent the position of the American Society of Missiology or of the Editorial Committee. Selection is guided by such criteria as intrinsic worth, readability, and accessibility to a range of interested persons and not merely to experts or specialists.

The ASM Series Editorial Committee
James A. Scherer, Chair
Mary Motte, FMM
Charles Taber

FOREWORD

Alan Neely is well known as a gifted professor of ecumenics and mission at Princeton Theological Seminary. In particular, he is recognized for his effectiveness in using case studies in his teaching. Each year he teaches a seminar at the Overseas Ministries Study Center, and I have observed his case study method with admiration and appreciation for the way in which he engages class participants in intensive dialogue and analysis about incidents and events in the lives of persons in mission.

Some years ago I urged him to prepare a book that could be used as a text in mission courses, to help teachers who are not familiar with the case study approach and also provide cases that could be used in classes. This book is the result, and we are greatly indebted to Dr. Neely for the superb work he has done. The book will encourage and facilitate the use of case studies by teachers, and it will introduce students to an exciting new way of thinking about problems and issues in Christian mission.

Case studies motivate students to think "in context" about difficult and ambiguous situations in mission. There is an element of immediacy about the discussion—"you are there"—that stimulates the dialogue. The student is challenged, as Dr. Neely observes, "to enter into the experience, face the dilemma, and imagine himself or herself as *the* decision-maker."

Because of my special interest in other religions, two of my favorite case studies included here are "Roberto de Nobili" and "What's the Matter, Abdaraman?" The experience of Roberto de Nobili, an Italian Jesuit in Madurai, South India, in the seventeenth century, is a landmark in the history of mission theory and strategy regarding the Christian attitude and approach to people of other faiths—in this case, Hinduism. The principal issue, it seems to me, is: How far can one go in accommodating Christianity to the culture? The case study about Abdaraman, a small Muslim boy in the desert of Algeria, gives a new twist to one of the most profound questions in mission theology—as readers will discover when they peruse the case.

In both these case studies—as in the sixteen other cases in this book—the issues become personal, so the question the reader or student faces is, "What should I do in this situation?"

The publication of this volume opens a window of opportunity in the teaching and study of the Christian mission. The open window offers not only a new view; it also lets in a breath of fresh air that is energizing to every thoughtful Christian.

Gerald H. Anderson
Overseas Ministries Study Center
New Haven, Connecticut

PREFACE

Almost twenty years ago I was introduced to the use of case studies in the teaching of theology. At that time I had been a professor of Philosophy of Religion and Christian Mission for fourteen years, but the opportunity to participate in the Case Study Institute in Cambridge, Massachusetts, opened for me new methods for teaching and learning—not only in the classroom, but also in the parish. Like others of my generation I was fortunate to be exposed to a number of competent and influential teachers, and surely their impact had much to do with my own sense of calling to teach. Because teaching for me was intensely fulfilling, always a challenge, and never routine, I regularly read and discussed with others essays and books on educational theory and teaching methodology, seeking continually to improve my pedagogical skills. During the Case Study Institute, however, my teaching—as well as that of the other participants—was observed and critiqued by experienced case teachers. And though this was alternately encouraging and painful, the net result was, I am convinced, highly beneficial. It became clear to me that students often times have as much to contribute to the learning experience as the professor, and their experience and knowledge are best tapped in situations of structured dialogue. Likewise, when I began to use case studies, I became as concerned with what was happening to the students as I was with the volume of information I wanted to impart.

The truth of course is that until 1977 I taught principally the way I had been taught and employed, by and large, the methods modeled by my teachers. Almost without exception they taught monologically, i.e., they lectured. Students listened, made mental and written notes, read assignments from the textbooks, and memorized everything we could in preparation for examinations. If questions were raised during class sessions, virtually no time was allotted or available to discuss them. When a professor responded, his or her comments were brief and often couched in the form of pronouncements or moralizations. Discussion, if there was any, was short and controlled. Analysis or debate among students took place in the halls, in the dorm rooms, or at meals. That a member of the class—other than the professor—might have something to contribute to the learning process was scarcely considered and never formally acknowledged.

Lectures clearly have a long and noble history, and they have their place in education. But they represent merely one pedagogical device and are not necessarily the best, nor are they the only way to teach and learn. It is my observation that with rare exceptions it is the teacher, not the students, who learns most from the lecture method.

The experience in the Case Study Institute radically altered my philosophy of teaching and motivated me to begin to try to use case studies. But no sooner had I made this decision than I encountered a significant impediment. Few cases in Christian mission were available—as a review of the Index of Case Studies in Christian Mission reveals (see pages 263–295). Even today, after nearly two decades, the number is relatively small. Of course most teachers of mission constantly use "cases" in the form of anecdotes or illustrations from their own and from others' experiences. Doubtless such narratives enliven lectures, but hardly ever are they subjected to reflection and analysis either by the teacher or by the class. Conclusions, if any are reached, are either implicit or they are asserted.

There are of course multiple ways to study and teach mission, even the history of mission. One can, for example, teach mission history by concentrating on the great historical epochs and/or on the missionary work of one's denomination—as is commonly done. One can also study mission history by centering on particular geographical areas such as Asia as a whole, the Indian subcontinent, or North China. One can study mission history by reading and discussing the lives of individual missionaries, or by studying their theologies, ideologies, or methods.

In a sense, case studies utilize all these approaches by selecting incidents in the lives of one or more persons, focusing on their experiences in their historical contexts, identifying the issues involved, and coming to individual and collective conclusions as to what should or what did in fact transpire. Careful analysis—reaching a conclusion and defending it—is the goal of doing a case study, not consensus within the group.

In the following pages, I have selected eighteen cases which illustrate the wide variety of issues missionaries have faced in the past and are still facing today. Some are descriptions of incidents that happened centuries ago, others occurred only a generation or a decade ago, while most are recent. A reader initially may wonder how a quandary faced by a seventeenth-century Italian Jesuit in India, for example, could in any way relate to doing Christian mission today. Similarly, reading about a dilemma faced by a Baptist in Kentucky or a Presbyterian in Kenya may appear to a Roman Catholic as extraneous given the historical, theological, and ecclesiological differences between Protestants and Catholics. Perusal of and reflection on the cases, however, will soon dispel any doubt about their relevance. One does not have to be a mission historian, anthropologist, or theologian to perceive quickly that Roberto de Nobili's questions about Christianity and Hinduism nearly four hundred years ago are not unlike those which Christians confront today whenever they encounter peoples of other cultures and other faiths. Moreover, the thorny issues arising from the clash of faith and politics faced by a Lutheran in Madagascar or a Japanese evangelical in Irian Jaya, are issues that will not go away. Rather than dealing with such momentous concerns abstractly and raising hypothetical questions and attempting to discuss them in a kind of experiential vacuum, case studies force us to confront and analyze concrete, authentic, historical situations. For the case studies of the kind included in this book are not fictitious. Neither have they been embellished nor cropped. Though names of the individuals involved and/or the places in some of the cases have been changed for obvious reasons, nothing else has been altered. These are accounts of actual people, and the incidents are genuine.

In order to put the cases in a broader context and facilitate individual study and group discussions, each case is preceded by an introductory historical or theological essay. Following the case is a sample study guide and a brief bibliography for additional reading.

During the past three or four years—when time for the discussion has been ample—I have selected a biblical passage or two which appeared to me to be related to the case being considered, and I have allocated time either before or following case discussion to talk about the Scriptural text. I am including, therefore, several bibical passages for each case which I have used in the past. All participants were urged to read and think about the suggested passage(s) as a part of their preparation for discussing the case, and the use of Scripture has worked best when someone in the group agreed beforehand to lead a fifteen- or twenty-minute reflection. Time given for these reflections not only involves students in the "teaching," more significantly, it is another means for drawing upon the vast reservoir of experience and knowledge latent in any group. Personally, I prefer to utilize the biblical material to conclude a case study, but using Scripture before, during, or following the discussion of a case study has always proved to be worthwhile.

Because of the widespread use of case studies during the last two decades, many individuals are already acquainted with the method. For others, however, it is a new experience. Without adequate preparation by the teacher and the discussants, case studies can be disconcerting and even intimidating. All, therefore, should read carefully and refer repeatedly to the first chapter, "The Case Study Approach to Teaching and Learning," which describes briefly the history and philosophy of the use of case studies, as well as a step-by-step method for preparing to discuss them. (An abbreviated version, "Cases: What They Are and How to Study Them," is found in the Appendix and can well be used as a handout.) Also included in the appendices is a brief outline of how to write a case and an annotated index of mission case studies currently available.

Several years ago Irwin T. Hyatt, Jr., said, "Understanding other peoples is by common agreement necessary for living in the same world with them."[1] Hyatt was, I believe, absolutely correct. Yet as he also noted, understanding

---

1. *Our Ordered Lives Confess* (Cambridge, MA: Harvard University Press, 1976), ix.

others is never easy nor is it a simple matter, given the disparity of backgrounds, cultures, languages, values, experiences, and perspectives. Difficulties, however formidable they may be, do not release us from trying to
understand others. Especially is this imperative for those of us who propose
to live and work in cross-cultural situations. Case studies, I am convinced,
facilitate our understanding of others, and even more important, they assist
us in understanding ourselves.

It is not possible to acknowledge the vast number of people who have contributed to this work, many of them missionaries whose names for obvious
reasons have been disguised. I must, however, express my profound gratitude
to several colleagues who have read portions of the manuscript and made needed
and helpful suggestions for improvement in the text. Among these are Professors Charles A. Ryerson III of Princeton Theological Seminary and Charles
Kimball of Furman University; Henry N. Smith, Executive Director of the
Tarrant Area Community of Churches in Fort Worth, Texas; Rabbi Melvin J.
Glazer of London, Ontario, and Chandra Shekar Soans of Princeton and Bangalore, India. No less helpful has been Robert Staats-Westover of Princeton
who patiently and skillfully designed and produced the maps which I believe
will aid readers in the use of the case studies.

Alan Neely
Princeton, New Jersey
February 1995.

CHRISTIAN MISSION

PART ONE

CONTEXTUALIZATION
and
CASE STUDIES

WHAT IS A CONTEXT AND WHAT IS CONTEXTUALIZATION?

The Gospel of John begins with a forthright declaration that "the Word" of God—enfleshed in Jesus of Nazareth—was perceived as God's spokesperson and believed by some, but neither recognized nor accepted by others of the people to whom the Word was spoken in Jesus Christ (1:10–11). Despite the fact that "the Word became a human being," a person, a Jewish person, born to Jewish parents in a first-century Jewish setting, who spoke their language and followed the Jewish customs, the contrast and dissonance between who Jesus was and what he said and did was so marked that he was not acceptable to many. Though the gospel was contextualized in Jesus, initially few who followed him were able to transcend their individual contexts and see the universal dimensions of Jesus' life and mission.

From the first attempt to translate the gospel from a Jewish to a non-Jewish setting, a philosophical, theological, and cultural dissonance ensued. The struggle to make the faith that is so closely tied to a Jewish context intelligible to non-Jews represents the core of the New Testament. It is also the essence of mission history.

Though in one sense the Christian faith transcends culture, it can never be communicated nor understood a-culturally. In order to be grasped and passed on, it must be transposed from one context to another whether the transposition is the incarnation into first-century Palestine (John 1:1, 10–14), from a Jewish man to a Samaritan woman (John 4:5–42), from a Jewish fisherman to a Roman military officer (Acts 10), or from a Hellenized Jew to Greek philosophers (Acts 17:16–34). Transposed or not, the gospel will not be understood or accepted by everyone. But unless there is a transposition, it will not be understood or accepted by anyone.

Two conditions appear undeniable and inescapable. First, the gospel is not nor can it be a-historical. If it is to be understood and appropriated, it will have to be rooted in a particular historical context. But as the gospel is never a-historical, neither can it be *a-cultural.* Christians assert that Jesus was a historical person, and being historical, Jesus was chronologically, geographically, religiously, and culturally a first-century Jew. He neither repudiated his humanity nor his Jewishness.

One can despise one's humanity, but one does not cease being human. One can reject one's culture and discard much of it, but in doing so one never becomes non-cultural. One simply sheds aspects of his or her culture and takes up the apparel of another. For every human being or group of human beings is a part of a culture, that is, everyone lives in a *setting* that includes a system of assumptions or "beliefs and practices that are built upon the implicit assumptions that people make about themselves, about the world around them, and about ultimate realities."[1] The "setting" is then the culture which Louis Luzbetak defines as "a design for living, a plan by which society adapts to its physical, social and ideational environment."

> Culture is not just an open-ended way of life. Rather, it is a plan, map, or blueprint for living that is always in the process of formation and adjustment. It is a code for action, for survival, and for success in life.[2]

Thus culture is a "set of norms, standards, notions, and beliefs"; it is "the ideational code *underlying* behavior"; it is a comprehensive plan for living a "purposeful, harmonious, and successful life"; and in many respects, it is "a unique plan" for living.[3]

Physical culture includes food, shelter, clothing, and technological skills. Social culture includes family and community organization, political systems, and laws. Ideational culture refers to knowledge, art, science, philosophy, and religion. A particular culture includes all of these.

As already indicated, whenever and wherever Christianity (or any other faith) is carried from one culture to another, intentionally or not, consciously or not, it is either adapted to that culture or it becomes irrelevant. A contemporary Buddhist scholar, Masao Abe, observes that the religions of the world fall into one of two categories: "missionary religions and nonmissionary religions."[4] Only Buddhism, Christianity, and Islam are indisputably missionary religions. As they spread geographically, they encountered "many different local and national cultures." An interaction followed. At times the result was various levels of cultural conflict, while at other times and places the result was various degrees of cultural mingling. All three religions, however, were successfully missionary because, as Abe notes, they "accommodated themselves to the national cultures in which they found themselves."[5]

Ideally, the accommodation or adaptation was made consciously. This appears to be the case both in early Buddhism and in Christianity as the words of the founders were intentionally translated into more than one language. A number of terms have been employed to identify and describe this adaptation, and though the terms are similar, they are not synonymous. The list includes the following: "accommodation," "adaptation," "indigenization," "inculturation," "autochthonization," and "contextualization." Though sometimes these

---

1. Paul Hiebert, *Anthropological Insights for Missionaries* (Grand Rapids, MI: Baker, 1985), 171.
2. *The Church and Cultures* (Maryknoll, NY: Orbis Books, 1988), 156.
3. Ibid., 156–158.
4. "Buddhism," *Our Religions* (San Francisco: Harper, 1993), 129.
5. Ibid.

words are used as if they were interchangeable or synonyms, when used correctly, each has its own shade of meaning and correct usage.

1. *Accommodation.* Missionary accommodation may be defined as adapting or adjusting one's thinking, vocabulary, and approach to the life of a people in order to narrow the gap between the missionary and that people. It requires distinguishing between what is essential and what is expendable. The latter then is deemphasized, ignored, or jettisoned. What is essential and non-essential is not, however, always a simple matter. Is the use of bread instead of rice cakes, for example, essential to the celebration of the eucharist? Is one or another ritual imperative for anyone professing to be a follower of Christ? Are certain prescribed foods or dress required of all Christians? Discussions of these matters have been going on for centuries and apparently figured prominently in debates in the early church (1 Corinthians 8:1–13; Acts 15:1–29; Mark 1:23–28). How far can one go in adapting Christianity before it ceases to be Christian? This is the issue.

Apparently the earliest recorded statement on the subject of "accommodation" was issued by the Jerusalem Council as described in Acts 15:1–29. A more debatable assertion on the subject, however, was that of Pope Gregory in 601 C.E. and is found in a letter sent to the abbot Mellitus. Evidently the Pope's comments were provoked by a series of questions raised by the missionary Augustine of Canterbury who with his colleagues had arrived in the south of England in 590. Augustine's inquiry revolved around a common question: How should he and his companions regard many of the Saxon customs, their holidays, and their places of worship—all of which appeared to the missionaries to be indisputably pagan. Gregory's response represents a significant bench mark in missionary strategy. He counseled:

> The heathen temples of these people need not be destroyed, only the idols which are to be found in them. . . . If the temples are well built, it is a good idea to detach them from the service of the devil, and to adapt them for the worship of the true God. . . . And since the people are accustomed, when they assemble for sacrifice, to kill many oxen in sacrifice to the devils, it seems reasonable to appoint a festival for the people by way of exchange. The people must learn to slay their cattle not in honour of the devil, but in honour of God and for their own food; when they have eaten and are full, then they must render thanks to the giver of all good things. If we allow them these outward joys, they are more likely to find their way to the true inner joy. . . . It is doubtless impossible to cut off all abuses at once from rough hearts, just as the man who sets out to climb a high mountain does not advance by leaps and bounds, but goes upward step by step and pace by pace.[6]

---

6. The Venerable Bede, *Ecclesiastical History of the English Nation,* Bk 1:30. Cited by Stephen Neill, *A History of Christian Missions* (New York: Penguin Books, 1989), 59.

One of the most dramatic instances of accommodation in Christian history can be found in the approach of the young Jesuit missionary to China, Mateo Ricci (1552–1610), who became convinced that if Christianity was ever to be accepted by the Chinese, it would have to become, as nearly as possible, Chinese. Ricci, therefore, discarded his European dress in favor of a Chinese robe, utilized a common Chinese name for God, *T'ien Chu,* Lord of Heaven, and insisted that the Chinese reverence for ancestors and the ceremonies practiced in their honor were cultural and civic, not religious acts. Roberto de Nobili's more sweeping accommodation in India shortly thereafter incited even more controversy (see case study, pp. 32–50).

As already implied, all Christian missionaries have not followed Pope Gregory's counsel nor Ricci's example, not even all Roman Catholic missionaries. In fact, if one regards either Ricci's or de Nobili's accommodations as representing one extreme, the antithesis may be found in innumerable examples among Roman Catholic and Protestant missioners who have followed what may be called the *eradication* approach, that is, attempting to rid a people of every vestige of what the missionaries regarded as manifestations of paganism. Eradication, many missionaries have insisted, is sanctioned in the Bible. They cite, for example, Elijah's destruction of the altar and priests of Baal (1 Kings 18:20–40) and the burning of their books by the new Christian believers in Ephesus (Acts 19:19–20).

Are there also examples in the Bible of *accommodation?* I believe there are many, such as Jesus' acceptance of the ontological reality of evil spirits (e.g., Mark 9:14–29); his approval of paying taxes to the Roman emperor (Mark 12:13–17); Paul's circumcision of Timothy (Acts 16:1–3; cf. Galatians 5:1–6) and the Apostle's conciliatory words spoken in Athens (Acts 17:22–31).

Any or all of these can be considered when studying the case of Roberto de Nobili. To what degree can the gospel be adapted to another culture, especially to a culture which is philosophically, theologically, and ethically clearly non-Christian?

2. *Indigenization,* from the word "indigenous" (within + L *gignere* to beget, i.e., being born into or a part of a particular place or environment), refers to making something (a thing, action, idea, or value) from one culture native to another culture. "Mexican" food, though once found only in certain areas of the United States, can now be found in New Jersey, North Carolina, and Boston. It has been indigenized.

3. *Autochthonization* is synonymous with the English "indigenization," but in Spanish and Portuguese the word "indigenous" connotes that which is Native American. Thus, the American Indian population is commonly referred to as *la gente indígina,* that is, the indigenous people. Though rare in English, "autochthonous" has a distinct meaning in Spanish and Portuguese.

4. *Acculturation* or *Inculturation* is sometimes regarded as synonymous with "socialization," i.e., the process by which one adapts in an active sense, or is forced to adapt in a passive sense, to another culture. An example is

motivating or requiring people with certain values, beliefs, names, dress, and customs to adopt different values, beliefs, names, dress, and customs.

Recently an article appeared in the *New York Times Magazine* regarding the less than forty people who today live on the tiny island of Pitcairn, a South Pacific atoll made famous by Fletcher Christian and the mutinous crew of the British ship *Bounty.* Pitcairn is located 3,400 miles west of Chile and 1,300 miles SE of Tahiti. In 1887 an itinerant American Seventh Day Adventist missionary came to the island and is reported to have converted all the islanders to Adventism. As a condition of their conversion, the missionary convinced the islanders that their pigs were spiritually unclean, and natives responded by driving the swine over the edge of the cliffs into the ocean. The giant crawfish was also declared to be unclean so that today they are no longer eaten but cut up and used as bait. Likewise, dancing was prohibited as was the importation of any alcoholic beverages or tobacco. The traditional Polynesian feast in which dancing was central and the suckling pig the favorite dish was abolished. "On the Sabbath—celebrated on Saturday—fishing, swimming, cooking and watching videotaped movies are not countenanced." Sabbath reading is limited to the Bible or *Reader's Digest*—"which the Pitcairners regard as a religious publication."[7]

Is this an example of Christianizing the culture of the Pitcairners? Hardly, but in the history of mission these kinds of changes have often been confused with Christianization. Is it then a kind of "socialization," that is, the process by which one learns to live with others and is accepted as a member of that social group? One of course may argue that even though the Pitcairners felt compelled to conform to the missionary's culture rather than his conforming to theirs, this had to happen if they were to become Christians. To be regarded as genuine believers, they had to be "socialized" to Christianity. The fact is, however, the islanders were socialized, that is, forced to conform to the missionary's version of Christianity.[8] Now, after more than a century, it is clear that rather than Christianity's being indigenized into the culture of the Pitcairns, the Pitcairn culture was adapted to a form of American Adventism.[9]

---

7. Dea Birkett, "Fletcher Christian's Children," December 8, 1991, 74 [total article pp. 66–78].

8. See Luzbetak, 182.

9. Cultural practices and habits are evident not only in *what* people eat, but also in the contrasting *ways* in which people eat. In the West, eating with "flatware,"—knives, forks, and spoons—is considered the only proper way to consume most food. Sitting down at a banquet table and eating with one's fingers would be considered uncouth or odd. Children, for example, are taught (read "acculturated") early to eat with a spoon and later with a knife and fork. Yet, even in the West popcorn or peanuts are commonly eaten with one's fingers. In Zambia or India, conversely, it is not considered ill-mannered to eat with one's fingers. Eating with one's fingers from a common bowl is not only acceptable, it is the way most Indians and Zambians eat.

So it was in New Testament days. One can better grasp the import of the story Jesus told about the rich man and Lazarus (Luke 16:19–31) if one understands that

What people eat, how they dress, and what they do for recreation are, of course, aspects of a culture most easily identified and subject to change.

Gustavo Gutierrez makes the point forcefully in his conclusions regarding Bartolomé de Las Casas. Unless the missionary recognizes the intrinsic worth of the people to whom the missionary has gone, "evangelization," Gutierrez insists, can be a guise to subjugate them. "This is precisely what happens," Gutierrez continues, "whenever the gospel is unduly linked to a particular culture," that is, when the missionary eschews what nowadays is called "the inculturation" of Christianity. "The word is new, but the reality is old. For believers it rings of incarnation and of a presence of God that is respectful of the human condition."[10]

5. *Contextualization,* a term first introduced by Shoki Coe of the Theological Education Fund of the World Council of Churches[11] differentiated between indigenization and contextualization as follows:

> Indigenization tends to be used in the sense of responding to the Gospel in terms of a traditional culture. Contextualization, while not ignoring this, takes into account the process of secularism, technology and the struggle for human justice which characterizes the historical moment of nations in the Third World.[12]

Thus contextualization attempts to see a culture not as a static system, but rather a system that is always in the process of change because of stimuli from within and from without. Moreover, it insists that the gospel should never be presented as otherworldly while ignoring the suffering, pain, and injustice within a culture.

What then is a context? Max Stackhouse in an essay written for the Boston Theological Institute asks the question, "How do we know a context when we see one?" He answers by asking other questions, e.g., How big is a context? How long does it last? Who is in it and who is out of it, and how do we know?[13]

Without repeating the intricacies of what Stackhouse says, the following are surely included in those things that determine a context:

---

the rich man ate with his fingers and used the bread to wipe his mouth and fingers. It was this bread that was tossed out for beggars such as Lazarus.

10. *Las Casas. In Search of the Poor of Jesus Christ.* Trans. Robert R. Barr (Maryknoll, NY: Orbis, 1993), 455–456. This is likewise the burden of Aylward Shorter's earlier *African Christian Theology: Adaptation or Inculturation?* (London: Geoffrey Chapman, 1977), and his recent *Toward a Theology of Inculturation* (Maryknoll, NY: Orbis, 1988).

11. "In Search of Renewal in Theological Education," *Theological Education* 9 (Summer 1973): 233–43.

12. Ruy O. Costa, ed., *One Faith, Many Cultures* (Maryknoll, NY: Orbis Books, 1988), xii.

13. "Contextualization, Contextuality, and Contextualism," ibid., 11.

- geography
- language
- ethnicity
- political, economic, and social systems
- class, gender, age
- time frame
- sense of identity
- religion
- values
- history.

Whereas for us in the West, especially historians and philosophers, the time periods designated as the "Middle Ages," "Renaissance," "Reformation," and "Enlightenment" are specific and very significant, these periodizations have no meaning whatsoever for indigenous tribal peoples in the Amazon Valley or for the Maasai in Kenya. Their contexts must be determined by events in their history. What a context is, therefore, depends on the people being considered.

Sometimes we assume that our understanding and application of the Christian message is not only an adequate and correct understanding and application, but the *only* understanding and application. Contextualization is an attempt to communicate the gospel in a way that is faithful to its essence, understandable by those to whom it is presented, and relevant to their lives.

When did the adaptation, indigenization, or contextualization of the gospel begin and how can we describe that context? It surely began well before the end of the first century, and it spread to areas far beyond Palestine. The context into which Jesus was born was primarily Jewish, but not hermetically so. The Romans were there, for example, as well as peoples of other cultures. Judaism, however, was the predominant faith and culture. In fact, Jewish religion and Jewish culture were two sides of the same coin. Judaism was a fiercely monotheistic culture-religion with its own developed traditions, rituals, holy places, and sacred literature. It was patriarchal. It had been impacted by foreigners and foreign cultures, of course, particularly by the Canaanites and the Persians.

Christianity, born in a first-century Jewish context, was inherently Jewish. Social structure, worship practices, values, and theological perspectives were distinctly Jewish. The Apostle Peter's experience in Joppa (Acts 10:9–14) surely reflects the contemporary Jewish attitude toward diet. But what about 1 Corinthians 11:1–10, where the Apostle Paul says that when women "prophesy" or pray in church, they must have their heads covered? Is this a universal value or an example of a particular context? Can the same question be raised about other things Paul is reported to have mandated?

One will look in vain, for example, for a specific biblical basis for opposing slavery. In fact, scriptural endorsement of slavery is easily found (Ephesians 6:5–8; 1 Timothy 5:23, 6:1–2). Yet, does anyone today defend slavery on the authority of the Bible? Why? Reluctance to use the Bible to defend slavery is in part at least the result of cultural influence on our hermeneutics. Several years ago I noted and put in my card file the comments of a European who adjusted his theology to that of an African.

> As to the adjustment of "our" theology to include an understanding of the cultural input of others, I offer this experience. While living in Nigeria I attended a service with a local pastor who always took copious notes on the sermon. One day, noticing that his pen had run dry, I gave him one of mine. He was overwhelmed at the "miracle" of God filling his need at the proper time. He had known his pen was about to give out and had prayed for another. Pens were not easy to come by in his area, and he was certain that God was in this act, as indeed God was. This seemingly common occurrence was a "miracle" for him and needs to be understood in light of his have-not world, and his perception of God providing "all his needs."[14]

To the African pastor, being supplied at the precise moment of his need was a miracle. To deny that it was is to impose one context upon another. Yet, the reverse is also true.

In the last analysis, the gospel needs to be accommodated, acculturated, indigenized, and contextualized to a culture if it is to make more than minimal impact. Any of these efforts can be excessive and compromise the gospel to the point that it is no longer "good news." When this occurs, however, it is often the result of thoughtlessness or naivete. Bernard Joinet tells of a well-meaning missionary priest who, in his attempt to identify with the people to whom he had been sent, called all the people of the village together. He professed his love for them and his determination to be one of them. To dramatize his words and decision to break with his own people, the missionary took out his passport and burned it in front of the shocked onlookers. What was meant as an act of solidarity, however, was not seen that way at all by the villagers. For them he had repudiated his own family and people. He did not, in their minds, know the meaning of love. "He rejects and despises those who gave him life," they said, "who fed and reared him. We can't trust him. He has rejected his father and mother. Perhaps one day he will also reject us whom he calls his brothers!"[15]

FOR FURTHER STUDY

Bosch, David J. *Transforming Mission.* Maryknoll, NY: Orbis, 1991, 420–432; 447–457.
    A helpful discussion of the history, strengths, and weaknesses of contextualization, inculturation, and adaptation.

---

14. However, I failed to note the source of this quotation. I will be grateful if readers of this volume can supply it for proper attribution in a future edition.

15. "I am a Stranger in My Father's House," *African Ecclesiastical Review* 14 (1972): 244–245.

Divarkar, Parmananda R. "The Encounter of the Gospel with Culture." *Zeitschrift für Missionswissenschaft und Religionswissenschaft* 61 (1977):214–220.

A brief historical reflection on the problems of inculturation in which the writer discusses the problems both for the Christian evangelist/missionary and those encountered in the new culture.

Hiebert, Paul G. "Critical Contextualization." *International Bulletin of Missionary Research* 11 (July 1987): 104–112.

A historical summary of how missionaries have responded to the beliefs and practices of the cultures where converts to Christianity were being sought and made. He then discusses the consequences of "noncontextualization" and why contextualization is necessary and why it should be based on sound exegesis of the culture and Scripture.

Kraft, Charles H. *Christianity and Culture: A Study in Dynamic Biblical Theologizing in Cross-Cultural Perspective.* Maryknoll, NY: Orbis, 1981.

The most extensive analysis of the missionary task in the light of the difficulties and challenges of cross-cultural communication available. Kraft defines and describes the "cultural matrix" and then reflects on the implications, especially the meaning of revelation and how the Christian message is shaped by and how it affects a culture.

Luzbetak, Louis J. *The Church and Culture.* Maryknoll, NY: Orbis, 1988.

One of the most recent and competent treatments of the nature of culture, levels of cultural integration, and the processes by which cultures are changed.

Nida, Eugene A. and William D. Reyburn. *Meaning Across Cultures.* Maryknoll, NY: Orbis, 1981.

A brief treatment of what communication means and how the Christian message should be shaped in order to make it meaningful.

Schreiter, Robert J. *Constructing Local Theologies.* Maryknoll, NY: Orbis, 1985.

Defines "local theologies" and describes how they relate to the universal church and Christian tradition. Particularly helpful is Schreiter's analysis of syncretism.

Shorter, Aylward. *African Christian Theology—Adaptation or Inculturation?* London: Geoffrey Chapman, 1977.

———, *Toward a Theology of Inculturation.* Maryknoll, NY: Orbis, 1988.

Two valuable works by a veteran Roman Catholic missionary in East Africa. Included are an analysis of the meeting of Christianity and African traditional religion, Africa's contribution to world theology, and various approaches to African traditional religions. He pleads for an incarnational theology.

Taber, Charles R. "The Limits of Indigenization in Theology." *Missiology* 6 (January 1978):53–79.

The writer goes beyond the issue of missionary adaptation to question whether the church can be contextualized.

———, *The World is Too Much With Us. "Culture in Modern Protestant Missions.* Macon, GA: Mercer University Press, 1991.

Especially helpful in defining "culture" and for tracing the attitudes of missionaries toward cultures, particularly during the nineteenth and twentieth centuries.

Ukpong, Justin. "What is Contextualization?" *Neue Zeitschrift für Missionswissenschaft* 43 (1987): 161–168.

Visser 't Hooft, W. A. "Accommodation—True and False." *Southeast Asia Journal of Theology* 8 (3):5–18.

A provocative discussion of authentic and unauthentic adaption of the gospel, and how one tells the difference.

THE CASE STUDY APPROACH TO TEACHING AND LEARNING

Case studies are not new. The story told to King David by the prophet Nathan (2 Samuel 12:1–14) about the rich man who had many flocks and herds but who, when an unexpected guest arrived, took a poor man's only ewe lamb in order to serve the guest, is a cleverly disguised and skillfully utilized case study. The King, as the prophet expected, entered into the case discussion with passion and indignation.

Likewise Plato's dialogues are examples of case studies in which Socrates engages the youth of Athens in philosophical discussions designed to establish universal truths. The philosopher asks questions and more questions. Whether discovering a point by a process of systematic doubt or by subjecting one's reasoning to group critique, dialectical conversation is still valid, even when a unanimous resolution to a dilemma is not forthcoming.

One does not have to accept the philosopher's assumptions—that all will act appropriately if they have sufficient knowledge and that no one knowingly does wrong—to benefit from examining our perceptions of reality by submitting them to others' questions and judgments.

It would be a mistake to conclude that case studies are therefore best used to entrap the unsuspecting or to expose the ignorance of those who assume themselves to be knowledgeable. In fact, a good case teacher will do neither. Case studies, particularly those in this book, are designed rather to motivate students to study and reflect upon the various aspects of difficult and ambiguous situations and to stimulate them to enter into discussions of those situations. Case discussions thereby draw from the reservoir of pooled knowledge and make possible well-grounded conclusions about the most appropriate course of action.

Case Teaching: A Brief History

The use of the case method is similar though not identical to the analysis of a case history by medical personnel in that it is a means of teaching and learning by the analysis of actual persons and events. Case studies were first utilized in Harvard Law School beginning in 1870 and since that time have been adopted by virtually all the law schools in the United States as a means of preparing fledgling attorneys for work in the real world. Rather than memorizing an unending string of legal principles and theorizing about hypothetical situations, law students are thrust into the analysis of an actual case.

Then from the student's own analysis of the case, he or she is expected to develop a line of argument and make a judgment based on sound rules of law. This method does not disregard the importance of knowing the legal principles, i.e., the law, but it has the advantage of forcing students to apply their knowledge and understanding of the law to actual legal disputes.

Shortly after the turn of the century the Harvard Business School began to utilize cases from the world of commerce as the central feature of its educational approach, and today cases are the exclusive means of teaching. The study of business cases is designed to prepare students—all of whom are post-baccalaureate—for managerial positions by developing in them the skills needed for analyzing complex and controversial situations and making the tough decisions necessary to resolve the conflicts. Real situations are the data used in the writing of the business cases, though at times—in contrast to the legal cases, all of which are a part of the public record—it is necessary to disguise the individuals and companies involved. But the facts are not altered in any way.

In the 1960s a small group of theological teachers initiated a discussion with some of the Harvard Business School professors regarding the possibility of employing case studies to teach theology. Encouraged to pursue the matter, a proposal was made to the Sealantic Fund for a grant sufficient to conduct a series of annual three-week case study institutes to be administered by the Association of Theological Schools. Approval of the grant resulted in seven annual institutes held in Cambridge, Massachusetts, beginning in the summer of 1971. And though most of the grant money was exhausted by 1977, case study institutes have continued each year at various sites: Pasadena, California; Wake Forest, North Carolina; Evanston, Illinois; and Toronto, Canada. Also, hundreds of cases have been written, published, and used in an increasing number of theological schools in the United States and Canada, as well as many other countries. Moreover, hundreds of theological professors, parish pastors, and lay leaders have been trained in the writing and teaching of cases. A large number of books of case studies are currently available together with individual cases, and an annual case study institute is still being conducted under the auspices of the Association for Case Teaching. (For information regarding cases, books, and case study institutes and workshops, see Appendix B.)

What is a Case?

A case is a carefully written description of an actual situation or event fraught with ambiguity in which a person or persons must make a decision based upon the information at hand. It can be a contemporary event or one selected from history. A case study is *always* written from the perspective of one person. It is not a description of an event as seen by various people. The data included are those factors that appear to be significant to the participant through whose eyes the case is written, but enough data are provided to allow the students to understand what has occurred as well as to enter vicariously into the situation. Usually, though not always, a case is left open-ended, that is, the reader is not told what decision was made nor how the issue was resolved. Initially, students want to know "what really happened." Sometimes a case teacher does not know how a case ended, and if he or she does know, it is not necessarily wise to share the information with the class. There are good reasons for not divulging how a case ended. First, simply because a particular decision was made is no indication it was the best decision. Also, students who have argued for a decision other than the one actually made could, if they are told what finally happened, wrongly conclude they were mistaken. The fact that a certain decision was made does not necessarily mean that it was the right decision. Finally, and most importantly, in a case discussion the challenge to the student is to enter into the experience, face the dilemma, and imagine himself or herself as *the* decision-maker, not theorize or try to divine how the person(s) described in the case decided. Thus the question the student faces is, What should I do in this given situation?

Paul Lawrence put it this way:

> A good case is the vehicle by which a chunk of reality is brought into the classroom to be worked over by the class and the instructor. A good case keeps the class discussion grounded upon some of the stubborn facts that must be faced up to in real-life situations. It is the anchor on academic flights of speculation. It is the record of complex situations that must be literally pulled apart and put together again before the situations can be understood. It is the target for the expression of attitudes and ways of thinking brought into the classroom.[1]

In a classroom context, therefore, the effective use of case studies not only demands a well-written and relevant case, but also a skilled case teacher and students who have thoroughly studied the case, researched the issue(s) related to the case, and are prepared and eager to discuss their insights and positions.

How to Study a Case

Initial impressions about cases sometimes lead a student to assume that a single perusal and then "playing it by ear" is all that is required. This may pass for preparation in some settings, but not in a case study discussion. Any experienced case teacher will quickly recognize inadequate preparation by students. After one or two sessions with a class, I always tell my students that if they have to refer repeatedly to the case during the discussion, I know

---

1. "Preparation of Case Material," *The Case Method of Teaching Human Relations and Administration,* ed. Kenneth R. Andrews (Cambridge, MA: Harvard University Press, 1951), 215.

they are not prepared. Also, if they are unable to recall names, dates, facts, and offer supporting information or data, they are not prepared. No more careful and diligent study is required of a student than preparing for the discussion of a case, and faithfully following the suggested steps will not only enable a student to enter the case authentically, but also to look forward to the discussion with excitement and anticipation.

Step 1: Read the Case

Begin by reading the case quickly and getting a feel for what is happening. Note how the case begins. Many case writers condense the story and pose the dilemma in the opening paragraphs. From whose perspective is the case written? Remember that a case describes a difficult problem for which there is no single obvious solution. Also, a case is a description of an actual, not a fictitious or hypothetical situation. Though names and places are sometimes disguised, cases are not embellished nor is the truth altered. A good case is about an issue or problem with which many people can identify. Kierkegaard once said, "There is truth that matters and truth that doesn't matter." A case is about truth that matters, not about secondary, provincial, or unrelated truths.

Step 2: Determine the Cast and the Chronology

Next, re-read the case carefully by immersing yourself into the situation and noting the details of what has happened or is happening. There are different ways of doing this, but I have found that if I am to grasp the intricacies of a situation I must write out the *cast of persons* involved in the case including their names, personal characteristics, roles or responsibilities, statements attributed to them, attitudes and feelings they reveal, relations with others in the case, and their circles of influence. Likewise, I have to chart with care the *chronology* or sequence of events in the case. Decisions almost always are affected by time, and some possibilities are suggested or eliminated according to the chronology or when certain things happened.

These first two steps of preparation will result in two or three pages of notes even for a brief and relatively uncomplicated case. Longer and more complex cases require more copious notes.

Step 3: Identify the Basic Issues

The third step can be compared with an experience in a zoological laboratory. The specimen is chosen, then dissected, and the various parts are identified and related. Then comes the most difficult part, namely, analyzing what you see. In studying a case this means *identifying the basic issue or issues*. Basic issues are those factors in the case which have provoked the crisis or that call for a decision to be made. Usually a class will agree on the most crucial issues, but not always. Whenever there is disagreement, it is the responsibility of the case teacher to enable the group to decide what issue or issues they choose to discuss.

Step 4: List the Possible Alternatives

Once the issues are decided, one should then *list the various alternatives* available to the decision-maker(s). The question, however, is not merely what should one do, but upon identifying the range of options, what is the appropriate decision? If only one decision is indicated or possible, or if everyone in the class agrees that only one option is appropriate, then the case is flawed. A good case will suggest a number of possible decisions about which reasonable people will disagree.

On occasions during the discussion of a case someone will say, "We don't have all the information we need to make a decision." In real life we never have all the information we need, and decisions have to be made on the basis of the information available. Only God is omniscient. Students therefore should assume that the decision-maker in the case is rational and is adequately informed.

The question faced by the student is, however, "What decision do I think is right and why?" In order to decide which option is best, students should examine the likely results of each possible option and be prepared to discuss them.

Step 5: Research Other Materials for Additional Insights

Assume, for example, that the case is related to the issue of missionary colonialism. Go to the library and read what you can find about the definition, history, extent of, reasons for, and objections to colonialism. You will discover there are books, chapters in books, monographs and essays aplenty on the subject of colonialism in general and missionary colonialism in particular. Do not limit your search to books. Investigate in the reader's guides of periodical literature for articles that may have been written on the subject. If you have difficulty, consult the reference librarian and ask for help in locating materials. Not only will this kind of study enlarge your reservoir of knowledge, it will also help to identify and clarify the issue(s) at stake and prepare you to make a well-founded decision and then defend it.

Step 6: Reflect and Meditate on What You Have Discovered

Once you have read the case several times, noted the persons involved and are acquainted with them by name, role, and relationship; charted the chronology, decided on the issues and possible courses of action; and researched the issue or issues in the case, it is time to let the facts of the case and the possibilities suggested ferment in your mind.

Step back mentally and emotionally from the case and casually brood over or ruminate about it. Some people discover it helps to do something physical such as taking a walk, jogging, or working in the flower garden while mulling over the case. Others simply think and make notes. Imagine that you are the person having to make the decision. What is the central, most crucial issue in the case? Allow your mind to make free associations. Have you considered all the possible options? Given the information you have, which is the best option, and why? Remember, no decision is free from risk, and in a case study there is no single right answer.

Whatever decision you reach, be prepared to hear the views of others and, if warranted, change your mind. The goal of a case study is not to win a debate, but to see the nature of the problem and make a decision about a course of action that is possible, reasonable, and ethical.

Step 7: Participate in the Discussion of the Case

For individuals who are extroverts, entering into the discussion of the case will be natural. For others it will be more difficult. One thing an experienced teacher has learned is that some students participate without speaking. But when doing case studies every participant has an obligation to share his or her understanding and insights as well as to listen carefully to what others are saying. To those who readily participate in group discussion, a word of caution is in order. *Avoid dominating the discussion.* Give the more reserved members an opportunity to speak. Encourage them to speak. In other words, be willing to pass the ball and let others score some points.

To those who are by nature reluctant to disclose their thinking and points of view, a word of encouragement is needed. *Speak up. Share your understanding, insights, and conclusions.* Do not hesitate to ask questions. In contrast to the more traditional kind of learning situation, especially the lecture, case studies demand and are enriched by the participation of everyone in the group. One can be mistaken about some fact, name, or date in a case, but other than these, there are no wrong answers. You may be the only person in the group who decides and argues for a particular decision. And in this particular instance, you may be right.

The Role of the Case Teacher

Though a teacher is commonly thought of as one who imparts knowledge and therefore should be a source of enlightenment and a cornucopia of information and insights, a competent teacher has skills that include much more than being a storehouse of data. A good teacher enables a student to know how to do something: to drive, for example, or to think, to reflect on an action or an attitude, to learn to reason and think for oneself. The best teacher is one who is able to act as a catalyst by probing and drawing out from the student what he or she already knows and assisting the student in weaving this knowledge into a pattern of insights for living.

In the teaching of case studies, the teacher is of course responsible to write or select a case which is relevant and applicable to the subject at hand; to be thoroughly familiar with the background and details of the case; and to involve every member of the class in a discussion of the case by probing, recording, and facilitating group analysis and stimulating group thinking or process rather than reproducing the kind of atmosphere and relationship wherein the students look to the professor for *the answer.*

As you become familiar with the case study method of teaching you will observe that learning depends much more on individual study and the interchange between students than it does upon information or facts provided by the professor.

Case studies done well are a *participatory means of learning* whereby the effectiveness of the class session depends upon careful preparation by the participants, teacher and students, and during which time everyone in the class enters into the discussion by sharing his or her knowledge and perspective. Conscientious preparation for the class discussion is not made primarily to ensure a good grade, but rather to be open to learning and to enable others to learn with you.

PART TWO

CHRISTIANS
and
OTHER FAITHS

INTRODUCTION

One of the most significant developments in history is now evident. It began in fact five centuries ago. Prior to the sixteenth century, Christianity was predominantly a European religion, and the other major religions of the world were likewise concentrated in various geographical regions: Hindus in India; Buddhists in East Asia; and Muslims in Africa, the Middle East, and the Indian subcontinent. Though the largest concentrations of adherents of the world's religions are still in the same geographical areas, a worldwide diaspora has taken place during the last half-millennium. First Roman Catholic and later Protestant and Eastern Orthodox missionaries were sent in ever increasing numbers to Africa, Asia, and Latin America. In a matter of four centuries, the Christian faith was evident in virtually every area of the world. Except for Eastern Europe where large populations of Muslims had long resided, Western Europe and North America were during most of this time almost exclusively Christian. Beginning in the 1950s, however, this began to change, and the change has continued unabated. It had begun, largely unnoticed, earlier.

The earliest known Europeans who came to the Americas during the final decade of the fifteenth century were professing Christians, and the indigenous people they found already here were considered non-Christians. Labeled "heathens," "pagans," or worse, the Amerindians were either exterminated, compelled to accept Christian baptism, or enticed by one means or another to espouse the Christian faith. The history of the efforts to evangelize Native Americans is, however, checkered both in terms of the methods employed and their effectiveness.

Beginning in the sixteenth century African Muslims began arriving in the Americas as slaves, and in the nineteenth century Buddhists and Hindus were brought as Chinese and East Indian indentured workers. Admission of Muslims, Buddhists, and Hindus as immigrants has been for the most part limited to the present century. Most of the African slaves and their descendants, at least outwardly, became Christians. Peoples whose religion was neither Christian nor Jewish almost all resided in the major industrial and urban areas and were almost as unnoticed as they were scarce. If they practiced their faith, it was unobtrusively. Until the last half of the twentieth century only a few Muslim mosques or Buddhist and Hindu temples were evident, and they were found almost exclusively in the largest cities such as New York, Chicago, San Francisco, and Los Angeles, not in Charlotte, Davenport, or Oklahoma City.

Children born in the U.S. before 1960 grew up with little or no direct contact with peoples of other faiths. This is one of the reasons Bible reading and prayer in the public schools was routine. Few teachers, administrators, or pupils had any knowledge of the Bhagavad Gita, the Tipitaka of Buddhism, or the Qur'an. The United States was predominantly and in most places overwhelmingly a Jewish-Christian culture. Later, when large numbers of Muslims, Buddhists, and Hindus began arriving as students and immigrants and settling in areas other than the largest cities, change was inevitable and Christians became unsettled and unsure as to how to react. Whereas the presence of practicing Muslims or Hindus was rare or unknown in most communities in the United States a generation ago, it is increasingly common today because of the dramatic difference that has come about during the past three decades.

The change in the religious landscape in the U.S. began almost imperceptibly in the last century. During the past thirty years, however, that is, since the new immigration act of 1965, the momentum of change has increased significantly as immigration patterns of previous generations have altered. Except for Latin Americans and Europeans, not all but more—some would say most—of the immigrants who have come to the United States since 1965 are religiously and culturally Muslims, Buddhists, Hindus, Jains, Sikhs, Zoroastrians, Confucianists, Taoists, and Shintoists. And whereas the issue of religious pluralism was largely academic for most U.S. Christians earlier, the presence of a growing number of peoples of other faiths challenges the heretofore Christian hegemony of the past. Also, direct contact with believing and faithful Hindus, Buddhists, and Muslims is raising for many Christians nagging theological questions about the traditional Christian claim of finality and the uniqueness of Jesus Christ. And though Christianity is still the religious faith boasting the largest plurality of followers in the world, Christianity is being challenged and appears to be no longer the most aggressive missionary religion in the world.

The following cases deal with the encounter of Christians with peoples of other faiths. Though most of these represent experiences missionaries have had in other parts of the world, they serve to introduce the issues Christians now must face in Europe and North America. Though they can of course be read, understood, and discussed with minimal knowledge of Hinduism, Buddhism, Islam, and primal religions, discussions will be greatly enriched if discussants have some basic knowledge of the world's religions.

FOR FURTHER STUDY

Carpenter, Joel A. and Wilbert R. Shenk, eds. *Earthen Vessels. American Evangelicals and Foreign Missions, 1880–1980.* Grand Rapids, MI: William B. Eerdmans, 1990.

Contains a number of valuable essays designed to enable the reader to understand the conflict between theological conservatives, moderates, and liberals in regard to the traditional missionary approach. Especially helpful are James A. Patterson's "The

Loss of a Protestant Missionary Consensus," Carpenter's "Propagating the Faith Once Delivered," Charles E. Van Engen's "A Broadening Vision: Forty Years of Evangelical Theology of Mission," and Grant Wacker's "Second Thoughts on the Great Commission: Liberal Protestants and Foreign Missions, 1890–1940."

Heim, S. Mark. *Is Christ the Only Way?* Valley Forge, PA: Judson Press, 1985.

Written primarily for laypersons, the author focuses on the historic claims of exclusivity and the reality of religious pluralism in the modern world. He evaluates the Christian missionary movement and the various options for responding to people of other faiths.

Knitter, Paul F. *No Other Name?* Maryknoll, NY: Orbis, 1985.

A provocative summary of various ways the issue of religious pluralism is approached—from the conservative evangelical, mainline Protestant, Roman Catholic models to the "theocentric" model of Hick, Panikkar, and Samartha.

Newbigin, Lesslie. "The Gospel and Other Religions." In *Mission Trends No. 5,* ed. Gerald H. Anderson and Thomas F. Stransky, 3–19. New York: Paulist, 1981.

The author, a former missionary and bishop in the Church of South India, describes and appraises how Christians who are committed to Jesus Christ respond when they meet those committed to other faiths. He advocates an approach of witness, not one of condemnation or compromise.

Thomas, M. M. *Risking Christ for Christ's Sake.* Geneva: WCC Publications, 1987.

Analyzes the contemporary challenge of religious pluralism and developments in ecumenical and Catholic thought. Examines in detail the thought of Panikkar and Paul Devanandan.

A LETTER FROM CLAIRE

The pastor of a university church is troubled because a student who has been active in the church has almost ceased to participate. He receives a letter from her in which she discloses the reason for her behavior, namely, she has begun to question the Christian assertion that Jesus is the only way to God and to salvation.

CONTEXT
Is Jesus the Only Way?

One may assume the letter from Claire in this case study could not have been written by a less likely member of the congregation. She had been reared in one of the most conservative churches in her denomination, was quite active in the student Christian group in the university, and was a regular participant in the university church. But contact and friendship with international students from India and the Middle East incited a change in her, and Claire began to ask fundamental questions about her own faith and the traditional claims of Christianity. The letter reflects the transformation that is taking place.

Claire's reaction to inter-cultural and inter-religious encounter, however, is not uncharacteristic of what happens to many Christians who have accepted unquestioningly the assertion that Jesus is the only Savior. They have heard or read the words of Simon Peter when he said,

> "Be it known to you all, and to all the people of Israel, that by the name of Jesus Christ of Nazareth, whom you crucified, whom God raised from death, by him this man is standing before you well. This is the stone which was rejected by you builders, but which has become the head of the corner. And there is salvation in no one else, for there is no other name under heaven given among men by which we must be saved" (Acts 4:10–12).

What the Apostle declares here is not different from what he is reported to have said earlier (Acts 2:17–39 and 3:12–26), but there is one striking exception. He asserts not only that salvation is found in Jesus Christ but *only* in him. Clearly it is the conviction that Jesus is the only Savior of humankind that has motivated the vast majority of Christian missionaries to leave their homes and families, to journey to other places, live among other peoples, and attempt to communicate the gospel to them.

On the other hand, it is the exclusive claim of Christians that Jesus Christ is the final and unique revelation of God to humankind that perplexes and offends most Hindus, Jews, Buddhists, Muslims, and followers of other faiths. Sensitive Christian believers have become increasingly aware of this, and many, like Claire, are confused about what they should think and do. A century or so ago Christians like Claire were, for the most part, ignorant of the religions of Africa and Asia. But as people in the West became more aware of the beliefs of other religions, their sacred literature translated and made available, and the study of comparative religions more widespread, the issues faced by missionaries and questions raised by scholars such as Ernst Tröltsch (1865–1923) and Max Müller (1823–1900) are being considered and discussed not only by university students, but generally among church peoples. How one responds to these issues will determine to a significant degree one's view of the Christian mission.

FOR FURTHER STUDY

See suggestions at the end of the Introduction to Part Two.

THE CASE
A Letter from Claire

"Here's the mail, Dr. Forsythe," the secretary said as she came into the pastor's study. The stack was quite small, Jim Forsythe thought, in comparison with what he usually received—only three letters, some church bulletins, and two catalogs.

He looked at each of the envelopes and noted one he had been hoping to receive from Claire Evans, a fourth-year student at the university. Forsythe had been anxious to hear from Claire since his conversation with her three weeks earlier in the university cafeteria, a chance encounter that occurred the day before she left to go home for summer vacation.

Forsythe opened the letter and read it quickly. "She certainly comes to the point," he said to himself. "I asked her to write and tell me more about how she was feeling and raise any questions she had. Well, she has obliged, and now I will have to respond." Jim laid the letter on the desk and muttered to himself, "Uh, this will not be easy."

The University Congregational Church

Jim Forsythe had been pastor of the University Congregational Church in Bowling Green, Ohio, for eighteen months. A number of factors had led him to accept this pastorate, and one of the principal reasons was the insistence by the Pastor Search Committee that "Bowling Green is truly a mission field . . . as much a mission field," they had said, "as Africa or India."

This had impressed the Forsythes, Jim and his wife, Katie, because they had talked repeatedly for more than five years about whether they should seek appointment as missionaries. Both expressed an interest in investigating the possibility of being foreign missionaries since their time in seminary, even before their marriage nearly thirteen years ago. Moreover, they had been in contact with their denomination's international board of missions for two years prior to coming to Bowling Green. They were now 33 years old, and their oldest child would be twelve in December. Jim and Katie knew that if they were to be accepted as missionaries by the board, they would have to be appointed before their daughter reached the age of thirteen.

The growth of the church numerically, the stimulating atmosphere of a university community, the challenge of working with and preaching to a congregation composed of people from everywhere, especially the large number of university students—many of whom were internationals—had many of the characteristics and challenges of mission work, at least as Jim perceived it. But there was still the unresolved question of foreign missions, and Jim had found himself thinking more about it now than he had earlier in his career.

Originally from Kentucky, Jim had done his undergraduate university study at Vanderbilt where he graduated with a B.A. in English literature and a minor in American history. Even before his senior year he had struggled with the question of where to attend seminary. His father had died during Jim's last year at Vanderbilt, so it seemed logical for him to return to Louisville, live in his mother's home, and attend Louisville Presbyterian Seminary. Thus, after some deliberation, this is what he did. It was at the seminary that he met and married Katie, and when she graduated, she was able to work and allow him to continue beyond the M.Div. program. Two more years were spent at the seminary, and Jim completed his residency for the Th.D. degree. University Congregational Church was his second pastorate, although he had served as an associate pastor during his time in seminary.

Claire Evans from Ashland, Kentucky

Claire Evans was one of a dozen students whom Jim had met when he came to talk with the Pastor Search Committee. A small reception had been arranged to allow the student leaders in the church to meet and talk with the prospective pastor.

Jim had been impressed with the whole group, but especially with Claire for several reasons: her cultural and church involvement, her beauty, and her winsome personality. Then after coming to Bowling Green, he had learned even more about her. Her home was in Ashland, Kentucky, where she had been reared in a large fundamentalist congregation.

Claire had spent her sophomore college year in France, and this had delayed her finishing the university in four years. But she was now fluent in French and Spanish and was intensely interested in world issues. She was an active participant not only in the University Church, but also in the InterVarsity Fellowship on campus. Even more significant, Jim thought, Claire sought and made more friends among the international students than anyone else he knew, except possibly Bill Taylor whose father was an agricultural expert with the U.S. Agency for International Development. Bill had spent part of his childhood and youth in the Philippines and India, and like Claire, he had many friends among the international students.

Hardly a Sunday passed that Claire did not bring one or more international students to worship, young men and women from various countries in the world. Her friendship with the male internationals did not appear to Jim to be romantic, but rather a desire to associate with and learn as much about other people and cultures as she could.

As the months passed, however, Jim noted that Claire seemed to be spending more time with the students from India, many of whom were Hindus and Muslims, than with the Latin Americans, Africans, or Europeans. One reason, Jim conjectured, was that there were many more students from India in the university than from other areas of the world.

Claire's cosmopolitanism was unusual, Jim thought, especially in view of her provincial childhood and youth. It was possible that Claire regarded the non-Christian internationals with whom she associated as potential converts, except for the fact that she gave little or no appearance of trying or wanting to evangelize them.

This was somewhat out of character, Jim felt, for one whose theological formation as a child and adolescent had been in a well-known fundamentalist congregation. And the apparent incongruity had prompted Jim at two different times to ask Claire about her experience in the Ashland church. But she had shrugged, smiled or laughed, and said something to the effect, "Oh, you know our pastor. I enjoyed the church when I was younger, and when I am home I attend because my mother and dad are there, but I probably would go somewhere else if I had my choice."

The fact was Jim did not know the pastor of Claire's home church except by reputation, and around the seminary his reputation had been that of a "fire-breathing fundamentalist." Jim sensed, however, that Claire was not comfortable talking about her former pastor and church experience, so he did not press the issue.

Claire's Encounter with Other Faiths

Shortly after the first of the year, Jim noted Claire's attendance in church had become spasmodic, and he said to her, at least on two occasions as she was leaving the morning worship, that he had missed seeing her. Also, when she came to church, she rarely came with anyone else.

Following the Easter break which was early in April, Jim remembered seeing Claire only once in worship. During final examination week at the university, he saw her in the university cafeteria. He spoke to her and told her jovially that he had "been wondering about her." She appeared to appreciate his stopping to speak to her and apparently did not resent his comment regarding her absence from worship.

She replied saying that she had been "doing a lot of thinking" and would like to talk with him when she came back to school in September. She said that she could not talk that day because she had an exam within the hour. But she said enough to indicate she was questioning some of the theological assumptions she had long held, especially the relationship of Christianity to the world religions. The only specific thing Claire said—which gave Jim a clue to what she was thinking—was a reference to the inclusiveness of Hinduism and the exclusiveness of Christianity.

He said, "Claire, I know we don't have time to discuss this now, but I would be glad to correspond with you about it while you are away for the summer. Why don't you write to me and spell out in more detail what you are thinking, the questions you have, and I will respond. This will give us a good basis for continuing our conversation when you return in September."

Claire said she would think about it and would try to write a letter as soon as she got settled at home. Jim, however, wondered if she would write, and he was especially anxious about her being in a fundamentalist church during the summer. Would this confuse her more?

Claire's Letter

The first weeks after the close of the spring semester were always a letdown for Jim. Attendance in worship services as well as participation in other church activities were less than half of what they were when the university was in session. Things would pick up, and new people would be arriving for the summer term, but in the meantime, Jim was having a "real downer."

He had thought of Claire several times since their last conversation, and as the days passed he became increasingly dubious that he would hear from her. When he saw that one of the letters the secretary had handed to him was from Claire, he opened it with a sense of relief and with a degree of apprehension.

The letter was handwritten and relatively brief:

Dear Dr. Forsythe,

It was thoughtful of you to stop and talk with me the day before I left school, and I appreciate your asking me to write to you.

I suppose I began to question what I believe after repeatedly hearing Christians say "Jesus is the only way." Is Jesus the only way? If He is, then why hasn't God revealed things in a like manner to all people who have earnestly sought to know and carry out His will? Why do they not have the same convictions about Christ that Christians have?

The founders of other religions and people like Gandhi surely must have had a strong conviction that what they were doing was the will of God. Why didn't the Lord straighten them out if they were so wrong?

When Christ said that only through Him could we come to know the Father, could He have meant through living a life like Christ without actually knowing him personally?

These are a lot of questions, I know, but they represent what I have been thinking. If you have time to write, I will be pleased. But I know you are busy, and this can wait until I get back to school.

I am glad to be home for the summer, and I am enjoying the change of pace. Haven't got a job yet, but I'm looking.

> Sincerely,
> [Signed] Claire Evans

Claire's letter did in fact pose a lot of questions, Jim thought. Yet his initial reaction was that she was raising only one question, and that question, he said to himself, is "Why isn't one religion as good as another?"

"Well, I can't answer this today, but I'll try to come up with something tomorrow." So he slipped the letter into the middle drawer of his desk and left to make some hospital calls.

STUDY QUESTIONS

Have you ever asked yourself the questions Claire poses in her letter? If so, you should find this case provocative.

1. Who are the principal characters in the case? What do you remember about them that you believe is significant?

2. Why is Jim Forsythe concerned about Claire?

3. Can you outline the sequence of events described in the case?

4. How old are the Forsythes? Why is this important?

5. When was Claire's letter written? What did she say in the letter?

6. What do you see as the basic issue(s) in the case?

7. Jim reduces Claire's letter to a single question. Do you agree with him?

SUGGESTED BIBLICAL TEXTS FOR REFLECTION

Genesis 12:1–3. God's commission and promise to Abraham.

Matthew 12:15–21. God's chosen servant.

Matthew 13:47–50. Parable of the net.

John 10:7–16. Jesus the Good Shepherd.

Acts 4:1–12. Peter and John before the Council.

ROBERTO DE NOBILI

A Case Study in Accommodation

Nearly four centuries ago, in 1606, a young Italian Jesuit, Roberto de Nobili, was sent to an inland town in Southeast India. Within two years he was convinced that the only way to influence and evangelize high caste Hindus was by accommodating Christianity to the culture. De Nobili's philosophy and his methods incited a storm of protest and provoke widely differing opinions today. How far can one adapt the Christian faith and it still be Christian?

CONTEXT
Hinduism and Christianity

In Part One "accommodation" was defined as adapting or adjusting one's thinking and approach in order to narrow the gap between the people of one culture and another.[1] Though there are examples of accommodation in the New Testament (e.g., Acts 15:6–29), the most celebrated instance occurred when Pope Gregory advised the missionary Augustine of Canterbury to consecrate the Saxon days, practices, and holy places to Christianity.[2] The Pope advised Augustine to adapt the heathen temples to Christian use, convert the pagan celebrations into Christian festivals, and patiently turn the hearts of the people toward God. "It is doubtless impossible," Gregory noted, "to cut off all abuses at once from rough hearts, just as the man who sets out to climb a high mountain does not advance by leaps and bounds, but goes upward step by step and pace by pace."[3]

Some missionaries, such as Mateo Ricci in China and Roberto de Nobili in India, followed this counsel. Others, however, either were unaware of what Gregory had said or they ignored it. A number of missionaries have followed what may be described as the *eradication* approach, that is, purging a culture

---

1. See above, pp. 5–6.

2. Ibid.

3. The Venerable Bede, *Ecclesiastical History of the English Nation,* Bk 1:30. Cited by Stephen Neill, *A History of Christian Missions* (New York: Penguin Books, 1986), 59. See the text of Gregory's letter, p. 5, above.

as thoroughly as possible of every belief and practice that is regarded as non-Christian. Prohibiting visible practices is, however, much easier than changing hearts—as Gregory recognized. The case of Roberto de Nobili readily lends itself to focusing on the question, To what degree can the Gospel be adapted to another culture, especially to a culture which is philosophically, theologically, and ethically distinct from the Christian faith?

Indian History and Hinduism

Indian history can be traced back at least five thousand years to 2,500 B.C.E., the era when a remarkable civilization began to develop and flourish in the Indus Valley, the northwest part of the country of present-day Pakistan. At the time India was populated by the bronze-skinned Dravidians and by the darker-skinned descendants of the Negritos and Austrics, the earliest settlers. Precisely when the Dravidians began migrating into India is not known. Approximately a millennium later, c. 1,500 B.C.E., light-skinned bands of shepherd warriors who called themselves "Aryans" (a Sanskrit word meaning "noblemen" or "lords of the land") began migrating into the Indus Valley, probably from central Asia, and soon began to spread out in several directions. It is generally believed they were not welcomed by the Dravidians, and a protracted conflict ensued. Some insist the story of the Aryan invasion and conquest is celebrated in the famous Hindu classic, the *Ramayana,* an epic poem of incredible beauty and length.

From the time of the Dravidians until the arrival of the Portuguese in 1498 and the early 1500s, the Indian civilization, including religious traditions, assumed the basic character it reflects today. The triumph of Sanskrit as the language of Indian nobility, the social structure built around a complex system of caste, and the religious philosophy and theology later known as Hinduism developed. Invasions were frequent—including that of Alexander the Great in 326–5 B.C.E.—and challenges from Buddhism, Jainism, and Islam threatened the cohesiveness of Indian civilization, but none of these developments was able to displace Indo-Aryan culture and religious views and customs, which included a wide array of gods, beliefs, peoples, and practices.

Several misconceptions about Indian religion need to be corrected. First, the word "Hinduism" is of recent European origin, appearing first in the early nineteenth century.[4] Second, its use can be misleading if one assumes that it refers to a cohesive set of doctrines and religious practices. A contemporary

---

4. At the beginning of the century, the Reverend William Tennant published a work on Indian history and customs in which he mentioned what he called "the Hindoo system," and a reference to the "goodly habits and observances of Hindooism" appeared in a Bengali-English grammar published in 1829. "Yet it was not until the inexpensive handbook *Hinduism* was published by the Society for Promoting Christian Knowledge in 1877 that the term came into general English usage." John Stratton Hawley, "Naming Hinduism," *The Wilson Quarterly* 15 (Summer 1991):20–21.

authority on Hinduism, Arvind Sharma, professor of comparative religion at McGill University, suggests there are "as many Hinduisms" as there are Hindus, for the primary characteristic of Hinduism is its inclusiveness and ability to assimilate an extraordinarily wide variety of beliefs. "Hindus choose the gods they worship," says Sharma.

> For instance, some might choose to worship god as male, some as female. Hindu polytheism is an expression of Hindu pluralism. But although there may be as many Hinduisms as there are Hindus, there is only one Reality. Reality has many names and faces, but it is one.[5]

Sharma also contends that military and political defeat has had much to do with the shaping of Hindu religious views, defeat at the hands of Muslim invaders in the eleventh century and by the British eight centuries later. Though a missionary form of Christianity was introduced in India after the arrival of the Portuguese, a more formidable challenge was presented by the victory of the British who, once firmly in control, not only permitted missionary activity, they encouraged it. The net result, however, was "the consolidation of Hindu identity in an unprecedented manner."[6] The liberation of India in 1947, followed by the creation of Pakistan as a separate Muslim country, probably did more to cause Indians "to think of themselves as Hindus."[7]

One can hardly overestimate, however, the impact of Islam on the Indian religious scene as wave after wave of Muslim invaders swept across the subcontinent in the eighth, eleventh, fourteenth, and sixteenth centuries. Their military skill enabled Turkish Muslims to subdue much of the land, and by the end of the twelfth century they had established political hegemony and cultural dominance, especially in the northern areas of the country. By the time the Europeans arrived—and they too came in increasing numbers beginning in the fifteenth century—Mogul preeminence had begun to wane. Millions of Indians, however, remained firmly committed to Islam, particularly in the areas now known as Bangladesh and Pakistan.

During the sixteenth and seventeenth centuries, Portuguese, Dutch, French, and English all sought to gain control of the country and its people, and it was in the midst of this colonial struggle between rival European powers that Roberto de Nobili arrived in southern India.

Though the Indian subcontinent is unified in many ways, its divisions and diversity can be traced back at least to the time of the Aryan invasions, if not earlier. And even though Bangladesh and Pakistan, predominantly Muslim, are now separate nation states, India still reflects a dizzying mosaic of competing and often conflicting customs, languages, and religious traditions.

---

5. "Hinduism," *Our Religions,* ed. Arvind Sharma (San Francisco: Harper, 1993), 57–58.

6. Ibid., 51.

7. Hawley, 23.

Hindu Religious Tradition

To understand the intricacies of this case, one needs a basic knowledge of the predominant Indian religious tradition known as "Hinduism." It is believed that the Muslim invaders were the first to give the name "Hindu" to the people who lived in the geographical area of present-day Pakistan and India.[8] " 'Hindu' therefore designated not a religion but a geographical attribute of all non-Muslim peoples south and east of the Indus River: that is, in 'Hindustan.' "[9] Etymologically, the word "Hindu" means "Indian." Foreigners, therefore, beginning possibly with the Muslims, designated the Indo-Aryans as "Hindus." This was not a name the Indians chose for themselves, nor did it necessarily have religious connotations until much later. For the Indians, however, their religious beliefs and rituals apparently had no name as such. Their "religious practices" were simply a part of the routine aspects of their daily lives. Today, Hindus refer to their religious beliefs as the "*sanatana dharma*," or the "eternal teaching" or "law."

Hinduism has no known founder nor are there creeds or prophets as such. Unlike Christianity, Hinduism lacks institutional structures. The emphasis, or so it is said by Hindus, is on the way one lives, not on the way one thinks. Central, however, is the reverence for life. All of nature is regarded as living and is therefore sacred. Particularly revered are rivers such as the Ganges, the most sacred. Likewise, Hindus stress a reverence for the land or "Mother India," its culture, and its social system.

Like all world religions, certain doctrinal ideas can be discerned in Hinduism. Yet, they are often vague and contradictory. There are rites and liturgies, as well as recognized holy places and holy people. Hinduism also has its sacred scriptures generically referred to as the *Vedas*. They include the ancient *Rig-Veda*, an Aryan collection of hymns, prayers, and liturgical formulas; the *Upanishads*, philosophical treatises designed to establish and preserve the Vedic heritage (and some believe to counter the spread of Buddhism and Jainism); and the extensive epic verses of the *Ramayana* and the *Mahabharata*, the latter containing the *Bhagavad Gita* which literally means the "song of the Blessed One," a long epic poem usually dated c. 200 B.C.E.

Though Hindus do not agree concerning which of these texts represents the highest form of divine revelation, all are regarded as sacred, and they are read and treated with deepest reverence and respect. Until modern times, foreigners and people of lower castes were not even allowed to see, much less own copies of Hindu scriptures. Today, however, they are readily available in Sanskrit editions as well as in multiple translations. For non-Hindus, especially western scholars, these ancient texts are viewed as the true classics

---

8. This may or may not be the case, for the Greeks had not only the word *hindoi* but also political representatives in India as early as the second century BCE. See ibid, 22, and Sharma, 49.

9. Hawley, 26.

of Indian literature, but to Hindus they are much more. They are divine revelation. They embody a vast collection of songs, poems, philosophy, and cultic instructions. Hinduism itself is, according to its adherents, a vast, complex, and comprehensive quest for truth. Intentionally, Hinduism would encompass all truth from any source and include everything and everybody. While Buddhism and Jainism, as does traditional Christianity, emphasize a single way to salvation, the *Bhagavad Gita* explicitly asserts there are many paths to ultimate truth and reality. Jawaharlal Nehru once wrote:

> Hinduism as a faith is vague, amorphous, many-sided, all things to all men. It is hardly possible to define it, or indeed to say precisely whether it is a religion or not, in the usual sense of the word. In its present form, as well as in the past, it embraces many beliefs and practices, from the highest to the lowest, often opposed to or contradicting each other. Its essential spirit seems to be to live and let live.[10]

In a sense, then, Hinduism may be described as one faith and as many faiths. Most Indians, but not all, are theists. Some, because of their reverence for life, are vegetarians, while others offer animal sacrifices. Some revere Shiva, others Vishnu or an incarnation (*avatar*) such as Krishna or Rama. Hinduism is therefore a kind of religious umbrella under which a large number of religious ideas are accepted. Ideally, it is a way or philosophy of life that theoretically is prepared to embrace all religions and all religious people. The late and highly respected philosopher and one-time president of India, Sarvepalli Radhakrishnan, often stressed the inclusiveness of Hinduism, saying it is neither dogmatic nor sectarian. Since all religious roads ultimately lead to the same God, he declared, religious people "should not quarrel about the road one should take." Unfortunately, however, neither Nehru's nor Radhakrishnan's tolerance is necessarily reflected in the day-to-day relations of the Indian people. There are today hundreds of Hindu sects, and not infrequently do they manifest a spirited intolerance for each other as well as for non-Hindus.

Given its professed tolerance and openness, how can one explain the central social (some would say "religious") pillar of Hinduism, namely, the system of caste? The term "caste" (from the Latin *castus,* "pure" or "chaste") is not a Hindu word. Its origin apparently can be traced to the Portuguese for whom the word *casta* meant "race" or "lineage" and who designated the Indian societal arrangement as a system of *castas.* Subsequently, the Portuguese word "casta" was transliterated into English and is now employed to refer to other forms of social stratification, even those outside India. Some observers insist that the caste system in India is a social, not a religious institution. This may well be true, and all religion should be judged by its highest

---

10. *The Discovery of India.* Meridian Press, 1946, p. 52. Cited by A. C. Bouquet. *Hinduism.* London: Hutchinson's University Library, 1948, p. 10.

standards, not by its inconsistencies or perfidious followers. Yet, it can hardly be denied that the concept of caste has been used in India to legitimize discrimination and oppression and rigidly enforced social and religious differentiations by claiming that caste was a part of the original creation, and separation by castes represents the most logical and workable organization of society.

The Hindi word for caste is "varna," literally "color," though it can also mean "group."[11] Possibly, the basis of the caste system—which may have originated with the earliest Dravidians to separate them from the darker Negrito and Australoid inhabitants of ancient India—was the color of one's skin. This is not, however, the basis of contemporary caste distinctions. Today, the explanation is much more intricate.

Broadly speaking there are five groupings in Hindu society, hierarchical divisions which, it should be noted, neither time, education, constitutional law, nor competing religions including Christianity have effectively proscribed. They are: *Brahmins*[12] (custodians of the sacred texts and rites), *Kshatriyas* (defenders or warriors), *Vaisyas* (early land owners and later merchants), *Sudras* (serfs or workers of the land, servants, and occasional artisans), and *Pariahs* (outsiders or non-caste people who today are euphemistically referred to as "Dalits").

No person chooses her or his caste, nor is it possible (theoretically) to change caste. One is born into his or her caste according to the immutable law of *karma* or actions. The more *karma* one accumulates, the less one will have to atone for past sins in one's next incarnation, and the higher the caste into which one will be born. The idea is extremely complicated, but in a word one accumulates good *karma* by living according to the rules of caste. The end of life and liberation from the unavoidable cycle of rebirths is *moksha* (salvation as it is sometimes translated) or final liberation into the ultimate reality, the Brahman.

Astute observers of the Indian scene, however, stress the fact that caste distinctions are not only illegal in India today, but they are disregarded in many of the modern Hindu sects, especially in the Bhakti or devotional movements.[13]

Jatis are exclusive in membership (one is born into them and cannot change) and inclusive in worship (a father and son can worship separate

---

11. My colleague Charles A. Ryerson says that *varna* means class, not caste for which the Hindus use the word *jati,* into which one is born and from which one can never change. "Christian Presence in Hinduism," a soon-to-be-published essay, 6, 10.

12. One should be careful to distinguish between "Brahmin," one of the Brahmana caste and "Brahma(n)," the divine absolute in Hindu philosophy and religion, i.e., God. "Brahmanic" signifies not God-like, but those aspects of Hindu religion derived from early Indo-Aryan traditions.

13. This has been emphasized particularly by Ryerson, a historian of religions and recognized authority on modern Hinduism.

particular deities). The sect is inclusive in membership (anyone from any *jati* can usually join) but exclusive in worship. At the center of the *jati* system is the Brahmin priest; at the center of *bhakti* is the *guru* who has gained freedom from the *dharmic* system. Most Hindus belong to a sect as well as to a *jati* and so participate in both *bhakti* and *dharma*.[14]

Moreover, in Bali—and perhaps in other places outside India—one's caste is determined by one's occupation or profession. "A businessman is a vais'ya, a teacher a brahmin, an employee a sudra, and so on. No inferior or superior status is attached, and if one switches profession—say from teacher to shopkeeper—one changes caste from brahmin to vais'ya."[15]

For millennia, only a brahmin could be regarded as a *priest,* though this is not necessarily the case today. On the other hand, a brahmin could not attract disciples as a Shadu or a Swami—a saint or spiritual leader—unless he manifested the gifts of sainthood and spiritual leadership.

Like any vital religious system, Hinduism today is constantly changing. Who would have thought a generation or two ago that great numbers of Hindus in India today would insist their religion is a single system of beliefs and therefore a separate legal entity? Moreover, who would have predicted that in 1989 a group of fanatics claiming to be Hindus—who traditionally have been prideful of their tolerance and inclusivity—would destroy the sixteenth-century mosque in Ayodhya? The Hinduism of future India, therefore, may not resemble in every respect the Hinduism of the past. The mixing of fervid nationalism and religious passion could well produce an Indian Hinduism that is neither tolerant nor inclusive.

An immense number of resources on Hinduism are available, and students are encouraged to investigate further the ever-expanding reservoir of materials, a small sampling of which is included in the "For Further Study" section of this discussion.

Christianity in India

No one can be certain about the time Christianity first arrived in the subcontinent. According to a third-century Christian document, the *Acts of Thomas,* the Apostle Thomas was missioned to India by Jesus Christ. A contemporary branch of Christianity is represented in the St Thomas Christians in Kerala, some of whom are Roman Catholics, others Jacobite or Orthodox Christians, and a third group known as the Mar Thoma (Syriac for "St Thomas") Church. A fourth group of St Thomas Christians became Protestants—principally Anglicans—during the nineteenth century and are now a part of the Church of South India formed in 1947. These are the principal branches of the St Thomas Christians, all of whom maintain that

---

14. Ryerson, 133–34.
15. *Hinduism Today* 14 (December 1992):26. Cited by Sharma, 25.

their heritage can indeed be traced back to Saint Thomas the Apostle who according to tradition arrived in India in C.E. 52, settled in Kerala in the extreme southwest part of the country, converted thousands of Indians to the faith, and was martyred there about C.E. 68.[16] Today, it should be noted, scholars are somewhat more reluctant to dismiss the long-standing claim. Moreover, vestiges of Christianity can be found in India in the earliest centuries of the common era.[17]

Nestorian missionaries also visited India early in the Christian era, and Orthodox Christianity is believed to have been established by C.E. 200. Marco Polo's assertion that he too passed through the land may not be, as was once believed, without foundation. Evidently, however, the first missionary representative of the Western Church to visit India was the Franciscan John of Monte Corvino who on his way to China stopped in Malabar in 1291–92 and supposedly baptized one hundred converts in the city of Madras. Some Roman Catholic historians claim that John was followed by other Franciscan and Dominican missionaries in the fourteenth century, but this cannot be verified. What is certain is that in 1500 the Portuguese explorer Pedro Alvares Cabral (who, while sailing for the Indies, was blown off course and accidentally touched the coast of Brazil and claimed it for his king) was accompanied by a small group of Franciscans who were followed in 1503 by five Dominicans.

---

16. Historians do not agree on the validity of this ancient tradition. It should be recognized, nonetheless, that the once prevailing dubiousness has been shaken by later archeological and historical study. Even those who question the tradition "admit that there is no intrinsic improbability in it, judging from the frequent communications between Kerala (the Malabar Coast, as it was then called) and the shores of the Mediterranean, which are attested by the quantity of the trade that plied between these parts of the world even before the days of our Lord. . . . The probability of an event is of course no positive evidence of its having actually happened." C. P. Mathew and M. M. Thomas, *The Indian Churches of Saint Thomas* (Delhi: I.S.P.C.K., 1967), p. 6. Those interested in this fascinating question should begin with this stimulating work by Mathew and Thomas.

17. Klaus Klostermaier says, for example, "it is not unlikely that Judeo-Christian influences were at work during the first centuries of the Christian era, molding certain aspects of Hinduism. During the time of the Roman Emperors, when anti-Semitic laws forced Jews from the heartlands of the Roman Empire to emigrate, a considerable number settled on the West coast of India. . . . According to an old tradition of the Christians in Kerala, Thomas, one of the Twelve Apostles of Jesus, preached his faith along the Malabar coast in South India and was martyred close to the modern city of Madras. . . . Despite strong arguments that suggest a link between the Syrian Christians of India and Nestorian communities in Asia Minor in the fourth century, it is not impossible that some Christians were already living in Malabar before then. These South Indian Christians maintained their numbers largely unchanged throughout the centuries. They lived in peace with their Hindu neighbors and had their own caste structure." *A Survey of Hinduism.* Albany, NY: State University of New York Press, 1989, p. 43.

The most famous Roman Catholic missionary in history, the Jesuit Francisco Xavier, sent by the King of Portugal to spread the Christian faith in the Portuguese colonies in India and the rest of Asia, arrived in Goa on the Malabar Coast in 1542, spent several months there—some say nearly a decade[18]—and supposedly baptized 60,000 converts to the Roman Catholic Church. Though Xavier's methods would be questioned today, he was an extraordinary and courageous pioneer who led the way for hundreds of missionaries who followed, including Roberto de Nobili.

No Protestant mission to India occurred until the first decade of the eighteenth century when two young Lutheran missionaries, Bartholomew Ziegenbalg (b. 1682) and Henry Plütschau (b. 1677), sent under the auspices of the Danish Halle mission, arrived in Tranquebar in 1706.[19] Ziegenbalg's successor was the remarkable Christian Frederick Schwartz (b. 1726) who as a missionary representative of the Society for the Propagation of the Gospel spent nearly a half-century in India. Upon his death in 1798, the Tranquebar mission boasted 40,000 converts. Schwartz and, to a lesser extent, Ziegenbalg are often overshadowed by William Carey (b. 1761) who arrived in India in 1793. Carey was later joined by Joshua Marshman (b. 1768) and William Ward (b. 1764), and there followed a steady stream of Protestant and Roman Catholic missionaries until the 1970s when the Indian government began restricting missionary visas.

The India Scene Today

The population of present-day India is not homogeneous. The dominant ethnic group is Indo-Aryan representing 72% of the people, followed by the Dravidians, 25%, and the Mongoloids with only 3%. No less than 16 different languages are spoken along with some 700 dialects. The official languages on the national level are, however, Hindi and English.

In 1993 the estimated population was 866,000,000, making India the second largest country in the world. Hindus are predominant with 83% of the population followed by Muslims (11%), Christians (3%), and Sikhs (2%).

FOR FURTHER STUDY

Hinduism
Chaudhuri, Nirad C. *Hinduism. A Religion to Live By.* New York: Oxford University Press, 1979.

---

18. Xavier's missionary career began in 1542 and extended to India, Malacca, and Japan. He died in 1552 within sight of China, his ultimate goal. Though it is possible to establish the approximate time he spent in each place, it is not possible to determine the precise length of Xavier's stay in India.

19. Few missionaries in Protestant history equal Ziegenbalg in ability, commitment, insight, and effectiveness. His methods stand in stark contrast not only to those of

Though the author is said to have abandoned his Hindu roots, his knowledge of the history, beliefs, and practices is formidable. The book is not only comprehensive, it is descriptive and analytical in approach.

Chennakesavan, Sarasvati. *A Critical Study of Hinduism.* New York: Asia Publishing House, 1974.
A series of insightful lectures by a Hindu philosopher and scholar to Christian missionary trainees. Its value lies in its objectivity and authoritative study of the original Hindu scriptures as well as surveying the rapid changes and developments in modern Hinduism.

Devanandan, Paul E. *Living Hinduism. A Descriptive Survey.* Bangalore: Christian Institute for the Study of Religion and Society, 1959.
An analysis of contemporary Hinduism, its complexities, contradictions, and appeal by a known and highly regarded Indian Protestant scholar.

Dumont, Louis. *Homo Hierarchicus. The Caste System and Its Implications.* Translated by Mark Sainsbury. Chicago: University of Chicago Press, 1980.
A carefully done history and appraisal of India's caste system. Critical but objective.

Hawley, John Stratton. "Naming Hinduism." *The Wilson Quarterly* 15 (Summer 1991): 20–34.
A synopsis of the emergence of modern Hinduism, together with a penetrating analysis of Roberto de Nobili's philosophy, methodology, and significance. Hawley's essay is one of several on the subject of "Hinduism and the Fate of India" (pp. 20–61).

Klostermaier, Klaus K. *A Survey of Hinduism.* Albany, NY: State University of New York Press, 1989.
One of the most complete, useful, and up-to-date studies of Hinduism available to the English reader. Highly recommended for the serious student.

Sharma, Arvind. "Hinduism." In *Our Religions,* ed. Arvind Sharma, 1–67. San Francisco: Harper, 1993.
A brilliantly written study by a contemporary Hindu scholar of the beliefs, literature, history, structure, and functioning of Hinduism today.

Younger, Paul and Susanna Oommen Younger. *Hinduism.* Publication of the Major World Religions Series, ed. Donald K. Swearer. Niles, IL: Argus Communications, 1978.
A brief introduction to Hinduism, its history and tradition, principal ideas, rituals, festivals, and myths. The illustrations and the glossary are helpful.

Roberto de Nobili

Clooney, Francis X. "Christ as the Divine Guru in the Theology of Roberto de Nobili." In *One Faith, Many Cultures,* ed. Ruy O. Costa, 2: 25–40. Boston Theological Institute Annual. Maryknoll, NY: Orbis Books, 1978.
An essay on de Nobili's background and missionary approach in which the author assesses the missionary as an innovator and the implications of his work for contextualization today. Based in part on de Nobili's own writings.

Xavier, but to many Protestants as well. See, for example, E. Arno Lehmann, *It Began at Tranquebar* (Madras: Christian Literature Society, 1956).

————. "Roberto de Nobili: Adaptation and the Reasonable Interpretation of Religion." *Missiology* 18 (January 1990): 25–36.

Similar to his earlier article, Clooney again examines de Nobili's adaptation of Christianity to the Indian context and contends that his theory and methods "anticipated by centuries" the contemporary emphasis on inculturation.

Cronin, Vincent. *A Pearl to India: The Life of Roberto de Nobili.* New York: E. P. Dutton, 1959.

One of the two biographical studies of de Nobili available in English. Delightful reading, but non-critical and somewhat hagiographic. The other is a work by the Indian Jesuit scholar, S. Rajamanickam, *The First Oriental Scholar,* published in 1972 by the Roberto de Nobili Research Institute in Tirunelveli, India. Unfortunately, Rajamanickam's work is not easily available to most students outside India.

Luzbetak, Louis J. "Adaptation, Missionary." *New Catholic Encyclopedia* 1: 97–99. New York: McGraw Hill, 1966.

An essay dealing with many of the issues faced by de Nobili.

THE CASE
Roberto de Nobili: A Case Study in Accommodation

In the year 1606 a young Italian Jesuit, Roberto de Nobili (1577–1656), was sent by his Superior to the strategic inland town of Madurai in southeast India. Within two years the fledgling missionary began to utilize an unfamiliar approach to evangelizing the high caste Indians, and by so doing he incited a storm of protest and controversy which continued for more than two decades. The dispute was so intense and widespread that it could only be resolved by the intervention of the Pope. In reality, however, the missiological issues raised by the de Nobili case remain unsettled, and they continue to provoke heated discussion today.

The Background of a Missionary

Roberto de Nobili was born in Rome in 1577, the first son of an Italian noble family that traced its lineage from Emperor Otto III (980–1002). Roberto's father, distinguished as a military leader, was a general in the papal army, and his mother, also from a family of nobility, was said to be a model of Christian piety and dedication to the Church.

When, however, at the age of seventeen—a year after his father's death—Roberto announced his intention to enter the Jesuit order and to become a missionary to the Orient, the family strenuously objected. Their opposition was not to the idea of his entering the priesthood, for the de Nobili family could boast that it had contributed numerous and eminent clerics to the Church, including several Cardinals and at least two Popes. Roberto's folly,

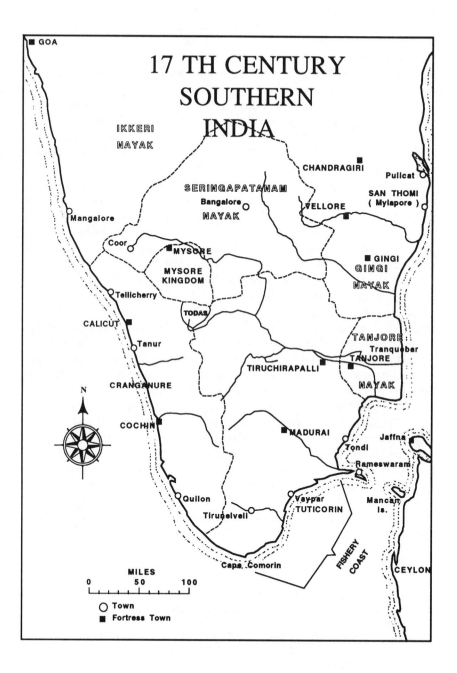

17 TH CENTURY SOUTHERN INDIA

GOA

IKKERI NAYAK

CHANDRAGIRI

Pulicat

SERINGAPATANAM

Bangalore

NAYAK

SAN THOMI
(Mylapore)

VELLORE

Mangalore

Coor

MYSORE

GINGI

GINGI

NAYAK

MYSORE
KINGDOM

Tellicherry

TODAS

CALICUT

TANJORE

Tanur

Tranquebar

TANJORE

TIRUCHIRAPALLI

NAYAK

CRANGANURE

N

COCHIN

MADURAI

Jaffna

Tondi

Rameswaram

Quilon

Vaypar

TUTICORIN

Mancar
Is.

Tirunelveli

FISHERY
COAST

Cape. Comorin

CEYLON

MILES

0   50   100

○ Town
■ Fortress Town

his family members insisted, was his choice of the Society of Jesus, a path which offered few possibilities for ecclesiastical advancement and position. Roberto could not, however, be dissuaded. "When God calls," he declared, "no human consideration should stop us." Thus in 1596, ignoring his family's wishes, he entered the Jesuit novitiate with the expressed intention of becoming a foreign missionary.

For a brief period de Nobili appeared to be destined for Japan, but in response to urgent appeals for reinforcements in India, he offered himself for missionary work in the Portuguese colony of South India. Because of the *Padroado,* a treaty between Portugal and Rome, the Portuguese monarch exercised almost complete political and religious authority over Portuguese colonies. Any missionary going to one of these areas was required by the stipulations of the treaty to obtain the approval of the Portuguese king and was obliged to travel only on Portuguese ships. Roberto was no exception, and therefore he journeyed to Lisbon to obtain royal confirmation. After a period of language study, political indoctrination, and the usual delays, he embarked for India the last week in April, 1604. It was more than a year later, May 1605, before he finally arrived in Goa, the Portuguese island stronghold off the southwest Indian coast.

Adjustment to the new living conditions did not come easily for the new missionary, and during Roberto's first months in India he became critically ill. Toward the end of the year, however, he was well enough to go to Cochin to meet his new Superior, Alberto Laerzio. Early in 1606 Laerzio sent Roberto to the Fishery Coast where he lived among the Paravas, a large tribe of outcastes who gained their meager livelihood by fishing and pearl diving.

Most of the Paravas lived along the coast, although by the time Roberto arrived some had migrated to inland areas of the country. By and large the Paravas of the Fishery Coast professed to be Christians, but it was common knowledge that in the 1530s several thousand of them had submitted to baptism in exchange for Portuguese protection from the Muslim raiders from the north. Roberto observed that the Paravas, like the other converts he had met in Goa and Cochin, had been given Portuguese names, that they dressed like Portuguese, and in general were expected to conduct themselves like Portuguese.

Early Missionary Experience

For seven months Roberto lived with the Paravas, immersing himself in the study of their culture and the Tamil language.[20] Possibly he would have

---

20. Tamil is a Dravidian language spoken in Southern India and in Northern Sri Lanka (Ceylon). De Nobili did not study Tamil from prepared grammars, for there were none. He learned it from close association with the Paravas whose limited vocabulary provided an adequate introduction. Proficiency in Tamil was, however, difficult to acquire. It bore no resemblance to any European language, neither to Italian, Latin, nor Portuguese. Its alphabet consisted of thirty letters plus a few

spent his entire missionary career working with these people and thus would have remained on the outer fringes of India's life, but for the fact that Laerzio reassigned him to the city of Madurai located five days' journey inland. Madurai, the capital of Madura, was the center of the Tamil culture. A mission had been established there in 1594 by a fifty-four year old Portuguese Jesuit, Gonçalo Fernández. Though not necessarily by choice, Father Gonçalo worked exclusively with Paravas who had immigrated to Madurai and with Portuguese tradespeople who traveled there. The hub of his activity was the missionary compound located on the outskirts of the city. Fernández lived in the mission house, said mass and heard confessions in the small mission chapel, directed the mission school for boys, and oversaw the mission dispensary. He had made attempts to attract higher caste people to the gospel and on several occasions had sought to interest the Nayak (the regional king) in Christianity. All of these evangelistic efforts among people of caste, however, had been rejected.

At the time de Nobili arrived in Madurai, India had a population of approximately one hundred forty million. Christianity had attracted only a small number of the people, and virtually all of those who had submitted to Christian baptism were outcastes and animists. Apparently one reason why Christianity appealed to them was because of the discrimination they experienced and the severe restrictions placed upon them by the caste Hindus. The Madurai mission had functioned already for eleven years, but there had been no converts from Hinduism. The one hundred or so individuals to whom Father Gonçalo ministered were all Paravas or Portuguese.

An Attempt to Understand the Indian Context

Roberto struggled to grasp the reason why the work of the Madurai mission was confined to outcaste Paravas and Portuguese. He felt himself fortunate therefore to become associated with the Hindu schoolmaster whom Fernández had placed in charge of the school. Over a period of several months the schoolmaster introduced Roberto to the complexities of the Indian culture. The young missionary was astounded to learn, for example, that the term used by the Indians to refer to the Portuguese and their converts, *"Parangis,"* was not, as the missionaries believed, Tamil for "Portuguese." Rather it signified in the most pejorative sense the polluted, uncultured, contemptuous foreigners and their proselytes. *Parangis* were despised, the schoolmaster explained, because they ate meat, drank wine (usually to excess), bathed irregularly, wore leather shoes, and ignored the rules of social intercourse.

---

borrowed from Sanskrit. Twelve of the letters were vowels called "souls," and the other eighteen were consonants referred to as "bodies." Seventeen of the "bodies" could be combined with the twelve "souls" making a total of 204 different characters. These, together with the thirty original letters, made a total of 234 different signs which Roberto had to master—all of them in script.

Thus by proudly referring to themselves and their converts as *"Parangi* Christians," the missionaries had unwittingly erected an insuperable barrier between themselves and the Hindus.

Besides learning of this linguistic *faux pas,* Roberto came to understand through the help of his mentor the significance of the caste system, namely, that it was the cornerstone of all Indian society and culture. To violate it was equivalent to threatening the divinely ordained structures of life. To the Hindus the single most important aspect about a person was his or her caste.[21]

When the Portuguese first came to India the initial question asked about them was, to which caste do these foreigners belong? It soon became evident, at least to the Hindus, that the Portuguese were ignorant, uncouth, unscrupulous people who were unworthy to associate with anybody except the outcastes. How else could one explain their total disregard for basic religious and social principles? No Indian, it was said, who valued his rank in society or who esteemed his religious faith would ever consider adopting the ways of these foreigners. This was the reason, according to the schoolmaster, why the Hindus avoided all contact with the Portuguese except when necessary for trading purposes. For to be touched or even gazed upon by a *Parangi,* Roberto learned, was believed to be contaminating.

Roberto had been in India hardly two years and in Madurai only a few months, but he was firmly convinced that the Hindus would never listen to the gospel until a formal and absolute break was made with *Parangi* Christianity. He therefore became determined to disassociate himself from the people and customs which identified him as a *Parangi.*

It was not possible for him to introduce such radical alterations without the approval of his superiors; but before appealing to them, he wanted the support of his older colleague. So he shared his findings and ideas with Father Gonçalo and attempted to persuade him to adopt a new approach. Fernández, however, had been in India since 1560, and he had worked virtually alone for nearly twelve years to establish a Christian base in Madurai. As vicar of the parish there he had the responsibility for all the believers in the area, and he listened to Roberto's proposals with increasing dismay. Roberto wanted to deny that he was a *Parangi,* to speak only Tamil, to avoid touching or even associating with the Portuguese and outcaste Christians, to bathe daily, to sit down cross-legged, to refer to himself as a *"sannyasi"* (a Sanskrit word meaning "one who has given up everything," but for a Brahman, being a *sannyasi* was the last stage of life), to eat no meat, and to wear wooden clogs and a saffron robe instead of the black cassock.

---

21. Indian society was composed of four principal castes: the *Brahman* (sacerdotal or learned), the *Ksatriyas* or *Rajas* (governors or warriors), the *Vaisyas* (traders or farmers), and the *Sudras* (serfs). Each of these principal castes was divided into innumerable subcastes. Finally there were the despised outcastes. The Hindu schoolmaster was, like the majority of caste people, a *Sudra.*

Fernández was straightforward with his young associate. What Roberto was advancing, said Gonçalo, would be not only a repudiation of three generations of missionary work in India, it would be, he declared, an irretrievable concession to the very social evils which Christianity should eradicate. In effect, Fernández continued, Roberto's approach would be a denial of the gospel. Hundreds of missionaries had given their lives in India in an attempt to plant the Church and root out the social evils. For Roberto and him now to withdraw from outcaste believers and accept the prohibitions of caste would be turning their backs on the very people who had first accepted the gospel. Furthermore, the other changes Roberto was suggesting, such as refusing to eat meat or wear leather sandals, wearing Indian clothing and speaking only in Tamil, calling himself a "*sannyasi,*" would be a denial of his priestly identity and a sanctioning of superstitions and prejudices which should be challenged by the gospel.

Roberto, however, was equally adamant, and he decided that he had no alternative but to appeal to his Superior, Laerzio, who after reflecting on the request confessed that he was disturbed by the unconventionality of it. Was it necessary, he asked, to go to such extremes? Laerzio affirmed that he longed for the conversion of Hindus as much as any missionary in India, but he could not himself grant permission for Roberto to make such a radical departure from the traditional missionary approach. Laerzio, nonetheless, indicated that he would consult with the Archbishop.

Several weeks passed before de Nobili received an answer, and he was granted considerably less than he had requested. According to Laerzio, Roberto could cease using the name "*Parangi,*" and he could refer to himself as a "*sannyasi.*" No mention was made, however, regarding his other proposals.

Meanwhile, the relationship between de Nobili and Fernández had deteriorated, and the breach widened as Fernández reiterated his objections. De Nobili in turn refused to associate with his fellow missionaries and isolated himself from the Christian community in Madurai. How was it possible, Gonçalo asked, for a new missionary who had been in the country less than three years to determine the best way to evangelize India?

Roberto, however, was not to be deterred. He simply ignored Gonçalo's protests and his growing disapprobation. As long as Roberto had the approval of Laerzio and the Archbishop, he would continue what he was doing, with or without his colleague's support.

A Radical Accommodation to Hindu Life

In his letters Roberto described the growing breach between himself and his older missionary colleague. It was evident, he said, that there was no possibility of reconciling two missionary philosophies so antithetical, so he decided to come to terms with what he believed to be the social givens. He would accept the restrictions of caste and refuse to condemn any social custom or idea, even the despised Hindu practice of *suttee*.[22] He moved from the missionary compound into a hut in the Brahman quarter of the city and shaved his head except for a small tuft of hair. He spoke only Tamil, hired a Brahman cook and houseboy, and became a vegetarian. Like all Brahmans, Roberto limited himself to one meal a day. He abandoned the familiar black cassock and leather sandals and wore instead the saffron robe and wooden clogs. To cover the "nakedness" of his forehead he put a sandalwood paste insignia on his brow, an indication that he was a Hindu *guru* or teacher. He referred to himself not as a priest but as a *"sannyasi."* Eventually he ate only with Brahmans, and for a brief period he wore the Brahman thread of three strands of cotton cord draped from the shoulder to the waist as an indisputable sign of rank. He bathed daily and cleansed himself ceremonially before saying mass.

Roberto's first Hindu convert was the Sudra schoolmaster whom he christened "Alberto," in honor of his Superior. By the end of 1608, two years from the time he arrived in Madurai, de Nobili had baptized at least ten young men of caste. As his circle of disciples expanded, he soon became friends with a Brahman Sanskrit scholar named Sivadarma who, after considerable hesitation, permitted de Nobili to see and study the Vedas and the Upanishads. (Roberto de Nobili is generally regarded as the first European to study Sanskrit and even to see the Hindu sacred writings.) Possibly Sivadarma believed that he was converting the personable European to Hinduism, but by 1609 Roberto had persuaded Sivadarma to read the Bible—which de Nobili referred to as the Christian Veda—and to accept Christian baptism.

Immediately Roberto faced two difficult questions. In the first place, he knew that neither Sivadarma nor any other Brahman would consent to worship with people of lower castes. Would it then be proper to segregate the believers according to caste? Secondly, was it necessary, as the other missionaries insisted, that Sivadarma discard the triple thread and shave the *kudumi* or single braid of hair which distinguished him as a member of the highest caste? Roberto resolved the first problem by forming a totally Brahman church, and he appealed to his superior Laerzio for an answer to the question of the thread and the *kudumi*. Roberto left no doubt, however, as to where he stood on the matter. He insisted that the thread and the *kudumi* were social, not religious symbols.

Opposition to de Nobili's Accommodations

Father Gonçalo did not hide his mounting distress. Roberto's innovations, and his *de facto* acceptance of the caste system, were for the older missionary inimical to the spirit of the gospel. He warned Roberto as well as others that

---

22. Suttee was the self-immolation of Hindu widows on the funeral pyres of their deceased husbands. Supposedly, it was an evidence of devotion. Roberto said he witnessed 400 widows burned to death in this fashion soon after he arrived in Madurai.

these moves, if not halted, would soon undo the Madurai work and ultimately would jeopardize the whole Christian mission in India. Fernández made a trip to the coast and confided to the priests there the level of his anxiety. He wrote a detailed denunciation of Roberto's activity and sent it to the Archbishop. Before many weeks had passed, the entire Jesuit mission in South India was debating the wisdom of de Nobili's approach. Some supported it, including Alberto Laerzio, but many of Roberto's friends and even members of his family in Rome manifested dismay when they heard of the extent to which he had adapted himself to Indian life. Laerzio, however, attempting to minimize the criticism of his young charge, wrote a letter to the Jesuit General defending de Nobili's work.

Toward the end of 1609 Roberto had gathered around him some sixty converts, a few of whom were Brahmans. None was obligated to violate the rules of caste nor to give up any custom which was not indisputably idolatrous. The signs of caste such as the thread and the *kudumi* were given a Christian blessing.

Official Condemnation

Two years elapsed before de Nobili's methods were officially condemned by a member of the hierarchy in India. The censure resulted from the written report submitted by Fernández and was issued by Nicolau Pimenta, the newly appointed Papal Visitor[23] to the provinces of Goa and Malabar. Pimenta declared that the accommodations by Roberto were excessive, superstitious, and schismatic. As Papal Visitor he lacked the authority to close the mission; only the Jesuit General in Rome could do that. But Pimenta's condemnation represented a serious threat to the continuation of the strategy de Nobili was following. Both Pimenta and Roberto wrote detailed reports to the General, and each appealed for his support. Communications between Rome and Goa were painfully slow, and another two years passed before a reply came. In the meantime, nearly twenty of Roberto's disciples lapsed, and his Superior, Laerzio, was replaced by Pero Francisco.

The letter from the Jesuit General arrived in Cochin in August 1613. Francisco read it, then sent a copy along with his own comments to Roberto. The letter, according to Francisco's interpretation, clearly indicated that de Nobili's methods were in error on three counts: the use of the Brahman thread, the sandalwood paste mark, and the wooden clogs, as well as his denial that he was a *Parangi*. The adaptation of Hindu ceremonies such as the baths was wrong. And the separation from his missionary colleague Fernández could not continue. "You must," the General wrote, "during the day and in the sight of all, deal freely with the Fathers of the other residence, go to their house and talk with them, and they, in their turn, must be allowed to

---

23. One commissioned by the Pope to make official inspections and report directly to him.

come to your house without any restriction and not by night only." Francisco's comments included a prohibition against de Nobili's baptizing any further converts unless he was prepared to submit to the conditions the General had stipulated.

Roberto responded by saying that to make these changes would have the effect of undoing all he had accomplished and would sound the death knell of his mission to the Hindus. He fixed his hope and based his refusal to change on a single sentence in the General's letter: "No change should be made which would compromise the existence of the mission."

Reconsideration: The Goa Conference, February 1618

The affair dragged on for another five years during which time Roberto could not baptize anyone. In 1617 Pope Paul V ordered a conference to be held in Goa the following February during which time de Nobili was to explain and defend his missionary methods. Twenty theologians and priests were present including two Papal Inquisitors. They were charged with deciding the future of Roberto's mission. The debate was intense. Then came the vote.

STUDY QUESTIONS

1. What are the principal characteristics about the religious beliefs and practices called "Hinduism" that distinguish a Hindu from a Christian?

2. In what sense can one say that Hinduism is one faith and many faiths? What are the doctrinal beliefs that are common to all who profess to be Hindus?

3. How would you define "accommodation" as exemplified in the missionary method of Augustine of Canterbury and Roberto de Nobili? Are there examples of this kind of approach in the New Testament?

4. Can you name and describe the seven or eight principal characters in this case?

5. What did de Nobili regard as the primary impediment preventing Indians of caste from becoming Christians, and what steps did he take to remove that impediment? How did his colleagues and superiors react to his innovation?

6. Imagine yourself to have been appointed by the Bishop of Goa to defend de Nobili (or to bring charges against him). How would you do it? Was de Nobili's strategy sound?

7. De Nobili insisted that the Brahman thread, the sandalwood paste mark, diet, and caste were all cultural, not religious distinctions. To what degree can a missionary accommodate aspects of culture without compromising the Christian faith and ethic? How can we distinguish between what is cultural and what is religious?

SUGGESTED BIBLICAL TEXTS FOR REFLECTION

Job 4:1–8. The doctrine of retribution declared by Eliphaz to Job.

John 1:1–14. The Word of God incarnated in Jesus Christ.

1 Corinthians 9:19–23. Adaptation for a higher purpose.

1 Corinthians 12:12–26. One body, many body parts.

FUNERAL FOR NORIKO-SAN

An evangelical missionary woman has developed a close friendship for many years with a Japanese business woman who dies of cancer. The missionary is invited by the deceased woman's daughter to speak at her mother's Buddhist funeral. If the missionary accepts the invitation, most if not all her Christian colleagues and friends will regard her act as compromising the Christian faith. If, on the other hand, she refuses, she risks offending the grieving family and losing any opportunity for future witness.

CONTEXT
Buddhism and Christianity

Christianity in Japan

Christian history begins in Japan with the arrival in 1549 of the greatest Roman Catholic missionary, Francisco Xavier. The country remained open for nearly a century, until 1639, after which virtually all traces of the church Xavier planted were obliterated. But during the period the Jesuits and others were in Japan, a large number of converts were baptized, a number of steps were taken to adapt the faith to the Japanese setting, a seminary was begun, and some national young men were accepted into the priesthood. It is estimated that by the end of the sixteenth century, the Japanese church boasted at least 300,000 faithful, an astounding figure given the tenuous beginning, the delay in opening the priesthood to national youth, and the traditionally closed attitude of Japanese people.

As early as 1587, however, the political situation in the country began to change, and for a number of reasons Japanese rulers became extremely suspicious of foreigners in general and of the effects of alien religion. Foreigners were ordered expelled, and harassment and persecution followed. At first the implementation of the expulsion was irregular and the persecution was localized and sporadic, but in 1614 it became widespread. So intense and effective were the efforts to isolate Japan from the outside world and suppress all vestiges of foreign religion that the church which had flourished for more than half a century was virtually wiped out by the swift verdicts, severe torture, apostasy, or brutal execution of all exposed believers.[1]

More than two centuries would pass before any Christian missionary was again able to enter Japan, and this was the result of forced treaties initiated by the threat of invasion in 1853 by Commodore Matthew C. Perry, U.S. Navy, who demanded that Japan establish formal relations with the United States. First to enter was a Roman Catholic priest in 1858, followed by an increasing number of Christian missionaries—Roman Catholic, Protestant, and Orthodox. Conversion to Christianity was, however, still regarded as a crime punishable by death, and it was not until the approval of a new Constitution in 1889 that civil penalties were annulled and "freedom of religious belief" legalized. By the end of the century, American Episcopalians, Presbyterians, the Reformed Church, and the Free Baptists all had missionaries working in the country. Converts were, nonetheless, few and the churches that existed were exceedingly small and weak. This is not to imply that little of significance occurred. Quite the contrary. The Japanese church has produced a remarkable number of renowned leaders including Jo Niijima or Joseph Hardy Neesima (1843–1890), Kanzo Uchimura (1861–1931), Masahisa Uemura (1859–1925), and Toyohiko Kagawa (1888–1960).

Prior to and during the Second World War, the church suffered many restrictions and most of the missionaries were expelled from the country, and a number of pastors and other church leaders were imprisoned. Immediately prior to the outset of the war, in 1940, for instance, the government attempted to compel all Protestant denominations to merge into a single body, the *Nippon Kirisuto Kyodan,* the Church of Christ of Japan. Most of them did.

Defeat at the hands of the Allies, however, sent shock waves through the whole of Japanese society, and the country became open as never before in its long history to outside influences and forces. The American General Douglas MacArthur, military ruler of the occupying forces, brazenly called for a thousand Christian missionaries to come to Japan. Missionaries, especially Protestants, began to pour into Japan by the hundreds, and at one point reached a high of more than four thousand. The expected Christian evangelization of the country, however, failed to materialize. What appeared in the late 1940s and 1950s as a burgeoning interest in Christianity soon evaporated, and the

---

1. Stephen Neil, *A History of Christian Missions* (1982), 136. The apostasy of Father Christovão Ferreira, the Jesuit Superior in Japan, October 18, 1633, was a grievous blow to the mission and has incited no little controversy. Ferreira is the historical figure who inspired Shusaku Endo's riveting novel *Silence,* Tr. Wm. Johnston (NY: Taplinger, 1969). George Elison deals with the period in his *Deus Destroyed. The Image of Christianity in Early Modern Japan* (Cambridge, MA: Harvard University Press, 1988), especially, 190–191. See also Neil S. Fujita, *Japan's Encounter with Christianity* (New York: Paulist Press, 1991); Masaharu Anesaki, *History of Japanese Religion* (Rutland, VT: Charles E. Tuttle, 1963); and C. R. Boxer, *The Christian Century in Japan 1549–1650* (Berkeley, CA: University of California Press, 1967).

number of converts remained small. Though the status and influence of the Christian church in Japan greatly exceeds its numbers, the baptized Japanese Christian community has yet to reach two percent of the total Japanese population.

Resistance to Christianity is the consequence of a number of factors: culture, tradition, nationalism, ethnocentrism, secularism, and the Japanese religious heritage which is a unique amalgam of Confucianism, Shinto, and Buddhism. Central in this heritage, however, is Buddhism.

Buddhism

Buddhism, the Way of the Enlightened One, arose in the Hindu world of northern India probably as a kind of Hindu reform movement. The "reformer," later called "The Buddha," was born c. 560 B.C.E. as the son of a wealthy rajah and given the name Siddharta (he who has reached his goal) Gautama (after a well-known Hindu teacher). The Buddha is a title meaning the "enlightened one" and was given to him by his disciples. Like the founders of other religious movements, a number of legends and myths are told about the Buddha's birth, life, and death. Generally accepted, however, is the account that after he married and fathered a son, he became disillusioned with his life of luxury and ease, left home and became a wandering ascetic. Four experiences led him to forsake forever his family and former life.

In three successive journeys the young prince came face to face with suffering, pain, and death. He encountered a sickly old man, an invalid afflicted with constant pain, and a procession of weeping mourners bearing the corpse of the deceased to the funeral pyre. This, Gautama concluded, was the destiny of all humankind. Then on his fourth journey, Gautama met a monk who, despite having renounced all attachments to life and living only from alms put in his begging bowl, appeared satisfied and fulfilled.

Seeking liberation and contentment like that of the monk, Gautama definitively left home to search for knowledge as a traditional Hindu *sannyasi* or mendicant ascetic. All he accomplished, however, was almost destroying his health without gaining enlightenment. Then, recalling his first insight under a fruit tree in his family's garden, he forsook the life of self-affliction and sought enlightenment by meditation. Seating himself under a fig tree, called the *bodhi* or enlightenment tree, he found that for which he had been searching, the secret of life and the essence of reality. Refusing immediate entry into *nirvana,* Gautama, now the Buddha, began to preach to others what he had experienced and began to attract an increasing number of disciples.

Though Gautama accepted the doctrines of *karma* and of reincarnation and in this sense could be regarded as a Hindu reformer, the religious life he finally modeled and taught became distinct, comparable to Christianity's breach with Judaism. A separation of Buddhism from Hinduism, given the Buddha's teachings, was inevitable. Following his enlightenment, for example, he rejected the idea of God as an ultimate being and repudiated absolutely the idea and practice of caste. Likewise, he denied the prevailing Hindu belief that an individual soul or *atman* that shed all *karma* would finally be absorbed into the great oversoul or *Brahma atman.* The way to religious awakening, enlightenment, Buddha insisted, was not cognitive but spiritual. It was beyond intellectual knowledge and experience. Moreover, enlightenment, if experienced, would come by following the physical and moral precepts of the law or teaching, the *dharma,* not venerating any divine or human being. What are these teachings? The Buddha was clear: all of life is characterized by change, and the rearrangement of life's components is determined by the laws of *karma* or of cause and effect. One's good and evil actions determine one's *karma.* What one is and what one will be in future incarnations depend on how one lives, that is, on one's thoughts, speech, and deeds. One can accumulate good or bad *karma,* depending on how one lives and has lived in this life or incarnation, as well as in previous and later incarnations.

The *Dharma,* or life principles and the path to *nirvana* or eternal peace, applies to all of reality—to the four fundamental elements of water, earth, fire, and air; to the senses and emotions; to sounds and colors; and to the episodes of life such as birth, learning, eating, sleeping, aging, and dying. All are interrelated, and though an individual regards himself or herself as an independent entity, this is an illusion, for all are merely components of the total stream of life or *dharmas.* Individuality, the self or *atman,* whether in this incarnation or another, is an illusion.

The *Dharma,* therefore, may be condensed in the "Four Noble Truths" the Buddha enunciated in his first sermon preached near Benares.

• The universal experience of suffering (physical and mental) resulting from *karma.*

• The cause of suffering is desire for that which is wrong or craving that which is right for the wrong reasons.

• Desire can be mastered.

• The way is the "Noble Eightfold Path."

The Noble Eightfold Path includes: right knowledge or understanding, right attitude, right speech, right action, right livelihood, right effort, right thought, and right concentration or composure.

Buddhists are required to live by Five Precepts. They are to refrain from killing anything, taking what is not given, sexual immorality, falsehood, and intoxicants (alcohol and drugs).

The dates of the Buddha's life are debated, but most Buddhist scholars say he was born in the sixth century B.C.E. Masao Abe indicates that he was born in 563 and died in 483 B.C.E.[2] Living a total of 80 years, he spoke often and did a great many things. It is said that after the Buddha's death, however, nearly five centuries elapsed before his words and teachings were committed to writing. Until they were written down they were preserved and passed on orally, though, according to Buddhist historians, the teachings were

2. "Buddhism," 101.

reviewed and agreed upon by general councils immediately following the Buddha's death and from time to time thereafter.

The Buddhist Scriptures are known as the *Pitakas* or Baskets of the Law. The Pali canon of Theravada Buddhism is often called the *Tripitaka* or Triple Basket containing accounts and legends of the Buddha's life (lives), rules and guidelines by which monks and all Buddhists are to live, and the higher teachings.

As in the case of other religions, the Buddha's disciples became hopelessly divided following his death, and today there are numerous branches of Buddhism: Theravada Buddhism (strict or conservative) which contends that only a few monks will be saved and enter *nirvana,* and then it will be by their own efforts. Theravada Buddhists do not practice any rituals, allow any images—even those of the Buddha—nor do they pray to the Buddha. They believe, however, that Gautama was not the only Buddha, for at least six preceded him and one, Maitreya, is yet to come.

Mahayana Buddhism is much more tolerant and inclusive, the name means "Great Vehicle" and suggests that all will ultimately be saved. Mahayana Buddhists hold that certain individuals—male and female—willingly decline entry into *nirvana* in order to remain in the world and lead as many others as possible in the right way. These special people are called *Bodhisattvas,* those destined for enlightenment or Buddhahood, who become not only examples, but in a sense they are saviors who teach, encourage, counsel others, and serve the needy.

Other forms of Buddhism have followed such as Vajrayana that originated in the first century CE in northern India and spread to Nepal, Tibet, China, and Japan. Unlike Theravada and Mahayana Buddhism, Vajrayana has incorporated a great deal of magic and the occult such as the use of magical words or phrases called *mantras,* mystical gestures or movements called *mudras,* and meditation diagrams or circles called *mandalas. Mantras* are repeated many times and may be written down and put on a "prayer wheel." "Ommmm"and "Hummm" are commonly used mantras. The *mudra* is sometime fused with certain erotic acts in a branch called "Shaktism," from the Hindu Shakti, an eternal feminine power. Concentration on a *mandala,* it is believed, will lead to enlightenment.

Lamaism is the principal form—some say the only form—of Tibetan Buddhism that originated in the seventh century CE when Buddhism was first brought to the land. Lamaism has passed through several stages and is now led by the Dalai Lama, the Great Teacher. The current Dalai Lama, who since 1959 has been in exile, is the fourteenth leader of Tibetan Buddhists.

Zen Buddhism, though it originated in China and is known there as *Ch'an Buddhism,* is much more associated today with Japan. It emphasizes a rigorous system of meditation, which appealed to the disciplined Samurai. Zen teaches that enlightenment comes not through reason or knowledge, but through intuition, meditation under the guidance of a Zen Master. Sitting and meditating in the lotus position, pondering unsolvable riddles, painting, dancing, flower arranging, and many other activities are avenues of spiritual insight.

Other than these main branches of Buddhism, there are a number of other lesser Buddhist movements such as the Japanese *Amida* or *"Pure Land"* Buddhism that teaches salvation not by one's own efforts, but rather by calling on Amida, and the lay *Soka Gakkai* or "Value-Creating Society."

One can find many similarities between Buddhism and Christianity, but none so striking as the missionary zeal of certain Buddhists, especially the Mahayana who carried Buddhism through most of Asia in the centuries following the death of the Buddha and who now have communities, worship centers, and temples all over the world.

As there are similarities, there are also contrasts between Christianity and Buddhism, none so obvious as the Buddhist denial of God. "Buddhism," says Abe, "does not believe in God, but it does believe in gods."[3] By this he means that Buddhists believe that those who have gained enlightenment and have acquired extraordinary *karma* speak as gods or become gods. But they do not have the attributes of a supreme deity as in monotheistic religions. For this reason, it is sometimes said that Buddhism is atheistic, that Buddhists do not believe in God. The distinction made by Buddhists, however, is subtle but crucial, namely, that Buddhism does not deny the existence of deity or deities. Buddhists simply refuse to ascribe to any being or beings absolute metaphysical attributes. Abe puts it as follows: "Buddhism rejects the metaphysical attributes of God while accepting the moral attributes."[4]

Like medieval Christianity, Buddhism functions around a community, the *Sangha* or monastic community—"it is the Sangha that sustains Buddhism. So long as the Sangha functions, Buddhism works; when the Sangha falls, Buddhism collapses."[5] In fact, many Buddhist authorities insist that the Sangha is "the only constant factor" in Buddhism.[6]

> This is an observation so elementary in its nature that it risks being overlooked on account of its obviousness. Buddhism is not designed to function as a religious system without a monastic order—even if the monks themselves decide to lead the life of householders, as in some Pure Land sects.[7]

In contrast to Christianity, however, the Buddhist *Sangha* or community is not composed of all believers, only of the monks and nuns. Thus it may be said that whereas the center of Buddhism is institutionalized monasticism,[8]

---

3. "Buddhism," 77.

4. Ibid., 78.

5. Ibid., 124.

6. Edward Conze, *Buddhist Texts Through the Ages* (New York: Philosophical Library, 1954), 48. Cited by Abe, 125.

7. Abe, ibid.

8. Abe contends that "Buddhism was the first major religious tradition in history—

the center of Christianity is the church, the institutionalized community of all Christ's disciples. Despite the contrasts between Buddhism and Christianity, Buddhism is appealing to many Westerners, especially to those who are weary of religious intolerance and violence and of our idolization of individualism. The simplicity of Buddhist teachings, the high ethical standards, the fact that one can be religious without the burden of creeds and complex theology, the apparent fairness of a system wherein one receives what one deserves—are all aspects of Buddhism which many find attractive and sensible.

FOR FURTHER STUDY

Christianity in Japan

Anesaki, Masaharu. *History of Japanese Religion.* London: Kegan Paul, Trench, Trubner, 1930, and republished by Charles E. Tuttle, Rutland, VT, 1963.

A carefully organized history of religions in Japan by epochs—Shinto, Buddhism, Confucianism, and Christianity—by a professor at the Tokyo Imperial University.

Cary, Otis. *A History of Christianity in Japan: Roman Catholic, Greek Orthodox, and Protestant Missions.* Rutland, VT: Charles E. Tuttle, 1976.

The nearest to a definitive history available. Covers from Francis Xavier to early twentieth century. Originally two volumes, now available in one.

Drummond, Richard H. *A History of Christianity in Japan.* Grand Rapids, MI: Eerdmans, 1971.

One of the most readable and informative books available on the history of Christianity in Japan from 1549 to 1970. Includes a section on the Orthodox Church in Japan.

Kitagawa, Joseph. M. *On Understanding Japanese Religion.* Princeton, NJ: Princeton University Press, 1987.

A recently published and valuable resource for understanding the history and development of Japanese religions. Concentrates principally on Shinto and Buddhism with a briefer reference to Confucianism. Christianity is only mentioned in passing.

Koyama, Kosuke. *Mount Fuji and Mount Sinai: A Critique of Idols.* Maryknoll, NY: Orbis, 1984.

A theological analysis of the history of Japan from the bombing of Hiroshima (1945) to the present. Critical of the idolatry in Japanese culture with an emphasis on the meaning of faith in God who "is passionately involved in history."

Phillips, James M. *From the Rising of the Sun: Christians and Society in Contemporary Japan.* Maryknoll, NY: Orbis Books, 1981.

A history of Christianity in Japan since 1945 with discussions on Christians and politics, education, social work, and ecumenism. Also deals with Christian "outreach," biblical studies and theology, and the role of missionaries.

---

with the possible exception of the Jains, a sect of ancient India—to institutionalize monasticism," 125.

Spae, Joseph J. *Christianity Encounters Japan.* Tokyo: Oriens Institute for Religious Research, 1968.
   Written from the perspective of a Japanese Roman Catholic. Unusually informative in regard to the sociological, psychological, and theological contexts Christians encounter in Japan.

Thelle, Notto R. *Buddhism and Christianity in Japan: From Conflict to Dialogue, 1854–1899.* Honolulu, Hawaii: University Press of Hawaii, 1987.
   Examines the early Christian missions to Buddhists in Japan, the methods employed, Buddhist defenses, anti-Christian campaigns, and ensuing Christian-Buddhist relations. Evaluates how each has been affected by the other. Extensively documented.

Buddhism

Conze, Edward. *Buddhism: Its Essence and Development.* New York: Harper, 1959.
   An introductory study of the history, beliefs, and practices of Buddhists.

―――. *A Short History of Buddhism.* Bombay: Chetana, 1960.
   Two concise and well-written studies of Buddhism, the first concentrating on the philosophical and theological, and the second on the history and evolution of Buddhism.

Metz, Wulf. "The Enlightened One: Buddhism." In *Eerdmans' Handbook to the World's Religions,* 222–244. Grand Rapids, MI: Eerdmans, 1982.
   A readily usable summary of the history, development, branches, and doctrines of Buddhism with illustrations and diagrams.

Rahula, Walpola Sri. *What the Buddha Taught.* New York: Grove Press, 1974.
   Considered the foremost introduction to the study of Theravada Buddhism.

Thomas, Edward J. *The Life of Buddha as Legend and History.* London: Routledge & Kegan Paul, 1949.
   One of a number of critical biographies of the Buddha.

―――. *The History of Buddhist Thought.* New York: Barnes & Noble, 1971.
   Somewhat dated, but still a valuable analysis of the development of Buddhist thought.

THE CASE
Funeral for Noriko-San

"Yes, I understand, Keiko. I am very sorry, but your mother has suffered so long and so courageously, and now she will not have to suffer any more." Rebecca Johnson listened patiently as Keiko sobbed.

"Yes, yes, that's right. We will miss her terribly.... I'm sorry, did I understand you correctly? You want me to speak during her funeral?"

Rebecca hoped her question did not reveal the shock she was feeling, nor leave the wrong impression on Keiko, but to be asked to participate in Noriko's funeral rites was not what Rebecca anticipated. An invitation to

attend the funeral, given her long friendship with Keiko's mother, would not have been unusual. But Noriko was a Buddhist, and Rebecca was a North American Protestant missionary.

The Acculturation of Rebecca Johnson, Missionary

After nearly twenty years in Japan, Rebecca Johnson had perceptibly adopted many of the customs, thought patterns, and outward expressions of the Japanese. One of those customs was to avoid manifesting discomfort or embarrassment, or in any way intentionally to cause another to feel distress or humiliation.

When she first arrived in Japan, she noted how modestly the Japanese women dressed, avoiding strong colors, especially red, and she dressed accordingly. She moved into an apartment rather than a missionary house, utilized public transportation, and learned how to greet people properly. She always provided guest slippers for persons who came to visit and as hostess always served tea to her guests before they left. When Rebecca was told by her language school teacher that cultured women spoke *teinei,* a formal type of Japanese used especially by women, she made it her goal to learn *teinei* even though for her it "required twice as long to say something." Rebecca enjoyed seeing the surprise and pleasure of Japanese women when she would speak to them in *teinei.*

Rebecca Johnson was born and reared in the suburbs of Philadelphia, attended public schools there, and very early in her life became deeply involved in the activities of her parents' church, a nearby congregation of the Christian and Missionary Alliance. Besides the weekly Bible study, morning and evening worship and youth group on Sundays, she was from her early childhood an active member in the missionary organizations. It was commonplace for missionaries on furlough to come to the church and speak in the worship service, to the women's missionary society, and to the young people and children.

It was no surprise to her parents, therefore, that when Rebecca was only twelve years of age, she announced that she wanted to be a foreign missionary. Her mother and father did not discourage her, but they did urge her to continue to think, to pray, and to prepare herself.

"If this is God's will for your life," her mother would say, "you will know it, and God will open the way." As far as Rebecca was concerned, God did open the way. She finished high school in the top of her class, attended and graduated from Nyack College, NY, and received from that institution the B.S. and M.R.E. degrees.

Many times during those years she thought about marriage, but she was unwilling to sacrifice what she believed was God's will for her life simply to have a husband and children. She often thought that if she met a young man whom she came to love and who also was a missionary volunteer, then marriage and a family would be possible. But that did not happen.

Following her college and seminary education, Rebecca worked for three years in a Christian counseling center and as a youth director in a large church. She grew to feel comfortable and competent in counseling, and reflecting on her experience, she was convinced that the counseling training had been excellent preparation for missionary service.

She was appointed by the Christian and Missionary Alliance as a missionary to Japan in 1970, and after two years of language study in Tokyo, she was assigned to teach English and journalism in a Christian college where she remained for the additional three years of her first term. She enjoyed the work, progressed rapidly in learning and speaking Japanese, and was particularly challenged by the college students she taught, many of whom became her closest friends. She adapted easily to Japanese ways, loved Japanese cooking, and made as many friends among non-Christian Japanese as among those who were professing Christians.

During her first furlough, Rebecca completed an M.A. degree in pastoral counseling. Her thesis subject was "Death and Funeral Practices in Contemporary Japan." Upon returning to Japan, she began what was known as an "encounter ministry" among college students in Kyoto, an assignment that she has continued for more than fifteen years. When asked what an "encounter ministry" involved, she described the Christian student center near the university, the bilingual program of English classes, Bible study, recreational activities, and "just being there, meeting the students where they are."

For three successive furloughs she did post-graduate work in pastoral counseling, receiving not only her M.A., but also becoming certified in the field of pastoral care. She did her work in Drew Seminary and two well-known medical centers in Pennsylvania and Virginia. Rebecca was convinced that her whole missionary career had been profoundly shaped and enhanced by learning to listen and see people and their needs as more important than her own predispositions, and more important than people's cultural eccentricities or their professed religious beliefs.

She grew to love the Japanese and not be troubled by their formality, reserve, or habitual deference, though at times she wondered if being single had enabled her to adjust more quickly to Japan than other North Americans she knew.

Friendship with Ms. Noriko Suzuki, Japanese Buddhist

This is Rebecca's story of her relationship with one Buddhist woman.

"I met Noriko Suzuki through a mutual Japanese friend shortly after I moved to Kyoto. Noriko had worked with the American military, and it was by a U.S. officer on the base that she became pregnant with her daughter Keiko who is now 27. Unfortunately, Noriko and the solider never married, and for reasons I do not know, she never revealed to Keiko the identity of her father.

"Keiko has become a lovely young woman, and from my observation, Noriko was a very good mother.

"Noriko was bilingual, an excellent translator and typist, and an extremely competent office manager. Thus, in the late 1970s, she decided to begin her own business, a public relations firm that catered to the English-speaking companies and community in Japan. She had far more ability to work cross-culturally than most people I have known. She could translate from Japanese to English with very few mistakes.

"This was, in fact, how I first began to work with her. She would ask me to read her translations of various things and correct her mistakes.

"Noriko was 43 years old when we met in 1980. Her business was growing, and she had more accounts than she could handle. She would come to my apartment, or she would ask me to meet her somewhere, and I would read the draft of her material, make the needed corrections, and then we would talk or go somewhere to eat.

"Two years after I met her, she had breast cancer. The treatment was radical, but it seemed that she would recover completely. Six years later, however, the malignancy reappeared and was discovered to have spread to her spinal column. As the months passed, she suffered terribly, but never complained. For the last two years of her life she had to walk with a cane.

"Besides helping her with translations, I would often recommend certain young American students to her to work as models in the Japanese department stores. There was an exchange program at the university, and American students would come there to study. The stores frequently wanted Americans to model and advertise their merchandise.

"I was in Noriko's apartment one afternoon, and she and I had been working on a translation. Her mother, Haruko, had come from Tokyo to visit, but she was in another room and was unable to hear us talking. Noriko said, 'Rebecca, I know I am going to die, but I'm not afraid. I believe in one God. As you know, Shintos and Buddhists are supposed to believe in many gods. But I believe in *one* God. My Shinto and Buddhist priest friends tell me I am a very strange woman.'

"She appeared to be saying to me that her belief about God was anything but orthodox Buddhism or Shinto.

"I then said, 'That sounds like the God I know.'

"Noriko replied, 'I don't know if your God and my God are the same, and I do not know about Jesus, but I believe that there is *one* God.'

"I tried to talk to her about Jesus. I attempted to explain the difference between God and Jesus and the Holy Spirit. I did not want to confuse her, so I avoided complicated terminology. I felt good because when I finished she said, 'I can believe that.'

"I asked her if she had talked with her mother concerning her death. 'No,' she replied. 'We cannot do it. We cannot express our feelings.' I urged her to talk with Haruko and with Keiko.

"She thanked me for talking with her, and she expressed deep gratitude for the persons in her life who had helped her. I did not know it then, but this would be our last visit together.

"When I stood to leave, Noriko asked Haruko to come in and accompany me to the elevator. She did, and as we were walking down the hall, I asked the mother if she knew how ill Noriko was. She said she did.

" 'Have you talked with her about this?'

" 'No,' she said, 'it is too difficult.'

"About ten days later Noriko was taken to the hospital, and during the two weeks she was there I talked with Haruko and with Keiko almost daily. I expressed a willingness (it was really a desire) to go see her, but they both said that she looked so bad that she had asked that none of her friends be allowed to come. 'She wants you to remember her as she has been,' they said.

"The Sunday before Noriko died, all of her immediate family went to visit her in the hospital. She was in great pain but was lucid. One problem especially bothered her. She had tried several times to persuade her brother to take over her public relations firm, but he had resisted because of his own business. On that Sunday, however, he told Noriko he would assume responsibility and manage her agency. Two days later she died.

"On Wednesday, Keiko called to tell me that her mother had passed away. 'My mother considered you a good friend, and I know she would want you to speak at her funeral. Will you do it?' "

The Japanese Funeral Rite: Description and Implications

Rebecca was honored but surprised. She knew well what was involved in a Buddhist funeral and how some of her missionary friends would interpret it if she accepted.

She described a Buddhist funeral as follows:

"By law in Japan, the body of the deceased must be cremated, and the funeral rites in cities like Kyoto and Tokyo are commonly held in the home or in the crematorium. The container with the ashes and a picture of the deceased are displayed on a home altar or in the front of the chapel. Those who are asked to speak during the funeral address the picture, not the mourners.

"The reason for this is they believe the spirit of the departed hovers over the family for forty-nine days. Thus, at the funeral, one talks directly to the picture, for the spirit of the dead one is hovering near and hears the speeches of his or her friends.

"Though there is a difference in Buddhist and Shinto beliefs, there has been a great deal of syncretism. Generally, the Japanese believe that when the faithful die they become gods. This is one of the basic Christian objections to the Japanese rites. Buddhists refer to these ancestral gods as *hotoke-sama,* and followers of Shinto believe these dead become *kami-sama.* This last word, incidentally, is the same word Japanese Christians use for God, although some Roman Catholics use instead *tennoue-sama,* a possessive form meaning "of heaven" or "heavenly."

"If the family is wealthy, several Buddhist priests may take part. If not, only one priest or no priest is present. Those asked to speak, other than the priest or priests, may be, for example, the deceased's best high school friend, best college friend, and a current friend. Each, however, will speak to the picture, not to the family and friends.

"If a priest is there, he will be dressed in his clerical robes and will be seated facing the altar and the picture. The ceremony begins with the priest or priests reading or reciting the sutras. At designated intervals there is the tapping of a bell. The priest then bows to the picture of the deceased and offers a prayer.

"During this part of the ritual, the family members as well as the priest(s) finger their meditation beads and repeat over and over, *'Namu Amida Butsu,'* meaning, 'I pay homage to Amida Buddha.' These are words of gratitude and faith that Amida will deliver the soul of their loved ones to the Pure Land.

"Then the friends will come and speak. Oh, I neglected to mention the incense. At every funeral incense will be burning throughout the service. There are two kinds of incense, sticks and powder. The priests and the family members, one by one, come forward and light sticks of incense and stand them up in sand in an incense bowl. They believe the aromatic scents are pleasing to the gods, and the rising smoke accompanies the spirit or soul to the Pure Land.

"The powdered incense will be in two bowls, one of which will be burning. As the service concludes, those present are expected to show their respect for the deceased by coming forward, taking a pinch of dry powder from one bowl and putting it into the bowl of incense that is burning. The mourner then will fold his or her hands in an attitude of prayer and will bow before the picture. As the incense burns, the priest(s), members of the family, and some of the other mourners continue repeating the prayer, *'Namu Amida Butsu,'* while passing the meditation beads through their fingers.

"Incidentally, Christian funerals in Japan are similar in some ways. A picture of the deceased will be placed at the front of the chapel, and rather than incense, there will be flowers. At the conclusion of the service, mourners customarily come forward, take a flower from one of the arrangements, place it on the table with the picture, fold their hands in an attitude of prayer, and bow before the picture.

"Those who speak usually say things such as, 'Noriko, do you see all of these friends and family who love you and who have come to honor you? I love you, and I am here to show you how much I love and respect you.'

"Following the speeches of friends, a member of the family will express gratitude to all the friends who have come for taking time from their very crowded schedules to attend the funeral ceremony, and for burning incense for the deceased.

"The priest will then say the final chant or requiem, entrusting the spirit of the departed one to the care and protection of Amida Buddha.

"This is the background of my relationship to this family. You see why I was unsure about what I should do. I was not prepared for Keiko's question. She said, 'Rebecca, my mother loved you, and she will be pleased if you speak at her funeral. Can you do it?'

"What would you have said?"[9]

STUDY QUESTIONS

1. Who is Rebecca Johnson, and what preparation did she have for being a missionary in Japan? Can you summarize the major events in her missionary career?

2. Rebecca developed a friendship with Noriko Suzuki. What is significant about Ms. Suzuki's life and her relationship with Rebecca?

3. Describe the final conversation between Rebecca and Noriko. Do you feel that Rebecca was sensitive, clear, and straightforward in what she said to Noriko?

4. What is there about the history of religion in Japan as well as the religious context that makes it difficult for Christianity to gain converts?

5. What do you know about the Japanese funeral rites? Are there fundamental differences as well as similarities between what you perceive as Christian and Japanese funeral customs?

6. More specifically, at what point would Rebecca's participation in the funeral of Noriko-San compromise her Christian witness? Should Rebecca accept the invitation to speak at Noriko's funeral?

SUGGESTED BIBLICAL TEXTS FOR REFLECTION

Psalm 116:1–19. Praise for being saved from death.

Ecclesiastes 1:1–11. The philosopher's soliloquy on the uselessness of life. Is this view akin to the Buddha's insistence that all of life involves suffering?

John 11:28–33. The death of Lazarus and the sorrow of Jesus.

2 Corinthians 4:16–5:10. Suffering, death, hope, and anticipation.

---

9. *Note:* There is a Part B of this case, and it together with a teaching note are found in the *Journal for Case Teaching* 3 (Fall 1991):51–57, or may be ordered from the Case Study Institute, Yale Divinity School Library, 490 Prospect Street, New Haven, CT 06511. Teachers are encouraged not to use Part B, however, unless they have a minimum of 90 minutes of uninterrupted class time.

"What's the Matter, Abdaraman?"

Carlo Carretto, a member of the Little Brothers of Jesus in the mountains of Algeria, North Africa, is a close friend of a small Muslim boy named Abdaraman. One evening the boy is uncharacteristically pensive and silent. When pressed by Carlo to disclose why he is not talking, Abdaraman begins to cry. Finally the lad gains composure and explains the reason for his sadness. Carlo then is unexpectedly confronted by the compassion and love of this simple, sincere Muslim child.

CONTEXT
Islam and Christianity

Muslim-Christian Relations: A Brief History

The history of Christian-Muslim relations is lamentable if not deplorable. Prior to the time of Muhammad (b. 570) the Prophet—as he is referred to by Muslims—there were small numbers of Syrian Orthodox, Jacobites, and Nestorian Christians living in Mecca as well as in other areas of the Arabian peninsula and in what today is North Yemen and Iraq. A few Arabian tribes as a whole professed Christianity. With the rise of Islam, however, most of these either chose to pay tribute to the Prophet or convert to Islam. A small minority challenged the Muslim forces militarily but were quickly defeated.

During the period when Muhammad and his small band of followers were struggling to survive, some of them fled to Abyssinia in 615, sought refuge there, and were provided sanctuary by the Christian king. This gesture was greatly appreciated by Muhammad and subsequent generations of Muslims. It is often cited as evidence supporting the Qur'anic affirmation of Christians as "people of the Book," believers in the same God, and worthy of certain rights.

After the Prophet's death in 632, however, Islam, which had already become much more than a religion, began its expansion throughout the Middle East and North Africa, clashing continually with Christian Byzantine and European armies. The fall of Jerusalem and the "holy land" to the Muslims in C.E. 638–640 became a thorn in the side of Christians and eventually incited the series of military adventures called the Crusades, to recover this region. The first Crusade began in 1095, and there were at least seven—some say more—Christian expeditions set forth to drive the Muslims from Palestine and liberate the Holy Land. Men young and old—even children on one occasion—were caught up in the fanatical emotions fanned by the Church's assurance that *"Deus vult,"* God wills this.[1] The last of the Crusaders were driven from Acre in 1299, ending the most tragic and futile series of ventures in Christian history.

One thing is clear, the Crusades were not efforts to convert Muslims, but to defeat, annihilate or expel them from territories believed to be historically and rightfully Christian. The Crusades were as a whole totally unsuccessful, and the atrocities committed and the suffering, destruction, plunder, and slaughter that followed "left a trail of bitterness across the relations between Christians and Muslims that remains as a living factor in the world situation to the present day."[2]

Not all Christians, of course, supported these adventures, but one of the first to speak negatively about them was Peter the Venerable (1094–1157), Abbot of Cluny, who advocated gestures of good will and dialogue rather than violence and conquest.[3] He likewise commissioned a translation of the Qur'an and portions of the *Hadith* (the sayings, decisions, and deeds of the Prophet as well as other documents of Islam), together with certain Arab-Christian apologetic treatises. Peter appealed for the conversion of Muslims, not their destruction.[4]

His efforts were admirable but largely fruitless except for the influence he exerted on others such as Francis of Assisi (1181–1226) and Ramón Lull (1235–1315), both of whom sought to evangelize Muslims rather than exterminate them. Francis is said to have made three separate attempts to present the gospel to Muslims by journeying to Morocco in 1212, to Spain in 1214, and finally in 1219 to Egypt. No evidence exists to suggest that any Muslims were converted to Christianity by the noble and courageous efforts of Francis, but his missions did represent a striking change in dealing with those long regarded as the principal adversaries of the Christian faith. Lull's importance lies not only in his valiant efforts to convince Muslims in North Africa to abandon Islam and accept Christianity—efforts that finally resulted in his martyrdom—but it was Lull who called upon the political and religious leaders of Europe to establish chairs of Arab studies in the leading European

---

1. The history of the Crusades has been extensively treated by western authorities, and hardly any defend them as justified or beneficial. See Steven Runciman, *A History of the Crusades,* 3 vols. (Cambridge: Cambridge University Press, 1951); Benjamin Z. Kedar, *Crusade and Mission: European Approaches Toward the Muslims.* (Princeton, NJ: Princeton University Press, 1984), 57–116; and Carl Eerdmann, *The Origin of the Idea of Crusade.* (Princeton, NJ: Princeton University Press, 1977).

2. Stephen Neill, *A History of Christian Missions,* 2nd ed. (1982), 97.

3. J. Peter Kritzeck, *Peter the Venerable* (Princeton, NJ: Princeton University Press, 1964).

4. Byron L. Haines and Frank L. Cooley, eds., *Christians and Muslims Together* (Philadelphia: Geneva Press, 1987), 32–33.

universities for the teaching of the Arabic language and philosophy as a means of preparing apostles (missionaries) to go to the Muslims.[5]

Between the time of Muhammad and Ramón Lull, a few Christian spokespersons did maintain contact with and engaged Muslims in discussions and debates. Most notable was John of Damascus (c. 645–c. 750), the reputed author of the tract entitled, "Dialogue Between a Saracen and a Christian," which described for Christians the Muslim belief system. The purpose of the treatise was apologetic, basically to prepare Christians for debates with the followers of the Prophet. It is significant that this eighth century document is the earliest known Christian work on Christian-Muslim relations, and that John did not regard Islam as another faith, but as a Christian heresy.[6]

Most significant and scarcely mentioned in mission histories is the impact of Greek philosophy on Arab and thus Muslim thinking. During the Middle Ages, the works of Plato, Aristotle, and the Neo-Platonists, together with many scientific and medical writings, were translated into Arabic, and later they found their way into European thought via the Muslims.[7]

After Christianity became the state religion of the Roman Empire in the fourth century, a sad but oft repeated phenomenon followed. Those who had once known and protested the discrimination and persecution they experienced became themselves intolerant and persecutors of those labeled as "heretics" and "pagans."

When Islam began its rapid spread across much of the known world, the steady Islamization of the Syrian, Persian, North African, and Turkish empires placed Christians living in those areas in difficult situations. Charles Kimball notes, however, that a negative mythology needs to be corrected.

> Contrary to popular opinion, the Muslims did not come out of the Arabian desert plundering everything in sight and forcing conversions at the point of a sword. Rather, the expansion of Islamic rule was a multifaceted phenomenon. The Arab conquest was facilitated by the religious and political situation in Syria, Palestine, and Egypt. The Syriac- and Coptic-speaking Orthodox churches were decidedly anti-Greek in sentiment. Their strong rejection of the Chalcedonian orthodoxy the emperors had endeavored to impose encouraged a subdued response to Islam, at times even welcoming the Muslims rather than resisting them.[8]

5. Neill, 115–117, and E. Allison Peers, *Ramón Lull* (NY: Macmillan, 1929).

6. Charles Kimball, *Striving Together. A Way Forward in Christian-Muslim Relations* (Maryknoll, NY: Orbis, 1991), 39.

7. Muslim civilization, it should be noted, reached its zenith during the European Dark Ages. "Muslim scholarship and knowledge were transmitted to Europe through North Africa and Spain by means of the works of people like Avicenna (Ibn Sina; 980–1037) and Averroës (Ibn Rushd; 1126–1198). Western mathematics and medicine, even the Enlightenment itself, were made possible by the accomplishments of Muslim scholars." Haines and Cooley, 31.

By the end of the seventh century, however, with the single exception of the Coptic Orthodox Church in Egypt, the Christian communities across North Africa were assimilated into Islam. This was true likewise in what is present-day Israel, Syria, and Lebanon. Those who resisted conversion to Islam emigrated or lived in what came to be called *millets* ("millet," Turkish meaning people, and from the Arabic *millah,* religion). Under the Ottomans, *millet* came to signify a non-Muslim group with its own religious leader who exercised both civil and religious functions.

In the West, as already implied, emphasis has been frequently given to the discrimination and adversity Christian believers suffered under Muslim rule, as well as what has been described as the forced conversion of many believers to Islam. Scholars now raise serious questions concerning the objectivity and accuracy of these depictions. But even assuming their validity, Christians likely suffered no worse at the hands of Muslims than Muslims suffered at the hands of Christians. For not only do Christians have to recognize the senselessness and tragedy of the Crusades, Christians must also acknowledge the excesses of the Inquisition which for more than a century in Spain demanded either conversion of Muslims and Jews to Christianity or decreed their execution or expulsion. "By the beginning of the seventeenth century, about three million Muslims had been either banished from Spain or executed by Christian leaders."[9]

With the rise of the Ottoman empire, beginning c. 1300, the threat of Islamic power put Christians, especially Orthodox or Byzantine Christians, under constant pressure as Constantinople fell, and Muslim forces spread into the Balkans and threatened to break through into the heart of Europe. For centuries, Muslims were seen not only as spiritual adversaries, but also as fearsome political enemies.

Some Roman Catholic and Protestant mission efforts to Muslims were initiated during the eighteenth century, and these multiplied significantly during the nineteenth century, that is, during the heyday of European colonialism. Conversions, however, were infrequent as missionaries often resorted to apologetics, that is, discussions and debates with Muslims, or indirect methods of Christian service through missionary educational institutions, clinics, and hospitals. The approach described in the following case study is simply one of many ways Christians have tried to gain a foothold in the most difficult of missionary fields, the world of Islam.

Though work with Muslims has always been difficult, nothing has complicated Christian-Muslim relations in modern times as did the creation of the state of Israel in 1948 followed by the uprooting of hundreds of thousands of Palestinians who became refugees, pawns, and victims in the political and military struggle between Arabs and Jews. The Palestinians are for the most part Muslim—eighty to ninety percent—while approximately ten percent are

---

8. *Striving Together. A Way Forward in Christian-Muslim Relations,* 38.
9. Haines and Cooley, 33.

professing Christians. These fourteen to sixteen million Palestinian Christians, however, are sympathetic to the Arab position. Though many tensions and schisms exist between the various Arab factions, the most serious rift is between Arabs and Jews and between Arabs and the West, principally the United States. This half-century disagreement and struggle profoundly affects Christian-Muslim relations everywhere, and the tensions and suspicion will not be reduced significantly unless and until there is a peaceful settlement of the Palestinian question. The final outcome of this conflict is of course yet to be seen, but no one can deny the severely adverse impact of the events since the Zionist dream of a homeland was realized.[10]

Islam

"Islam" is the name given by Muslims to their religious beliefs and practices, and the word is from the Arabic root *Silm* and *Salam* meaning peace. The way to peace, Islam teaches, is by submission to the One God, Allah, and the results of submission will be peace with God the creator and sovereign Lord, peace with others, peace with oneself, and peace with the environment. Islam for faithful Muslims is more than a religion. It is a complete way of life with spiritual, economic, political, social, and personal implications.

To refer to Islam as "Mohammedanism"[11] is offensive to Muslims because it suggests, they insist, that they worship Muhammad rather than God.

• The basis of Islam is the belief in the One and Only God, Allah, who is known by ninety-nine "beautiful names," such as: the Merciful, the Beneficent, the Creator, the Gracious, the All-Knowing, the All-Wise, the Lord of the Universe, the First and the Last. Allah is the fountain of all of life, the Creator and Sustainer. "Allah" is simply the Arabic word for God, as is *Dieu* in French, *Dios* in Spanish, and *Gott* in German. Muslims believe that one God, Allah, is the God of Muslims, Christians, Jews, Hindus, Buddhists, Confucians—of all. Like Jews, Muslims are strict monotheists.

• The beginnings of Islam, according to Muslims, was in creation. Islam is not a new faith nor did it originate with Muhammad. Adam, Abraham, and Moses are all reverenced as God's messengers. Abraham is regarded as a Muslim for he was the father of Ishmael, and Ishmael was the progenitor of all Arabs. Non-Muslims, however, see Islam as beginning with the Prophet Muhammad.

• Muhammad, Islam teaches, was the last of God's prophets, and it was to him the archangel Gabriel appeared in a series of visions and gave Muhammad God's message which is contained in the Qur'an. The message, however,

---

10. Haines and Cooley, 38–39.

11. The spelling of the Prophet's name and his followers has caused some problem for non-Arabic speakers. Because there is no "o" nor "e" in Arabic, "Muhammad" and "Muslim" are the accepted transliterations. The only vowels in Arabic are a, i, and u. Also, the preferable name of their scriptures is the Qur'an, not the Koran.

was not new. It simply reaffirmed the eternal will of God which had been given to the patriarchs centuries before. These patriarchs and prophets included John the Baptist and Jesus.

Muhammad was born of the tribe of Quraish, descendants of Ishmael and Abraham, in the city of Makkah (Mecca) c. 570 C.E. His father died before Muhammad was born, and his mother six years later. Reared by extended family members, his earliest contacts with the faith of his family, and with Judaism and Christianity as well, was in Mecca. As a lad, Muhammad became involved in the business of caravans and trading, and at the age of twenty-five married a wealthy widow, Khadijah, for whom he had been acting as an agent. Fifteen years later, when Muhammad was forty years of age, he was, Muslims say, chosen by God to write and teach God's message of peace, that is, Islam. The revelation of God to Muhammad is the Qur'an, and the message of God is Islam. But Islam is a message not merely to Arabs. It is to Christians, Jews, Buddhists, and all people.

Muhammad's earliest disciple was his wife, and others soon followed. But his denunciations of idolatry incited fierce opposition, and six years after his first sermon, he and his followers were driven from Mecca. Some found refuge in Christian Abyssinia, and six years later, 622 C.E., the people of Yathrib invited Muhammad to come and be their leader. He regarded the invitation as a summons, and the journey to Yathrib (later named *Madinat an-nabi,* "City of the Prophet" or simply "Madina") is one of the most important events in Muslim history. It is known as the *hijra* or migration, and the year 622 became the first year of the Muslim era.[12]

The Prophet's fortunes rapidly improved and what began as a rag-tag force of relatively few disciples began to grow rapidly in numbers, power, and wealth. Muhammad's religious genius at this point was matched by his ability as a leader and administrator. At first he was highly regarded not only by Muslims, but also by Christians and Jews with whom he initially enjoyed a cordial relationship. Likely this explains why his followers were enjoined at first to face Jerusalem when they prayed, a mandate that was later changed probably because of growing conflicts the Prophet experienced with Christians and Jews.

After a series of skirmishes and battles, Muhammad's followers defeated the powerful tribes of Mecca in 629, followed by the Prophet's peaceful entry into Mecca in a "farewell pilgrimage" and the cleansing of the Ka'bah. The succeeding three years witnessed the submission of more and more Arabian desert tribes to Muhammad's authority, and by the time of his death in 632, Arabia was irreversibly Muslim. The growth and expansion of Islam, however,

---

12. Muslims writing for non-Muslim readers will often give two dates for important events, the first being the year in the Muslim lunar calendar and the second the year according to the Gregorian calendar. Sayyed Hossein Nasr, for example, says that the Crusaders were defeated and expelled from Jerusalem "in 583/1187." "Islam," *Our Religions,* ed. Arvind Sharma (1993), 489.

had just begun, for within a century, it spread as far West as Morocco and Spain and as far East as China.

• The Qur'an, Islam teaches, is the word of God, or more specifically, the words are the specific, literal words of God. They were given to the Prophet in a series of visions, the first in a cave which he frequented outside Mecca. The visions, however, continued intermittently for twenty-three years, that is, until his death. As a single book or collection, the Qur'an is about the same length as the Christian New Testament, but in contrast to the New Testament, the words of the Qur'an are understood as God speaking, not the Prophet.

Unfortunately for those accustomed to the arrangement of the Bible, the Qur'an appears totally unorganized following neither a chronological nor topical order. Its 114 *suras* cover a wide range of topics from the creation of the world to the Last Judgment, Heaven, and Hell. All the verses are written in Arabic rhyme. Besides the eternal truths contained within the message, there are warnings to the unfaithful and the wicked, and there are words of hope and encouragement to the weak and discouraged. But there are likewise *suras* directing the way Muslims are to live and how a Muslim community is to be organized and function, that is, moral, social, civil, and legal precepts. Theoretically, all that one needs to know and live is found in the Qur'an.

As in other religions, however, there are additional authoritative writings, and the principal collection is called the *Hadith,* the recorded sayings, deeds, and blessings of the Prophet. His life story is called the *Sirah* and his deeds and sayings *Sunnah.* The sayings and the actions of the Prophet are, after the Qur'an, the second source of authority in Islamic law.

• The primary beliefs of Islam stem from the principle of the absolute oneness of God. God is One, and God, Allah, is the Only God. There are no other gods, either divine or human. Thus, God cannot be said to be two in one or three in one, for God is but one.

Muslims also believe in:

—The oneness of humankind. All forms of racism, caste, or ethnic superiority are rejected. The way one lives determines who is better, and this is known only to God. No one, therefore, should assume or claim superiority over anyone else.

—The oneness of the messengers and the message. Muhammad was not God's only prophet. He was simply the last and final prophet. God sent many different messengers, but until Muhammad, people distorted the message. Muslims nonetheless believe in and reverence Adam, Noah, Abraham, Isaac, Ishmael, Jacob, Moses, David, John the Baptist, and Jesus. Those whom Christians believe to have been God's messengers are thus reverenced also by Muslims.

—The innocence of all at birth. Muslims believe that everyone is born innocent, that is, without the infection of sin. Sin is committed after people reach the age of puberty and knowingly do what is wrong and thereby become accountable. No one is answerable for the sins of anyone else, and God's grace and forgiveness is offered to all.

—The existence of angels, the coming Judgment, Heaven and Hell. Islam teaches that there are invisible beings—angels—created by God for God's work. The words of the Qur'an, for example, were delivered to Muhammad by the archangel Gabriel. All humankind, Muslims believe, are facing a final judgment for the things done in their earthly lives, and how they live will determine whether their eternal destiny is heaven or hell.

—Islam is more than a religion, it is a way of life in which all that one thinks and does is to be directed by God and what one does determines one's destiny. There is, therefore, no division of the sacred and the secular, no separation between the state and religion. Everything, every institution, every system, and every relationship is to be governed by the will of God found in the Qur'an and in the teachings and example of the Prophet.

• The five pillars of wisdom or practice are:

—*The belief that God is One and that Muhammad is God's prophet.* This declaration of faith called the *Shahadah* is a simple formula whispered in the ear of a Muslim baby at birth and whispered again in the ear of the faithful at death. In Arabic it is: *La ilaha illa'llah. Muhammadun rasulu'llah.* "There is no god (*ilaha*) except God (*illa'llah*), and Muhammad is the messenger of God." These words come nearest to being a creed in Islam, and one can become a Muslim simply by saying sincerely the *Shahadah,* "There is no god apart from God, and Muhammad is the Messenger of God."

—*Prayer is to be offered five times daily* facing Mecca. A translation of the Call to Prayer is:

> God is most great. God is most great.
> God is most great. God is most great.
> I testify that there is no god except God.
> I testify that there is no god except God.
> I testify that Muhammad is the messenger of God.
> I testify that Muhammad is the messenger of God.
> Come to prayer! Come to prayer!
> Come to success (in this life and the Hereafter)!
> Come to success!
> God is most great. God is most great.
> There is no god except God.

—*Fasting,* that is, the complete abstinence from food and drink, sexual intimacy between married couples, and other pleasurable activities, is required from sunrise to sunset *during the month of Ramadan.* Not only does this experience contribute to a sense of the equality of all, but it is a stern reminder of the suffering of the poor and less fortunate.

—The annual tax or *Zakat* (meaning both "purification" and "growth") is a designated percentage of one's income (depending on how it is made, but generally two-and-one-half percent of one's overall capital) that must be given for distribution among the needy. Some of the Muslim social services and the building of mosques, for example, are funded through the *Zakat* offerings.

—Once during a Muslim's lifetime, if physically and economically possible, he or she is to make a pilgrimage, a *Hajj,* to Makkah to commemorate the ordeals of the Prophet Abraham, his wife Hagar, and his eldest son Ishmael. One who has made the pilgrimage is a *Hajji.*

• Islamic life revolves around the following:

—The lunar calendar (though daily life can follow the solar or Gregorian calendar). Because Muslims observe the lunar calendar, religious days and observances, such as the month of Ramadan, vary.

—The Muslim holy day is Friday. Joint prayer and worship are to occur shortly after noon (1:00 P.M., for example), led by an *Imam* (literally, "the one in front" or the leader of the prayer) who usually gives a sermon.

—The month of Ramadan with the celebration or *Eid* of sacrifice and the feast or *Eid* of Fast-Breaking. The ceremony of sacrifice commemorates the willingness of Abraham to offer his son, and the celebration of Fast-Breaking concludes the month of Ramadan.

—Muslims are required to abstain from pork in any form as well as from alcohol and other addictive drugs.

—Though Muslims are taught they can pray anywhere and even alone, prayers are best said in the mosque with a congregation of the faithful. The physical center of worship is the mosque or *masjid* (Arabic meaning prostration), and the three most revered are the Mosque of Ka'bah in Mecca toward which all faithful Muslims pray daily, the Mosque of the Prophet in Medina (where the Prophet is buried), and the Mosque adjacent to the Dome of the Rock in Jerusalem.

• As indicated above, Muslim and Christian relations since the seventh century have been characterized and complicated at times by animosity, suspicion, and violence. The reasons are multiple, but central to the causes are the Muslim advance across much of the ancient Christian world, the ensuing Christian Crusades to drive the Muslims from "the Holy Land" (1096–1291), and the commercial, political, and military expansion of Portugal, Spain, England, the Netherlands, and France beginning in the sixteenth century. Former Islamic kingdoms fell to the Christian explorers and colonialists in the Near East, Africa, India, Ceylon, Malaya, Indonesia, and China.

The Crusades, the Inquisition, and modern European colonialism are the principal causes of the distrust and conflict of the present century, and can be traced back to events that occurred generations, if not centuries ago. And though Christians have distinguished between colonial adventures and Christian missions, Muslims have regarded them as two edges of the same imperialistic sword.

Often in the West, Muslims and Arabs are thought to be synonymous. But Muslims may be Arabs, Turks, Iraqis, Iranians, Bosnians, Bulgarians, Afghans, Moroccans, Tunisians, Egyptians, Somalis, Sudanese, Central Africans, Nigerians, Kenyans, South Africans, Syrians, Jordanians, Pakistanis,

Bangladeshis, Indians, Malaysians, Chinese, Indonesians, Filipinos, French, English, and Americans. Of the nearly one billion Muslims in the world today, approximately one-fifth or 200,000,000 are Arabs. Not all Arabs, however, are Muslims. As indicated above, some fourteen to sixteen million Arabs are Christians, others are Jews, Baha'is, or members of other small communities of faith. Some Arabs profess no religion.

The language of Islam is Arabic. The Qur'an, the Scriptures for Muslims, is written in Arabic, and all faithful Muslims study and try to gain enough proficiency in Arabic in order to read the Qur'an. Muslims pray in Arabic, although they believe that God hears their supplications in any language.

To understand why relatively few Muslims have converted to Christianity, one need only read the history of Muslim-Christian relations.[13] No less significant are the doctrinal differences and the firm conviction among Muslims that Muhammad was the last of God's prophets, and thus Islam is the final revelation.

FOR FURTHER STUDY

Christianity and Muslims

Haines, Byron L. and Frank L. Cooley. *Christians and Muslims Today.* Philadelphia: Geneva Press, 1987.

    A summary of the history and status of Christian-Muslim relations in various areas of the world. Includes a theological analysis on the issues.

Kimball, Charles. *Striving Together.* Maryknoll, NY: Orbis, 1991.

    The author, formerly the Middle East Director for the National Council of Churches of Christ, not only surveys the history of Christian-Muslim encounters, but interprets the recent events, such as the upsurge of Muslim fundamentalism. This is a concise and helpful volume.

Latourette, Kenneth Scott. *The Thousand Years of Uncertainty,* 286–342. Vol. 2, *A History of the Expansion of Christianity.* New York: Harper, 1938.

    The history of the rise and conflict between Muslims and Jews from the seventh to the sixteenth centuries.

Parshall, Phil. *New Paths in Muslim Evangelism.* Grand Rapids, MI: Baker Book House, 1980.

    An innovative evangelical approach to Muslims. Parshall outlines the Muslim worldview, the theological bridges available, Muslim religious and social practices, and concentrates on the question of Christian baptism for Muslims.

---

13. Nasr's "Islam" is an excellent beginning. *Our Religions,* 484–503. See also Carl Brockelmann, *History of the Islamic Peoples* (New York: Capricorn Books, 1960), J. M. Gaudeul, *Encounters and Clashes: Islam and Christianity in History,* 2 vols. (Rome: Pontifical Institute of Arabic and Islamic Studies, 1984), and Haines and Cooley, eds., *Christians and Muslims Together.*

Speight, R. Marston. *Christians and Muslim Relations: An Introduction for Christians in the United States of America.* 3rd ed. Hartford, CT: Office on Christian-Muslim Relations of the NCC, 1986.
>A practical guide written primarily for Christians interested in establishing relations with Muslims.

"You Shall Love Your Neighbor." *Church & Society* 84 (January/February 1994): 1–152.
>One of the most thorough, up-to-date, and helpful collections of information available for Christian and Muslim relations. Includes maps, a glossary, study guides, and audio-visual resources.

Islam

Denny, Frederick M. *An Introduction to Islam.* New York: Macmillan, 1985.
>One of the more recent and readable texts for those who want an introduction to Islam.

Esposito, John. *Islam: the Straight Path.* New York: Oxford University Press, 1988.
>An analysis of recent developments in Islam written by one who can best be described as objective but sympathetic.

Lings, Martin. *Muhammad: His Life Based on the Earliest Sources.* Rochester, VT: Inner Traditions, 1983.
>One of the most authoritative treatments of the life of Muhammad available. Utilizes sources only recently available to English readers.

Nasr, Seyyed Hossein. *Ideas and Realities of Islam.* Winchester, MA: Unwin Hyman, 1983.
>Written from the perspective of traditional Islam, the author explains the significance of the Prophet, the Qur'an, and other Islamic basics including the differences in Shi'ism and Sunnism.

———. "Islam." In *Our Religions,* ed. Arvind Sharma, 427–532. San Francisco: Harper, 1993,
>Nasr's most recent introduction to the history, theology, ethics, and practices of Muslims, including their divisions and relations with other religions.

Nazir-Ali, Michalel. *Islam: A Christian Perspective.* Philadelphia: Westminster Press, 1984.
>Islam as viewed by a Pakistani Christian.

Speight, R. Marston. *God is One: The Way of Islam.* New York: Friendship Press, 1989.
>An introduction to Islam written for Christian readers.

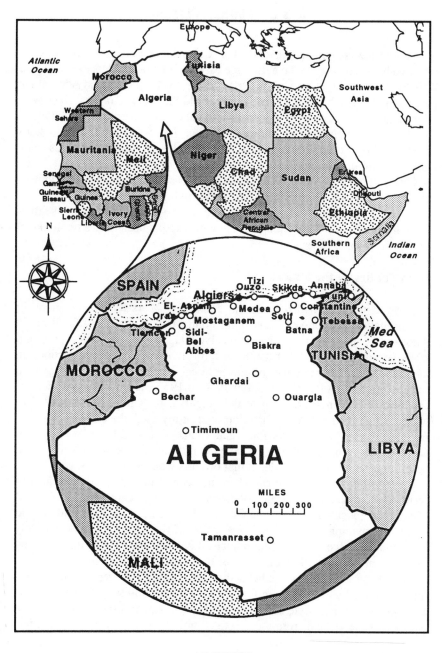

ALGERIA

THE CASE
"What's the Matter, Abdaraman?"

Darkness was approaching as Brother Carlo emerged from his cell to walk the two hundred yards to the hermitage for evening prayers. His eyes adjusted quickly to the twilight, and, as he expected, he saw his little friend Abdaraman waiting for him. Abdaraman, an eight-year-old Muslim lad, often walked with Carlo, and when invited he shared tea and cakes with the monk. Abdaraman, however, never entered the hermitage; when they were ten or fifteen steps away, the boy would always pull back as if he feared some mysterious force inside would do him harm.

This particular evening, Abdaraman was pensive, melancholy, and unusually quiet. He took Carlo's hand but said nothing.

"What's the matter, Abdaraman?" There was no answer. "Perhaps his father has punished him," Carlo thought. "He will respond because we do not keep secrets from each other."

From Politics to the Desert

Carlo at the time had been in the desert five years living as a monk in contemplation and prayer—a striking contrast to his earlier life. Born in Alessandria, Italy, Carlo Carretto received his degree in philosophy, and while in the university he became deeply involved in Catholic Action, an international anticommunist religio-political movement which began in Europe prior to World War II. From 1946 to 1952 Carretto was president of Catholic Action in Italy. Then at the height of his career he responded to what he described as "the most serious call of my life," the call to separation from the world. Thus at forty-four years of age, Carlo said "yes" to the inner voice which commanded him, "Leave everything and come with me to the desert. It is not your acts and deeds that I want. I want your prayers, your love."

Carretto left Italy for Algeria where he soon joined the Little Brothers of Jesus, a Roman Catholic order of hermits begun to carry on the work of Charles de Foucauld. At the time Carlo had never heard of Foucauld nor did he know anything of the history and rules of the Little Brothers. He only knew that he was entering a community established as a silent witness among the Muslims deep in the mountains of the North African Sahara.

Charles de Foucauld was educated to be a military officer, abandoned his faith, and lived a dissolute life for a time before committing himself to God and the Church. He wrote that he heard Jesus saying to him, "Your vocation is to shout the Gospel from the rooftops, not in words, but with your life."

This case study was adapted from Carlo Carretto's book *Letters from the Desert* (Maryknoll, NY: Orbis Books, 1972), and the material is used by permission. All rights reserved.

After a time with the Trappists, Foucauld became a hermit in Tamanrasset, Algeria, in an attempt to reach Muslims by a life of sacrifice and love. No one joined him in his effort, and he did not live to attract a single disciple. It was not until after his death in 1916 and the publication of his personal papers that the order of the Little Brothers of Jesus was founded in 1933, and the Little Sisters of Jesus in 1936, to continue his work.

In many respects, Carlo Carretto's change in life patterned that of Foucauld. Ivan Illich, who knew Carretto as a political leader in Italy, met him again years later in Algeria. Illich, known for his activist community in Cuernavaca, Mexico, said of the meeting, "I came to know Carlo: the man who was dying to the world of power, the world of good causes, the world of big words, and the world of political parties. I came to experience the naked simplicity in the statement of his love for the Lord. I came to marvel at his lack of embarrassment at being judged escapist because he refused to be militant."

Encounter with Submission

Like the other Little Brothers, Carlo lived in a cave near Tamanrasset, high in the mountains of Ahaggar. Though living in relative solitude, he came to know Abdaraman and his father Aleck, a devoted follower of the Prophet. Carlo was unable to ignore the faithfulness of Aleck to the Muslim traditions of prayer, fasting, and sacrifice. Five times daily he prayed; strictly he observed the month of Ramadan; and annually, in homage to Abraham, Aleck sacrificed a sheep in the presence of his family. His absolute trust in and reverence for the will of Allah were as evident as they were impressive to Carlo. Furthermore, though Aleck was dreadfully poor, he continued to work diligently and refused to steal.

On one occasion a detachment of the French Foreign Legion camped along the bank of a small stream that Aleck had kept clear and from which he channeled water for his meager crop of corn. Yet because of the thoughtlessness of the soldiers, the water was being wasted in their washing vehicles and throwing it on each other in jest. The result was that very little water reached Aleck's corn.

Carlo was irritated by the soldiers' lack of consideration, and he admonished the Muslim farmer, "Aleck, unless you say something, your corn is going to dry up and die. Why don't you go to the Captain and tell him that the stream is yours, that you need the water, and they should either use it sparingly or camp somewhere else?"

"No, Allah is great," Aleck replied. "He will provide for my children." So the legionnaires continued to waste the water, and the corn became stunted and died. Aleck's faith in Allah, nonetheless, remained unshaken.

The Question

As they left the entrance to the cave and walked toward the hermitage, Carlo was puzzled by the apparent sadness of his little friend. Was it the water problem or something else?

"What's the matter, Abdaraman?" There was no response.

"Are you hungry?" The boy always had a ravenous appetite, but tonight he was silent.

"Did your father punish you?" Still no answer.

"Did your little bird die?" The boy remained mute.

"Abdaraman, why don't you answer me? You know I am your friend, and it makes me sad when you will not talk."

Suddenly the child burst into tears, and his whole body shook. The tears ran down his cheeks and onto his naked chest and abdomen. Now Carlo remained silent, waiting for the emotional outburst to subside. Then as they approached the perimeter of the hermitage he asked again, "Why are you crying, Abdaraman?"

"I'm crying . . . I'm crying . . . because you don't become a Moslem! . . . If you don't become a Moslem you'll go to hell like all Christians!"

They stopped outside the little mud structure dedicated to Christian worship, a building constructed by Charles de Foucauld who wanted all people to regard each other as little brothers, but who was killed by Muslim fanatics from the same tribe as Aleck and Abdaraman.

Carlo would leave his little friend in a moment and enter the hermitage for prayer. There in the awe and introspection prompted by the Eucharist he would weep as he reflected on the depth of the sectarianism which prevailed and the stain which had penetrated his own soul. On his knees he would recall a traumatic experience from his own childhood when a man came through his village selling a book he had never seen nor of which he had ever heard—the Bible.

He remembered a woman leaning from a second floor window and screaming, "You rascal! Get out of here. We don't want your books! We don't need your religion!" He recalled another woman—who evidently moments before had purchased a Bible—throwing it at the man who was walking slowly down the middle of the street. Particularly painful was the image of the man putting down the heavy bag he was carrying, bending to retrieve the book, and being struck in the back by a stone thrown by a child. The children, many of them carrying stones and urged by the shouting of the women, followed the man as he quickly left the town. Carlo could almost hear the priest congratulating the townspeople that evening, especially the children, for defending the parish from contamination by a "representative of the devil."

Forty years had passed since that afternoon in May, and now the monk was hearing his own faith challenged, not menacingly by an unknown child with a stone, but by his little friend beset with compassionate anxiety. "If you don't become a Moslem you will go to hell. . . ."

Abdaraman, whose knowledge of the intricacies of theology was nil and who was possibly bewildered by the contrasting lives of this Christian hermit and the "Christian" legionnaires, was heart-broken because Brother Carlo had not converted to Islam. Carlo was stunned. No one had ever manifested this kind of concern for him, and he struggled for something to say.[14]

STUDY QUESTIONS

1. Who are the principal characters in this case, and what do you know about them?

2. Describe your reaction or feelings when you discovered why Abdaraman was crying.

3. What beliefs do Carlo and Abdaraman share? Is there enough common ground so they could discuss their respective faiths? If you feel there is a common set of beliefs, can you specify convictions they likely hold in common?

4. In what ways are their respective faiths different?

5. Why does Abdaraman believe Carlo is destined for Hell?

6. What is the significance of Carlo's remembering the incident from his own boyhood?

7. Knowing what you know about this case, how should Carlo respond to Abdaraman's anxiety?

SUGGESTED BIBLICAL TEXTS FOR REFLECTION

Genesis 16:1–15. Abram, Sarai, and Hagar: problems and promises.

Genesis 21:9–21. Hagar and Ishmael are sent away from Abraham's house. (See also Genesis 25:12–18, the descendants of Ishmael.)

Galatians 4:21–31. The Apostle Paul's analogy of Hagar and Sarah as symbols of the two covenants.

Hebrews 11:8–12. Abraham's faith and innumerable descendants.

---

14. *Note:* There is a Part B for this case which can be obtained from the Case Study Collection, Yale Divinity School Library, 409 Prospect Street, New Haven, CT 06511. See Appendexes B and E for information on obtaining cases.

"WHAT KIND OF GOD WOULD LET THIS HAPPEN?"

A Jewish-Christian Encounter

A theology professor meets an elderly Jewish couple in a restaurant near a Protestant mission center. When they learn the professor's vocation, they tell him their son has just died of a heart attack, leaving his wife and children. The title of the case is the question asked by the Jewish father.

CONTEXT
Judaism and Christianity

Christianity and Judaism

Christians are aware—or should be—of the close historical and theological relationship between Christianity and Judaism. Consequently, Christians for the most part are more familiar with Judaism than with other world religions, though, it must be admitted, Christians' knowledge of their parent faith is woefully inadequate and often distorted.

Judaism is traced back to Abraham with whom, Jews—as well as Christians and Muslims—believe, God made a covenant promising to make them a great people and give them a land in perpetuity. Belief that they are a covenant people is the foundation of Judaism. The essence of the faith is the belief in one God, creator and sustainer of all. God's nature and will, Jews contend, have been revealed in the Torah or the Law—specifically "the five books of Moses"—and in the history of the Jewish people whom God chose as a light to all the peoples of the world. Judaism, because of what Jews believe about God's promise to Abraham, is closely tied to a particular land, now called Israel.

Unlike Christianity, Judaism has no creeds. The essence of their belief is found in the six Hebrew words of the *Shema* (meaning "Hear"): "Sh'ma Yisra'el, Adonai Eloheinu, Adonai Ekhad" meaning "Hear, O Israel, the Lord is our God, the Lord is One" or "Hear, O Israel, the Lord is our God, the Lord Alone" (Deuteronomy 6:4)—a resounding declaration of mono-theism or one-Godism. Faithful Jews are expected to recite these words four times a day, twice in morning prayers, once in the evening prayers, and finally before going to sleep. This affirmation is often combined with additional commands, such as:

> "And you shall love the Lord your God with all your heart, and with all your soul, and with all your might (Deuteronomy 6:5). And these words which I command you this day shall be upon your heart (Deuteronomy 6:6), and you shall teach them diligently to your children, and shall talk of them when you sit in your house, and when you walk by the way, and when you lie down, and when you rise. And you shall bind them as a sign upon your hand, and they shall be as frontlets between your eyes. And you shall write them on the doorposts of your house and on your gates (Deuteronomy 6:7–8)."

Living according to these mandates, Judaism teaches, will assure God's blessings, both spiritual and material, and disobeying or ignoring them will inevitably result in punishment (Deuteronomy 11:13–17).

The entire written Law is contained in the first five books of the Jewish Scriptures (called the *Torah* or *Humash,* meaning five, viz., the Pentateuch): Genesis, Exodus, Leviticus, Numbers, and Deuteronomy which contain not only the well-known Ten Commandments, but a total of 613 laws and regulations.

As Judaism became institutionalized, worship took place around an altar that eventually was set up in a tent, then a tabernacle, and finally in the Temple. As Jews were dispersed by forced exile and persecution in 729 and 587/6 B.C.E., the *Bet Haknesset* or synagogue(s) (Greek for meeting place) began to be established. Finally, when the Romans destroyed the Temple in 70 C.E., the synagogues became the only places for congregational worship.[1]

Sabbath worship takes place weekly, and faithful Jews also observe a number of special religious days and festivals: *Rosh Hashanah,* New Year; *Yom Kippur,* the Day of Atonement; *Sukkot,* the week-long Feast of Tabernacles; *Simkhat Torah,* the Feast of Rejoicing with the Torah or the Law when the last part of Deuteronomy and the first verses of Genesis are read; *Hanukkah* or the Festival of Lights, an eight-day festival (during which time the *menorah* or eight-candlesticks are used) celebrating the victory of Judas Maccabeus over Syria and the rededication of the Temple in 164 B.C.E.; *Purim* commem-

---

1. When the required number of Jewish males was not available to establish a synagogue, some scholars state that worship was conducted in homes or outdoors near a river or stream. (Whether this was true or not, the lack of a quorum required the skipping of certain prayers thought to be essential for worship.) New Testament scholars often indicate that for this reason the Apostle Paul and his companions when they arrived in the Roman colony of Philippi in Macedonia "went out of the city to the riverside" on the Sabbath expecting to find whatever Jews there were gathered there for worship (Acts 16:13).

orating in February or March Esther's foiling of the plot by Haman to kill the Jews and his own execution; *Pesach* or Passover, the most widely celebrated Jewish holiday commemorating the liberation of the Jews from Egyptian slavery and "the beginning of Jewish nationhood";[2] *Shavuot* or Pentecost, the festival celebrated fifty days after Passover commemorating the giving of the Law to Moses and also the "First Fruits" of harvesting; and *Tishah B'Av,* a day of fasting and mourning observed in July or August when Jewish people remember the destruction of the Temple in C.E. 70.

Who are the Jews today? To say they are the descendants of Abraham or followers of the religion of Moses is minimally helpful. Muslims also consider themselves the children of Abraham, as do Christians, and both Muslims and Christians revere Abraham and Moses. Jews are not an ethnic, racial, physiological or anatomical group. There are Semitic, black African, Latin, Anglo, Germanic, Scandinavian, and Asiatic Jews. Some authorities contend that Jews cannot be distinguished by culture, language, or even by religion. The fact is Jews do not agree concerning what constitutes being Jewish.[3] The modern state of Israel has recognized as Jews those who have Jewish mothers, but this has hardly solved the question. Mordechi Kaplan, founder of Reconstructionist Judaism, calls Jews "a civilization," and he makes an impressive case for this claim.[4]

Comparatively few Jews speak and read Hebrew, and though many—perhaps most Jews—observe certain Jewish traditions and practice some form of Jewish religion, many do not. Culturally, the differences are numerous and marked. "The gap between the black Falasha Jews in Ethiopia and the Indian Jews in Mexico, for instance, is immense."[5]

Doctrinally and functionally, there are three main branches of modern Judaism. *Orthodox* or classical Jews[6] are committed to following the Torah in the strictest sense, for the Torah is God's unchanging and unchangeable word. Orthodox Jews believe not only that God revealed Godself in the Law given to Moses, but that the words of the first five books of the Bible are fully inspired, unalterable, and authoritative. All of life is to be governed by the Law, and an Orthodox Jew is supposed to study it daily and to fashion his or her life according to its teachings. Sabbath observance, diet (including laws of *kashrut,* "kosher" being the adjectival form), work, prayer three times daily, wearing apparel, business, recreation—all of one's activities and relationships are to adhere to the precepts of the Law. In Orthodox Judaism

2. Joseph Telushikin, *Jewish Literacy* (New York: William Morrow, 1991), 581.
3. Jacob Neusner makes this clear in his splendid essay on Judaism in *Our Religions,* ed. Arvind Sharma, 293–299.
4. *Judaism as a Civilization* (New York: Macmillan, 1934) was Kaplan's most influential work. See Marc Lee Raphael, *Profiles in American Judaism* (San Francisco: Harper & Row, 1984), 179–180.
5. Marvin Wilson, "Branches of Judaism," *Eerdman's Handbook to the World's Religions,* 292.
6. Sometimes referred to by other Jews as "fundamentalists."

the rabbi occupies a central role in the total life of the community. Children are educated in separate schools according to Orthodox traditions, that is, the boys are separated from the girls in different classrooms or schools, and are, of course, separate from the public schools. Jewish holy days are faithfully and precisely observed, and the coming of a personal Messiah is fervently anticipated. Understanding and applying the Law is aided by use of the Talmud, the authoritative rabbinic interpretations of the Law. In a word, Judaism is Law, God's Law for God's chosen people.

Reform Judaism began in the early 1800s in post-enlightenment Germany as a result of a number of forces: reaction to the authoritarianism, backwardness, and insularity—social and intellectual—of Orthodoxy at a time when the liberal political and social milieu allowed Jews freedoms and rights as citizens they had not known. Though Reform Jews reverence and respect the Torah, they are not literalists. They teach that much of the Torah has to be understood in its historical context and is selectively relevant and applicable today. For Reform Jews, Judaism is more a way to restore or revamp the world than it is a ritual and legal regimen. Services in the synagogues of Reform Jews are considerably different from those of the Orthodox. Whereas Orthodox worship depends solely on the cantor, and the playing of musical instruments is forbidden on the Sabbath, Reform worship often includes organ as well as other instrumental music. The use of Hebrew in sermons and in prayers has been largely replaced by the use of the language of the people, be it German, French, Spanish, Italian, English, or whatever.

Rather than following in an exacting way the Talmud with its multiplicity of ritual requirements, Reform Jews emphasize what they refer to as "ethical monotheism," behavior shaped by the prophets and belief in one righteous God.

Reform Judaism is clearly the most liberal branch of Judaism as well as being the most involved in social action, if measured by the number of organizations, and in inter-faith dialogue. Likewise, Jewish partners in inter-faith marriages are most frequently Reform. Their first seminary in the United States, New York's Hebrew Union College, was begun in 1875 by Rabbi Isaac Wise, and in the 1970s the school accepted and later ordained the first Jewish women as rabbis.

Conservative Judaism began late in the nineteenth century by Jewish leaders who could no longer accept the rigidity of the Orthodox, nor what they regarded as the radicalism of Reform Judaism. They hold to many of the traditions of the faith, but are more open to change than are the Orthodox. Some of their congregations allow the use of an organ, but not all. Conservative congregations observe the traditional dietary regulations, and they represent what may be rightly called the moderate wing of modern Judaism when it comes to tradition and change/renewal. The Conservative movement is the largest of the three major branches of Judaism, and they are committed to the centrality of Jews as a people, no matter what individual levels of observance may be.

Though one may assume that the Orthodox are the most traditional and conservative Jews, the fact is there is the ultra-orthodox branch known as the *Hasidim* who are even more strict than the majority of the Orthodox. Voluntarily segregating themselves in separate communities, each is led by its own *rebbe.* Hasidic males can be identified by their black coats, black hats, and braided ear locks.

Besides these and other smaller branches, a significant number of people who identify themselves as Jews are non-religious, at least in the traditional sense. Often known as "secular Jews," they constitute the majority in the state of Israel. Many of the "non-practicing Jews" are deeply committed to and involved in humanitarian and other causes. They often contribute large amounts of money to educational institutions and community endeavors. Some, like many religiously active Jews, are supporters of the state of Israel, not for religious reasons, but as a means of protection against persecution and genocide.

Many Christians have mistakenly concluded that Jews do not engage in efforts to convert non-Jews, that is, in evangelistic or missionary endeavors. This is true of some Jews, but it is not true of all Jews nor is it an accurate representation of all Jewish history. There have been times when many were welcomed into the Jewish faith and community, and there have been Jewish leaders who sought converts. Jesus, in fact, is reported to have spoken harshly of certain Pharisees who went over land and sea to make converts (Matthew 23:13). Conversions nonetheless evidently continued well into the Christian era, but virtually ceased when both Christian and Muslim governments made conversion to Judaism a capital offense. By the late Middle Ages, because of the danger to the Jewish community itself as well as to the converts, conversion to Judaism was infrequent and openly discouraged. The Enlightenment and the founding of democratic states that allow freedom of religion have resulted in losses as well as some gains for Judaism. Many Jews have ceased to practice the faith of their forebears while some non-Jews have converted to Judaism. Orthodox, Conservative, and Reform branches all accept converts, although the Orthodox do not recognize as Jews those converted by Conservative or Reform rabbis. Only a few Reform leaders advocate aggressive attempts to gain converts. It is estimated that between five and ten thousand persons convert annually to Judaism in the United States.[7]

FOR FURTHER STUDY

Goldscheider, Calvin. *Jewish Continuity and Change: Emerging Patterns in America.* Bloomington, IN: Indiana University Press, 1986.

    A valuable source for information, statistics, and analysis of Judaism in North America.

---

7. Telushikin, 625.

Neusner, Jacob. "Judaism." In *Our Religions,* ed. Arvind Sharma, 293–355. San Francisco: Harper, 1993.

A recently published essay on the history and essence of Judaism. Neusner is a well-known and highly regarded interpreter of Judaism.

————. *Death and Birth of Judaism: The Impact of Christianity, Secularism, and the Holocaust on Jewish Faith.* New York: Basic Books, 1987.

A concise analysis of the changes in Judaism resulting from the impact of history.

Sachar, Howard M. *The Course of Modern Jewish History.* New York: World Publishing Co., 1958.

Somewhat dated, but still a helpful history of modern Judaism.

Schiffman, Lawrence. "Judaism: A Primer." Baltimore: Institute for Christian-Jewish Studies, n.d.

A pamphlet that provides an introduction to Judaism. Others available from the same publisher are Beverly Schneider, *A Guide to Jewish Holidays and Special Days;* and Claudia Setzer, *Jewish Worship,* both of which are written to help non-Jews understand Jewish holy days and celebrations as well as the place of worship in their religious life.

THE CASE
"What Kind of God Would Let This Happen?"

This was not the first time David Thompson had conversed with Jewish people, but his experience in discussing theological issues with them was very limited. Now suddenly, in the most unlikely place—a small pizzeria in Ventnor, New Jersey—a Jewish father and mother were telling him of their grief and pain, and they were raising profound questions about the nature of God, suffering, and premature death. For David, it was a totally new experience, for he had never been confronted in this way by one who did not have basically a Christian world view. This was unfamiliar territory for him, and he struggled for an appropriate response.

Seminar for Seminarians: A Week in Ventnor

David was in Ventnor for a January seminar at the Overseas Ministries Study Center, an ecumenical center that offers a varied program for the study of the Christian world mission. (The Center has since moved to New Haven, Connecticut). Because of the large number of residents at the Center—missionaries on leave and international Christian leaders from various countries—the January seminars offer seminary students ecumenical, cross-cultural preparation for ministering in an increasingly pluralistic world. David, who was a professor at the Presbyterian Seminary in Richmond, Virginia, had brought several students with him for the first week of "seminars for seminarians."

Following the first afternoon session some of his students asked him to go out that evening for dinner, but he told them he was very tired and would go with them later that week. "Tonight," he said, "I am going to eat somewhere nearby, take a shower, and 'hit the sack' early."

A Chance Encounter

About 5:30 p.m. David left the Center and walked south down Ventnor Avenue, looking for a place to eat. He had gone less than a half-block when he came to a small, apparently newly-opened pizzeria. It looked clean and appealing, so he went in, studied the menu, and ordered a pepperoni pizza and a large coke. He was somewhat surprised that he was the only customer, but it was early, he thought.

He selected a table in the corner of the small dining area, opened the newspaper he had bought, and was reading it when an elderly couple came in and sat down at the next table. David greeted them. "Good evening," he said. The couple responded, "Good evening." Their accent, David thought, was distinct, but he too, it seems, had an accent, for the man said, "I sense you are not from this area. Right?"

"No," David chuckled, "I'm from Virginia."

"Oh, that's nice. And what are you doing in Ventnor?"

"I'm here at the Overseas Study Center," he replied.

"Are you a priest?"

"I suppose you could call me a priest, although I am a Protestant, not a Catholic. We usually refer to ourselves as ministers or pastors. I have been a pastor, but now I teach in a theological seminary in Virginia."

"We're Jewish, but since you're a minister, maybe you could answer a question we've been struggling with," the man said. "By the way, my name is Sam Epstein, and this is my wife, Jean."

"I'm David Thompson. What's the question?"

Rather than responding immediately, Sam looked for a long time at the table. When he finally spoke, it was slowly and with deep emotion.

"Three weeks ago our son, Daniel, who lived in Margate, came home from work, and while his wife was preparing dinner, he was playing with their little three-year-old daughter on the living room floor. He was lying on his back, holding Rachel in the air, pretending to throw her up and catch her. Suddenly, he had a massive heart attack and was dead before the paramedics arrived."

As Sam recounted the story, Jean began to cry.

"Oh my," David said. "I am terribly sorry. How old was your son?"

"Forty-two," Sam replied.

"Are there other children?"

"Yes, they had three children."

David sensed the hurt and bewilderment of this couple whom he had not known ten minutes earlier, but now in a pizzeria in Ventnor, New Jersey, they were disclosing to him in the most intimate way the sorrow and pain they were experiencing.

After some moments, Sam said, "You're a minister. Tell me, what kind of God would let something like this happen? My son was in the prime of life, a loving father, a devoted son, and a faithful husband. I'm old, as you can see. I've been sick with heart problems for several years. Why not me?"

David had taught philosophy of religion earlier in his career, and Sam's question was not new to him. But David had never sought to deal with the issue Sam had raised except in a Christian context and on the basis of Christian presuppositions. Sam and Jean, however, were not Christians. They did not, David assumed, accept the New Testament as Scripture nor view Jesus as the Christ who suffered and provides for Christian believers a means whereby one copes with suffering.

"What kind of God would let something like this happen?" Sam asked again.

David did not know what to say. He wanted to be true to his own belief, but how could he respond in a way not to offend, and how could he give a Christian witness and at the same time not jeopardize the level of trust that had been established? He groped for an answer.[8]

STUDY QUESTIONS

1. Is it unusual for people to "bare their souls" as the Epsteins did to David Thompson? How would you explain Sam's willingness to share his grief with someone he has known only a few minutes?

2. We do not know if Sam and Jean Epstein identified themselves as Orthodox, Reform, or Conservative Jews, or if they practiced their faith at all. Are they, however, theists? If so, how would you describe the God in whom they believe?

3. There are many individuals in Jewish tradition who dare to question God. In the Jewish scriptures some authors—for example, the writers of Job, certain Psalms, Ecclesiastes, Lamentations, as well as the prophets Jeremiah and Habakkuk—challenged God's righteousness and purpose when they encountered examples of inexplicable suffering. Do Christians share with Jews the belief that history is redeemable, that some things happen by chance, and that God can redeem evil and tragedy?

4. We know little about David Thompson's view of God and of suffering. Assuming he is evangelical in his views, is this the appropriate time for him to give Sam and Jean a Christian perspective on suffering? If you believe it is, how should David respond? If you believe it is not, what then should David say?

SUGGESTED BIBLICAL TEXTS FOR REFLECTION

Genesis 18:25. Can one rightfully question God? "Shall not the Judge of all the Earth do justice/justly?"

---

8. *Note:* This case has a Part B which may be found, along with a detailed teaching note, in the *Journal for Case Teaching* 3 (Fall 1991): 149–158. The case (Parts A & B) and teaching note may also be ordered from the Yale Divinity School Library, 409 Prospect Street New Haven, CT 06511.

2 Samuel 18 & 19, esp. 19:1. King David laments the death of his son Absalom. "Oh, Absalom, my son, my son. If only I had died instead of you." Is the pain and anguish caused by death of a child not the worst possible tragedy that can befall a parent? How can this be reconciled with the God of justice?

Job 23:1–17. Job's complaint against God. Note also 24:1–17, in which Job, by implication, compares his behavior to that of the grossly wicked and wonders, Why?

Psalm 10:1–18. An imprecatory prayer for justice. (See also Psalms 58 and 83.) Most familiar of the imprecatory Psalms is 137, especially verses 8–9, a gruesome petition.

Psalm 88:1–18. A plea for divine help, but without the customary positive finale as, for example, in Ps. 102:25–28, or 108:13.

Ecclesiastes 3:16–4:3. The Jewish philosopher's pessimism, doubt, and cynical view of life. (See also 8:16–17.)

Jeremiah 20:7–18. The prophet's complaint to God and vacillating faith in God.

Habakkuk 1:2–4, 12–17. The prophet challenges God's passivity in the presence of blatant evil and injustice. God's answer is found in 2:1–4. Note how the writer of the New Testament epistle to the Romans employs verse 4. Does the original context need to be recovered?

"BUILD YOUR CHURCH HERE"

A Lutheran missionary in Madagascar wants to begin an evangelistic work among a people heretofore ignorant of the Christian faith. Initial contacts with the local shaman are rebuffed, but a month later when the missionary and two colleagues return to the village, they are invited into the shaman's house. After a ceremonial meal, the shaman unexpectedly announces that he is not only willing for a church to be started, he even offers a piece of land nearby for the construction of a church building. Bewildered by this sudden change of attitude, and not a little suspicious of the shaman's motives, the missionary wavers about what he and his companions should say and do.

CONTEXT
Primal Religion and Christianity

The following case has—as do all cases—an immediate and a general context. The general context is that of primal religion, and the case cannot be appreciated nor be adequately discussed without some basic knowledge of primal religion. The following comments merely touch on the complexities and nature of primal religions. Furthermore, attitudes toward them have changed significantly as they have been observed and studied.

Primal Religion

In 1832–33, when the ship *the Beagle* anchored off the coast of the Argentine Patagonia, Charles Darwin, the eminent biologist, observed for a period the indigenous peoples and concluded that they had no religion and were devoid of religious impulses. His reasoning was simple. The Patagonians manifested no apparent religious patterns, they practiced no visible or regular religious rites, they had no designated worship buildings or shrines, and they had no identifiable priests or holy men. Darwin's conclusion, therefore, was reasonable.

Westerners, long exposed to *organized* religions with their elaborate ceremonies and liturgies, their priesthoods and creeds, their temples and churches, have often assumed that if a people are truly religious, they will have some familiar religious accoutrements. The fact is, however, millions of people in the world—some authorities say as many as 200 to 300 million in all the continents—practice what is now precisely called "primal" religions. More-over, these followers who hold to primal spiritual beliefs are far more religious than most Westerners. They are religious in that they live in constant reverence or awe of the invisible, transcendent powers which are beyond their control but at the same time apparently determine their lives. Primal religious views and practices, therefore, are manifestations of the desire and attempt to relate to these unseen and largely capricious powers.

Most of us are aware that nowadays certain epithets are inappropriate and offensive to the descendants of people our ancestors routinely called "sav-ages," "heathen," and "natives," and we wisely avoid using these names. Yet, it is not unusual to hear or read descriptive labels of the beliefs and religious practices of these people as "primitive," "animistic," "superstitious," or "pre-literate." The more accurate term now employed to designate and describe the religions of these people is "primal," meaning *primary* or *prior to* the religions that later appeared in Asia—such as Hinduism, Judaism, Zoroastrianism, Confucianism, Buddhism, or Taoism, and of course preceding the emergence of Christianity in Asia and subsequently in Africa, Europe, and America.

Primal religions have their own systems of belief and often have their own priesthood, places of worship, and defined rituals. Usually, though not always, they lack, however, the written history and theology, the majestic temples and shrines,[1] the elaborate network of institutions, and the wealth and power characteristic of the "world religions." Primal religions, nonetheless, are still vibrant religious systems, and though they differ from place to place and frequently from tribe to tribe, they share a common core of beliefs.

• Belief in a transcendental existence of spirits.

Common to all primal religions is the belief in the ontological reality of spiritual beings. (The word "spirit" is a translation of the Latin *anima,* meaning "spirit," from which we derive the word "animism.") These spirits inhabit the whole of the universe. They dwell in various places and things, in moun-tains, rivers, forests, and rocks. They sometimes move from place to place. They even wander aimlessly. They have the ability to enter into or possess a living person and work good or evil. Some are benevolent while others are malevolent, i.e., demonic. Spirits can be appeased and spirits can be angered. Spirits have power, often called *mana,* that can benefit or can injure and kill.

• Belief in life after death.

Most, if not all, adherents of primal religion believe in some kind of life after death. Many also insist that ancestors and animals, though physically dead, continue to exist as spirits. These "living-dead" not only know what

---

1. Monuments such as England's Stonehenge, Mexico's Chichen Itza, Egypt's Luxor, Easter Island's monoliths, and excavated Harappa, the prehistoric capital of the Punjab—all evidence an astonishing magnificence that has survived.

is happening to their survivors—their family, their friends, their tribe—they affect and can even determine those happenings. Thus, not to remember and honor these deceased ancestors would not only be disrespectful, it would be imprudent. Whether the honoring of these ancestors can be rightly called "ancestor worship" is debatable. Surely it evidences a belief in the continuing life and presence of those who have died, and it reflects a desire to garner from them any power or influence they may be able to exert as benefits and blessings.

• Belief in a Supreme Spirit or god.

While primal religionists often believe in multiple gods and are therefore called "polytheists," many reverence a single spirit as the Supreme or Highest Spirit. Don Richardson, the first missionary to the Sawi people in Papua New Guinea, discovered that even the Sawi did not regard all spirits as equals.[2] The Maasai in East Africa continue to speak of *Enkai,* sometimes translated as "God" or the "Sky God," as the highest deity,[3] and Native Americans have manifested a belief in and reverence for the one whom they call the "Great Spirit."

In the past, outside observers have hastily concluded that the spirits in the primal religions function in effect as surrogate gods, and in some cases this is true. Certain spirits—and they inevitably have names—oversee and govern particular places or areas. Other spirits act as patron deities of certain peoples, such as those who fish, or farm, or fight. The warriors thus revere their god, farmers a different god, and those who fish a third god. Above all these lesser gods, however, is a high or the highest god.

• Belief that life is determined by one's relationship to the spirits.

In contrast to a cardinal belief found in several contemporary religions, such as the Hindu or Buddhist doctrine of *karma,* primal religions do not view life as necessarily and strictly retributive, that is, that one is consistently rewarded or punished according to how one lives. Primal religions, for example, teach that the rains can come or the rains can be stopped, depending on the gods and whether they are appeased or satisfied. Moreover, misfortune, suffering, and even death can be inflicted on another person or group, regardless of their past behavior, if the power of a spirit, usually an evil spirit, is harnessed and utilized to afflict such malevolence.

An initial introduction to the nature of primal religions often leaves observers wondering. Without written scriptures and records, formal creeds, grand and glorious temples, hierarchies of religious functionaries, highly developed liturgies, and a means of technological communication, how do primal religions survive? The answer lies in two additional beliefs.

---

2. See his *Peace Child* (Glendale, CA: Regal Books, 1974). Also the case study "Peace Child" written by Jack Rogers. Appendix E, p. 284.

3. See the case study in this book, "Should I Baptize Them . . . Now?" pages 168–78.

• An established system of ritual, admonition, and prohibition—symbols of reverence for and fear of the spirits.

As already indicated, primal religions are still very much evident in many parts of the world. They have often been forced to retreat as more vigorous, missionary religions have challenged them. They continue to endure, nonetheless, and have since prehistoric times without most of the trappings we ordinarily associate with the practice of religion. This is not to say there are no rituals or rites observed by the devotees of primal religion. They communicate regularly with the spirits by prayers, rites, and symbols. They make offerings to the spirits in the form of sacrifices or by placing, using, or wearing certain emblems such as body paint, masks, beads, or amulets. Animal and sometimes human sacrifices are offered. Ritual libations are drunk, sprinkled, and/or poured. Ceremonial meals consisting of designated foods and drink are consumed by the family or the whole community. In some instances the food and drink are shared with the god(s) in a kind of communion meal.

All this is to say that though life as a whole and the gods in primal religions are regarded as capricious, daily life is regulated by specified rituals that are strictly observed and passed on from one generation to another. For in every community, among every people there are established customs and rules concerning what is permissible and what is forbidden. And these rules, it is believed, were originally delineated by the gods.

• Belief in legends, myths, dreams, and visions.

In contrast to modern societies, primal religious groups do not maintain or pass along their beliefs in the form of scriptures or written histories and theologies, though the carved objects, paintings, sculptures, scrolls, and other tangible signs of their faith have been found. When these have existed, however, it appears they were created and maintained primarily to enhance their reliance on *oral traditions*. For the essence of the faith is passed on through legends and myths developed, memorized, and repeated by father to son, mother to daughter, priest to priest, and shaman to shaman. The latter function in many ways as clergy among their people: healing, advising, praying for, and manipulating spiritual powers. Insights often come in trances, visions, or dreams.

Westerners educated in science and technology have commonly dismissed these functionaries as charlatans and derogatorily labeled them "witch doctors," "medicine men," "sorcerers," or "shamans."

Religions of every kind, however, develop their own experts, the specialists or professionals who fulfill the role or act as religious guides in the community. Whatever titles they assume or are given—priest, shaman, or witch doctor—they stand between the spirits (or the Spirit) and the people.[4] Those who fill

---

4. Sometimes the various titles for primal religious functionaries are used as if they were synonymous. Each, however, has its own particular meaning. *Shaman* (fr.

these places usually are regarded as designated or gifted from birth, they profess a divine call or summons, or they learn their art through apprenticeships.

In every case, however, primal religions represent the earliest and most solemn attempts by humankind to make sense out of life, to establish beneficial connections with unseen powers, and to live in harmony not only with the gods but also with nature which can sustain and can destroy.

Madagascar and Christian Missions

According to Madagascar folklore, the country was settled by Malaya-Indonesian people who sailed westward and landed on the main island more than 2,000 years ago. Their descendants are the predominant ethnic group today.

Though commonly referred to as "Madagascar," the official name is "The Democratic Republic of Madagascar." The more than nine million inhabitants are divided into two principal groups, those of Malaya-Indonesian origin called the "Merina" or "Hova," and those of African-Arab lineage. There are at least sixteen other ethnic groups including French, Indian, and Chinese.

Located in the Indian Ocean some 240 miles east of Mozambique, the main island is an area of 226,658 square miles (587,041 sq. km.) and is 980 miles long and 360 miles wide. Slightly smaller than the state of Texas, Madagascar is the fourth largest island in the world.

The Afro-Arab peoples live for the most part in the coastal regions of the country while the Merina occupy the central and south central highlands. Not only are these groups separated geographically, but deep-seated political and cultural rivalries also divide them. The blacks for the most part favor political and economic alliances with the West while the Merina strongly advocate closer relations with non-Western countries.

---

sham or trick, hoax) refers to one who employs magic to discern the future, to heal, or to manipulate events. *Diviner* or soothsayer, one who practices divination or the foretelling by seeing the future, what can or is to happen, hidden for example in the stars, a crystal ball, tea leaves, or chicken viscera. *Medium,* one who acts as an intermediary between the living and the dead, i.e., the spirits. *Medicine man/person,* one who utilizes herbs, potions, incantations, and other charms such as fetishes, talismans, amulets, or signs to heal the sick. *Sorcerer* or necromancer, one who employs the powers of evil spirits for divining or for the working of evil. *Witch,* (*wicca* in Old English) one who utilizes the powers of the spirits to do good or, as in most cases, to do evil through the Devil, devils, or demons. A witch can be male or female, but more commonly is thought of as female. *Warlock,* a male who practices witchcraft. *Wizard,* a utilizer of enchantment or magic. There are many other names given to people who are believed to have spiritual powers or the ability to tap the powers of the spirits, e.g., magician, dowser, conjuror, or exorcist, but these describe particular functions or they are synonymous with the terms above.

The earliest European contact with Madagascar was in 1500 when the Portuguese explorer Diego Dias landed on the island. The primary value of Madagascar during the sixteenth and seventeenth centuries was as a naval base and center for slave trading, and there was a prolonged struggle, principally between France and England, for control of the harbors and the trade. French colonists were sent to the island in 1642 but were unable to secure a firm foothold until much later. France finally prevailed, and Madagascar was recognized first as a French protectorate and then in 1895 as a colony. Madagascar was granted full independence by France in 1960.

The population of Madagascar is predominantly rural (nearly 85%) and is directly dependent upon agriculture. The Merina, formerly called "Hova" after one of their social classes, is the country's best educated, most populous and influential ethnic group. Illiteracy, however, remains a major problem with hardly more than 50% of the people being able to read and write.

Discalced Carmelite and Lazarist missionaries were sent to Madagascar in 1643 to minister to the French colonists, but their efforts were short-lived primarily because of death from illness or at the hands of the indigenous people. The last of these early missionaries departed in 1657. Further attempts were made by the Lazarists in the eighteenth century, but none was successful until the Jesuits began to evangelize the people in the southern part of the country in the 1850s.

The first Protestant missionaries to Madagascar were David Jones and Thomas Bevan of the London Missionary Society (LMS). These British representatives arrived in Tamatave on the eastern coast of the island in 1818 or 1820. They were welcomed, protected, and patronized by King Radama I (1810–28) who, though not disposed to become a Christian himself, regarded the missionaries as a means of introducing European culture and technology to his people. Radama especially wanted missionary teachers and artisans, many of whom came and opened schools and began small industries. It was during this period that a written form of the Malagasy language was developed, and the translation of the Bible was begun and was finally completed in 1836. That same year Queen Ranavalona I (1828–1861), who opposed Christianity from the time of her inauguration, intensified her persecution of Christians by expelling all Europeans, banning all Christian teaching, preaching, and public worship, and unleashing a wave of atrocities that led to the death of many Malagasy believers. Until her death in 1861 Christians were fined, flogged, jailed, and often killed, but the number of believers more than quadrupled. Until 1864 all Protestant believers were associated with the work begun by David Jones and the LMS, and they formed the *Eglise de Jesus-Christ a Madagascar*, now by far the largest Protestant body.

Both Roman Catholic and Protestant missionaries began openly to return to Madagascar in 1861 when Radama II (1861–68) opened the kingdom again to Europeans. At the time of her coronation in 1869 Queen Ranavalona II professed the Christian faith, and the number of Christians began to increase dramatically—from 5,000 in 1869 to more than a million by the end of the century. According to current government statistics, more than four million of Madagascar's inhabitants are now professing Christians, and they are almost evenly divided between Roman Catholics and Protestants. At least 50% of the people, however, are still animists, and some 5% are Muslim. The practice of tribal religions with the worship of ancestors and spirits, together with offering cattle in sacrifice, is widespread among the coastal peoples.

Protestantism is the predominant faith among the upper classes of the Merina society, while the peasant masses and the Christian peoples of the coastal regions are predominantly Roman Catholic.

The Norwegian Mission Society sent missionaries to Madagascar as early as 1866, and two U.S. Lutheran churches sent their missionaries to the island in 1892 and 1895. These three Lutheran groups united in 1950 to form the Malagasy Lutheran Church which is now Madagascar's second largest Protestant body. There are at least thirty-nine separate denominations in Madagascar today.

FOR FURTHER STUDY

Primal Religion

Appiah-Kubi, Kofi and Sergio Torres, eds. *African Theology en Route.* Maryknoll, NY: Orbis, 1979.

Papers given during the Pan-African Conference of Third World Theologians, December 17–23, 1977, Accra, Ghana. Contain valuable insights into the evangelization process utilized by the missionaries, the history of theology, the task of African theologians today and the options open to them, and the indigenous African religions.

Dickson, Kwesi A. *Theology in Africa.* Maryknoll, NY: Orbis, 1984.

An appraisal of theological developments among African Christians in light of the impact of colonialism and the African-cultural situation. The author, a Ghanaian Methodist theologian, also includes a discussion of the "theological unreality in the Church in Africa."

Kalilombe, Patrick. "The Salvific Value of African Religions." In *Mission Trends No. 5,* ed. Gerald H. Anderson and Thomas F. Stransky, 51–68. New York: Paulist, 1981. Also in the *African Ecclesial Review* 21 (June 1979): 143–157.

A Roman Catholic bishop from Malawi differentiates between individual salvation and the salvific value of religions. He analyzes past readings of the biblical passages by non-Africans who came to evangelize Africans and concludes with "a contextualized" reading of the Bible. He does not give a definitive answer to the question posed, but he does set forth some helpful guidelines.

Oduyoye, Mercy Amba. *Hearing and Knowing. Theological Reflections on Christianity in Africa.* Maryknoll, NY: Orbis, 1986.

A history of Christianity in Africa and an analysis of the principal themes in contemporary African theology written by a Ghanaian female theologian.

―――. "Ways to Confront Africa's Primal Religions." *International Christian Digest* 1 (February 1987): 14–18.

> Oduyoye analyzes African primal religions as a way of contextualizing the Christian message, and includes her own definitions of "acculturation," "inculturation," and "indigenization."

Sarpong, Peter K. "Christianity Meets Traditional African Cultures." In *Mission Trends No. 5,* 238–248. Also in *Worldmission* 30 (Summer 1979): 16–23.

> A plea for the Church in Africa to become less foreign and more African by changing symbols, thought-forms, values, and practices. A sensitive evangelical will discover that one can thus avoid preaching "a new God" and tap into the theological ambience of the African experience.

Shorter, Aylward. *African Christian Theology—Adaption or Incarnation.* London: Geoffrey Chapman, 1977.

> A Roman Catholic priest and lecturer in anthropology at the Makerere University in Uganda provides a comprehensive treatment of African traditional religion, Africa's contribution to world Christianity and theology, together with an analysis of the comparative approaches to the study of African religion.

Setiloane, Gabriel M. *African Theology. An Introduction.* Johannesburg, South Africa: Skotaville, 1986.

> A brief (45 pp) but unusually helpful discussion of the sources of knowledge according to African theologians together with their understanding of "Genesis," community, being a person, ancestors, and the nature and place of theology.

Tippett, Alan R. "The Evangelization of Animists." In *Perspectives on the World Christian Movement,* ed. Ralph D. Winter and Steven C. Hawthorne, 629–640. Pasadena, CA: William Carey, 1981.

> Tippett defines animism, presents what he sees as the biblical perspective on animism, and gives six specific suggestions to those who propose to communicate the Christian message to animists.

Turner, Harold. "World of Spirits." In *Eerdmans' Handbook to the World's Religions,* 128–132. Grand Rapids, MI: Eerdmans, 1982.

> A brief introductory essay on primal religion written by the director of the Project for the Study of New Religious Movements in Primal Societies, University of Aberdeen, Scotland.

Christian Missions in Madagascar

Ellis, William. *The Martyr Church.* London: John Snow, 1869.

> A brief description of the island and its history, the religious ideas and practices of the people followed by an account of the growth of Christianity in the capital and major provinces from the early 1800s to 1869. Written by one of the early missionaries who was in Madagascar for fifty years.

Fletcher, John Joseph Kilpin. *The Sign of the Cross from Madagascar, or, From Darkness to Light.* Boston: United Society of Christian Endeavor, 1900.

> A history of Madagascar with a glowing account of the beginnings of Protestant missionary efforts. Hagiographic, but contains some helpful insights, especially the history of Hova rule from 1810–1885.

Hardyman, J. T. *Madagascar on the Move.* London: Livingstone, 1950.

An analysis of the social, educational, and religious changes resulting from the impact of Christianity, both Roman Catholic and Protestant. The author was born in Madagascar.

Jordaan, Bee. *Splintered Crucifix. Early Pioneers for Christendom on Madagascar and the Cape of Good Hope.* Capetown: C. Struik, 1969.

Though lacking in documentation, the book contains two interesting and helpful chapters on Christianity in Madagascar.

Matthews, T. T. *Thirty Years in Madagascar.* London: Religious Tract Society, 1904.

The history and characteristics of the island and its people. Recounts the entry of Protestant missionaries until the end of the monarchy and "the triumph of the gospel." Major emphasis is on the work of the London Missionary Society.

McMahon, E. O. *Christian Missions in Madagascar.* London: Society for the Preaching of the Gospel in Foreign Parts, 1914.

Written to celebrate fifty years of missionary work by the Society for the Propagation of the Gospel. The author describes the people, their religious beliefs and practices, the entry and progress of Christianity, missions under French rule, comity, and a view of the future. Author gives the dates for the arrival of each Protestant mission.

Missions and Martyrs in Madagascar. Boston: American Tract Society, c. 1864.

Though dated, the book is a helpful source for understanding the people and the history of Christianity during the first fifty years of Protestant mission work.

Mondain, Gustave. *Un siecle de mission a Madagascar.* Paris: Societe des missions evangeliques, 1948.

A newer edition of a work first published in 1920. Valuable for the early as well as the recent history of Christianity in Madagascar. The author worked for more than fifty years in the country.

Sibree, James. *Fifty Years in Madagascar.* London: George Allen & Unwin, 1924.

Though primarily autobiographical, the book is thorough and interesting, especially in regard to Malagasy religious beliefs and habits.

Townsend, William J. *Madagascar: Its Missionaries and Martyrs.* New York: Fleming H. Revell, n.d.

One of a number of histories of the first fifty years of Protestant mission work in the country.

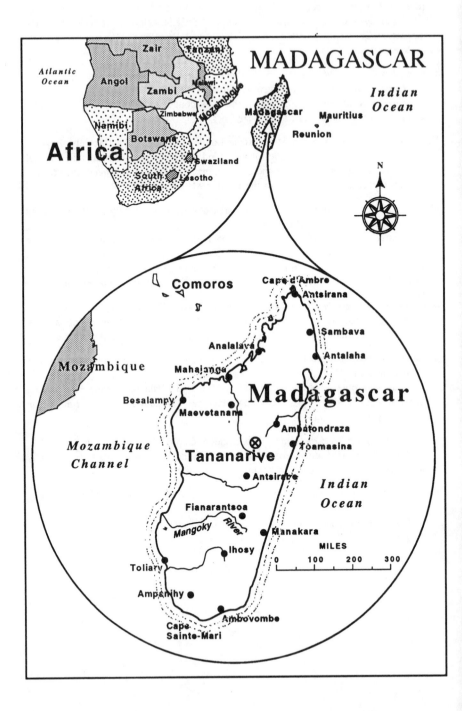

THE CASE
"Build Your Church Here"

The three missionaries were finishing their tea when the village shaman in whose home they had shared a meal suddenly appeared to fall into a trance. Several moments passed before anyone spoke, and then it was Ratefy, the shaman. What he said and did caught his three visitors by surprise. Gesturing toward an open field across from his house, he said, "You can build your church here," implying, it seemed to Daniel, that he was not only giving permission, but offering them the land also.

Daniel Razivelo, a Malagasy Lutheran missionary who had first come to the village nine months earlier, looked imploringly at his two companions. Emmanuel Ramambasoa, a former missionary and now a national pastor, and Ted Jacobson, a representative of the American Lutheran Church and long-time missionary to Madagascar, appeared stunned. Daniel was totally unprepared for Ratefy's announcement and was unsure about how he or his companions should react.

The First Missionary Attempt in Ramaholimar

More than a year earlier Daniel, a young Malagasy pastor, had been commissioned by the Lutheran Church in Madagascar to begin evangelization work in an area south of the Mangoky River and north of Toliary. More than 10,000 people lived in the 1200 square miles, and it was one of the most underdeveloped sections of the country. In fact, Daniel had often remarked to his wife Mariette that he thought the people lived no differently than they had lived some fifty or a hundred years ago.

Prior to Daniel's initial efforts, the Lutheran national missions and evangelism board had sponsored an extensive survey of the area and had found only six professing Christians among the entire population. The area was quickly designated by the board as their number one priority for missionary and evangelistic work. Daniel was invited to be the area missionary. He was given an adequate stipend, slightly more than what he had received as a pastor, and he was provided a motorcycle and a small budget for travel and other expenses. His work plan, approved by the board on missions and evangelism, consisted primarily of going from village to village, meeting people, making friends, beginning Bible studies in homes, and training local leadership; and when a group appeared strong enough, he encouraged them to secure a worship center or construct a small chapel.

On one of his early trips, Daniel had spent two days in the village of Ramaholimar where there was no church, Catholic or Protestant, and—as far as he could determine—not a single professing Christian. Several families, however, had shown marked interest in the Christian faith, and Daniel was able to begin monthly Bible studies alternating between two homes. But this had been the extent of his work for several months. Even so, attendance grew, and the homes were not large enough to accommodate everyone who attempted to crowd into the limited space.

Daniel suggested on two occasions that the people would do well to secure some land and build a chapel. He indicated the mission board would likely help them buy some of the necessary building materials. No one responded. The third time he spoke of a chapel, however, several people shook their heads, and then someone said, "To get land and construct a chapel, you would have to see Chief Ratefy. He is a very powerful man." Everyone hummed in agreement. Daniel understood the last comment to mean that Ratefy exerted great spiritual powers and was a person the villagers feared. He surely had authority over them, Daniel thought, for not only was he the recognized chief, he was also a widely known shaman who served as the animistic priest in the village.

The truth was that Daniel did not relish the thought of trying to talk with Ratefy about a church building. But he also sensed that the people, because of their obvious fear, were not likely to take the initiative. The first time he came to Ramaholimar Daniel had sought to meet Ratefy, but the shaman refused to talk to him. The second time he went to the shaman's house, Ratefy had threatened Daniel and driven him away.

After talking with Mariette and praying with her about the matter, Daniel decided to make a trip to the capital city of Tananarive to seek the counsel of Ted Jacobson and his friend Emmanuel Ramambasoa. They met in Ted's living room, and Daniel described in great detail the work he had done in Ramaholimar, the response of the people, and the difficulty he had experienced with Ratefy.

I know it is important to gain Chief Ratefy's goodwill if at all possible, but he refuses to talk with me. The first time I went to the village, I asked directions to the chief's house. When I rode up on my motorcycle, he was sitting out in his yard under a tree, staring up at the sky. I parked the cycle, saluted him, walked over and squatted down [a gesture of respect], and began to talk to him. I told him I was a Christian pastor, that I would like to visit his people and teach them the Bible. He never responded. He never even looked at me—just kept staring up into the sky. I waited for a while, but he never said a word, so finally I left.

I went back a second time. This time it was late in the afternoon, almost dark. I tried the same approach, but again he refused to say anything. I had given up and was beginning to stand when he looked at me and said, "You must leave. I will not allow you to come into this town. You cannot build a church here nor try to bring my people into your church."

I tried again to tell him I came with the good news of the gospel, but he became very angry. His face darkened, and he reached for his spear that was leaning against the side of his house. "You leave now!" he said.

"Right now you leave or I'll put this spear through you!" I left frightened and very discouraged.

Daniel paused a moment and then said if Ted and Emmanuel would accompany him to Ramaholimar, perhaps they could talk with the shaman and try to persuade him to allow Daniel to continue his visits and Bible studies. After considerable discussion, it was agreed they would make a trip together the following week, and they would attempt to gain an audience with Ratefy. They also decided nothing would be said about land or a chapel. They would be satisfied to get permission for Daniel to return to the village.

The Visit to the Shaman

When the three arrived at the priest's house, Ratefy was sitting in his yard under a tree. He was dressed in his full regalia, and his hair was braided in a Rastafarian style. As the three visitors approached, Ratefy sat staring into space. They squatted down in front of him in a semi-circle and again explained why Daniel had come to the village and why they were there. The shaman said nothing. His eyes seemed to be fixed on a point in the sky. Daniel later described the rest of the meeting to his wife Mariette:

We waited and waited for a response, and finally Ratefy made a sweeping gesture with his arm and said to Emmanuel, "Come here." Emmanuel got up and walked over and shook the shaman's hand. Then Ted did the same thing, and I followed. Ratefy shook all our hands.

Then he said he was not going to fight with us and did not want to argue with us. He would greet us as friends coming to his village.

This was quite a surprise, considering his previous attitude toward me. Then Ratefy began to stare into space again. It was as if he had gone into a trance. He looked up into the sky for a long period, and then he spoke what sounded like a kind of prophecy.

"We were here before, but now someone has come who is stronger. I am not going to fight with them. They are our friends. We don't understand their customs, but we want to welcome them, and we don't want to fight with them."

Then he came out of the trance, said a few other things, and motioned to us saying, "Come with me." We did not know what was going to happen at that point, but he invited us into his house for a meal. It was clearly a ritual for him. After we had eaten, Ratefy sacrificed a chicken. Then he made another wide sweep with his arm and said as he pointed to a large area across from his house, "Here is where you can build your church."

This was not only a surprise, it was unsettling. It seemed to me that Ted wanted to delay a formal acceptance by responding, "We likely would want quite a bit of space in the future. We probably would like to build a home for the pastor and even a school, a church school. So it may be that we would want more land than you are prepared to offer us."

"That's no problem," Ratefy replied. "Take all you need. How much do you want? I'll get someone to pace it off now."

"Will there be any conditions?" Emmanuel asked.

"Only one," Ratefy said. "You cannot have your services on Sunday because that is when I have mine. Sunday morning is when I offer sacrifice for the whole village."

I was so bewildered by what was happening that I did not know what to say. I wondered what Emmanuel and Ted were thinking. I felt we needed to make a graceful exit and have time to discuss the matter. I was terribly fearful that we were being drawn into a position of irreversible compromise. Ratefy was now looking straight at Emmanuel and Ted. He was obviously waiting for a response.

"What did they say?" Mariette asked.

STUDY QUESTIONS

1. The names of persons and places in the case are unfamiliar. Can you name each of the characters, groups, and the principal places?

2. How would you describe the missionary strategy and policies of the Lutheran Church in Madagascar?

3. What is the principal issue in this case? Are there other important issues? If so, what are they?

4. There appear to be several views as to what Christianity is and what is the gospel. Can you delineate these?

5. If you were sitting where Daniel, Emmanuel, or Ted is sitting, what would you say or do?

SUGGESTED BIBLICAL TEXTS FOR REFLECTION

The following texts are often appealed to as biblical bases for Christian separatism. They are given without prejudice. The question is, in light of these admonitions, are there accords Christians today can reach with non-Christians?

Exodus 34:10–16. The demands of the Covenant and warning against treaties with "foreigners."

Deuteronomy 7:1–11. What is required to continue as God's people?

Nehemiah 13:29–31. The governor reflects on what he has done to purify the people and their society.

2 Corinthians 6:14–7:1. The Apostle Paul's warning against affiliations with unbelievers.

PART THREE

CURRENT ISSUES
in
CHRISTIAN MISSION

THE CALL

The Recruitment Secretary for the American Reformed Church Mission has worked with a young couple seeking missionary appointment. Their records, recommendations, and motives appear good, but the Secretary has a lingering doubt. Should he recommend them to the administrative board?

CONTEXT
The Question of the "Missionary Calling"

Anyone who has read more than a few missionary biographies knows that people who have become missionaries are not alike. Until recently, however, nearly all—were they Catholic or Protestant—maintained they had been called of God to be missionaries. The "call" therefore has been a kind of common denominator. Some calls have been dramatic, rivaling the experience of Moses before the burning bush (Exodus 3:1–20), others mystical such as that of the prophet Isaiah in the Temple (6:1–8), or the Apostle Paul's vision of the man from Macedonia (Acts 16:6–10). A contemporary biographer of Ramón Lull (1235–1315) describes in detail his call to be a missionary to the Muslims. The young Spaniard, a courtier and troubadour living a dissolute life, was attempting to compose a ballad when he casually looked up from the paper on which he had drafted some music and lyrics and saw the figure of Jesus Christ hanging on the Cross. Jesus' eyes were piercing and gazed intently at Ramón. The face of the crucified one, Lull remembered, bore "great agony and sorrow." The courtier was awestruck and could write no more. The next day he had the same experience, only the suffering of Jesus was more vivid. Three additional times Lull tried to return to his composition, and each time he saw the Christ "in great agony and sorrow" staring at him in a kind of silent appeal. Like other young men of his era Lull interpreted these visions as Christ's call to "abandon the world and devote himself to His service." Specifically, what did this mean? How should he go about it? He would relinquish his position, forsake his family, give himself as a sacrifice to Christ and the Church by becoming "a missionary," thereby devoting the rest of his "life to preaching the Catholic Faith, until it should please God to grant him the crown of martyrdom."[1]

---

1. E. Allison Peers, *Fool of Love. The Life of Ramon Lull* (London: S.C.M. Press, 1946), 12–14.

Others have described their callings in much less melodramatic terms, more akin to that of Amos (7:14–15) or the call issued by Jesus to the four fishermen (Mark 1:16–20). Still others have been called through proxies, such as the experience of Barnabas and Saul in the church at Antioch:

> "While they were serving the Lord and fasting, the Holy Spirit said to them, 'Set apart for me Barnabas and Saul, to do the work which I have called them.' They [therefore] fasted and prayed, placed their hands on them and sent them off" (Acts 13:2–3).

The sense of divine call to be a missionary, though experienced in different ways and described in different terms, is so frequent that most sending agencies in the past—and some today—have either refused or have been reluctant to encourage anyone to consider being a missionary who could not profess to having a sense of divine calling. The following paragraph is indicative of how some have described the call to be a missionary:

> "To me the call is that divine urge, that compelling impulse, that passion within that makes it impossible to resist. There is something within that is calling, ever calling. I am restless. I am like a hunter's dog on the leash, straining to get away. It is that irresistible 'must.' "[2]

Not all mission spokespersons, however, regard as sound the idea of being compelled as expressed in the preceding statement, nor are they ready to elevate the missionary call to a level of being distinct from the call to discipleship which Jesus Christ extended to everyone.[3] Typical is the account of a missionary who went to Japan shortly after the end of World War II. His calling to Christian ministry, he said, had come five years earlier, and it was later he faced the question of where that ministry would take place.

> The quiet conviction that in the Lord's own good time he would make known his will regarding the question of missionary service was not ill-founded. But when this leadership came it was not through a sudden revelation or blinding flash of light, but through a growing conviction that the call which had come to me December 12, 1945, was genuine and that it had not been revoked. The clarification came so gradually that it is difficult to say exactly when the decision was made. However, by the beginning or middle of my last year of graduate

---

2. Quoted by Norman L. Cummings, "What is a Missionary Call?" (Washington, DC: Evangelical Foreign Missions Association, n.d.), 3.

3. J. H. Kane, a conservative Evangelical Protestant, dismisses the notion that one should not be considered a potential missionary unless he or she affirms a special calling from God. *Understanding Christian Missions* (Grand Rapids: Baker, 1974), 38–49.

work the decision to seek appointment as a foreign missionary was rather definite.[4]

A "call" to become a missionary is not necessarily theologically sound or even emotionally healthy. In an autobiography published several years ago, the writer describes in vivid detail the conflict engendered in his home when he expressed his desire to leave the Lutheran church of his parents and began attending an evangelical congregation. His father ridiculed him, insisted that he continue to go to Lutheran worship on Sunday mornings, and in every way sought to discourage his walking the five miles to the evangelical services. On a particular wintry Sunday night, he arrived home late and found that his father had locked the doors and refused to get up and allow his son into the house. He hoped either his mother or father would respond to his entreaty.

"I hated to wake them up, but I had to get in, so I rang the doorbell. I watched the window of their bedroom, waiting for the light to go on. It didn't. I rang the doorbell again. No response.

"My mother could sleep through that noise, but my father was too light a sleeper. I knew he was awake. I called to him.

" 'Dad, it's me, Bruce. Come down and open the door for me, please. I'm freezing.'

"There was no reply. Although I didn't want to, I started to cry, the tears freezing on my face.

" 'Dad, please. It's Bruce. Please let me in.'

"I took a deep breath and held it in. Then I felt a little more calm. I looked up at the dark window again. It seemed to be looking back at me, like a dark, hooded eye. Finally I thought of the Langes. I knew they would take me in. But it was two miles to their house, back along the way I had come.

" 'Please, Dad,' I called, and waited. There was no response. I turned on my heel and began to run. I ran as hard as I could until I couldn't run any farther. When I stopped, I was already across the bridge. My breath was heaving and the cold air burned my lungs each time I breathed.

"I made it to the Langes, exhausted and shaking. They got up and gave me a warm place to sleep."[5]

Is it any wonder that as Bruce Olson continued to attend the interdenominational evangelical church and be exposed more and more to missionaries and their adventurous accounts of their lives in other countries, that he would

---

4. Robert H. Culpepper, *God's Calling: A Missionary Autobiography* (Nashville: Tennessee, 1981), 58.

5. Bruce Olson, *For This Cross I'll Kill You* (Carol Stream, IL: Creation House, 1973), 31–32.

have a growing sense that God was calling him to be a missionary? The account of his application to an evangelical mission and their rejection of him, his decision to go to South America on his own, and his subsequent mission work there—all reflect the complex forces that shape and influence people to become missionaries.

During the last half-century, however, a number of changes have ensued which have tended to diminish the traditional emphasis on being called to be a missionary: (1) the decrease in the number of persons willing to offer themselves as vocational missionaries, that is, missionaries for life; (2) the difficulty in obtaining permission for such persons to enter many countries as vocational missionaries and/or to remain there indefinitely; (3) the new models of what it means to be a missionary;[6] (4) the inclination on the part of many young people today to ignore the traditional and "artificial division between mission in Jerusalem and mission to the ends of the earth";[7] (5) the relative ease and speed of travel which is prompting an increasing number of individuals who think of mission work as a short-term task; (6) and the increased readiness of many missionary sending agencies to depend more and more on short-term personnel. Despite these various changes, many sending agencies—especially those of an evangelical tradition—still give a great deal of emphasis to being called to missionary work.

Recently I wrote to thirty-six United States and Canadian missionary sending agencies[8] inquiring about their criteria for vocational appointees. Among those I contacted were the denominations and missionary groups that send out the largest numbers of missionaries annually, and they represent a wide range of theological and methodological approaches. I received thirty-four responses to the two questions I asked:

(1) Does your agency require a statement from a potential appointee about his or her calling? Twenty-six responded "Yes," and eight "No." One agency

---

6. Leif E, Vaage, "On Being a Missionary: Models of Self-Understanding," *Missiology* 15 (April 1989): 131–141.

7. Samuel Escobar, "Recruitment of Students for Mission," *Missiology* 15 (October 1987): 542.

8. These comprised denominational agencies and para-church groups, and included the following: American Baptist Churches, USA, Anglican Church of Canada, Assemblies of God, Canadian Baptist Ministries, Christian and Missionary Alliance, Church of God in Christ (Mennonite), Church Ministry Among the Jews, Church of the Nazarene, Cooperative Baptist Fellowship (SBC), Cumberland Presbyterian Church, Evangelical Covenant Church, Evangelical Free Church of America, Evangelical Lutheran Church, General Mennonite Conference, Gospel Missionary Union, Inter-Varsity Fellowship, Jews for Jesus, Latin American Mission, Mennonite Board of Missions, Mennonite Central Committee, Moravian Church, OMS International, Operation Mobilization of Canada, Presbyterian Church in America, Presbyterian Church, USA, SIM Canada, Southern Baptist Convention, United Methodist Church, United Church of Canada, World Vision, Wycliffe Bible Translators, Youth With A Mission, and Liebenzell Mission of USA, Inc.

indicated they do not require a statement as such, but would not appoint anyone who did not give some indication of being "called."

(2) Would a person be considered for appointment who did not or could not affirm such a sense of calling? Eight answered "Yes," and twenty-six "No." To this second question, three agencies said they do not ask for nor expect a statement of calling. Two agencies indicated that they ask for statements of calling, but appointment is not contingent upon the candidates' affirming a specific call to missions.

Several agencies responding added that they do not require a statement of calling from those being considered for short-term appointments.

FOR FURTHER STUDY

Carey, William. "An Enquiry into the Obligation of Christians to Use Means for the Conversion of the Heathens." In *Perspectives on the World Christian Movement,* ed. Ralph D. Winter and Steven C. Hawthorne, 227–236. Pasadena, CA: William Carey Library, 1981.

> Selections from Carey's famous tract that changed the way the foreign mission responsibility and effort was viewed by Protestants beginning in the late eighteenth century.

Escobar, Samuel. "Recruitment of Students for Mission." *Missiology* 15 (October 1987): 529–545.

Japinga, Lynn. "Who Are We Called to Be?" *Reformed World* 43 (March & June 1993): 63–68.

> A theological analysis of the concept of calling.

Kaiser, Walter C. Jr. "Israel's Missionary Call." In *Perspectives on the World Christian Movement,* ed. Ralph D. Winter and Steven C. Hawthorne (1981), 25–34.

> An evangelical view of the missionary calling given to Israel as a people.

Kane, J. Herbert. *Understanding Christian Missions,* 38–49. Grand Rapids, MI: Baker Book House, 1974.

> An evangelical but unconventional view of the "missionary calling" as seen by a one-time missionary to China and later professor of missions at Trinity Evangelical Divinity School.

————. *Life and Work on the Mission Field,* 1–12. Grand Rapids, MI: Baker, 1960.

> A traditional but important evangelical perspective.

Mott, John R. "The Responsibility of the Young People for the Evangelization of the World." In *Perspectives on the World Christian Movement* (1981), 261–271.

> An address given by Mott in 1901 and an example of the thinking that led to the founding and the impact of the Student Volunteer Movement. Mott was the principal spokesperson and long-term chair of the movement.

Neill, Stephen. *Call to Mission.* Philadelphia: Fortress, 1971.

> A moving and persuasive case for involvement in the world mission of the church.

Taylor, J. Hudson. "The Call to Service." In *Perspectives on the World Christian Movement,* ed. Ralph P. Winter and Stephen C. Hawthorne (1981), 237–243.

The founder of the China Inland Mission sets forth the basis for becoming a missionary in the nineteenth century.

Vaage, Leif E. "On Being a Missionary: Models of Self-Understanding." *Missiology* 15 (April 1989): 131–141.

THE CASE
The Call

Scott Dressler, recruitment secretary for the Protestant Reformed Churches of America Mission, finished reading the biographical statements of James and Carol Anne Reist. The Reists were seeking appointment with the PRCAM to go as missionaries either to Singapore or Japan. Their recommendations from friends, former teachers, and pastors were positive, and their statements regarding their call to missions were conventional. They had passed their medical examinations, and their psychological profiles were satisfactory. Academically, they were well prepared, and their church experience was more than adequate. Why did Scott have a lingering question?

The Reist Files

James and Carol Anne Reist's files had been given to Scott Dressler nearly seven months earlier. He had read carefully their applications, talked with them by phone several times, and three months later went to Elizabeth, New Jersey, to meet them. On the plane Scott re-read the materials in their files.

James Reist was a native of New Jersey, born in 1955 into a Christian Reformed home in Camden where he had spent his childhood and youth. He was a graduate of Calvin College in Grand Rapids, Michigan, of Westminster Theological Seminary in Philadelphia, and because he was planning to enter the Christian Reformed ministry, to fulfill the denomination's requirement, he had gone back to Calvin Seminary for an additional year of theological studies. His academic record was strong, especially in languages and Bible. He had worked on the docks of a major trucking firm while he was in seminary, as well as serving as a youth pastor in a Philadelphia church.

Carol Anne likewise was from Camden. She and James met when Carol Anne was only thirteen years old, and they began dating soon thereafter. As the months and years passed—six years in all—they talked increasingly of marriage and a life together. He had indicated that he sensed a call to Christian ministry, and she stated that she wanted to become a nurse. Carol Anne graduated from high school in 1975 and enrolled in a nurses' training program in a nearby community college. James meanwhile completed his last year in college, and they married in July of 1976. She continued her studies in the community college and completed an Associate degree in nursing the year before James finished Westminster Seminary. Their first child was born the year they went to Grand Rapids for James to do the year of study in Calvin Seminary.

Meeting with the Reists

Seated comfortably in their small living room in Elizabeth where James was serving as pastor of a small Christian Reformed congregation, Scott asked them to tell him more about their parents, siblings, and home life growing up in Camden. James spoke first.

"My grandfather was a Christian Reformed pastor who, as my father told it, moved his family from Chicago to South Dakota in order to take a church there. My dad was fifteen years old when they left Chicago. He said he was so lonely and unhappy in South Dakota that he dropped out of school after finishing the ninth grade and eventually apprenticed to be a plumber. He became a licensed plumber and followed this trade until he retired.

"He regularly attended church, and I have not had any reason to doubt his faith, but he never was involved in any church activity or organization. Even though he had a beautiful voice, he would not sing in the choir, nor would he consider becoming a deacon or an elder. He simply attended worship and encouraged me to be faithful to the church.

"When I was in high school I learned for the first time that my father had a drinking problem. In fact, on a date with Carol Anne, I found a half-empty liquor bottle under the car seat. Later I discovered a cache of bottles in our basement. Dad was a very intelligent man, good to his family, and he provided for us. But I think of him now as being very unhappy. His unhappiness, I believe, stemmed from his regret and resentment for having dropped out of school, and also because of the difficulties with my older brother, Frank.

"Frank caused a lot of stress in our family. He was epileptic, and never was accepted by his peers. He did not do well in school. He was on medication as far back as I can remember. As he grew older, soon after entering puberty, he often became violent and took out his frustrations on my mother. He would harass her, abuse her verbally, and a couple of times at least he hit her. Once, I remember, she locked herself in the bathroom to get away from him, and Frank broke down the door and struck her several times. To deal with this, Mother began taking tranquilizers—stelazine, I think it was called—and eventually she became dependent on the pills to cope with life.

"Despite her problems, Mother was active in church, much more involved than my father.

"When Frank was seventeen—I was a sophomore in high school—my parents decided to institutionalize him in a mental hospital operated by our church. It was a traumatic experience for the whole family. My father said that leaving Frank at the hospital 'caused something inside him to break,' and I think that is true because his alcoholism worsened."

Scott interrupted at this point. "Tell me something more about your mother."

"My mother? Oh yes, I should have said something about her background. She was reared on a farm close to Lancaster, Pennsylvania, was valedictorian in her high school class, and graduated from college. She was proud of her education and frequently talked to me about going to college. When my brother and I were small she was a housewife. Later she became a secretary in a law office in Camden. I think it fair to say that she was the stackpole in our home, and until she became addicted to tranquilizers, she was the steadying influence. I think I was closer to her than to my father.

"Seeing my father drinking and my mother becoming more and more dependent on drugs—because of their feelings of guilt and failure with Frank—their example was less than positive. I did not want to become like them. Also, I had a growing sense of wanting to be useful to the Lord and help people like my parents deal with difficulties. These were experiences and feelings that probably contributed more than anything else in my decision to enter the ministry. For a while I considered a medical and psychiatric career, but I felt God was leading me into the ministry."

Turning to Carol Anne, Scott said, "And what about your home and childhood?"

"In some ways our homes were similar. My younger brother was mentally retarded and he had to be institutionalized in his late teens to protect my mother. My parents were strong Christians, and though the situation with my brother was very difficult for them, they seemed to handle it well.

"My father worked in the Navy yard in Philadelphia, and my mother was a housewife. I had no other brothers or sisters.

"James and I became friends when I was quite young, and we dated for six years before we married. We were fully aware of each other's family life, and I think it created a bond between us. The experiences we had growing up matured us beyond our years.

"We often discussed what kind of life we would have together and what our vocations would be. As James said, I knew he wanted to be a minister and he knew I was planning to be a nurse."

Carol Anne paused as if she were waiting to say something more, but she did not. James then told of his mother's dying of cancer when he was in Westminster Seminary, and of his brother's being released from the institution shortly thereafter. "Since he got out of the hospital," James said, "he has worked at odd jobs of one kind or another. Presently he is a dishwasher in a restaurant in Philadelphia."

"What about your call to missions?" Scott asked. James spoke first.

"During the year Carol Anne and I were in Grand Rapids together we attended a church where Roger Peterson was the pastor. It was during that time that we first considered foreign missions."

"How did that come about?" Scott inquired.

"I think it was Roger's influence as well as other factors at work . . . factors such as where we could fit into the Kingdom of God. Also, I had very definite ideas about the kind of ministry I wanted to do. I was especially drawn to an evangelistic ministry. I wanted to work in an urban area similar to the area where I grew up. I can trace my love for evangelism back to childhood days. During my first year in high school my mother was involved in a church planting project sponsored by our home church. The mission was located in a very poor black community in North Camden. I went with my mother every Sunday afternoon to distribute literature and to attend the preaching service. Once I remember Dad's going with us. The work started with a daycare center and Sunday evening worship. Mother worked in the day care center for a period of time. Carol Anne and I also were counselors for a summer camp we had for the children of the community.

"Also, I remember missionaries coming to our church, and what most impressed me was their emphasis on evangelism. All of these feelings and experiences were reinforced by Roger Peterson."

Though Scott had never met Roger Peterson, his name was familiar. "Didn't he write a book on urban evangelism?" Scott inquired.

"Yes, more than one. He now teaches missions and urban evangelism at Westminster Seminary." James then continued:

"The year Carol Anne and I were back in Grand Rapids and I was attending Calvin Seminary, she became pregnant with our first child, and this had an interesting psychological effect on us. To me it made the matter of deciding about our future more urgent.

"Soon after the baby was born I saw a bulletin from your agency describing the need for missionaries and the positions open in Asia. I think I had not seriously considered serving overseas until I read that bulletin. I took it home and showed it to Carol Anne. She read it, and I said, 'Let's contact them and see what they say.'

"Her response was, 'Are you crazy?'"

James and Carol Anne both laughed as he told this, and Scott smiled. The atmosphere had become comfortable, and he sensed both James and Carol Anne were being candid and honest.

"As you know," James continued, "we did call and talk with a secretary, and a few days later your colleague Paul Zirkle called us. He invited us to come and see him.

"He talked to us for about two hours, mostly about the Philippines. We were not totally unwilling to go there, but for some reason, we were more drawn to Japan."

Carol Anne then said, "We had a new baby, and I was fearful of tropical diseases."

"I was not particularly interested in going to an underdeveloped area of the world," James added. "I wanted to live and work in an urban area and have something of the life style we were accustomed to.

"Paul Zirkle then asked us how we would feel about going to Japan, and immediately we both indicated this would be fine. That is how we began to think of Japan."

Scott then asked, "Have you studied much about our work there, and does it still interest you?"

"Very much so," James replied. "The opportunities in Japan for urban evangelism and church planting fit in with the idea of ministry I have had."

"How are you at learning languages?"

"I do well," James responded. "I made straight A's in Greek and Hebrew, and I did very well in French both in high school and college. Japanese will be harder, I'm sure, but it doesn't frighten me."

Carol Anne then spoke.

"To tell the truth, I was less excited about all of this than James. After all, we had just had our first child who was also the first grandchild for both sides of the family. I thought it was not fair to be separated from my parents and from James' father by thousands of miles."

"I basically had to persuade her," James added. He went on to say that he had a growing conviction that what they were doing was God's will, and their conversations with Roger Peterson confirmed this. "Carol Anne was very responsive to Roger's preaching, and we sought his advice."

"What did he tell you?" Scott asked.

"He said by all means we should serve on a foreign mission field. But this was not surprising and not an unusual thing for him to say because about a third of the seminarians at Calvin end up as missionaries."

"The idea of travel and living overseas appeals to Roger. He is adventurous," Carol Anne commented. "He was quite open about it."

"Anyway," James said, "we decided to pursue this seriously." He then concluded:

"I knew I had to have some full-time pastoral experience, and that is why we took this church here in Elizabeth. We may not spend the rest of our lives in Japan, but it is something we are willing to try for a while."

"How have your families responded to the idea of your going overseas?" Scott queried.

"We decided together—I'm not sure who thought of this first—that we would be guided by how our parents reacted."

"Can you be more specific?" Scott asked. James responded:

"We agreed that if they opposed it, it would not be God's will, and we would give up. If they consented, we would take this as a sign that God was leading us. Also, we were praying all this time that God indeed would lead us.

"We called my dad first and told him what we were thinking—of going to Japan as missionaries. Carol Anne then talked to her parents. She was straightforward and asked them if they had any objection or advice. None of them objected. So here we are."

"Yes," said Scott, "here we are."

The Recommendation

The rest of the visit was uneventful. Scott reviewed the possible schedule for appointment, provided they were approved. They then had prayer and Scott left.

Now he was back in his office, and he was expected to make his recommendation to the administrative board that morning. What should he do? Were the Reists good candidates for missionary appointment?

STUDY QUESTIONS

1. Have you ever heard the expression "the missionary call" or "the missionary calling"? What does it mean? Are there expressions in most Christian traditions that are similar?

2. Think a moment about some missionary you have read about or heard speak. Was there any emphasis given to that individual's "calling" to be a missionary?

3. Assuming there is some theological basis for believing that God does impress some people to be missionaries, what would you suggest as sound and healthy components of that impression or proclivity?

4. James and Carol Anne Reist are seeking appointment as missionaries. What factors contributed to their understanding of their call to mission?

5. What are the aspects of their background and training which prepare them to be missionaries? Is there anything in either of their resumes or elaborations that would cause you to question whether they should be appointed?

6. If you were Scott Dressler, knowing what you know, would you recommend that the Reists be sent to Japan as missionaries of the Protestant Reformed Churches of America?

SUGGESTED BIBLICAL TEXTS FOR REFLECTION

Exodus 3:1–20. The call of Moses to return to Egypt.

Isaiah 6:1–8. God's call to the prophet Isaiah.

Mark 1:16–20. Jesus calls Andrew, Peter, James, and John.

Luke 9:57–62. Some would-be followers of Jesus.

Acts 16:6–10. The Apostle Paul's vision at Troas and his call to go to Europe.

"I WANT TO BE A PRIEST"

Mario, a Guatemalan Roman Catholic lay leader, tells his friend, a North American Maryknoll missionary, that he wants to become a priest. His age, his lack of education, and the reluctance of the bishop to consider Mario's request places the missionary in a difficult position. In view of the critical shortage of priests in Guatemala, should the missionary encourage Mario to persist or be satisfied in his role as a catechist? What is the best way for a person like Mario to serve the people in the highlands of his country?

CONTEXT
Orientation of a National Layworker

One of the most serious problems the Roman Catholic Church has faced for generations in Latin America has been the desperate shortage of trained clergy. The reasons are many and complex, but likely they can be traced back, in part at least, to the reluctance of Europeans who dominated the Church during the colonial era to ordain native Latin Americans to the priesthood. During the three hundred years of colonial rule, a Spanish, not a national nor an indigenous, Church was established. Even as late as 1800, as many as fifty percent of the clergy were Spanish-born. The remainder were almost entirely Creole. Hardly any were indigenous. Moreover, very few Creoles became bishops, much less archbishops. While it is true that there was no official policy against developing a native priesthood, it can also be asserted that there was no official and consistent policy encouraging the development of a native priesthood. Consequently, the clergy in Latin America for the most part were foreign born. Since that time there has never been a sufficient number of national or foreign clergy.

Shortly after World War II, the intrepid John Considine, M.M., returned from an extended journey through Latin America as the Extraordinary Visitor of the Maryknoll Missions and wrote his moving *Call For Forty Thousand.*[1] Though largely anecdotal, the account was sufficiently documented with facts and statistics to sound a convincing alarm.

Citing the words of a South American bishop, Considine wrote:

---

1. New York: Longmans, Green, 1946.

"I believe we can say," the bishop lamented, "that as many as fifty million Catholics [of the then current population of 140 million] in Latin America are living what is tantamount to a priestless religious life. Each receives from a priest baptism and marriage, and occasional visits, sometimes as often as once a year, at the local fiesta. But for some three hundred and sixty four days out of three hundred sixty five these hosts of our people are priestless."[2]

In 1953, less than a decade after the publication of Considine's book, some three hundred lay delegates, men and women, along with several clerical moderators, gathered in Chimbote, Peru, to talk about the state of Catholicism in their respective countries. Though differing in details, the consensus of the delegates was that the vast majority of Catholics in their nearly twenty countries were *"Católicos solo de nombre,"* that is, Catholics in name only. Most Latin Americans, Coleman wrote, professed Christianity, but they did not allow "it to influence their daily lives in any appreciable degree." A major part of the problem was the lack of clergy, and one agreed-upon solution was an aggressive program to develop a lay apostolate.[3]

According to the Considine data of 1946, the ratio of priests to communicants in Central America was as poor as anywhere else on the continent. In Guatemala, for example, he reported only 125 priests for a combined community of 3,450,000 or one priest for every 27,600 communicants. It was somewhat better in Honduras (1 to 12,860), El Salvador (1 to 9,314), and Nicaragua (1 to 9,200). One may question the accuracy of those data, especially for those of Guatemala, but subsequent investigations have tended to support Considine's overall statistics.

Though the situation today has improved in Guatemala and Nicaragua, it has grown steadily worse in Honduras and El Salvador. According to the 1994 edition of the Catholic Almanac, the current ratio of priests to communicants is as follows: Guatemala, 766 priests for 7,634,000, or one for every 9,996; Honduras, 310 priests for 5,260,000, or one for every 16,967; El Salvador, 485 priests for 5,380,000, or one for every 11,092; and Nicaragua, 325 priests for 4,000,000, or one for every 12,307 communicants. The situation in Mexico is even more critical with one priest for every 17,603 communicants.

For Protestants in Latin America the problem is somewhat different in that most of the evangelical denominations from their earliest beginnings in the nineteenth century recognized and soon began to ordain nationals as ministers and pastors. In one sense, this practice has been Protestantism's greatest strength and perhaps one of its greatest weaknesses. While on the one hand the phenomenal growth of Protestantism in Latin America has been greatly facilitated by the ease with which any individual may declare himself/herself

---

2. Ibid., 11.

3. William J. Coleman, *Latin American Catholicism: A Self-Evaluation* (Maryknoll, N.Y.: Maryknoll Publications, 1958), 20, 78–84.

"called of God to preach," this open-ended system has created some major problems. Formal theological education is required by many and certainly preferred by the other churches associated with the older denominations such as the Anglicans, Presbyterians, Methodists, Lutherans, and Baptists. But the Baptists, for example, have never insisted that a pastor must be seminary trained. In 1990 the Brazilian Baptist Convention reported a total of 4,614 congregations plus 8,254 missions or "preaching points." Yet they had only 4,815 pastors, and many of these with minimal or no formal theological education. This is true in Brazil, although to a lesser extent in other Latin American countries as well.

Among the innumerable newer Protestant groups, especially among the independents and Pentecostals, traditional theological study is not regarded as necessary. In some of these churches the only prerequisite to being accepted as a minister is to declare oneself to be "called of God." Formal education, theological or otherwise, is even denigrated in some denominations. The result has been an incredible and uncontrolled proliferation of Protestant sects, the continual emergence of new ecclesiastical *caudillos,* and a persistent unwillingness to enter into serious ecumenical dialogue or cooperation with anyone beyond one's own self-contained and self-assured church and community.

What was said of the Pentecostal churches in Chile more than twenty years ago is more or less true of the many other Protestant groups in Latin America.

> The Pentecostalist congregation is organized like a large extended family
> . . . whose undisputed head is the pastor. The latter amply fulfills the
> pattern of the ideal *patrón* of their dreams; he is the incarnation of the
> father-figure who has been lost—or rejected. . . . The pastor is the person
> who protects, who finds work for the unemployed, who gives counsel.
> Often very authoritarian, he nevertheless ensures the protection of the
> congregation, and it is possible to have faith in him, since he is the
> depository of God's gift, the person whose election is marked by His
> [God's] baptism. Pentecostalism both offers equality of opportunity
> (rupture) and also recreates the old seigniorial form of society by fulfill-
> ing its ideal of protection and trust in vertical human relationships (conti-
> nuity).[4]

One must acknowledge that ordination to ministry among the traditional Protestant denominations in Latin America was not always as easy as it may have appeared to the outsider. In many cases, the North American missionaries retained as long as possible the authority to determine who would and would not be ordained. And even though they eventually were forced by circumstances to divest themselves of this feature of their control, nationalization

---

4. Christian Lalieve D'Epinay, *Haven of the Masses* (Lutterworth Press, 1969), 38–39.

of the work as a whole often was achieved not because of the initiative of the missionaries, but over their vigorous protests.

In the following case study, Mario Domínguez, a Guatemalan lay worker, is not satisfied to continue as a catechist (*delegado de la palabra*) and expresses his desire to become a priest. Father John Dawson is evidently sympathetic but ambivalent because of Mario's age and lack of education, not to mention other cultural questions.

Though the individuals and institution involved in this case are Roman Catholic, the issue of ordination of nationals to the ministry or priesthood is not unique to any one denomination, and this case can be profitably considered by Roman Catholics and Protestants alike.

FOR FURTHER STUDY

Baptism, Eucharist, and Ministry. Geneva: World Council of Churches, 1982.
> The most recent statement from the World Council of Churches on the sacramental beliefs and practices Christians hold in common and issues that divide them. The section on ministry is especially relevant.

Cleary, Edward L. *Crisis and Change. The Church in Latin America Today.* Maryknoll, NY: Orbis, 1985.
> A recent overview of the new direction and leadership in the Latin American Church, including the impact of the theology of liberation, base Christian communities, and "the emergence of the laity."

Coleman, William J. *Latin American Catholicism: A Self-Evaluation.* Maryknoll, NY: Maryknoll Publications, 1958.
> The noted 1953 Chimbote Report wherein Latin American Roman Catholics critique the status of the faith in their countries. Includes a call for a "new apostolate" for Latin America.

Considine, John Joseph. *Call for Forty Thousand.* New York: Longmans, Green, 1946.
> After making an extensive journey through Latin America, Considine was one of the earliest to sound an alarm about the severe shortage of priests.

———, ed. *The Church in the New Latin America.* Notre Dame, IN: Fides, 1964.
> A more thorough examination of the situation in the church with chapters on the "new army of catechists in the Andes," the problems and promises of vocations, and the emerging role of laity in the church.

D'Epinay, Christian Lalieve. *Haven of the Masses.* London: Lutterworth, 1969.
> An important and insightful sociological study of the Pentecostal movement in Chile which includes the alienation many of the poor feel in relation to society and to the Church.

Foy, Felician A., ed. *1994 Catholic Almanac.* Huntington, IN: Our Sunday Visitor, 1993.
> Published annually, the *Almanac* includes data regarding the number of Roman Catholics, and the number of priests and other religious in every country in the world. For example, in 1993, of the total population of 302 million in Latin America, 270 million were Roman Catholics. For these 270 million, there were 36,698 priests or a ratio of one priest for every 7,350 communicants.

Haddox, Benjamin Edward. *Sociedad y religión en Colombia.* Translated by Jorge Zalamea, 64–78. Bogota: Ediciones Tercer Mundo, 1965. A translation of "A Sociological Study of the Institution of Religion in Colombia." A Ph.D. dissertation for the University of Florida, 1962.

An accounting and analysis of the Roman Catholic clergy in Colombia, the most Catholic country in Latin America, their origins, numbers, and distribution together with their impact on the society as a whole.

Pironia, Bishop Eduardo F. "Foreign Priests in Latin America." In *Between Honesty and Hope.* Translated by John Drury, 235–247. Maryknoll, NY: Maryknoll Publications, 1969.

A report by the secretary general of CELAM (Latin American Bishops Conference) in Rome stating forthrightly the positive and negative aspects of the phenomenon with theological reflections and recommendations.

"The Role of the Layman." In *Between Honesty and Hope* (1969), 151–155.

The functioning of the layperson in the world and in the church as seen by various lay apostles.

Stoll, David. *Is Latin America Turning Protestant?*, 24–41. Berkeley, CA: University of California Press, 1990.

Though journalistic in approach, Stoll's analysis of the state of the church in Latin America and the role of the Catholic clergy is insightful.

THE CASE
"I Want to be a Priest"

" 'I want to be a priest.' Those were his words," John said to the bishop and his four colleagues. " 'What must I do to become a priest?' "

Father John Dawson, an American priest and missioner, had been in Guatemala for nine years. Most of the time he had spent working in the highlands with the indigenous people, and for the past six years he had been director of the Apostolic Center for the training of layworkers. It was at the Center that he had first met Mario Domínguez when he came nearly three years earlier for his first course of study. Now Mario says he wants to become a priest, and John is torn between Mario's apparent sincerity and dedication and the reality of the situation.

No one responded immediately, and it seemed to John that his co-workers were as perplexed and pained as he was by Mario's request and the bishop's lack of encouragement.

Two Guatemalas

For John Dawson there were really two Guatemalas, and Mario was virtually a stranger to one of them. There was the Guatemala described in the

This case was written by Marcella Hoesl, M.M. It is copyrighted by the Case Study Institute and used here by permission.

GUATEMALA

tourist brochures and seen by those who came for brief visits as well as for those who lived insulated from the dismal existence of more than half the people. It was the land of exquisitely beautiful mountains, deep blue volcanic lakes, cedar forests, and quaint Indian people who dressed, lived, and worked as their ancestors had for centuries. It was a land of ancient ruins of the Maya culture, archeological treasures that dotted the landscape and that could be found all the way from Tikal, Cotzal, and Cobán in the North to Antigua and Atitlán in the South.

The cities and towns of Guatemala were no less impressive to John now than when he first came to the country, cities like Quezaltenango, Huehuetenango, Antigua, and Guatemala City with its broad avenues, spacious homes, luxury hotels, exclusive clubs, private schools, and ancient churches together with modern office buildings and industrial and technological complexes—all evidence of the wealth and opulence of some people in the country.

But herein lay a terrible irony for John, for there was another Guatemala, not one of tranquil beauty or unique little people in their fanciful dress and *cosas típicas* (souvenirs), but a Guatemala of violence, earthquakes and destruction, political and social oppression, rightwing death squads who along with the police and the army systematically killed and wiped out all suspected opposition. It was the Guatemala of grinding poverty and indescribable suffering and want, of torture and murder, of 200,000 refugees who chose to flee to neighboring countries to escape the hunger, the violence, and the widespread killing.

The indigenous people, the Indians, John knew, represented some 55% of the Guatemalan population, and they had suffered exploitation and oppression since the coming of the first European conquerors. Their lands had been taken from them, and they had been forced into lives of servitude and squalor. When they protested or attempted to challenge the institutionalized injustices, they were ruthlessly suppressed. For more than fifteen years, even before John had come to Guatemala, the Indians had been targeted by several military leaders. General Lucas García, for example, had attempted to eliminate key segments of the Indian leadership as a means of checking the growing insurgency. General Efraín Ríos Montt was little better. John believed that this was a Guatemala most visitors never saw, one which many Guatemalans themselves preferred not to see.

Having worked for most of his missionary career with the Indians, Father Dawson was committed to developing a trained and competent indigenous leadership. He saw and appreciated the profound role religion played in the lives of the Indians, a role that he was satisfied had been constant since colonial times. All the important moments of life and death were integrally woven into their religious practices, rites, and celebrations. This reverence, this individual and collective participation in religious life should, he thought, be preserved.

Yet John had come to believe that one of his tasks, as well as a task of each of his missionary colleagues, was to help the Indians be aware of their dignity and rights, to enhance their knowledge of and appreciation for their own religious traditions. At the same time, he was committed to awakening them to the detrimental effects of accepting fatalistically—as they had for generations—the injustices, suffering, and repression of their marginal existence. For these reasons John saw the Apostolic Center in Huehuetenango as an ideal means for achieving some of his missionary goals.

The Apostolic Center

There was a growing consensus in the Roman Catholic Church following the Second Vatican Council (1962–65) that the shortage of priests in Latin America, as well as other places, would continue, and that if the masses of believers were to receive ministry, a lay apostolate would have to be prepared to fill this critical need. With this broad objective, the Apostolic Center was founded in 1968 by the bishop of Huehuetenango. As it developed, a team of eight American Roman Catholic missioners serving in Guatemala were eventually called upon to staff the Center and direct its programs.

By the time Father Dawson became the director, more than three hundred men had been trained and had assumed leadership roles in their various communities. Recommended by their parish priests and encouraged by their families and friends, the men would come with beans, rice, or corn, and a few *centavos* or a *quetzal* or two. Some would arrive by bus, but many would walk long and arduous distances to reach the Center.

Mario Domínguez

Mario Domínguez had not been among the first to come. The delay was not because of any lack of ecclesiastical or community support, but because of the physical condition of his mother and the fact that several of his younger brothers and sisters depended on him to supplement their meager incomes to feed and clothe the family. Mario was *ladino,*[5] thirty years old and single—an uncommon status for a man of his age and culture. He had completed only two years of formal schooling.

He was from Los Aldes, a coffee-growing village of less than a thousand inhabitants, and he had worked for more than ten years on a large farm owned by a wealthy landlord who lived most of the time in the capital city. Mario's family and extended family were leaders in the village and were very active in the religious life of the community, several of them serving as catechists for the parish priest. For the past several years, however, the priest rarely came to the remote area.

---

5. The name *ladino* is used principally in Guatemala and El Salvador to refer to non-indigenous people, that is, to the *mestizos* and whites, although those of the middle and upper classes would resent the term's being applied to them.

When Mario first came to the Center, he attended the three-week basic *evangelization course*. He struck John as exceedingly shy, but capable. "He is so timid," John had said to Miguel Ortiz, one of the Guatemalans on the staff, "but he is really a hard worker. What a determination to study!" In the evenings, Mario took extra classes in reading and writing, and others on the staff remarked about his *buena voluntad* and energy. He would volunteer for any job that needed to be done.

In September of the following year, Mario returned for a second course that would prepare him to be a *delegado de la Palabra* (a minister of the Word), a task that would include teaching, preaching, and sharing the Bible with his people. Nine months later he returned for a third time, for preparation to be an *animador de la fé* (energizer or stimulator of the faith). When he completed the course, Mario was authorized in certain situations to distribute the Eucharist to the people, to baptize, comfort the sick, and prepare couples for marriage. The bishop of Huehuetenango traveled to Mario's village, more than a hundred kilometers away, to install him publicly and admonish the villagers to support him in his ministry. It was a jubilant celebration, the bishop later told John, and nearly four hundred people crowded into the church, and several hundred others stood outside.

After serving as *animador* for more than a year, Mario returned to the Center for a month-long renewal course. He was one of fifty-five men from all over the diocese who came when the planting and harvesting had been completed. During the final week of study, the leadership team and all the students went on a *paseo* (outing)—walking from the Center to the ancient Maya ruins on the outskirts of Huehuetenango.

Mario and John walked along together. Suddenly Mario said, "Padre Juan, I want to become a priest. What must I do now to become a priest?" John put his arm around Mario's shoulder without saying anything for several moments. He had come to admire Mario as much as any man who had come to the Center, but he was concerned about the rigors of the celibate priesthood and conscious of the long years of training required for ordination. Both of these presented formidable obstacles for men anywhere in Latin America, John believed, but especially for those of the Guatemalan highlands.

"First, Mario, you would have to complete your *bachillerato* [high school]. You possibly could get some credit for the work you have done at the Center, but even so, I believe we are talking about two to three years. Then you would have to do your licentiate and master's in theology which would take at least five more years. *Amigo*, would it not be better for you to continue your fine service to your people in Los Aldes?"

"I love my work, Padre Juan," Mario replied, "but I want to be a priest! I have a calling to the priesthood."

"I understand, Mario, but it is a very long road. I will promise you, nevertheless, that I will talk to the bishop. Let's see what he says."

The following week, as he had promised, John requested an appointment with the bishop. He took with him four of the leadership team, and together they related the results and the problems they were facing at the Center. Finally, John presented Mario's case and his desire to become a priest.

The bishop was not encouraging. Mario was not the first student at the Center to express a desire to become a priest. The Center, the bishop reminded them, was not begun as a pre-seminary school. Moreover, he said, a man thirty years old with less than a primary education would find the difficulties too great.

"How in the world can a man like Mario acquire the necessary education to enter and complete seminary? Even if the Minor Seminary in Quezaltenango would receive him, would he have the determination to complete his studies for the priesthood, given all the pressures? I believe he can do much better continuing where he is."

John wondered if he should press the matter any further. He looked at his colleagues to see if one of them would speak. None did.

STUDY QUESTIONS

1. Make a list of the principal characters in this case. If you were called upon to role play one of these, what characteristics would you attempt to reveal to the other members of the class?

2. What are the issues in this case, and which of these do you think is the most important?

3. Though this case is about a male wanting to be a priest, are the same dynamics related to the question of ordination of women to the ministry or to the priesthood?

4. Missionaries, like other persons in leadership, often face the dilemma of what is best for an individual and what is best for the community. Is what is best for Mario in this case different from what is best for the community?

5. What would be the best strategy for John Dawson if he wants to support Mario for the priesthood or counsel him to continue as a catechist?

SUGGESTED BIBLICAL TEXTS FOR REFLECTION

Matthew 9:9–13. Jesus calls Matthew.

Luke 9:1–6. Jesus sends out the twelve disciples.

Mark 7:1–8. Jesus responds to the traditions and teachings of ancestors.

1 Timothy 3:1–7. Criteria for elders or pastors.

INITIATION

A U.S. missioner with many years of experience in East Africa is assigned to work in partnership with a young Ugandan who has just graduated from seminary. Their task is to establish a mission church. Soon the village elders come to the Ugandan and ask him to serve the eucharist prior to their celebrating the traditional rite of Imbalu, the circumcision of tribal youth as a sign of induction into adulthood. The young minister, however, voices his profound reluctance to mix the two rites, the second of which he regards as non-Christian. The missioner, committed to the indigenization of Christianity in East Africa, struggles with whether to question his young associate's position and thereby jeopardize their partnership, or remain silent and forfeit an opportunity for integrating the gospel and the culture.

CONTEXT
Contextualization and Primal Religion

The setting of this case is East Africa where Christianity spread southward from Egypt and Abyssinia, probably earlier than records attest. The eastern part of this the second largest continent was, it now appears, not only the cradle of the oldest civilizations, but also the locale for some of the earliest forms of humankind. Study a map of Africa and note the proximity of present-day Ethiopia (ancient Abyssinia) to Somalia, Kenya, and Uganda. Ethiopia or Abyssinia along with Egypt were major political forces during biblical times.

Although some have sought to establish Christianity in Ethiopia during the first century C.E.,[1] the earliest record of its being there is associated with the entry of two young Greek Christians from Syria, Frumentius and Aedesius, when the ship on which they were traveling down the Red Sea was wrecked off the Ethiopian coast. Somewhat like the story of the Old Testament Daniel and his friends, Frumentius and Aedesius were made slaves in the royal court

---

1. They suggest that c. 35 C.E., a high official of Ethiopia, who was also a "God-fearer" was converted through the intervention of Philip while returning to his homeland from Jerusalem (Acts 8:28–40). Other than the New Testament reference, there is no record of this event. Lemuel C. Barnes fantasizes about subsequent developments, but he admits that the evidence does not exist. *Two Thousand Years of Missions Before Carey* (Philadelphia: American Baptist Publication Society, 1900), 196–197.

and eventually won the respect and favor of King Ezana. The two slaves not only were named to positions of prominence and power, they were permitted to witness to their Christian beliefs. So effective were their efforts that c. 350 C.E. the King Ezana proclaimed Christianity the faith of the land. After returning to Alexandria, Frumentius was named bishop of the Abyssinian church by Athanasius, and was accompanied back to Axum by other Egyptian Christians. The Ethiopian church functioned under the authority of the bishop of Alexandria of the Egyptian Coptic Church from the fourth century until after World War II, though a coup d'etat in 1937 sought to separate the church from Egyptian control. The first Ethiopian bishop was finally consecrated in Cairo in 1950.

Besides Ethiopia, there is a tradition that Christianity entered the ancient kingdom of Nubia (now a part of southern Egypt and northern Sudan), but the confirmation of this account has not been possible. The area today is overwhelmingly Muslim. Whether Christianity was known in the regions immediately south of Abyssinia prior to the 16th century is not known, but it is not difficult to imagine it was.

Roman Catholic missionaries began work in East and North East Africa after Portuguese explorers began to report on the area, and though their efforts have been disparaged and dismissed as superficial by some critics,[2] David Livingstone wrote positively of the Roman Catholic pioneers and of his indebtedness to them. He said:

"Indeed, missionaries of that body of Christians established themselves in a vast number of places in Eastern Africa, as the ruins of mission stations still testify; but not having succeeded in meeting with any reliable history of the labors of these good men, it is painful for me to be unable to contradict the calumnies which Portuguese writers still heap on their memory."[3]

The first Protestant missionary to arrive in Kenya was the indomitable Johann Krapf (1810–1881) of the Anglican Church Missionary Society who landed in Mombasa in 1844. Krapf had been among those of the same society who had attempted to do evangelization in Ethiopia as early as 1836, but their efforts were for the most part unsuccessful. Within two months from his arrival in Mombasa, Krapf's wife and infant daughter were dead and he was critically ill with a tropical fever, probably malaria. He recovered, however, and began to study Kiswahili and lobby for a "a chain of mission stations across Africa from east to west and north to south, in the form of a cross, each station being named after an Apostle."[4] In 1846, Krapf was joined

---

2. E.g., Robert H. Glover, *The Progress of World-Wide Missions* (New York: George H. Doran, 1924), 235.

3. In Ibid., 216–217.

4. Glover, 242.

by a fellow German, Johann Rebmann, and together they established the mission station at Rabai, near Mombasa, and began to make treks inland. Krapf's achievements were more linguistic and anthropological than evangelistic, but his *Travels and Missionary Labours in East Africa* published in 1860, and his language texts made Europeans aware of the possibilities and difficulties of doing mission work in this largely unknown region.[5]

The Church Mission Society dispatched additional missionaries to neighboring Uganda in 1876, among them the renowned Alexander Mackay (1849–1890), a Scotsman trained as a teacher and engineer. Involved in a bevy of activities including roadbuilding, printing, construction, teaching, and evangelization, Mackay was joined eventually by other Europeans and their first converts were baptized in 1882. Mackay, the only one of his group of eight sent to Uganda in 1876 who lived there more than two years, died in 1890 of a fever. He and those who aided him, however, laid a foundation for one of the strongest churches to develop in East Africa. In summary, despite the difficulties posed by many reversals, continual opposition, fierce persecution, torture, and martyrdom, Christianity spread through the Baganda tribal people in incredible fashion.[6]

The French Roman Catholic White Fathers arrived in 1879, and they too established a strong presence there. The spread of the Christian faith, however, was due not merely to the missionaries, but more importantly to the responsiveness of the people, the support of various chiefs, and the widespread use of catechists who multiplied the work of the missionaries many hundredfold.

Subsequently, other groups of Bantu-speaking people were attracted to the gospel, but Islam and the traditional or primal religious views have continued to be significant impediments. No less formidable is the strength of Islam that spread down the East African Coast beginning in the latter half of the seventh century by traders and slavers and today claims large percentages of the population in Sudan, Somalia, Uganda, Kenya, Tanzania, Zaire, Chad, the Central African Republic, Niger, and Nigeria.

In the following case study, the dilemma arises out of the apparent conflict between Christianity and primal religious beliefs and practices. Students are encouraged to review the discussion of primal religions that precedes the case entitled "Build Your Church Here." Primal religions often lack the organizations and structures of the more visible world religions, but they usually retain the devotion of people who are born in an environment in which belief in ancestral spirits and the gods of nature are prevalent. Divesting oneself of beliefs inculcated since early childhood is difficult if not impossible.

---

5. David Barrett, "Johann Ludwig Krapf," *Concise Dictionary of the Christian World Mission,* ed. Stephen Neill, Gerald H. Anderson, and John Goodwin (Nashville: Abingdon, 1971), 329.

6. Stephen Neill, *A History of Christian Missions,* revised ed. (Baltimore: Penguin, 1986), 324–327.

Anastasios Yannoulatos, the well-known Greek Orthodox missionary bishop in East Africa, tells of witnessing a formal sacrifice to the Nigerian iron god, Ògún. A chicken was sacrificed as well as a dog, he says. Libations of oil, roots, and shells were employed. Prominent on the altar, however, were the remains of an old automobile engine, a bumper, and other assorted parts. When the bishop inquired of the king "if a car manufactured in a European or American factory was suitable material for an altar of Ògún," this important Yoruba god, the chief replied, "Any iron thing, no matter where it is or where it comes from, belongs to Ògún."[7] The synthesis of ancient religious rites with the accoutrements of modern technology is common in all religions, but it is most striking when one encounters the fusion in another's sacred ceremony.

FOR FURTHER STUDY

Desai, Ram, ed. *Christianity in Africa as Seen by Africans.* Denver: Alan Swallow, 1962.
      Fascinating and insightful perspectives on the history of Christianity, missions, missionaries, and the future of the church(es).

Faupel, John Francis. *African Holocaust. The Story of the Ugandan Martyrs.* London: G. Chapman, 1962.
      A revision of a work published in 1941, *Black Martyrs* by René Lefèbre. Well-documented account of the tragic history of the victims of King Mwanga between 1885–1887.

Gale, H. P. *Uganda and the Mill Hill Fathers.* London: Macmillan, 1959.
      The history of the work of the Mill Hill missionaries during the crucial period from 1895–1914.

Hastings, Adrian. *African Christianity.* London: Geoffrey Chapman, 1976.
      A history and analysis of the first century of Christian missions in Africa, the church's ministries, the missionaries, the politics, poverty, and cultural changes.

Ikenga-Metuh, E. *Comparative Studies of African Traditional Religions.* Onitsha: Imico Publishers, 1987.

Kalu, Ogbu U. "Precarious Vision: The African's Perception of His World." In *African Cultural Development,* ed. O. U. Kalu. Enugu: Fourth Dimension Publishers, 1978.
      An examination of the contemporary African view of life, history, and religion.

Mbiti, John S. *African Religion and Philosophy.* London: Heinemann, 1969.
      An introductory study of African religion and views by a recognized Christian leader and spokesperson.

———. *Introduction to African Religion.* New York: Praeger, 1975.
      A basic and comprehensive introduction to the study of African religion. Includes definition, historical summary, manifestations, views of the universe, God, the spirits, origin of humanity, rituals, religious leaders, morals, and the value of religion.

---

7. "Christian Awareness of Primal World-Views." *Mission Trends No. 5,* ed. Gerald H. Anderson and Thomas F. Stransky (New York: Paulist, 1981) 251.

Setiloane, Gabriel. *African Theology. An Introduction.* Johannesburg: Skotaville, 1986.
Possibly the most concise and readable introduction available to Sub-Saharan African theology.

Shorter, A. *African Christian Theology—Inculturation or Incarnation?.* London: Geoffrey Chapman, 1975.
The last two chapters are especially relevant to this case.

Sundkler, Bengt. *The Christian Ministry in Africa.* London: SCM Press, 1960.
A thorough and useful discussion of the African pastor, ordination to ministry, the ministry of word and sacrament, the pastor and the missionary, and the pastor as "mid-man."

Taylor, John Vernon. *The Growth of the Church in Buganda.* London: SCM Press, 1958.
A concise history of Christian missions in Buganda, the world view of the people, and the pastoral and theological questions that must be faced. Valuable for this case study.

Tourigny, Yves. *So Abundant a Harvest. The Catholic Church in Uganda 1879–1979.* London: Darton, Longman, & Todd, 1979.
A thorough history of the Catholic Church in Uganda during its first one hundred years.

Uka, E. M. *Readings in African Traditional Religion.* Bern: Peter Lang, 1991.
A collection of readings by various African scholars on the African perception of the world, understanding traditional religion and its sources, the African concept of God, humanity, spirituality, and ethics. Also includes a chapter on the "salvific value of African traditional religion."

THE CASE
Initiation

In many ways it was the realization of a dream for the Bagisu people in this area when Misaeri Magambo came back to the East African mountain village of Butato with Peter Howell, an American missionary for many years, to establish a new Christian church. Misaeri, a recent graduate of Bishop Thurmon Theological Seminary, was returning to his own people in his new role as minister. Peter had written his bishop that he and Misaeri were warmly welcomed by the people who were excited about a church being built in their village.

Peter and Misaeri had been there only a few days when three village elders approached the hut which they had been given by the people. The men greeted Peter graciously, but it was clear they came to speak with Misaeri. The alternate year celebration of *Imbalu* (the initiation rites of adult male circumcision) was approaching, and the elders wished to discuss with their

---

This case was written by Professor Robert A. Evans and Alice Frazer Evans. It is copyrighted by the Case Study Institute and used by permission.

EAST AFRICA

new Christian minister the four 18-year-old boys to be initiated. The five men sat in the cool shade of the palm-thatched roof and drank *bursara* as they talked. Gatu, the eldest and the most respected leader of the village, expressed joy that for the first time a man of their own kin would administer the Christian sacrament of Eucharist when many in the village gathered prior to beginning the three months of ceremonies in preparation for "the cutting." Gatu declared, "First the missionaries, and now you have shared Christianity with us. We have come to know Jesus and believe in Him. It is important that the juice and bread are shared among us before *Imbalu,* for this is the time of *mana,* when the wisdom of the elders is given to the boy and he becomes a man." Gatu continued, "In years past the white missionary came from many miles away to give us the blessing of the Church. We rejoice that this blessing now comes from a son of our village."

As the old man spoke, Peter noted the unusual quietness of Misaeri. In Peter's estimation, Misaeri was a man of warmth who usually spoke with an open smile and genuine enthusiasm. On this occasion, however, Peter noted Misaeri's solemn face as he politely thanked the men for coming and nodded as they stood to leave. When the three men had left the compound, Misaeri spoke softly as his pent-up thoughts tumbled out. "Peter, when I was a boy, *Imbalu* and the sense of personal identity and wholeness my village imparted to me were crucial. But as a Christian I have come to profess my identity and salvation in Christ alone. Paul speaks for me: 'We are not circumcised or uncircumcised ... slave or free men. Christ is all.' This is the message I must bring to my people.

"Forty years ago the colonial government and many of the mission priests absolutely forbade the rite or insisted it be performed in a hospital. The people continued the practice in spite of tremendous opposition. I do not want to restrict my people in the celebration of this important ritual, but I do not want it confused with the most meaningful symbols of the Christian faith. The Gospel, in the body and blood of Christ, would then become watered-down to become part of a social ritual. Gatu is an exception in the village. He is a deeply committed Christian. Most of the people are unaware of the meaning of the Eucharist, and some even resent the intrusion of the Church into the *Imbalu* rites. The missionary who came in the past wanted the Faith to become an accepted part of the people's lives. But in my own understanding of the Faith, I must separate the sacred from social custom, or the Faith becomes insignificant. Peter, I don't want to jeopardize the new mission, but I must be a strong leader for my people and hold to my convictions. The Eucharist cannot be served during *Imbalu.* I must now struggle with how to explain this to my people."

Peter sensed the deep sadness of the young minister as Misaeri turned and walked slowly out of the hut. Peter was aware that Misaeri had not asked his advice. He was also aware of the sensitive balance he sought to maintain in this mission. He and Misaeri had been officially declared "co-pastors," but Peter saw his primary responsibility in using his years of mission experience to provide administrative assistance to Misaeri. Peter felt he technically had a right and possibly a moral responsibility to counsel Misaeri. But he was also cautious about undermining the younger man's self-confidence. Peter was committed to the gradual removal of a missionary presence as Africans assumed leadership in the Church.

Now alone in the hut, Peter moved to the window where the late-afternoon sun streaked down on the notes he had been preparing for a special church conference in Nairobi next month. He had been struggling with what he felt was the too-frequent imposition of Western cultural values along with the introduction of Christianity. His primary thesis, however, was the need for the Western Church to realize the tremendous insights the African culture and people had to offer the West. Peter had written in his notes that he had learned more from his African brothers and sisters about the essence of a community of Christ than in any other setting. He was aware of the genuine care and concern of the community for one another. *Imbalu* was not new to Peter. He had often encountered the initiation rite of circumcision in his ministry in East Africa during the past fifteen years. As he had written, "I see *Imbalu* as a spiritual as well as a social ritual. Along with birth, marriage, and death, it is a rite that clearly marks the passage from one stage to another. It is crucial to the establishment of a male's identity—a landmark which our Western society has sadly lost."

Peter's eyes focused on a quote he had cited from John Mbiti's *African Religions and Philosophy*. "Religion permeates into all departments of life so fully that it is not easy or possible always to isolate it. . . . Wherever the African is, there is his religion." Peter had written that at the time of *Imbalu,* when the people in a given community so identify with the candidate "under the knife" that their own values and commitments are also being tested and affirmed. The people visit the ancestral graves to call on the "spirits" as well as the creator God, *Were,* to enable the boy to succeed in his ordeal. Peter saw this as a statement that the boy's successful initiation (to show no fear or pain at the time of circumcision), as well as future struggles in life, are not primarily dependent upon the candidate's ability, but on the strength his God and his community, both living and dead, give to him. In the moment of trial for the boy there is a sense of the whole community affirming the boy's personal identity and dignity. Peter thought, "What a message for our misguided, self-sufficient Western mentality."

In rereading his notes, Peter reaffirmed his conviction that *Imbalu* was a central rite not only for the boy, but for the whole village. Rather than rejecting that crucial ritual, Peter felt the need for the Church to create a constructive integration between *Imbalu* and the essence of the message of Christianity. Peter smiled at the thought. Could he separate his own Christian faith from Western cultural values to reach this "essence of the Gospel"? Peter wondered how he could help Misaeri appreciate the intrinsic values which Peter as a Westerner saw in the African culture, but more important, did he have a right to question Misaeri's understanding of his own faith in relation to that culture? With a bemused smile, Peter realized he was struggling with essentially the same quandary as Misaeri. How could he share his feelings with his co-worker?

STUDY QUESTIONS

1. Mercy Amba Oduyoye distinguishes between primal and traditional religions. "Primal" religions, she says, are those religions unadulterated by Islam, Christianity, or any other system of belief. "Traditional" religion, she insists, suggests a religion that is a part of the customs, that is, something practiced without modification or unthinkingly carried on just because it has always been. Does this distinction fit this case study?

2. Who are the characters in this case, and what do you know about them?

3. Were you surprised that Misaeri Magambo would oppose linking the traditional *Imbala* and the Christian Eucharist? How do you explain his position?

4. Why is Peter Howell concerned about Misaeri's attitude?

5. Can traditional non-Christian ceremonies be integrated into Christianity, as Peter seems to suggest? Has it been done before?

6. Assuming Peter is correct, should he intervene? What effect would such intervention have on Misaeri's leadership role?

7. Assuming Misaeri is correct, what should he do? How is the best way to inform the elders?

8. Was the unidentified missionary to whom Misaeri refers wrong in participating in the rite followed by the Eucharist?

9. Is Misaeri partially right? If so, what would be an adequate substitute for *Imbala* as a rite of passage?

10. Misaeri appeals to Scripture by quoting what the Apostle Paul said about circumcision. Are the two situations comparable?

SUGGESTED BIBLICAL TEXTS FOR REFLECTION

Genesis 17:1–14. Circumcision as a sign of the covenant.

Exodus 30:1–10, 34–38. The incense and the altar.

Leviticus 1:1–17. Sacrifices to be burned whole.

Numbers 27:12–23. Learning God's will through the Urim and Thummim.

Galatians 5:1–15. The admonition of the Apostle Paul regarding circumcision.

Acts 16:1–3. Timothy circumcised before accompanying the Apostle Paul on his second missionary journey.

"YOU MUST PURIFY THIS HOUSE!"

A British Wesleyan Methodist couple have returned to Nigeria from a year of leave in England. The second day after their arrival they discover a colony of bees in the wall of their house, and they proceed to exterminate the insects. When their Fulani Muslim neighbors discover what has happened, they are shocked that the missionaries would recklessly kill the bees that God had beneficently sent. Later, several Fulani elders come and declare that the house must be purified by the shaman or else the missionaries will suffer the wrath of God. Unsure as to how they should respond, the missionaries seek counsel.

CONTEXT
Contextualization and Primal Religion

The Fulani (pron. Foo-lahn-ee) are a nomadic people concentrated principally along the Sahelian belt in West Africa. As their numbers grew they scattered over what are today at least eighteen African countries including Mauritania, Senegal, Guinea, Mali, Burkina Faso, Benin, Niger, Nigeria, Cameroon, Chad, Sudan, and Ethiopia. They number from 10 to 14 million people and thereby represent the largest nomadic group in the world today.

Much like the Maasai, they are traditionally cattle-owners dependent economically and emotionally on the well-being of their herds. Because of the steady encroachments brought about by population growth, modernization, and government controls, the Fulani are being forced to settle and live in permanent villages. Although there is an increasing scarcity of grazing lands, the national governments consider cattle a part of national wealth and refuse to allow the Fulani to move their cattle across national borders. The prolonged droughts, the steady pressure to develop more farmland along with restrictions on land use for grazing and the imposition of fees for grazing of land—together with the other developments—threaten the Fulani way of life. As recently as 1983 the Fulani paid nothing in Nigeria. Now in many areas they must pay as much as ten dollars U.S. per day.

There is a steady social disintegration among the Fulani in West Africa. Their traditional way of life is being profoundly affected by the environmental changes, government regulations, and a knowledge of how to raise cattle but not how to adapt to change.

Contact with the larger world has revealed that the cattle suffer from a number of common diseases, maladies that are easily treated such as intestinal parasites. But the Fulani tribespeople often resist outside help, and their cattle grow weaker and often die.

Religiously, the Fulani are either animists or Muslim. Some of their ancestors began to accept Islam as early as the fourteenth century when they were introduced to the teachings of the Prophet by Muslim traders. But, like many other tribal people in Africa, the Fulani faith even of those professing to be Muslims is an admixture of Islam and primal religious ideas. Historically, the Fulani have been intensely ethnocentric, and they have regarded all other peoples as socially inferior. Nowadays, among the Muslim Fulani, there is strong resistance to what they regard as the menace of Christianity, and conversion to the Christian faith usually brings immediate and severe social consequences such as expulsion from the family and tribe, the loss of all property including one's cattle, and the proclamation, "He/She is no longer alive!"

Though there were isolated and sporadic attempts to evangelize the Fulani as early as the 1920s,[1] it was after 1949 that a consistent effort by a number of Christian missions was begun. Their efforts were doubtless aided by the prolonged Sahelian drought of the 1960s and 1970s that brought the normally isolated Fulani herders into direct contact with various Christian communities. It was not until the late 1970s that the first Fulani convert was able to withstand the pressure to return to the traditional tribal faith and remain faithful to the Church.

A consultation on how to minister to the Fulani was called by the Nigerian Lutheran Church in 1974, followed by annual consultations in 1976, 1977, 1978, and 1979. As a result of these meetings, the constituent assembly of the Joint Christian Ministries in West Africa convened in Jos, Nigeria, in November 1979, attended by representatives from twenty-seven different mission organizations. Fourteen Lutheran missions and the Anglican Church Missionary Society became the founding members, each of which committed personnel and economic resources to work among the Fulani. More than twenty missions are members of the JCMWF today, and thirty others send representatives to the biannual sessions.

Today, there are at least a hundred Protestant and Roman Catholic missionaries representing some fifty different missions working with the Fulani in West Africa, and though the number of converts has steadily increased, observers report that there are less than fifteen hundred Fulani Christians

---

1. A Lutheran missionary, the Reverend Adolphus Gunderson from the U.S. moved from Nigeria to Cameroon in the 1920s to work among the Fulani. A Sudan Interior Mission representative sought to present the Gospel to Fulani animists in Benin in the same decade and a Christian and Missionary Alliance missionary made a separate attempt in Mali in the 1930s. The responses were minimal to none.

among the fourteen million Fulani people. "The ratio of Christian to non-Christian Fulani is 1/10,000."[2]

FOR FURTHER STUDY

Victor Azarya. *Aristocrats Facing Change: The Folbe in Guinea, Nigeria, and Cameroon.* Chicago: University of Chicago Press, 1978.

A historical analysis in which the author compares the changes pastoral peoples in three West African areas underwent from pre-colonial times, through the colonial era, to independence. The focus is predominantly on the Fulani or Fulbe peoples, and the main issue considered is the means by which the "aristocrats" or controlling groups maintained their dominance during times of social change.

Charles Frantz. "Fulbe Continuity and Change under Five Flags atop West Africa." *Journal of Asian and African Studies* 16 (1981): 89–115.

Frantz concentrates on the Mbororo-en (people) who live along the southern border between Nigeria and Cameroon. He appraises both the change and the constancy in Fulbe life following 1915, and especially after independence in 1960.

Donald D. Martin. "The Fulanis of Africa: Changes Hobble a Way of Life." *The Commission* 54 (October–November 1991): 6–23; and his "Recipe for Fulani Evangelism: Cattle, Care and Christ." *The Commission* 54 (October–November 1991): 24–33.

Two essays published in the monthly magazine of the Southern Baptist Foreign Mission Board indicating the interest in and efforts being made by Baptist missionaries to evangelize Fulanis in West Africa.

Ron Nelson. "Some Crucial Dimensions of Ministry to Fulbe." *Missiology* 11 (April 1983): 201–218.

An unusually insightful essay on the recent history and impact of change on the life of the Fulani. This should be required reading for the study of this case.

Paul Riesman. *Freedom in Fulani Social Life: An Introspective Ethnography,* trans. Martha Fuller. Chicago: University of Chicago Press, 1977.

Especially valuable for Riesman's description of Fulani social structure, village life, authority patterns, and religious and ethical ideas. The glossary and index of Fula terms is also helpful.

Emily A. Shultz, ed. *Image and Reality in African Interethnic Relations: The Fulbe and Their Neighbors.* Williamsburg, VA: College of William and Mary, 1981.

A more recent analysis of the interaction and conflict of the Fulbe with other groups.

Hans G. T. van Raay. *Fulani Pastoralists and Cattle.* The Hague: Institute of Social Studies, 1974. Also, his *Rural Planning in a Savanna Region.* Rotterdam: Rotterdam University Press, 1975.

Two studies based on fieldwork done in the early 1970s, but worthwhile in understanding the radical changes that have come in the lives of these historically pastoral people, their altered relationships, and deteriorating conditions.

---

2. John Gorder, "JCMWA: A People-Orientated Network." A paper presented to the Jos-Bukuru Theological Society, December 3, 1990, 6, n.7.

THE CASE
"You Must Purify This House!"

"As most of you know, Dana and I have been working with the Fulani for more than three years," Ian said, "and we have had no converts." He and Dana were speaking to a session of the "Joint Christian Ministries of West Africa," an organization composed of missioners working with the Fulani. The Fulani, a nomadic tribal people numbering about fourteen million, are scattered through eighteen to twenty African countries stretching from Senegal to Sudan and Ethiopia.

"Two days after we returned from furlough," Dana continued, "less than a month ago, we discovered a large nest of bees inside the wall of our house. I went outside and found the hole where they were entering and leaving, and after spraying and killing most of them, Ian removed some siding and discovered their nest. Killing the bees was relatively easy. Explaining what we had done to our Fulani neighbors was the difficult part. They were very upset and insisted we have our house ceremonially purified. We did not know what to do."

Mission to the Fulani

Ian and Dana Heath, British Wesleyan Methodist missionaries, had been in Nigeria for more than four years. Ian first taught agricultural science in a secondary school established by the Methodists in the 1930s, and his first contact with a Fulani occurred when two of his students spoke of the need to inoculate Fulani cattle for intestinal parasites. They introduced Ian to Yohanna Abdu, a Fulani herdsman whom the students, after several extended conversations, were able to persuade to allow Ian to treat his cows. The cows did well, but Abdu did not become a Christian. He did, however, serve as the Heaths' first contact with a wide network of Fulani families. By the end of Ian's second year of teaching, he and Dana decided to devote more of their time to working with these intriguing people. They began by studying the Fulani language, Fulfulde, moved into a small bungalow located close to two Fulani villages, and began what the Heaths regarded as a process of inculturation. This, they believed, was the first step toward any effective evangelization.

The Fulani, Ian and Dana learned, were among the most resistant people in Nigeria to Christianity. Their ancestors became Muslims in the fourteenth century when Arab traders introduced them to the teachings of the Prophet, and today virtually all Fulani are followers of Islam. What was not clear to Ian and Dana was whether Fulani resistance to Christianity was primarily theological or cultural. Islam indisputably was a part of the Fulani culture, and to cease being Muslim was equivalent to being no longer Fulani.

About a year before their furlough, Ian and Dana attended for the first time a meeting of the "Joint Christian Ministries in West Africa," an ecumenical biannual assembly that brings together missionaries from nearly fifty different groups—Protestant and Catholic—who are doing or attempting to do Christian ministries among the Fulani. It was in this meeting that the Heaths first heard a formal presentation on the history of Christian missions to the Fulani. The speaker said, for example, that the first Christian effort to evangelize the Fulani began in 1949, and though a few isolated individuals showed interest and some began to identify themselves as Christians, hardly any were baptized. One man who was baptized in 1963, the speaker said, had died less than a month later, poisoned, it was believed, by his own family. Thus the threat of being disowned by one's family, losing one's cattle, suffering complete social alienation from one's tribe, and possibly even death was too heavy a price for converts to pay. The Heaths' optimism waned that day as they faced the reality of what they had set out to accomplish.

They decided, therefore, to attempt to gain their Fulani neighbors' confidence, help them in whatever ways they could, and try to develop genuine friendships with them before making any attempt to present the Christian message. The year they spent on furlough in England studying at Selly Oak College convinced them of the rightness of this approach. The incident with the bees, however, seemed to jeopardize the progress they thought they had made before leaving for England.

Attending Again the Joint Christian Ministries Meeting

Less than a month after they returned to Nigeria, Ian and Dana drove to Jos to attend the meeting of "Joint Christian Ministries in West Africa." Ron Martin, the program chair, asked Dana and Ian after they arrived if they would speak to a plenary session about their experiences before and during their furlough. The Heaths decided they should relate what had happened to them since moving their residence into the Fulani area, a few things about their year at Selly Oak, and conclude by describing their experience with the bees.

Those in attendance included nearly fifty missionaries and a small number of Fulani Christians. Ian spoke briefly about how they came in contact with Yohanna Abdu and why they decided to move closer to the Fulani, stressing his and Dana's belief that before attempting any evangelization they needed to go through a process of inculturation, " 'contextualization' it is now called," Ian said, "and this conviction was strengthened by our experience and by our year of study. Since returning to Nigeria, however, we have encountered a problem which we want to share with you because we need your advice and help."

Encounter with the Bees

"We had been back from furlough only two days," Dana continued, "when I heard what sounded like a low humming noise in the wall of our little house. I suspected it to be a swarm of termites that had taken residence while we were away. I went out and found the hole in the wall where the insects were entering and leaving. But they were not termites, I discovered. They were bees.

"We had brought with us from England some cans of very powerful insect spray, so I placed the nozzle of the can over the hole, held the button down for five or ten seconds, and backed away. Bees began to crawl out, but they quickly died. I sprayed a second time. More bees came out and died."

Dana noted the faces of the Fulani who were listening to her and continued the story. "Ian thought we should take off some siding because we could still hear buzzing in the wall. So he got a claw hammer and gingerly pulled off a piece [of siding], and though there were still some bees in the nest, it was obvious they were dying. We sprayed some more and killed the remaining bees. To our delight, we found a large comb filled with honey. So we carefully removed it and laid it on the ground a couple of meters from where most of the bees had fallen.

"I swept the dead bees into a pile—there were hundreds of them—picked up the comb, put it in a large pan, and set it on a stool near the front door."

A Fulani Reaction

"A short time later I heard a greeting from one of our neighbors. When I went to the door, he and two other Fulani men were squatted several meters from the house. I responded and invited them to come in. They approached the front of the house, all the while eyeing the pan and the honey comb. Saidu spoke, 'Ah, what a large honey comb. What do you plan to do with it? Where did you find it?'

"By this time Ian had come out, and he explained to them how we had found the hive in the wall, had sprayed, killed the bees, and taken out the comb. He led them around to the side of the house and showed them the dead bees.

" 'Oh, you have made a great mistake,' Hassan exclaimed. At first, we assumed he was objecting to our using the spray, that we had contaminated the honey comb. But we soon realized this was not the problem. Our mistake, he made clear, had been in killing the bees which he connected with their cows and with God as Creator.

"The discussion was enlightening for us, but it was also very troubling. We quickly realized that to our neighbors bees are a blessing. In fact their words were, 'The bees came from God.' It was not that the honey had been contaminated, not a matter of our destroying food. We had, in their eyes, unwittingly destroyed something God had sent.

"Shaking their heads, they left. We were upset, but we did not know what to say or do. In our ignorance we had committed what to Hassan and his friends was a grievous mistake."

A Visit from the Fulani Elders

Ian continued the story. "Late that afternoon before dusk, several of the Fulani elders came to visit us. They asked us to tell them what had happened. In the course of the conversation one of them suddenly demanded that we pay them for having killed the bees. We did not respond. Another said ominously, 'You will pay, but not in money!'

"The oldest one, however, spoke solicitously, 'This house must now be purified. I will send some women at dawn with gourds of milk to begin the purification ceremony. Then the shaman can come and complete the rite.'

"Our initial reaction was to try to explain our point of view, to tell them again that we meant no harm. The truth is we were afraid of the bees and did not know that we were doing something wrong.

"I really wanted to say," Ian concluded, " 'If we have offended God, then we will pray to God because God hears our prayers. We will ask *God* for forgiveness.' I did not believe that a Fulani rite of purification was needed." Ian then quipped, "As long as we had the spray cans, we didn't need the shaman. At the same time we did not want to make matters worse."

At that point Dana turned to the senior missionaries and asked, "What should we have done? What would you have done?"

STUDY QUESTIONS

1. Who are the Fulani, and how do they differ from other West African tribal groups?

2. What is the Joint Christian Ministries of West Africa (JCMWA), and why is it significant in this case?

3. Name and describe the principal characters in this case.

4. Do you see a clash of cultures in this case? How would you explain the conflict to a European or North American?

5. Why were the Fulani neighbors anxious about what the missionaries had done? In what ways did they express their anxiety?

6. What do the Fulani elders propose? What should be the response of the missionaries to the proposal?

SUGGESTED BIBLICAL TEXTS FOR REFLECTION

1 Kings 18:20–40. Elijah and the prophets of Baal.

Matthew 12:43–45. The return of an evil spirit.

Mark 5:1–20. Jesus and the man with the evil spirits.

Mark 9:14–29. Jesus heals a boy with an evil spirit.

Acts 19:11–20. The Apostle Paul and the evil spirits.

"DON'T COME OVER AND HELP US!"

Serious objections are voiced by Thai Karen church members when a group of Karen students from Myanmar come and utilize ancient myths in dramas designed to present the Christian message. The church is divided as are the missionaries as to whether the gospel is being compromised.

THE CONTEXT
Contextualization and Syncretism

Though established borders exist between Thailand and Myanmar (formerly known as Burma), tribal peoples usually far removed geographically from their nations' capitals and often alienated from the ruling parties, ignore the national boundaries that legally separate them from others of their group, tradition, and language. This has been true of the Karen people and others in Myanmar whose villages can be found on both sides of the Myanmar-Thailand border.

Syncretism, a Threat or an Essential?

In this case study, however, the Karen students who came into Thailand entered legally, so this is not a problem. What is at issue, however, is the response to the way they structured their presentation of the gospel which—according to those who objected—imprudently utilized pagan myths in their presentation of the Christian message. Their dramas were, according to the opponents, dangerous examples of *syncretism*.

What is syncretism and why is it regarded as a serious mistake? By definition syncretism (fr. Greek *synkretismos* or a federation of Cretan cities) is usually defined as the blending, mingling, or fusing of differing beliefs and practices.[1] A contemporary Roman Catholic scholar, Leonardo Boff,

---

1. Hendrik Kraemer, in his preparatory volume for the third meeting of the International Missionary Council in 1938 in Tambaram, questioned the prevailing definition of syncretism. He wrote, "The term syncretism has always more or less the connotation of expressing the *illegitimate* mingling of different religious elements." Thus he advocated a more precise term, one "devoid of any value-judgment," and he proposed "amalgation." *The Christian Message in a Non-Christian World* (Grand Rapids, MI: Kregel Publications, 1977), 203.

The Japanese Christian scholar, Masatoshi Doi, however, observed that in Japan

insists that there are at least six different ideas about what constitutes syncretism: an addition to the gospel, an accommodation, a mixture, an acceptance of "diverse paths for encountering divine reality," the utilization of "the categories, cultural expressions, and traditions of another religion," and the adaptation, assimilation, reinterpretation, and recasting of ideas, words, and practices from another religion.[2]

Since the second meeting of the International Missionary Council in Jerusalem in 1928, Protestant Christians have engaged in an unending debate regarding what constitutes syncretism and how Christians should respond to it. Roman Catholic theologians and missiologists have likewise addressed the issue, but less polemically. Despite efforts to the contrary, the word "syncretism"—as Boff suggests—has acquired more than one or two definitions. They are not necessarily similar, and some clearly are pejorative.[3]

Without entering into the disputation over the nature and menace of syncretism, it is evident from the study of history that when the gospel of Jesus Christ as Savior is introduced into another culture, inevitably there are traditions, customs, and conventional modes of thought, as well as religious ideas, practices and terminology, which are either affirmed, accommodated, or adapted and incorporated by the church, or they are challenged, condemned, rejected, and prohibited. Head-hunting, cannibalism, human sacrifice, idol worship, the burning of widows, and temple prostitution are examples of practices which have been condemned consistently by Christian missionaries, despite the fact that such practices often have been deeply rooted in particular cultures. Other notions, rites, mores, and conventions, however, such as food, dress, festivals, music, and words—some of which have been closely

---

[and this is true in other cultures as well], syncretism has at least two meanings. "One is the fusion of two or more religions into one system," and the other signifies a religious devotee's "adherence to two or more religions." How else can one explain the fact that "the total number of adherents reported by all religions organizations" in Japan consistently exceeds the total population, while nearly twenty percent of the population professes to hold no religious beliefs? "Christianity and Other Religions in Japan," *The Theology of the Christian Mission,* ed. Gerald H. Anderson (New York: McGraw-Hill, 1961), 170. I was recently told by a Japanese Christian leader that current statistics indicate that the number of religious affiliations claimed by the Japanese people surpasses 210,000,000, but the total population of the country is only 125,000,000.

2. *Church: Charism & Power* (New York: Crossroad, 1988), 90–91.

3. Peter Schineller, "Inculturation and Syncretism: What is the Real Issue?" *International Bulletin of Missionary Research* 16 (April 1992): 50. This essay together with another by Robert J. Schreiter, "Defining Syncretism: An Interim Report," Ibid. 17 (April 1993): 50–53, not only set forth the various definitions of syncretism, they frame the limits of the debate. Schineller, however, believes the word to be so contaminated in theological circles that it should be abandoned in favor of a more acceptable and less loaded term.

associated with the indigenous religion(s)—have been adapted without question or with minimal objection.

Most of us are aware that unless the gospel is translated into the language of the people and adapted to their thought-forms and customs, it will never take root. The question is, How much adaptation of the faith can occur without its being so adulterated and compromised that it is hardly distinguishable from the religion it seeks to replace? This is the question so intensely debated since the Jerusalem Conference of 1928.[4]

When the IMC began to plan its meeting in Tambaram, Madras, India, scheduled for 1938, the Dutch theologian and former missionary Hendrik Kraemer was asked to write the preparatory volume. His theological analysis was forcefully stated in his *The Christian Message in a Non-Christian World* (1938), and it deserves careful study by any serious student of mission history and theology. Kraemer, however, did not sound the final word, and in many respects, the controversy over syncretism intensified. M. M. Thomas, a contemporary Indian theologian, calls attention to the fact that many scholars, Protestant and Catholic, conciliar and evangelical, regard a certain amount of syncretism as evident in the faith of Israel, the early Christian church, as well as in contemporary Christianity. Furthermore, he says, a degree of syncretism is necessary and inevitable if one desires the faith to be understandable and acceptable in another culture. All Christians, Thomas continues, are partially pagan, and therefore, syncretism "with a sense of Christian direction is all that we can now realize."[5] Many evangelicals, however, are discomfited by or disagree entirely with this assertion.[6] Thus the dispute persists regarding the nature and the degree of adaptation of the gospel that is permissible.

Christianity among the Karen

Though the idea prevails that Christianity was introduced in nineteenth century Burma by the famed North American Baptist missionary couple, Adoniram Judson (1788–1850) and his wife Ann Hasseltine Judson (1789–1826), the first Christian missionaries to arrive in what was then called the Kingdom of Ava were unnamed Portuguese Roman Catholics about whose endeavors little is known. Documentation does exist, however, about two Italian Roman Catholic missionaries, Sigismond Calchi and Joseph Vittoni,

---

4. Students are encouraged to read Carl F. Hallencreutz chapters on "Continuity and Discontinuity" and "The Tambaram Controversy" in his *New Approaches to Men of Other Faiths* (Geneva: World Council of Churches, 1970), 20–39, for an excellent discussion of the debate prior to and following the 1938 meeting.

5. "Syncretism," *Dictionary of the Ecumenical Movement,* ed. Nicholas Lossky, et al (Geneva: World Council of Churches, 1991), 966.

6. See, for example, Arthur F. Glasser, "A Paradigm Shift?" in his and Donald A. McGavran's *Contemporary Theologies of Mission* (Grand Rapids, MI: Baker, 1983), 211.

who arrived in Burma in 1720, having been sent by Pope Clement XI with specific instructions to establish a mission. They were successful and other Catholic fathers followed, some of whom were martyred. Converts were won, however, albeit few, and churches and chapels constructed. By the end of the eighteenth century, events in Europe, a Buddhist renaissance in Burma, and a struggle between western colonial powers for hegemony in India and adjacent areas threatened to end all Christian missionary presence in the kingdom. A priest and the bishop were ordered executed by the king for complicity with Burma's enemies, and although this represented a formidable setback, the mission managed to continue.[7] It was functioning, therefore, when the first Protestant missionary representatives arrived from Serampore in 1807, Richard Mardon and James Chater of the Baptist Missionary Society in London, who were charged "to investigate the possibility of a mission in Burma."[8] Mardon soon returned to India and Chater was joined subsequently by Felix Carey, the son of the famed William Carey.[9] By the time the Judsons arrived in 1813, Felix Carey was ready to quit the effort, and he permanently left Burma six months later.[10]

Though Adoniram Judson devoted the remainder of his long life to evangelizing the Burmese, mastering their language, translating the Bible into their

---

7. Father Vincentius Sangermano, the Italian missionary who labored there from 1783 until 1806, became a recognized authority on Burma, publishing in Latin (and later translated) an impressive work on the kingdom, *A Description of the Burmese Empire* (Rome: Oriental Translation Fund, 1833).

8. Brian Stanley, *The History of the Baptist Missionary Society, 1792–1992* (Edinburgh: T & T Clark, 1992), 54. See also the letter to William Staughton, July 30, 1807, *The American Baptist Missionary Magazine* 2 (March 1808): 5. Cited by Helen G. Trager, *Burma Through Alien Eyes* (New York: Frederick A. Praeger, 1966), 20.

9. Francis Wayland mentions Chater and Mardon in his two volume work on Judson, *A Memoir of the Life and Labors of the Rev. Adoniram Judson, D.D.* 1 (Boston: Phillips, Sampson, 1853), 157, repeating almost verbatim what Ann Hasseltine Judson had earlier reported. See James D. Knowles, *Memoir of Mrs. Ann H. Judson* (Boston: Lincoln & Edmands, 1831), 123–124. Both Wayland and Mrs. Judson note that after the arrival of Felix Carey, he and Chater were joined by "Messrs. Prichett and Brain, from the London Missionary Society," but Brain died shortly thereafter, and Prichett, "after a year's residence, removed to Vizagapatam." Chater, they say, continued for four years, but then moved to Ceylon without having gained a single convert. This explains Ann H. Judson's assertion, "Thus had every attempt of the English Missionaries failed," (124) and Wayland's comment, ". . . Mr. Judson was obliged to commence the work almost *de novo* and, as he advanced, to prosecute it by his own unaided efforts" (158).

10. Carey and Chater gave themselves principally to learning the language, translating portions of the Bible, and making notes for a Burmese-English dictionary and grammar. The London Missionary Society dispatched three additional missionaries between 1810 and 1812, but one died soon after arrival and the other two transferred to other fields. Numerous difficulties—some of which are unclear—prompted Felix Carey to turn the station over to the Judsons. See Trager, 20–21.

language, and producing a massive Burmese-English dictionary, their response was meager. Six years would pass before he could count his first convert, and in 1824 when he was arrested and imprisoned by the Burmese authorities, only nineteen Burmese had submitted to Protestant baptism, a modest harvest for over a decade of work. For the most part, missionary efforts by Roman Catholics and Protestants among the Burmese produced minimal visible results, but a series of events soon prompted the missionaries to seek converts among the tribal peoples.

The history of the spread of Christianity among the Karen in Burma (and Thailand) is recounted in numerous chronicles, and the first Karen convert was a notorious bandit and killer, Ko Thy Byu, who was purchased from slavery by Judson. Two of Judson's missionary colleagues, George Dana Boardman and his wife Sarah evidently saw the potential in Thy Byu, for it was Boardman who baptized him on May 26, 1828. Shortly thereafter, Byu began what can only be described as a remarkable evangelistic career among his own people, one in which the Boardmans and other missionaries at first observed and later participated.

> Immediately after his baptism, Ko Thy Byu set out for the Karen villages in the hills. He was shortly to confirm a tradition then current among the people, to the effect that one day their long absent "white brother" would return to them from across the great waters, bringing the Lost Book which they had looked for with unabated expectation. His message of good news was received with wonder and surprise by the elders in the jungles. Delegations accompanied him to Tavoy to see the "white brother" [Boardman] and listen to his teaching. Among those who came was a prophet, who a few years before had bought from a white sailor in Tavoy a book that he had since regarded as a fetish. On examination this book proved to be a Book of Common Prayer; but the elders accepted the message of their white brother, Mr. Boardman, as the fulfilment [sic.] of their own prophesies, and a number of them were soon baptized. They wished to learn to read, and Ko Thy Byu became their teacher.[11]

The Bible would be the book that the Karen would come to regard as the recovered Lost Book, and it was no small task to lure them away from worship of the book itself. The Christian faith, nonetheless, spread phenomenally among them for reasons too complex to enumerate here. Statistics in these early years are not totally reliable, but nearly twelve thousand communicants were reported in 1856, increasing to 55,353 by 1919. Few comparable examples of growth can be found in Protestant mission history, and according

---

11. Harry Ignatius Marshall, "The Karen People of Burma: A Study in Anthropology and Ethnology," *The Ohio State University Bulletin* 26 (April 29, 1922): 297.

to one writer, by 1940 the Karen congregations both in Burma and Thailand had "earned the noble title of truly indigenous churches."[12]

The majority of Karen Christians are until today Baptists, but Roman Catholic missionaries began working among them in the 1840s, and they too baptized thousands of converts. Church of England missionaries likewise established the Anglican mission to the Karens in 1871, and in the years that followed baptized a significant but lesser number.[13]

Following World War II, specifically in 1948, Burma withdrew from the British Commonwealth and became an independent nation. Initially tolerance and freedom of religion were guaranteed, but from the beginning there were indications that national life would soon be intrinsically linked with Buddhism. Then in 1961, five years after the close of the Sixth Buddhist Council in Rangoon, the government declared Buddhism to be the state religion.

As early as 1948, however, it was evident that entry into Burma by Christian missionaries was going to be increasingly difficult, and after 1950 almost no new visas were granted. Occasionally, a limited number of temporary visas were issued, but these were revoked shortly after 1961, and in 1965 all Christian schools and hospitals in the country were nationalized and Christian missionaries were notified that they would have to leave the country. The last foreign Christian missionaries left Burma in 1979,[14] and from that time the work in all the churches has been directed entirely by nationals. It is in light of this history that the case study of the Karen in Thailand should be considered.

FOR FURTHER STUDY

Syncretism

Anderson, Gerald H., ed. *The Theology of the Christian Mission.* New York: McGraw-Hill, 1961.

> A collection of valuable essays on themes and issues in mission theology. It is significant that "syncretism" has the largest number of references in the Index, even more than the "Great Commission of Christ."

Boff, Leonardo. *Charism and Power.* Translated by John W. Diercksmeier. New York: Crossroads, 1988.

> In his provocative chapter, "In Favor of Syncretism," a well-known Brazilian Roman Catholic theologian distinguishes between what he calls true and false syncretism.

Conn, Harvey M. *Eternal Word and Changing Worlds.* Grand Rapids, MI: Zondervan, 1984.

---

12. Randolph L. Howard, *It Began in Burma* (Philadelphia: Judson Press, 1942), 77.

13. Marshall, 301.

14. Father Edward Fischer's account of the Columban Fathers' work among the Kachin tribal people relates the struggle and the cost of trying to remain in the country. *Mission in Burma* (New York: Seabury, 1980), 139–158.

A recent statement of the evangelical position including the history of evangelical responses to the emphasis on contextualization and the danger of syncretism since the 1974 Lausanne International Congress on World Evangelization (see 176–184).

Gort, Jerald D, ed. *Dialogue and Syncretism: An Interdisciplinary Approach.* Grand Rapids, MI: Eerdmans, 1989.
Seventeen essays originally written for a symposium held at the Free University of Amsterdam in 1988. Six of the writers deal with various approaches to the issue of syncretism and ten with "case studies" of inter-religious encounter. The final paper summarizes the findings.

Hallencreutz, Carl F. *New Approaches to Men of Other Faiths.* Geneva: World Council of Churches, 1970.
A valuable source for understanding the history of the questions raised in relation to Christianity and peoples of other faiths. Especially helpful is the discussion on Hendrik Kraemer's treatment of syncretism.

Kraemer, Hendrik. *The Christian Message in a Non-Christian World.* Grand Rapids, MI: Kragel, 1977 (reprint of the 1956 edition).
The preparatory volume for the Tambaram meeting of the International Missionary Council, and the most extensive and forceful statement opposing syncretism.

Lindsell, Harold. *An Evangelical Theology of Missions.* Rev. ed. Grand Rapids, MI: Zondervan, 1970.
The chapter entitled "A Final Theology—The Inadequacy of the Non-Christian Religions" is a classic evangelical rejection of any tendency toward syncretism. For a later version of this position, see David Hesselgrave, *Communicating Christ Cross-Culturally.* Grand Rapids, MI: Zondervan, 1978.

Schineller, Peter. "Inculturation and Syncretism: What is the Real Issue?" *International Bulletin of Missionary Research* 16 (April 1992):50–53.
A concise and helpful essay on the meanings of syncretism. The author proposes moving beyond the debate and seeing the need and means for inculturation of the gospel.

Schreiter, Robert J. "Defining Syncretism: An Interim Report." *International Bulletin of Missionary Research* 17 (April 1993): 50–53.
A continuation of the discussion initiated by Peter Schineller. Somewhat technical but useful. Schreiter points out the problems in trying to substitute a less contentious word for syncretism, and attempts to move the discussion into a wider arena.

Smalley, William A. *Translation as Mission.* Macon, GA: Mercer University Press, 1991.
See his chapter, "Translation and Indigenous Theology," in which he discusses the issue of syncretism in communication of the gospel, particularly in translating the Bible.

Thomas, M. M. "Syncretism." *Dictionary of the Ecumenical Movement,* ed. Nicholas Lossky, 964–966. Geneva: World Council of Churches, 1991.

Turner, Harold W. "Syncretism." *Concise Dictionary of the Christian World Mission,* ed. Stephen Neill, 580. New York: Abingdon, 1971, 580.
The position advocated in this article, though brief, is mediating and informative.

Visser't Hooft, W. A. *No Other Name: The Choice between Syncretism and Christian Universalism.* London: SCM, 1964.
An attempt to put the debate in a different framework written by one of the major ecumenical leaders of the time.

Christianity and the Karen

Anderson, Courtney. *To the Golden Shore. The Life of Adoniram Judson.* Boston: Little, Brown, 1956.
> A magnificently written biography of the Judsons. Includes a condensed discussion of the Boardmans and their work among the Karen.

Howard, Randolph L. *Baptists in Burma.* Philadelphia: Judson Press, 1931.
> A missionary account of the history of Baptist work in Burma and Thailand. Uncritical but informative.

———— *It Began in Burma.* Philadelphia: Judson Press, 1942.
> A missionary account of Christian beginnings in Burma. Particularly beneficial is the author's account of how Christianity spread into Thailand and the work among the Karen people.

Marshall, Harry Ignatius. "The Karen People of Burma: A Study in Anthropology and Ethnology." *The Ohio State University Bulletin* 26 (April 29, 1922): vii–329.
> Though dated, this is one of the most extensive and authoritative studies of the Karen people available in English, and it includes a section not only on the impact of Christianity on them, but also a longer discussion on their indigenous religious beliefs and practices.

Mason, Ellen B. *Tounghoo Women.* New York: Anson D. F. Randolph, 1860.
> A fascinating account of the effects of Christianity on Karen women.

Purser, W. C. B. *Christian Missions in Burma.* London: Society for the Propagation of the Gospel in Foreign Parts, 1911.
> Though lacking in documentation, this is a helpful narrative on the history of early Christian missions in Burma. Includes chapters on Roman Catholic, Baptist, and Anglican beginnings as well as work among different groups, including the Karen.

Robbins, Joseph C. *Boardman of Burma.* Philadelphia: Judson Press, 1940.
> The most readily available biography of George Dana Boardman, pioneer missionary among the Karen.

Torbert, Robert G. *Venture of Faith.* Philadelphia: Judson Press, 1955.
> The official history of the American Baptist Foreign Mission Society with extensive comments on the Judsons, Boardmans, and work among the Karen.

Trager, Helen G. *Burma Through Alien Eyes.* New York: Praeger, 1966.
> A valuable and informative history of Burma, the arrival of Christianity, and especially the beginnings and development of Baptist work. Particularly significant is the analysis of how the Burmese people were represented by the missionaries "to whose country they had come uninvited."

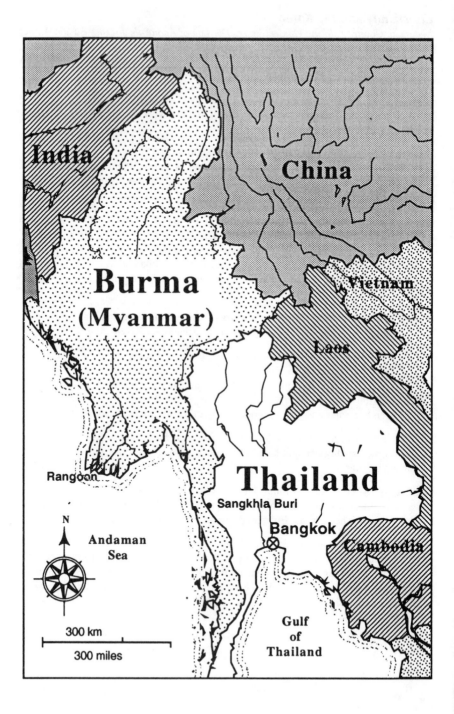

THE CASE
"Don't Come Over and Help Us!"

"Peggy, I am sick and tired of missionaries telling us what we can and cannot do. Claudia has never understood us or our work, and she has no right to try to control what evangelistic methods we use. You missionaries have been here how long? Twenty-five years? And how many Pwo Karen became Christians before the Bible school group came two years ago? Less than six, right? What those young Bible School students are doing is innovative and effective, and I think we should invite them again in June."

Peter Chaviwan, the Thai director of the local Baptist association, was responding to an appeal by Peggy Murphy to try to reach a compromise with the church members, the retired pastor, and two of the missionaries who opposed inviting the young people from the Burmese Pwo Karen Bible School to return the following summer and present their evangelistic programs.

Baptist Missionary Work in Sangkhla Buri

Early in the 1960s the Baptists and the Disciples of Christ entered the area of Sangkhla Buri in a joint effort to bring the gospel to the people there. Sangkhla Buri is adjacent to the Myanmar border where the Dutch railroad crosses from Thailand en route to Moulmein and Rangoon. The area is populated with indigenous Karen—Sgaw Karen and Pwo Karen—as well as Karen formerly from Thailand. The entire area in which the Karen live spans Thailand and Myanmar. Though related, each group has its own dialect. Also, the Sgaw Karen tend to look down on the Pwo Karen and often speak of them as "little brothers and sisters." Nearly all the Karen living in Thailand are either Mon Buddhists (Theraveda) or animists. One of their Buddhist beliefs is that the fifth Buddha will soon return to earth, gather all the faithful, and take them to his heavenly abode. "The faithful," it is believed, will be those earning merit when the fifth Buddha arrives.

The original Christian mission team in the area was composed of two missionary families, including Frank and Peggy Murphy and a missionary doctor, a Thai evangelist named Peter Chaviwan, and their respective families. A single woman missionary, Claudia Fillmore, joined them a short time later. Of the original group, only the Murphys, Peter Chaviwan—now head of the Baptist association—and Claudia Fillmore are still there.

Shortly after they began their work they learned that a prestigious Burmese Baptist pastor, Duh Shwe Wa who had been involved in the struggle of the Burmese Karens to gain independence from Burma and had been imprisoned for five years, was released suddenly and forced to leave the country. He and his family entered Thailand and sought political refugee status. The missionaries quickly invited him to come and help them. Being Sgaw Karen, Reverend Wa was able to gather a small number of Sgaw Karen Christians around him, and they became the nucleus of the church that grew from fewer than twelve to more than eighty baptized members in the twenty-plus years. Unfortunately, however, though Pastor Wa was aware of the missionaries' desire to evangelize the Pwo Karen, he conducted all the church services and other activities in the Sgaw dialect. The Pwo Karen meanwhile remained uninterested and unreached, primarily, the missionaries agreed, because the Pwo Karen dialect was never used.

The Attempt to Evangelize the Pwo Karen

Recently, a new evangelistic approach using the Pwo Karen dialect was introduced by a group of young Karen students from a Baptist Bible School located in the Kyimindaing township in Rangoon, and a number of the Pwo Karen became professing Christians. But one of the missionaries, Claudia Fillmore, along with Pastor Wa, now retired, and nearly all the Sgaw Karen church members are fervently opposed to the approach used by the Bible school students to attract the Pwo Karen.

Peggy describes what happened:

"Two years ago, a group of 40 young people and two teachers from the Karen Bible School in Burma crossed the border and came to our area with a well-developed program of evangelization. It involved Pwo Karen native dances and a series of dramas, the core of which were Pwo Karen folk tales and animist mythology, which the young people skillfully used as a basis for presenting the Christian gospel.

"One of the dramas enacted the story of a young Pwo Karen couple who lived at the edge of the forest. One morning the husband told his beautiful wife that he was going hunting, and no matter what happened, she was to remain in their house. Shortly after her husband left, however, the young woman heard one of their pigs squealing. Without thinking she rushed outside to see what was happening. A large python was attacking the pig. The woman tried to wrest the pig from the python, and the snake, seeing his chance to capture the woman, released the pig, seized the woman, and spirited her off to his cave.

"A dove observed what happened, flew to where the husband was hunting, told him that his wife was in distress—that she had been abducted and was now a prisoner of the python—and offered to guide him to the snake's cave. Frantic, the husband, following the dove, ran as fast as he could until he reached the mouth of the cave. He called out to the python and demanded that he free his wife. The snake, however, said he would release the woman only if the man gave him a liter of his blood.

"The young husband, terrified for his wife, rushed back to his hut, killed a chicken, and returned to the cave with a liter of chicken blood. But the wily python rejected the blood, saying it was not that of the husband. Successively the man tried to deceive the snake with the blood of a pig and a buffalo. Each time the python rejected the offering, saying, 'This is not your blood. Either you bring me a liter of *your* blood or you will have no further opportunity to save your wife. This is your last chance.'

"In desperation, the man ran again to his hut, punctured his wrist, drew a liter of his own blood, gave it to the python and succeeded in rescuing his wife. By this time, of course, he was so weak from running back and forth, from the emotional strain, and from the loss of blood that he died.

"The Bible school teachers who accompany the young people always conclude the presentations by adding to the drama a Christian message, saying, for example, that Jesus also shed his blood, that he too died for our sins, that he was resurrected by God and now wants to be our eternal savior.

"The Pwo Karen came from everywhere to see the young people give these performances. They were captivated by the dramas, and working through the Pwo Karen elders and families, the Bible school teachers challenged them to make a decision to become Christians. Many of them did.

"The most controversial part of what the Bible school group did was to identify Jesus Christ as the fulfillment of the people's hope for the return of the fifth Buddha. This may be questionable, but even so, many of the Pwo Karen who believe in the return of the Buddha and in life after death evidently saw this as a theological bridge and declared their faith in Christ. Our church could have reaped a great harvest. But the Sgaw Karen Christians were very upset by what happened. They said the gospel was being compromised and that the dances, dramas, and identification of Jesus as the fifth Buddha were syncretism. It was, they insisted, heresy 'pure and simple.'

"The first time the Bible School group was here for about six weeks, and some of the Sgaw Karen had been asked to be responsible for them only for the first few days and for a day or two before the young people left. After the initial drama presentations, the Sgaw were so angry—saying the young people had not presented the gospel and what they were doing was not evangelism—they would have nothing to do with them. So during the entire time the group was here, except for the first three days, they were cared for by the Pwo Karen, hardly any of whom were Christians. By 'cared for,' I mean they were given food, a place to sleep, and other necessary amenities.

"The head of our Baptist association, Peter Chaviwan, is from northern Thailand. He was sent to help us as an evangelist soon after we moved here. When the Burmese group left the first time, he invited them to return, and they did last year. The reception among the Pwo Karen was tremendous. Large numbers began to ask for baptism, even though there had not been a half-dozen Pwo Karen converts since we came. But the Sgaw Karen Christians were incensed. Then about a month ago when they heard that Peter wanted to invite the young people a third time, it became a major issue in our church. The debate among the Sgaw Karen Christians was as intense as anything we've experienced. Reverend Wa, the retired pastor, now over eighty years of age, objected strenuously, and he was supported by Claudia, one of our older missionaries, who, incidentally, will retire next year. In effect they were saying to the Burmese young people, 'Don't come over and help us!'

"Peter's brother, a deacon in the church, however, spoke in favor of the plan, saying this was God's way of opening the Pwo Karen to the gospel. But of the eighty-five church members, only three voted in favor of inviting the young people to come back. This has been a very difficult time for Peter as well as for Frank and me.

"Three days ago, trying to be a reconciler, I went to Peter to ask if there were not some way to reach a compromise. He was very upset and said Claudia did not understand the Thai people. 'She has no idea of how evangelism needs to be done among the Pwo Karen. The Bible School young people are the only Christians I've seen,' Peter said, 'who know the Pwo Karen culture well enough to put the gospel in words and actions they understand and will accept. They have responded as never before, and as you know several are ready for baptism. Any time the gospel is presented in a different cultural frame, there will be some syncretism. But that does not make it heresy. I believe if we are really serious about wanting the Pwo Karen to become Christians, we will use methods they can identify with and that are appealing to them.'

" 'Claudia has been influenced by Pastor Wa, and in turn she is influencing the Sgaw Karen women in the church. Claudia has never understood us or our work, and I don't think she has a right to try to control what evangelistic methods we use.'

"He concluded by saying, 'I hope you and Frank will support me in this. I don't want to go against the whole church, but I am convinced that if we allow the Sgaw Karen and a reactionary North American missionary to determine our future, it will not be a promising one for the Pwo Karen.' "

" 'Can I count on your help?' Peter asked."

"I was stunned, hurt, and bewildered," Peggy added. "I knew I had to say something, but what?"

STUDY QUESTIONS

1. Who are the principal characters in this case? Name them and give some basic facts about them.

2. When did the missionaries enter the Sangkhla Buri area of Thailand, and with whom did they begin their missionary work?

3. Why would it be considered different from the Christian missionary efforts in the other areas of Thailand?

4. Why is there a problem or dispute in the church?

5. List what you see as positive as well as questionable about the method(s) utilized by the seminarians from Myanmar (Burma).

SUGGESTED BIBLICAL TEXTS FOR REFLECTION

Judges 6:25–32. Gideon's altar constructed on the mound of his father's Canaanite shrine and grove.

Hosea 2:14–23. The prophet employs Canaanite religious imagery and terminology to illustrate his message to Israel.

John 1:1–16. Jesus is declared to be the *Logos,* agent of creation, unrecognized and rejected by the very people to whom the Word was sent.

Acts 17:22–34. The Apostle Paul's dialogue with the Greek philosophers. (Note especially v. 28.)

"SHOULD I ACCEPT?"

A young Roman Catholic girl, Meijung, accepts an invitation to celebrate a Buddhist holiday with three of her friends, one a Roman Catholic, another a Baptist, and the third a Buddhist in whose home they meet. After going together to the temple with her Buddhist friend's family, seeing and learning the significance of the rite, her Buddhist friend's mother invites Meijung and the others to return to the home and share the food that had been used in the Buddhist ceremony. One of the girls accepts immediately, but the second declines saying that she could not eat food that had been used in a Buddhist rite. It is an awkward moment and Meijung does not know what she should do.

CONTEXT
Contextualization and Syncretism

Though this case study is set in Taiwan, it could have taken place in any Chinese community in East Asia: Taiwan, Hong Kong, Singapore, Malaysia, the Philippines, South Korea, Japan, or even in mainland China. The event, however, did occur in Taiwan where the traditional religions of China are well established.

Chinese Buddhism, however, like Confucianism and Taoism, has its own unique history, and it has been influenced both by Confucianism and Taoism. Conspicuous in this case is the ancient practice of ancestor veneration, or what some have referred to it as "ancestor worship."

Mahayana Buddhism was introduced into China during the first or second century of the present era, but initially it provoked formidable resistance from Confucianists and Taoists. With the founding of the first Ch'an school in the sixth century C.E., however, Buddhism began to spread rapidly, and by the twelfth century Ch'an Buddhism was gaining adherents in Japan where it became known as Zen.

In one sense it can be said that Buddhism conquered China. Yet, Chinese Buddhism was significantly altered by the indigenous Confucianism and Taoism. One of the distinguishing features of Chinese Buddhism—as well as Korean and Japanese Buddhism—was the incorporation of the concern for genealogies, family registers, and ancestral rites.[1] A central feature of

---

1. Tu Wei-ming, "Confucianism," *Our Religions*, ed. Arvind Sharma (San Francisco: Harper, 1993), 167.

Confucian ethics is the emphasis on "filial piety," respect that is attested by the ancestral rituals.[2]

Unlike other developed religions, Confucianism began as an ethical, educational, humanistic movement that evolved into an ethical-religious system, but this development occurred slowly and without the building of temples or the founding of a priesthood as such. Confucianism teaches and promotes "self-cultivation, family cohesiveness, social stability, political order, and world peace."[3] Confucianism involves therefore much more than reverence for family and ancestors, but filial homage is integral. It was Taoism, the religion of the Way, that institutionalized ancient Chinese religious ideas and practice by promoting the belief in polytheism, polydemonism, and spiritism, and by establishing offerings, sacrifices, a priesthood, and shrines.[4] Even so, in China, according to a contemporary Taoist scholar, "Taoist religion is more important as a part of cultural tradition than as an organized religion."[5]

Though there has been a great deal of religious synthesis in China, it would be a mistake to assume that there is no real difference between Taoism and Confucianism. The fact is, some of the early Taoist philosophers were very critical of many of the political and moral teachings of Confucianism. In terms of loyalty to family and to rulers, however, religious Taoists and Confucians agree. Anyone who desires to be immortal, declared Ko Hung, a fourth-century C.E. religious Taoist, "must have loyalty for the ruler and filial piety for parents" as the fundamental guiding principle of his or her life.[6]

---

2. I suspect that Tu Wei-ming's recent statement on the subject is designed to emphasize the distinction between the western penchant for individualism and the Chinese tradition of family solidarity. Wei-ming's comment, nonetheless, can enhance our understanding of the reason for the Confucian reverence for one's ancestors. "Confucius," Tu Wei-ming says, "sees filial piety as the first step toward moral excellence. The way to enhance personal dignity and identity is not to alienate ourselves from the family but to cultivate our genuine feelings for our parents and siblings. To learn to embody the family in our hearts and minds is to enable ourselves to move beyond self-centeredness, or, to borrow from modern psychology, to transform the enclosed private ego into an open self. Indeed, the cardinal Confucian virtue (humanity) is the result of self-cultivation. The first test for our self-cultivation is our ability to cultivate meaningful relationships with our family members. Filial piety does not demand unconditional submissiveness to parental authority but recognition of and reverence for our source of life." Ibid., 186.

3. Ibid., 220.

4. It is important to note two things at this point. First, Taoism as a philosophy and Taoism as a religion are two different phenomena. Second, in Chinese culture religious Taoism and Confucianism are so integrated that a distinction between what is cultural and what is religious is arbitrary. In fact, "Confucianism" was a term created by the seventeenth century Jesuit missionaries, and there was no "specific word in Chinese for 'religion' until modern times, when one was coined to match the Western term." Liu Xiaogan, "Taoism," *Our Religions,* 235.

5. Ibid.

6. Ibid., 239.

One should also be aware of the fact that there are clear philosophical and theological distinctions between Confucianism, Taoism, and Buddhism.[7] Chinese people, however, do not necessarily observe those distinctions, especially in religious practice. The conscious fusion of Confucianism, Taoism, and Buddhism can be traced to the time of the Ming dynasty (1369–1644), when several religious leaders in China sought to blend or harmonize the three religious traditions. Today, "it would not be far wrong to say that most religious Chinese are in fact a mixture of all three great religions," so much so that it is not uncommon for a devout Chinese to regard himself or herself as Confucian, Taoist, and Buddhist.[8]

Ancestor veneration is variously designated as a ceremony, a commemoration, a ritual, or a manifestation of "filial piety." To call it worship, however, may be imposing a western thought-form on a practice which, in Confucianism at least, is other than and perhaps more than what is usually connoted by worship. Confucius, for example, did not urge simply the veneration of the dead. Rather, he advocated loyalty to parents, grandparents and other family members while they were alive, and continued loyalty in the form of reverence and service to them after they have died. In the *Analects* (2:5) he says:

"When parents are alive, serve them according to the rules of propriety. When they die, bury them according to the rules of propriety; and [then] sacrifice to them according to the rules of propriety."

Thus, filial loyalty is to be displayed in life, in death, and after death, and it is, according to Confucian teaching, the most important integrating principle of life, the Mandate of Heaven.

In Christian circles, debate over the legitimacy and permissibility of ancestor veneration erupted in the seventeenth century shortly after the death of the famous Jesuit missionary to China, Mateo Ricci (1552–1610). It was Ricci who gained a hearing for Christianity with the Chinese imperial court, gathered about him more than two thousand converts, and among other accommodations adopted for himself Chinese dress and allowed the continuation of the Chinese ceremonies honoring Confucius and other ancestors. Ancestral rites, Ricci contended, were a social and political act, not religious. They did not, therefore, violate any Christian principle.

When other Roman Catholic missionaries arrived in China, however, especially the Dominicans, they were horrified by what they saw as the sanctioning of idolatry. They therefore protested vehemently against what Ricci and the

---

7. Liu Xiaogan, for example, observes, "Theoretically speaking, Buddhism wants to escape from human life and Taoist philosophy is indifferent to human life, whereas Taoist religion seeks to prolong it. While Confucianism emphasizes social interests, Taoist religion prizes the values of individual life." Ibid., 285.

8. John Berthrong, "Sages and Immortals: Chinese Religions," *Eerdmans Handbook to the World's Religions* (Grand Rapids: Wm. B. Eerdmans, 1982), 254.

Jesuit community had permitted, and soon appealed to Rome to put a stop to what they regarded as pagan practices. The debate raged on for decades until 1739 when Rome finally issued a prohibition against any Christian's participation in what the Dominicans and others called "ancestor worship." Included in the decree was the requirement that all missionaries had to swear an oath of submission to the papal ruling, and further discussion of the matter was strictly forbidden.[9] Not until 1938 did the Vatican rescind the prohibition and oath of submission, and Chinese Roman Catholics were again free to participate in events venerating Confucius and other ancestors.

What is called "ancestor veneration" or "ancestor worship" of course is practiced in many parts of the world other than China. Especially is this true in Oceania and Africa south of the Sahara. Many theologians and other scholars from those areas dispute the use of the expression "ancestor worship," saying that it misrepresents the meaning of the practice and is a cultural and religious imposition by people who do not understand what is signified. The purpose of reverencing ancestors, they insist, is to enhance familial and tribal solidarity by recognizing that their dead continue to exist, although in spirit forms, and that these deceased ancestors still have proprietary rights in the community, particularly in regard to the land. Moreover, if they are ignored or displeased, they can adversely affect the lives of the living. Maintaining a healthy relationship with deceased ancestors, therefore, is "more important than 'religion' in most of its more generally accepted forms."[10]

Though the Roman Catholic Church in 1938 officially lifted the ban on Christian participation in ancestral rites, a decision ratified by the Second Vatican Council (1962–1965), ancestor veneration continues to be a divisive issue among Asian Christians everywhere. Objections are based on what some Christians regard as distorted or heretical ideas about life after death, or the practice is condemned as a flagrant example of syncretism.

Generally, ancestral rites consist of recording on tablets or registers the names of the deceased family members and preserving these in a special shrine. On specified days, the tablets or records are removed from the shrine, and a ceremony of recollection, thanksgiving, and entreaty follows. Believing

---

9. The experiment of Roberto de Nobili (1577–1656) in India also came under fire, and his attempts to accommodate Christianity to the Indian culture were likewise prohibited. See Albert J. Nevins, "Rites Controversy," *Concise Dictionary of the Christian World Mission,* ed. Stephen Neill, Gerald H. Anderson, and John Goodwin (Nashville: Abingdon Press, 1971), 528.

10. Raymond J. Hammer and the editors, "Ancestor Worship," *Concise Dictionary of the Christian World Mission,* ed. Stephen Neill, Gerald H. Anderson, and John Goodwin (Nashville: Abingdon, 1971), 20. Hammer continues: "The ancient Chinese believed that their ancestors, upon death, continued to exist in heaven and to exert a very definite influence upon human affairs. It was felt that the welfare of family or clan depended on the favour of the ancestral spirits. In both China and Japan the Obon festival (now linked with Buddhism) speaks of the annual return of the ancestral spirits to their former home—there to join with the present 'living.' "

the spirits have returned and are near, incense is burned, food and drink are proffered, and a prayer is said inviting the ancestors to be aware of the family's love and esteem. Attention is called to the gifts of food and drink that have been prepared, and then in a gesture of respect, the family members withdraw from the room or place temporarily in order that the spirits may eat and drink the offerings undisturbed. Then after an appropriate interim, family members return, the food and drink are collected, the tablets are returned to the shrine—or sometimes records are maintained on a special paper which is burned—the family bows again in respect and departs.

Whatever may be in the minds of the participants, ancestor rites obviously are a kind of memorial service conditioned on the belief that the deceased are living as spirits who join in the ceremony and whose good will is needed. Critics, however, have been quick to point out that the ancestral tablets are regarded by some as the abode or resting place of the departed spirits, and that the practice is a reflection of superstition and fear. Others, however, such as Mateo Ricci, see the rites as cultural manifestations of love, respect, and gratitude for those who gave them life and shaped their destinies. The genealogical records as such are simply tangible mementos of their deceased loved ones and do not necessarily have any more spiritual significance than a western Christian's invoking a saint or maintaining a picture of a deceased loved one.

FOR FURTHER STUDY

Addison, James Thayer. "The Meaning of Chinese Ancestor Worship." *The Chinese Recorder* 55 (September 1924): 592–599.

Argues for a sensitive approach to ancestor worship by becoming aware of the motives behind the practice rather than the outward forms. The meaning, Addison says, is determined by those who practice it, not by outsiders. Scientific knowledge and progress will purify the practice.

Berkowitz, Morris I., Frederick P. Brandauer, and John H. Reed. *Folk Religion in an Urban Setting: A Study of Hakka Villagers in Transition.* Hong Kong: Christian Study Centre on Chinese Religion and Culture, 1969.

Visits to the graves of one's ancestors reinforces "clan solidarity among resettled villagers," the authors contend, even when the practice is no more than a social occasion.

Berthrong, John. "Sages and Immortals: Chinese Religions." *Eerdmans Handbook to the World Religions* (Grand Rapids, MI: William B. Eerdmans, 1982): 245–254.

A concise and helpful history and analysis of Chinese religion written from an evangelical perspective.

Busia, K. A. "Ancestor Worship." *Practical Anthropology* 6 (January–February 1959): 23–28.

Written by an African Ashanti sociologist who argues that religious practices should be viewed not from a doctrinal perspective, but in terms of their cultural significance.

Ela, Jean-Marc. "Ancestors and Christian Faith: An African Problem," trans. John Maxwell. In *Liturgy and Cultural Religious Traditions,* ed. Herman Schmidt and David Power, 34–50. New York: Seabury Press, 1977.

Pleads for seeing the practice of ancestor worship in the context of African cultural traditions, and proposes presenting the Gospel in terms understandable by a people whose belief in ancestors is a deeply-rooted experience.

Eng, Lim-Guek. "Christianity Encounters Ancestor Worship in Taiwan." *Evangelical Review of Theology* 8 (October 1984): 225–235.
Contends that ancestor worship among Minnan Chinese in Taiwan has its roots in primitive animism, not in Confucianism. Should therefore be rejected.

Hwang, Bernard. "Ancestor Cult Today." *Missiology* 5 (July 1977): 339–365.
Despite the anticipation that modernity would "purify" the cult of ancestor worship, it has not only survived the impact of rationalism, secularism, and urbanization, it is experiencing a resurgence among Chinese people. Author calls for new research and theological reflection sensitive to the Chinese world view as well as to the biblical and authoritative Christian norms.

Martin, W. A. P. "The Worship of Ancestors—A Plea for Toleration." In *Records of the General Conference of Protestant Missionaries of China, Held at Shanghai, May 7–20, 1890,* 619–631. Shanghai: American Presbyterian Mission Press.
Recognizes ancestor worship as a great impediment to conversion to Christianity, but insists that direct attacks on it are futile. To call the practice "worship" is misleading, says Martin, and does not necessarily imply idolatry. Better to be patient than antagonistic. In the same conference, other missionaries take strong exception to Martin's position, and a resolution is approved condemning his position. (See also 631, 654–660, 690–702.)

Smith, Henry N. "Ancestor Practices in Contemporary Hong Kong: Religious Ritual or Social Custom." *The Asia Journal of Theology* 3 (April 1989): 31–45.
Sees the "appropriate Christian response to this ancient cult" as it is "practiced by its adherents," not on the bases of the outsider's own "cultural biases, inherited theologies, or emotional impressions." Includes statistical analyses of the practice.

———. "Christianity and Ancestor Practices in Hong Kong: Toward a Contextual Strategy." *Missiology* 17 (January 1989): 27–38.
Calls for accommodation to traditional values and practices reinterpreted in the light of biblical faith, Christian theology and ethics. "By accommodation, reinterpretation, and innovation," the author says, "Chinese Christian churches can express their cultural loyalty, maintain biblical integrity, and pursue the transformational goal of contextualization."

———. "A Typology of Christian Responses to Chinese Ancestor Worship." *Journal of Ecumenical Studies* 26 (Fall 1989): 628–647.
An analysis of the four historical Christian responses to the Chinese practice of ancestor worship: rejection and condemnation (the displacement model), substitution of another rite, fulfillment, and accommodation. The latter, Smith says, holds the greatest promise.

Wei-ming, Tu. "Confucianism." In *Our Religions,* ed. Arvind Sharma, 141–227. San Francisco: Harper, 1993.
A thorough and sympathetic essay on the history and significance of Confucianism. Written as a part of the volume published for the one hundredth anniversary of the Parliament of the World's Religions, Chicago, 1993.

Xiaogan, Liu. "Taoism." In *Our Religions,* ed. Arvind Sharma, 231–289. San Francisco: Harper, 1993.

A detailed essay on the history, beliefs, and practices associated with Taoism. Likewise written as a part of the volume published for the one hundredth anniversary of the Parliament of the World's Religions, Chicago, 1993.

Yates, Matthew T. "Ancestral Worship." In *Records of the General Conference of the Protestant Missionaries of China, Held at Shanghai, May 10–24, 1877,* 367–387. Shanghai: Presbyterian Mission Press, 1878.

This veteran Baptist missionary contends that though ancestor worship was not considered by the Chinese as a part of their religious system, it has, he says, become a religious rite and should be condemned. Yates was followed by C. Hartwell of the American Board and D. G. Sheffield who spoke on "Questionable Practices Connected with Marriages and Funeral Ceremonies," (387–396). The plenary discussion is revealing (396–406).

THE CASE
"Should I Accept?"

Meijung, Shuching, Reyhei, and Shuo had been close friends since they met in primary school in Taipei when each was nine years old. They shared everything: clothes, experiences, opinions, and beliefs. At school they were inseparable and frequently attended social events together. Though of different faiths, they often talked of the common features of their respective religions, and on a few occasions disagreed about their points of view. And though these conversations were usually animated and sometimes intense, their friendship was not threatened.

Today, however, Meijung was shocked and confused. For the first time in their almost eight years of friendship, suddenly a breach occurred, and it happened so quickly, so unexpectedly, that she was unprepared. Meijung and Reyhei were Roman Catholics, and Shuching a Baptist. They had been invited by Shuo, who was Buddhist, to celebrate a religious holiday with her.

After arriving at Shuo's home and engaging in "girl-talk" for a half-hour or less, Shuo said, "Let me explain to you about this day and the ceremony we will attend.

"Buddhists have many different feast days throughout the year. Fortunately, the one today falls on a Saturday when we are not in school. My mother, like all faithful Buddhist women, has prepared special food for today: pork, fish, fruit, and wine. We will take this food and some flowers to the temple, and my family and I will dedicate these offerings to God. After placing the food at the altar, we will worship and pray for about half an hour, giving the gods time to eat the food, drink the wine, and smell the flowers. Then we will return home. Any questions?"

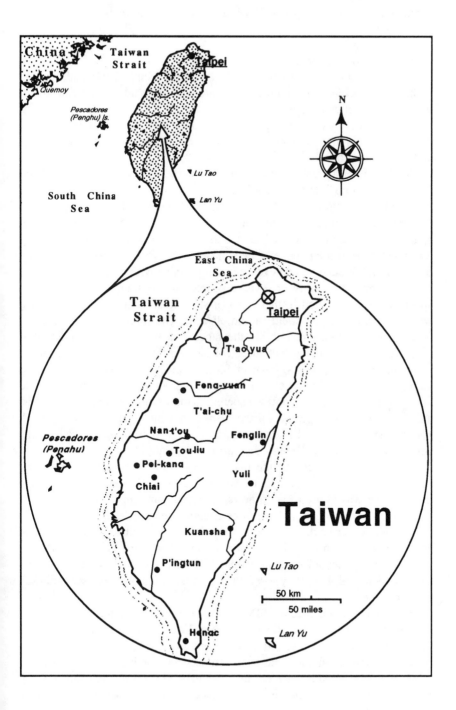

Shuching asked, "Do you believe the food and wine really are consumed by the gods?"

"Oh, yes," replied Shuo.

"Does any of it ever disappear?"

"Not that I can tell; but I believe they eat and drink," Shuo said.

Shuching appeared incredulous to Meijung, so she said, "I can understand. It is like our belief in transubstantiation."

"Yes," said Reyhei. "Though the bread and wine of the Eucharist don't *appear* different after they are consecrated, we believe they become the true body and blood of Christ."

Shuo's mother, father, and two brothers entered the room. "Are you young ladies ready to go?" the father asked.

"I think so," said Shuo. The girls stood, and they all left for the temple.

The walk was pleasant, only about ten minutes from Shuo's home. Each of the girls—Meijung, Reyhei, and Shuching—had seen the temple many times, but none of them had ever been inside. It was a 200-year-old structure, beautiful on the outside, and even more impressive within, thought Meijung.

There were some sixty or seventy people already there, but each family appeared to be engaged in their own private ritual. Shuo indicated a place where her three friends could sit and observe. The ceremony of placing the food, wine, flowers, and lighting the incense at the massive wooden altar took only a few minutes, but there followed a time of quietness, lighting more incense, and prayers. Each of Shuo's family appeared to Meijung to be deep in thought. Eventually the father stood, and so did the others. Shuo turned to her three friends and whispered, "God has had enough to eat." She and her mother then picked up the dishes on which the food was placed, poured the wine from the glasses back into the bottle, and placed all the containers in a basket. Quietly they all left the temple.

No sooner were they outside than Shuo's brothers excused themselves. "We're going to watch the regatta which begins at 12:30." The father also indicated he was going to get a newspaper and some pipe tobacco.

As Shuo, her mother, and her three friends began walking toward Shuo's home, the mother said, "It is lunch time. Would you girls like to come and share this food with us? I have more at home, because I prepared a lot."

Immediately Reyhei said she would like that, but Shuching stopped and said, "I apologize. I am very sorry. Please do not think me rude or ungrateful. But I cannot."

"Why not?" laughed Shuo. "Do you have a date this afternoon?"

Lowering her head, Shuching said, "No, I do not have a date."

"Then why don't you join us? We have plenty of food."

"I . . . I cannot eat food that has been used in worship."

Meijung had already guessed the reason for Shuching's reluctance, but it was a terribly awkward moment. Shuo's mother did not appear to be offended, but Shuo blanched.

"Meijung," Shuo said in a tone of hurt and bewilderment. "What about you? Will you come and eat with us?"

STUDY QUESTIONS

1. The names in this case are unfamiliar and difficult for many westerners to remember. Memorize the names and then write down as many things as you can remember to describe each of the principal characters. What important differences are there in the young women?

2. How long have they known each other, and what are some of the indications of their friendship?

3. Why did they gather at Shuo's home, and what took place soon after they arrived, that is, before they went to the temple?

4. What occurred at the temple? Describe the ceremony.

5. What parallels and what distinctions do you see between the reverence for ancestors among Chinese and other peoples and beliefs and practices in the West among Christian people?

6. Should the Christian young women have agreed to go to the Buddhist temple for the ceremony?

7. Given the fact that they did go, should they accept or decline the invitation to return to Shuo's home for the meal?

SUGGESTED BIBLICAL TEXTS FOR REFLECTION

Matthew 15:1–9. The disciples of Jesus are criticized for not observing tradition regarding parents, and Jesus responds.

Mark 7:14–23. Jesus' words that eating food as such does not defile one.

Romans 14:13–23. The Apostle Paul addresses the issue of eating food that has been previously used in pagan worship.

1 Corinthians 8:1–13. The Apostle deals with the same issue in his letter to the Corinthian congregation, an indication that the question was being raised in several of the early churches.[11]

---

11. The Oxford Edition of the New Revised Standard Version of the Bible includes the following footnote: "Much of the meat sold in the market places had come from animals sacrificed in pagan temples. Some Christians, *weak believers* (v. 11), had scruples about eating such meat (Rom ch 14). Others, however, felt superior to such scruples and contemptuous toward those troubled by them. Their views are quoted in vv. 1, 4, and 8. These superior people with their *'knowledge'* Paul rebukes. His principles are *love* for others that *builds up* community (v. 1) and renunciation of one's rights for the sake of others (v. 13)."

"Should I Baptize Them . . . Now?"

A group of Maasai women in Kenya request Christian baptism from missionaries whom they have come to know and trust. The women, however, are wives of polygynous husbands.[1] Baptists in the country have thus far refused to baptize such persons. The missionaries, therefore, wonder if they should continue this policy or risk trying to change it.

THE CONTEXT
Contextualization and Multiple Wives

In the movie version of *Out of Africa*, the actress Meryl Streep is frightened and conceals herself from a group of Maasai warriors who pass and fail to see her. To portray these tall, proud, and resilient people of East Africa as dangerous has not been uncommon. Until the last twenty or thirty years, they were for the most part a nomadic people moving their herds of cows and goats as well as their families in search of fertile grazing land. As is brought out in the case study, however, modernization (for want of a more descriptive term) has brought about drastic changes in the lives not only of the Maasai, but of most pastoral and nomadic peoples in Africa south of the Sahara. The rapidly growing populations, together with the increasing scarcity of land, have prompted governments—led by individuals and political parties unsympathetic to the traditional ways of minority groups—to impose restrictions on these wandering tribes. Forced to limit their movements or to settle in designated areas, the Maasai became increasingly receptive to visits from outsiders.

One missionary couple sought to live among the Maasai, first in a tent and later in a simple house. They dressed like Maasai and learned the language. In times of severe famine they accepted responsibility for a large number of babies whose mothers could not care for them. Conversions to the Christian faith, however, did not occur. The effort made by Harold and Betty Cummins should not be considered the only example of Protestant attempts to evangelize the Maasai, for other missionary groups, particularly the Sudan Interior Mis-

---

1. Polygamy is the generic term indicating that one person, male or female, has multiple spouses. Polygyny refers to a male having multiple wives, and polyandry to a female having multiple husbands.

sion (SIM) and the African Inland Mission (AIM), sought to preach the gospel among them. Results, however, were meager and discouraging.

Polygamy, central to the social structure of the Maasai, has for generations posed a major dilemma for Christian missionaries and churches in Africa, not only because of its long history and deep roots in the life of the people, but also because Christians themselves have not been able to reach an agreement regarding how best to deal with it.

According to data gathered in 1967, there were at the time nearly seven hundred fifty tribes in Africa who lived south of the 15th parallel north.[2] Of these nearly seven hundred fifty tribal units, polygamy was regarded as the preferable form of marriage in nearly six hundred, that is, in nearly eighty percent of them. This was not an indication that all adult men in a tribe had multiple wives. It simply indicated that polygyny was the preferential form of marriage.

Any adequate discussion of polygamy in Africa deals with the causes— some would say advantages—of polygamy. These include the numerical predominance of women, tradition and social pressure to be married, the custom of levirate marriage, economic benefits of large families and many children, and certain sexual taboos, such as, prohibition of intercourse between a husband and wife during her pregnancy and lactation or nursing of the baby—a period which can extend beyond two years. It is generally agreed among those who have studied the practice that polygamy is not the result of concupiscence. Rather it has much more to do with tribal traditions and social pressures, including status. The more wives one has, the more wealthy and important one is in the community.

In the late 1970s I was teaching in Zimbabwe, then Northern Rhodesia. At the close of one of the sessions, a young pastor stood, made a statement, and then asked a question. He said that his father was one of the first to accept the gospel in his village.

> "He has been a faithful follower of Christ and active in the church since the day he professed his faith in the gospel. He is recognized as a Christian, but my father cannot be baptized. He cannot receive communion. He cannot hold any office in the church. Do you know why?"

When I acknowledged that I did not know, the young man replied, "Because he has more than one wife. What do you think about this?"

Before I could respond, one of the older leaders stood and said that he wanted me to know the reason behind the policy of their church. "To baptize a polygamist would be to open the door, to approve in effect what is clearly

---

2. This figure should be understood to count the number of tribal units living within each nation. The Maasai, for example, were counted as two because they live both in Kenya and Tanzania.

prohibited in the New Testament. If this young man's father wants to be baptized, he knows what the church requires. He must give up all but his first wife." There followed an intense debate among the nearly fifty pastors who were attending the seminar, and no resolution of the differences was achieved.

For the next several years as I traveled from one African country to another, I inquired of Protestants and Roman Catholics about their church's policy regarding the baptism of polygamists. I found at least four different practices: (1) Some churches refuse to baptize any adult, man or woman, involved in a polygamist marriage. To be baptized, the husband must "put away" all his wives except one, usually the first wife. (2) Some churches will baptize the first wife, but not the husband or any of his other wives. (3) Some churches refuse baptism to the husband, but will baptize any or all the wives who profess the Christian faith. (4) A few of the churches in certain countries have set aside the requirement of monogamy as a condition for baptism. Polygamy, nonetheless, remains a divisive issue among African Christians. The fact that it is permitted in Islam, some insist, places the church at a notable disadvantage, given the long and widespread practice of multiple wives.

Biblically, the following passages are usually cited as authority for prohibiting polygamy: Matthew 5:31–32; 19:3–9; Mark 10:2–23; and Luke 16:18 in the Gospels; 1 Corinthians 7:12–13; Galatians 2:1–10; Ephesians 5: 21–33; 1 Timothy 3:2, 12; and Titus 1:6.

Historically, Christians in the West have espoused monogamy as the only form of marriage sanctioned by Scripture and have therefore rejected polygamy as being a violation of the Christian ethic. Some authorities insist, notwithstanding, that monogamy is not explicitly taught in Scriptures, nor was it necessarily the view of the early church. Rather, it *became* the Christian view because it was the recognized legitimate form of marriage in the Greco-Roman world.[3]

Harold Cummins faces a very difficult problem in Kenya because in his church there is the strict prohibition against baptizing either husbands or wives living in polygamous relationships. His dilemma, however, involves much more than the thorny question of polygamy.

---

3. Karl Barth, for example, says that the New Testament passages usually cited to sustain the view that monogamy is the only Christian form of marriage actually address other issues, and they do not unambiguously sanction monogamy. "We can hardly point with certainty to a single text of the New Testament in which polygamy is expressly forbidden and monogamy universally decreed," Barth contends. *Church Dogmatics,* ed. G. W. Bromiley. Trans. G. T. Thompson and H. Knight (Edinburgh: T. & T. Clark, 1961) III.4. 199. Edward Schillebeeckx agrees. "Nowhere in the New Testament," he says, "is there any explicit commandment that marriage should be monogamous or any explicit commandment forbidding polygamy." *Marriage: Secular Reality and Saving Mystery,* trans. N. D. Smith, 2 vols. (London: Sheed and Ward, 1965), I, 284.

FOR FURTHER STUDY

The Maasai

Donovan, Vincent J. *Christianity Rediscovered.* Maryknoll, NY: Orbis, 1978.

Originally subtitled, "An Epistle from the Masai," Donovan, a missionary to the Maasai for seventeen years, reflects on his own experiences in attempting to contextualize the gospel for the Maasai. The "African Creed" at the end is a poignant example of the gospel inculturated.

Hillman, Eugene. *Toward an African Christianity. Inculturation Applied.* New York: Paulist, 1993.

Hillman, a long-time missionary priest in East Africa, devotes a section of this his latest book to religion among the Maasai. He includes their concepts and practices in praying to God, blessings and curses, ritual slaughter of animals, fertility rites, and the role of prophets and elders.

Mullenix, Gordon R. and John Mpaayei, "Matonyok: A Case Study of the Interaction of Evangelism and Community Development Among the Keekonyokie Maasai of Kenya." *Missiology* 12 (July 1984): 327–337.

Authors discuss "how the gospel is spreading" among a group of Maasai and how their social and political history have affected their response to the efforts to evangelize them.

Neckebrouck, Valeer. *Resistant Peoples. The Case of the Pastoral Maasai of East Africa.* "Inculturation." Working Papers on Living Faith and Cultures XIV. (Rome: Pontificia Universita Gregoriana, 1993).

The author, a priest with doctorates in anthropology and theology, after working in Zaire and Rwanda for a decade, spent five years among the agricultural Kikuyu and nomadic Maasai in Kenya. One of the principal questions with which he deals is why "the Christian missions have not been able to take foothold among the Maasai." Includes an impressive bibliography.

Priest, Doug. *Doing Theology with the Maasai.* Pasadena, CA: William Carey Library, 1990.

The focus of this study is the author's own engagement in cross-cultural ministry among the Maasai. He deals with the thorny issue regarding whether Maasai who become Christians should be expected to abandon their social traditions and rites of passage, and whether Maasai sacrifices, for example, are incompatible with the Christian faith.

———. "Do the Maasai Know God? An Exercise in Cultural Exegesis." *Africa Theological Journal* 20 (1991): 81–88.

Priest, who went to Africa in 1978 as a missionary to the Maasai in Kenya and Tanzania, bases his comments on what he calls "cultural exegesis," that is, exegesis of the historical context. He concludes that the Maasai know and worship the same God as Christians, but their knowledge is inadequate.

———. "The Maasai Purification Ceremony." *Unto the Uttermost,* ed. Doug Priest Jr. Pasadena, CA: William Carey Library, 1984, pp. 199–215.

Author describes the history and social structure of the Maasai, how they are reacting to modernization, and their world view; he analyzes in detail the *Oikiteng' loo lbaa,* literally the "Ox of wounds" ceremony in which the celebrant sacrifices an animal in order to be forgiven and purified by God. It is a mistake, Priest contends, for the Maasai to abandon this practice. Rather, it should be adapted as the gospel is contextualized.

Waweru, Moses K. "African Missionary to Cattle People: Kikuyu Pastor Looks at His Job Among the Maasai People of Kenya." In *Windows on Africa,* ed. Robert T. Parsons, 38-49. Leiden: E. J. Brill, 1971.

    An African Presbyterian missionary from one tribal group (Kikuyu) discusses his Christian conversion, calling to the ministry, and his work as a pastor in a Maasai parish.

Polygamy

Bricknell, K. "Reader's Response (Monogamy and Polygamy, A Reply to C. R. Taber, with Rejoinder)." *Practical Anthropology* 18 (July-August 1971): 181–84.

    A reader, missionary in New Guinea, responds negatively to what he perceives as an inference by the editor that Christian missionaries should no longer uphold monogamy. He offers three "strands of evidence" to support monogamy as the only valid Christian view of marriage. Includes Tabor's reply.

Bujo, Bénézet. *African Theology in Its Social Context.* Translated by John O'Donohue. Maryknoll, NY: Orbis, 1992.

    "Marriage is a burning issue for the Church in Africa today," declares the author. A diocesan priest from Zaire, Bujo is professor of moral theology in the University of Friebourg, Switzerland. In the closing chapter of his book he addresses the issue of "trial marriages" in African tradition, as well as touching on the matter of polygamy. (See pages 115–122.)

Fountain, O. C. "Polygyny and the Church." *Missiology* 2 (January 1974): 111–119.

    The author, from New Zealand, went to Papua, New Guinea, to do post-graduate research in social and economic geography, and in 1967 became a missionary with the Christian Missions from Many Lands. He describes polygyny as "an integral part of the framework" of many societies and calls for a "rethinking" of the issue based on specific situations he found in New Guinea.

Gatima, C. "Christian Marriage and the Christian Family." *African Ecclesiastical Review* 16 (1974): 108–15.

    This essay along with two others, J. Njenga's "Customary African Marriage," (115–122), and S. Wellens' "Preparation for Marriage," were prepared for a 1973 study conference at the St. Thomas Aquinas Seminary in Nairobi on "Planning for the Church in Eastern Africa in the 1980s."

Harris, Lyndon. "Christian Marriage in African Society." In *Survey of African Marriage and Family Life,* ed. Arthur Phillips, 329–460. New York: Oxford University Press, 1953.

    The third part of Phillips' extensive study. Harris discusses the early conflict between missionaries and nationals over the practice of polygamy and the custom of "bride price," the clash of cultures and social structures, doctrinal views, and changing attitudes. Includes an extensive bibliography. One of the most thorough treatments available.

Hastings, Adrian. *Christian Marriage in Africa.* London: SPCK, 1973.

    A comprehensive report dealing with the history of traditional marriage in Africa together with contemporary views, civil requirements, and some brief case studies.

Hillman, Eugene. *Polygamy Reconsidered. African Plural Marriage and the Christian Churches.* Maryknoll, NY: Orbis Books, 1975.
A carefully done history and analysis of the place of polygamy in African culture. The author spent years as a priest among the Maasai in Tanzania, and his own questions regarding African marriage practices stimulated the research and writing of this provocative book.

————. "Polygyny Reconsidered." *Practical Anthropology* 17 (March-April 1970): 60–74.
Author deals with the historical, sociological, biblical, theological, and ecclesiological questions arising out of the practice of polygyny. Suggests reasons why many in Africa consider it the preferable form of marriage.

Horan, Hubert. "Polygamy Comes Home To Roost." *Missiology* 4 (October 1976): 443–53.
This one-time missionary to Tunisia and Tanzania compares marriage practices in Africa with those in North America. Though be believes that polygamy is a "problem faced by all churches in Africa," he maintains that U.S. Christians have little reason to feel morally superior.

Kisembo, Benezeri, Laurenti Magesa, and Aylward Shorter. *African Christian Marriage.* London: Macmillan, 1977.
Though written in the mid-1970s, the descriptions and examples of polygamy in Africa then are still current. The authors discuss the prevalence and socio-economic and domestic effects of polygamy, as well as the reasons for its acceptance. The theological reflections and models for pastoral response are useful.

Newing, E. G. "Baptism of Polygamous Families: Theory and Practice in an East African Church." *Journal of Religion in Africa* 3 (1970): 130–41.
An essay based on a survey of three Anglican dioceses in Kenya and Tanzania. Four questions were asked: "Are polygynists baptized?"; "Conditions for baptism?"; "Are wives baptized?"; and "Are children of baptized wives baptized?" The responses indicated that there was no uniform practice even among the Anglicans.

Price, Arthur, ed. *Survey of African Marriage and Family Life.* London: Oxford University Press, 1957.
Though dated in some respects, this is still the most comprehensive study of marriage and family relationships available. Includes numerous references to polygamy. The essay by Lyndon Harris, for example, "Christian Marriage in African Society," is especially helpful.

Price, Thomas. *African Marriage.* London: SCM Press, 1954.
The author's discussion of "How Many Wives?" summarizes the traditional missionary view on polygamy.

Taber, Charles R. "The Missionary: Wrecker, Builder, or Catalyst?" *Practical Anthropology* 17 (July-August 1970): 145–52.
An editorial in which a veteran Protestant missionary anthropologist analyzes the traditional missionary attitude toward polygamy and the "bride price" or dowry and suggests some provocative alternatives.

Tippett, A. R. "Polygamy as a Missionary Problem: The Anthropological Issues." *Practical Anthropology* 17 (March-April 1970): 75–79.
Written by a well-known former missionary to the Fiji Islands and later professor of missions and anthropology at Fuller Seminary's School of World Mission. Tippett evaluates six different missionary attitudes toward polygamy.

Ware, Helen. "Polygyny: Women's Views in a Transitional Society." *Journal of Marriage and the Family* 41 (February 1979): 185–95.

An appraisal of Nigerian women's viewpoints regarding polygyny. More than half of those surveyed were living in polygynous relationships. Data is based on research done in 1975, but the conclusions are still relevant.

THE CASE
"Should I Baptize Them . . . Now?"

"Ethical decisions are easy to make here in the living room, if they are made abstractly," Harold said. "But when they have to be made in the context of real life and in regard to real people, decision-making can be an ambiguous, agonizing experience."

Harold Cummins had just finished describing his two-year attempt to establish a relationship with a Maasai *enkang* or village and the decision he would have to make the next day. He and his wife Betty had worked in Kenya as Southern Baptist missionaries for more than sixteen years, principally in the Machakos area with the Kamba tribal people. Then a series of circumstances had given the Cumminses an opportunity to relate in several ways to a large group of Maasai people who, because of government pressure, had begun to settle in a barren area known as "El Mamin," some 120 kilometers southwest of Nairobi.

During the twenty-eight months since Harold and Betty had first visited El Mamin, they had made regular safaris there to help in the construction of a rather large school building as well as a small, rustic outbuilding designated for worship. They had also conducted Bible studies and some simple worship services with the hope of establishing a church among the Maasai. No Baptist had thus far been successful in evangelizing the Maasai, and no Baptist congregation existed among them in Kenya.

"No one so far has been able to 'plant' a Baptist church among the Maasai," Harold remarked. "Twenty-five to thirty women and a larger number of younger and older children have participated in the Bible studies and worship services. The Maasai men, however—with the exception of the school director, Michael Mbiti, himself half Maasai and half Kikuyu—haven't shown any interest.

"Two months ago," Harold continued, "more than ten of the women told us they wanted to be baptized. Betty and I were pleased, because if they are baptized they can be the nucleus of a Maasai church. But we were also surprised, because we haven't given much emphasis to baptism, only when it appeared in the Bible studies such as the passages regarding the Ethiopian eunuch and the Philippian jailer."

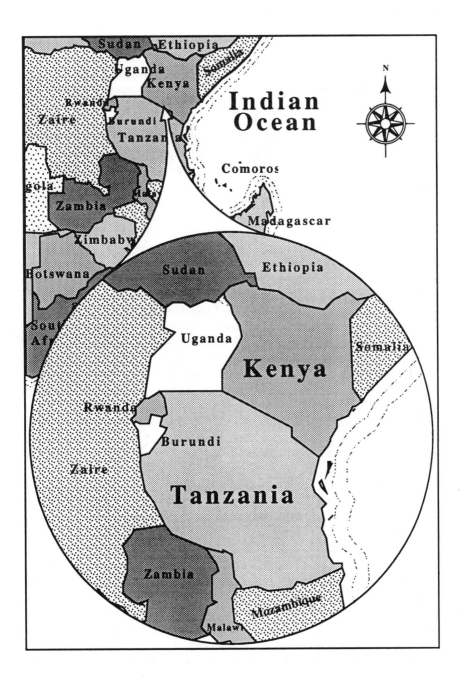

The Maasai

Harold continued by giving some background information about the people to whom he and his wife were ministering. "The Maasai are a nomadic people, descendants of the Nilotes, a tall, slender Negroid sub-race who migrated across eastern and central Africa from the southern regions of the Nile basin. Some of the ancestors of the Maasai who settled around Lake Victoria attempted to cultivate the soil. But repeated failures prompted them to turn to the less difficult and less problematical raising of cattle sometime between the ninth and the sixth centuries B.C.E. Following their herds in a perpetual search for grassland and water, the Maasai became pastoral nomads. Until the middle of the present century they led simple, uncluttered lives, wandering freely across Kenya and northern Tanzania. The continual encroachment of civilization, however, has led the governments of these two countries to restrict the movement of the Maasai. Official efforts are now being made to tie them to certain land areas.

"The Maasai are a simple, handsome people, devoid of complex political organizations. Their societal strata are determined by age. Their diet consists of meat, blood, and milk; the blood is obtained from living animals with a small arrow stuck into the jugular vein. Their dwellings are small, low, loaf-shaped huts made of a frame of branches plastered on the outside with cow dung. Circumcision of boys and clitoridectomy of girls are rites of passage. Polygamy is customary, and corporate decisions are usually made in a thoroughly democratic gathering of the elders of the *enkang*. Theirs is clearly, however, a man's society, though remarkably egalitarian and without overt manifestations of coercive authority. Wealth consists in the number of cows a man possesses and the number of sons his wives produce.

"Until the coming of Europeans, the Maasai had no chiefs or headmen as such. Questions then, as now, were settled in a gathering of the elders. The concept of individualism is absolutely alien to the Maasai, and as a whole they have been wedded to their traditions and are highly resistant to change.

"Religious concepts are, as one might expect, uncomplicated. *Enkai*— variously translated as "god," "the sky," or "the sky god"—was once, it is believed, one with the earth. Eventually there came a separation, and *Enkai* benevolently sent cattle to the Maasai, who were favored above all people on the earth. This central religious myth is interpreted quite literally, and for a Maasai to abandon his cattle is not only demeaning to himself, but an insult to the mercy and blessing of *Enkai*. There are some Maasai groups—especially in Tanzania—who have been forced to abandon their nomadic ways and to settle into designated areas. But most of the Maasai here in Kenya are strongly linked to their traditional ways, refer pejoratively to farming as 'scratching in the earth like a chicken,' and remain completely dependent on their cattle. All of life revolves around their cattle as can be observed in the everyday greeting, 'I hope your cattle are well,' and in their high ritual or ceremonial slaughter of a bullock.

"Today there are approximately 120,000 Maasai living in Kenya and Tanzania—some feeling the full impact of change, while others attempt to retain the simplicity and purity of their past."

The Decision

"Tomorrow we will go to El Mamin," Harold continued. "I indicated to the women several weeks ago that we would make a decision about their baptism before our next visit. But I don't know what I should do.

"I have asked for a meeting with the men, but if I tell them their wives want to be baptized, they could react negatively and prohibit my continuing to come to the village. Or they could agree to the baptism of the women, and I would face a more difficult dilemma.

"If I baptize the women now, I may fix in the minds of all the villagers that Christianity is a faith for women and not for men. Also if I baptize the women now, I will appear to be accepting without question their practice of polygamy. Betty and I have not faced the polygamy question before, except in isolated instances, but among the Maasai polygamy is commonplace. To accept a polygamist for baptism is something of a problem for me," Harold said, "and also it is an issue for many of the Kenyan pastors and lay leaders. Protestant churches here in East Africa have their own set of traditions, and the traditions regarding polygamists are long-standing and deeply ingrained.

"On the other hand, there is no uniform position on polygamy among Christian groups in East Africa. In fact, there are varying ideas and practices. But generally and historically, Protestants have refused baptism to any man who is a polygamist unless and until he puts away all but one of his wives. Some denominations insist that all the wives except his first wife must be put away, while others allow the husband to keep the wife of his choice. Theoretically, the man continues to be responsible for all his wives, but he lives conjugally with only one.

"Some Protestant churches have been willing to baptize *only* the first wife. Other congregations will baptize all the wives but not the husband. If I baptize any of these Maasai women, I am running the risk of alienating a sizable number of our national pastors and lay leaders. Also there is the question of how the Maasai men will feel about Christianity if it begins only with women. The Maasai culture is strictly patriarchal. I'm afraid to baptize the women without the approval of the men; but if they agree, I still don't know what is the wisest course.

"What do you think?" Harold asked.

STUDY QUESTIONS

1. What is the irreducible minimum that one should consider to the gospel, that is, what should be the requirement(s) for baptism?

2. Are there matters of ethnocentricity evident in this case? Elaborate.

3. Should Harold and Betty Cummins be attempting to evangelize the Maasai?

4. How much should he tell the men at this time about the Christian faith?

5. Do you believe the women in this case should be baptized at this time? If so, on what basis to you support their baptism? If not, what would you recommend?

6. Should Harold confide his dilemma to the Maasai women?

7. In view of the fact that polygamy is a very divisive issue in the African church, should Harold decide on his own what to do?

SUGGESTED BIBLICAL TEXTS FOR REFLECTION

Genesis 2:18–25. The Genesis writer depicts the first marriage.

Deuteronomy 21:15–17. Law concerning sons of multiple wives. See also Exodus 21:10–11.

Matthew 19:1–12. Jesus responds to some Pharisees who want to entrap him with a question about divorce. (One will do well to study the question of women's rights in Jesus' time as they related to the question of divorce.)

Acts 15:1–28. The Jerusalem council decides on what is required for Gentiles to become Christians. (It is curious that in the Bible, both in the Old and New Testaments, there is a clear prohibition regarding eating and drinking of blood. This has not, however, been a part of the church's evangelistic message or ethical demands. If, as some say, there is not clear condemnation of polygamy in the Bible, how do we explain why this has become a part of the norms expected of Christians everywhere?)

Singing the Lord's Song

A missionary couple, appointed as music missionaries, attempt to introduce indigenous instruments and hymn tunes in the seminary and churches in Zimbabwe. The national pastors, however, appear satisfied with Western hymns, and missionary colleagues voice their concern about the couple's tendency to syncretize animism and the Christian faith. The matter becomes an issue in a meeting of missionaries, and the couple is invited to respond.

THE CONTEXT
Contextualization and Church Music

A knowledge of missionary history can be invaluable if it is more than sectarian, anecdotal, and hagiographic. It is now generally acknowledged that one of the major mistakes missionaries made, a blunder no longer concealed nor defended, was the imposition of Western values on national converts and churches, an imposition that included modes of dress and behavior, world views, theologies, ethical requirements, and even church architecture and forms of worship. Only in the last generation, however, were studies published indicating the *role of church music* in the Westernization of African, Asian, and Latin American churches.[1]

Though it is unnecessary to recount the significance of music in Christian history,[2] until recently almost no attention has been given to the role of Christian music in mission history. One can read innumerable histories of Christian missions and find little or nothing about music and the spread of the faith.[3] This is not true, however, of the histories of Christian music.

---

1. E.g., the writings of A. M. Jones, "Hymns for the African," in *Books for Africa* (London: Christian Literature Council, 1957–1958), and "Music in Evangelism and Worship," *Concise Dictionary of the Christian World Mission*, ed. Stephen Neill, Gerald H. Anderson, and John Goodwin (New York: Abingdon, 1971), 428–429.

2. See, for example, David Breed, *The History and Use of Hymns and Hymn-Tunes* (New York: Fleming H. Revell, 1934; Lewis F. Benson, *The Hymnody of the Christian Church* (New York: George H. Doran, 1967); Edward Dickinson, *Music in the History of the Western Church* (New York: Charles Scribner's Sons, 1902); and Friedrich Blume, *Protestant Church Music. A History* (New York: W. W. Norton, 1974).

3. Kenneth Scott Latourette in his seven volumes, *A History of the Expansion of*

Edward Dickinson in his *Music in the History of the Western Church,* for example, observes that the Roman chant was an integral part of the Roman Church's eventual domination of Europe; the chant was regarded an essential part of the Church's liturgy. Those responsible for leading worship, namely clergymen, were trained in music, and they went out from Rome or they came to Rome in order to equip themselves liturgically, which included acquiring knowledge of and skills in church singing. No missionary went forth without such preparation, and

> "(e)very monastery founded in the savage forests of Germany, Gaul, or Britain became at once a singing school" from which wafted the music and words taught and learned in the sacred city of Rome.[4]

It is generally recognized that Christians from the first century, influenced by Jewish patterns of worship, have included music as an integral part of corporate worship. Moreover, in the expansion of Christianity, music transcended national, cultural, and even linguistic boundaries, for as Longfellow said, music is "the universal language" of humankind. In a worship setting, music enriches and enhances the experience by capturing and expressing in rhythmic, melodic, and usually familiar reiteration what is both cerebral and emotive. For music helps focus the human spirit on the primary purpose of worship, namely, the adoration of God.

Questions regarding the kind of music—the melodic formula or cadence, i.e., chant or hymn; sung by clergy, cantor, choir, or congregation; accompanied or unaccompanied by instruments; whether the text set to music is a biblical psalm or other verse—have incited both accord and conflict in the course of Christian history. There is, nonetheless, virtually universal agreement that music is a crucial, even an essential element in the corporate worship experience. Furthermore, there are no known people for whom music in one form or another is not inherently a part of their culture. Some anthropologists go so far as to declare that in the sequence of human development, singing preceded speech.[5]

Christianity (New York: Harper, 1937–1945), mentions music twice (vol. 2, pp. 382-3; and vol. 3, p. 380).

4. 117–118.

5. "Hymns," *Dictionary of the Ecumenical Movement,* ed. Nicholas Lossky, et al. (Geneva: World Council of Churches, 1991), 488 [entire article 488–494]. Sosa adds, "In individuals singing is one of the most intimate and profound expressions of the human being, coming from the very heart. Sung sound, technically defined as 'the musical expression through the voice, of every emotion suggested by thought and imagination (*Grove's Dictionary of Music and Musicians*), thus becomes an expansion of the singer's spirit and was recognized as such by the church fathers, who described tunes sung to the word 'Hallelujah' as the climax of the believers' praise and prayer, poured out when they could not organize their ideas articulately to express their feelings. Augustine commented insightfully, 'In singing we are doubling our prayers.' " (Ibid.).

Missionaries have, therefore, consciously taken their music with them as they crossed geographic, political, cultural, and linguistic boundaries. In the case of the Roman chant, it was not translated but memorized and sung in Latin. In the Byzantine tradition the same was true, only the chants were originally sung in Greek and subsequently translated into other languages, though not without provoking controversy.[6] Protestant hymnody, in contrast, was never limited to a particular language. When their missionaries, therefore, went to other lands with different languages, once they learned enough of the local vernacular, they proceeded to translate the words of the hymns they knew into the language of the people of that locale. The idea of utilizing indigenous tunes and/or instruments, however, was not considered.

One need but examine any pre-1960 Protestant hymn books in Latin America, Africa, or Asia to see that virtually all the music consisted of translations and adaptations of hymns and gospel songs written and sung in Europe and North America. Yet, not only were many of the translations inadequate and clumsily rendered, they served as *prima facie* evidence that the religion of the missionaries and of their converts was foreign. The older the Christian community, the more fixed and accepted were the worship styles and liturgies that had been brought to them.

Brian E. Schrag comments on the irony of missionaries' laboring so intensely to learn other languages, but manifesting no concern to understand and appreciate indigenous musical systems. The result has been singularly unfortunate.

> Every year, thousands of missionaries in cross-cultural environments work arduously to learn the language of the people with whom they are working. Most of these same missionaries also daily encounter a foreign music system, but there is no parallel effort put into its mastery or comprehension. The reasons for this are many: the historical and rightful priority on linguistic communication over other missiological endeavors; the paucity of musicians trained in the study of foreign music; the assumption since the birth of Western European missions that Western music was somehow more "civilized," and therefore, more godly; and a general lack of theoretical and practical tools necessary for the process of understanding a foreign music system.[7]

Schrag proceeds to offer both biblical and practical reasons for becoming bicultural musically, and he sets forth what he calls "a cognitive model" for doing so.

---

6. See Dimitri Conomos, "The Byzantine Legacy in Slavonic Chant," *The Legacy of St Vladimir,* ed. J. Breck, J. Meyendorff, and E. Silk (Crestwood, NY: Vladimir's Seminary Press, 1990), 57–68, and Vladimir Morosan, "Liturgical Singing or Sacred Music?: Understanding the Aesthetic of the New Russian Choral Music," Ibid., 69–78.

7. "Becoming Bi-Musical: The Importance and Possibility of Missiology Involvement in Music." *Missiology* 17 (July 1989): 311–312.

One of my long-time colleagues and friends, C. Michael Hawn, now professor of church music at Southern Methodist University's Perkins School of Theology, has for more than a decade traveled and spent extended periods of time in many areas of the world studying the role of church music in the lives of local Christians. Hawn carries Schrag's suggestions a step further, urging that music be composed in the language of the people, following "its rhythms, cadences, accents, [and] pitches." He does not discount the contributions made by "imported" hymnody to local patterns of worship, but translated music "from the West," he insists, is simply inadequate. Church music, like other music, Hawn says, "is a medium that combines emotional experience (melody/rhythm) with intellectual content (text)." When the music does not follow rhythms and melodies indigenous to the culture, and when hymn texts are incorrectly or ineptly translated or interpreted, an emotional and intellectual dissonance ensues. Add to this the increasing spirit of national-ism characteristic of every formerly colonized people, and one begins to sense the urgency and significance of developing musical forms that arise out of the context.

The writing of indigenous music is, however, more easily advocated than done, for anyone who has made an effort to encourage nationals to write their own Christian music soon uncovers an instinctive reluctance as well as sundry technical difficulties. Walbert Bühlmann describes his own attempt as a missionary in Tanzania to compose some simple indigenous Christmas carols using African lullabies.

> In 1951, before Christmas, I asked some other missionaries whether Christmas carols might be composed on the basis of African lullabies. "There are no African lullabies," the missionaries replied. Unconvinced, I paid a visit to a schoolteacher who knew something about music and even about musical notation. I asked him to listen to his wife singing their baby to sleep and then to write down the melody to fit the text of a carol I had brought along. He had a scruple: "You couldn't sing that kind of thing in church." I explained that our European carols were often based on lullabies, and that was why they were so appealing. After all, Mary had been a mother too, just like most other women. That did it. "Then I won't just listen to my wife, I'll go next door—the woman there can sing a lot better!" (Aha! So there was such a thing as an African lullaby.) After a few days he came around with a carol. But he was right, it would have been simply unthinkable to sing it in church in those days. First there had to be an awakening of national and ecclesial consciousness.[8]

A. M. Jones, more than twenty years ago, wrote that any effort to develop "vernacular music in Christian worship" depends finally on the willingness

---

8. *With Eyes to See. Church and World in the Third Millennium* (Maryknoll, NY: Orbis, 1990), 80.

and musical abilities of indigenous Christians. Ordinarily, however, those who are able to do this have been trained in, are accustomed to and comfortable only with Western hymnody. Besides, many of them feel that the tunes and musical instruments of their land are not Christian. Thus, asking or expecting them to write new words for indigenous melodies raises serious questions in their minds. Though the missionary, Jones adds, may encourage nationals with musical skills to compose hymns and songs that correspond to their context, "what is needed," he insists, "is a Christian music born of deep Christian experience" of indigenous Christian musicians.[9] Are Bühlmann and Jones saying that this will happen, not because missionaries think it is important or necessary, but it will be the result of an irrepressible desire and inspirational overflow from the hearts and souls of national Christians?

G. William Supplee, speaking to a group of church musicians, said that modern Protestant and evangelical missionaries have manifested one or more of the following eight attitudes toward indigenous music: (1) Only European and North American church music qualifies as good sacred music; (2) Only gospel songs written by Europeans and North Americans are acceptable; (3) Only certain writers of gospel songs, such as William Doane or Ira Sankey, have written suitable Christian music; (4) European and American melodies are adaptable to the pentatonic scale; (5) Some people have no musical ability and cannot be taught to sing; (6) Attempts by indigenous writers to compose Christian music are never acceptable; (7) Texts for some indigenous tunes can be written; and (8) Nationals are encouraged to compose, and the music out of their own musical traditions and styles and written in their languages is used.[10]

Yet, as one observer has noted, "Both in the East and the West, church music from the southern hemisphere deserves to receive greater attention than it does at present."[11]

FOR FURTHER STUDY

Benson, Lewis F. *The Hymnody of the Christian Church.* New York: George H. Doran, 1927.
   Traces Christian hymnody from inauguration of Christian singing in the early Jewish-Christian congregations to the hymns and Christian music of modern times.

Breed, David. *The History and Use of Hymns and Hymn-Tunes.* New York: Fleming H. Revell, 1934.

---

9. "Music in Evangelism and Worship," *Concise Dictionary of the Christian World Mission,* ed. Stephen Neill, Gerald H. Anderson, and John Goodwin (New York: Abingdon, 1971), 428–429.
10. Principles of Incorporating Music of Other Cultures in the Music of the Church." A paper presented to the National Church Music Fellowship Convention, Grand Rapids, MI, 1971, 1–4.
11. William T. Flynn, "Church Music," *Dictionary of the Ecumenical Movement,* ed. Nicholas Lossky, et al. (Geneva: World Council of Churches, 1991), 182–184.

Recounts and analyzes ancient Christian, Greek, and Latin hymnody from the first to the twentieth century.

Eskew, Harry and Hugh T. McElrath. *Sing with Understanding.* Nashville: Broadman, 1980.
   The authors' chapters on "The Hymn in History and Culture" deals with music in the early church and Middle Ages, the Reformation and post-Reformation periods, and through modern British and American traditions.

Flynn, William T. "Church Music." *Dictionary of the Ecumenical Movement,* ed. Nicholas Lossky, et al. (Geneva: World Council of Churches, 1991), 182–184.
   A brief but penetrating article on the importance of music in Christian worship. Summarizes many of the insights of the study of liturgy.

Hunt, T. W. *Music in Missions: Discipling Through Music.* Nashville: Broadman, 1987.
   Elementary in some respects, but valuable in that this is one of the few monographs on the subject of music and mission. The two chapters, "Indigenous Music" and "Indigenization," are particularly insightful.

Jones, A. M. "Music in Evangelism and Worship." *Concise Dictionary of the Christian World Mission,* ed. Stephen Neill, Gerald H. Anderson, and John Goodwin (New York: Abingdon, 1971.
   One of the earliest articles on the importance of developing indigenous Christian music.

Reynolds, William J. *A Survey of Christian Hymnody.* Carol Stream, IL: Hope Publishing, 1987.
   Concisely recounts music in the early church and analyzes the Lutheran chorale, psalmody, and English and American hymnody. Nothing is said about music in the southern hemisphere.

Routley, Erik. *Christian Hymns Observed.* Princeton, NJ: Prestige Publications, 1982.
   Summarizes the history of Christian hymnody for the first fifteen hundred years and then until 1955. Then follows a chapter on Roman Catholic hymnody since 1964, and another on "Main Stream" hymnody since 1955. Non-European or non-North American music is not mentioned.

Schrag, Brian E. "Becoming Bi-Musical: The Importance and Possibility of Missionary Involvement in Music." *Missiology* 17 (July 1989): 311–319.
   Contends that missionary responses to indigenous music have not only been negative, but have proved destructive. Also, he believes that all missionaries can and should become "bi-musical" as well as bi-lingual, and he proposes a conceptual model based on Mary Louise Serafine's description of how music is produced. Note also Schrag's references cited.

Sosa, Pablo. "Hymns," *Dictionary of the Ecumenical Movement,* ed. Nicholas Lossky, et al. (Geneva: World Council of Churches, 1991), 488–494.
   A substantive treatment of the history, kinds, use, and theology of Christian hymnody with several examples. Author's comments on "Third world hymnody" are brief but noteworthy.

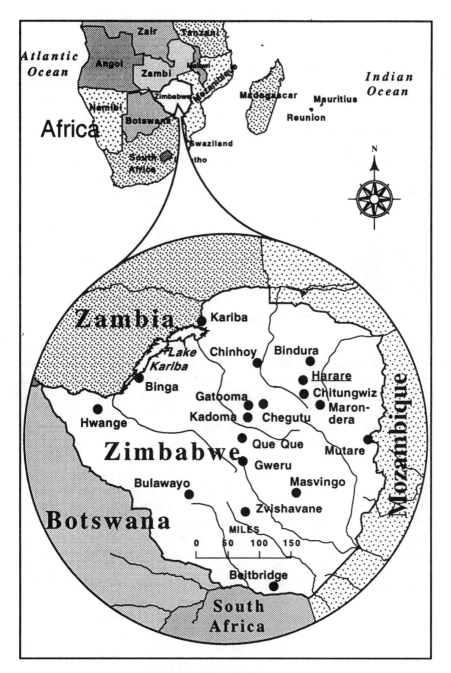

ZIMBABWE

THE CASE[12]
Singing the Lord's Song

Mitchell Hutchison listened with growing dismay and resentment to Richard Farmer's evaluation of the musical innovations Mitchell had introduced in Zimbabwe during the last two years. If there ever has been an example of being "damned by faint praise," thought Mitch, this is it.

Two years earlier Mitchell and his wife Janie had arrived in the East African country with the assignment of teaching in the evangelical seminary and developing a program of musical education and resources for local congregations. Though in his mid-thirties, Mitch had graduated from Princeton Seminary and Westminster Choir College with degrees in Christian education and in music. Furthermore, he had almost nine years of experience working in churches, first in the area of youth and music and subsequently as the minister of music for a large suburban Methodist congregation in Fairfax, Virginia. Those who knew him prior to his missionary appointment described him and Janie as very gifted musicians and effective leaders. Mitch did not consider himself merely a missionary musician, but also a communicator of the gospel and an evangelist.

A Zimbabwe Surprise and New Approach

Extensive readings and courses in missiology had convinced him of the need for contextualizing the gospel not only in spoken word, but also in song. But to his surprise, when he arrived in Zimbabwe, he noted almost immediately how little evidence of awareness there was among the missionaries regarding the "foreignness" of the music in the churches. Neither was there any indication of a desire on the part of the missionaries to reduce the amount of missionary control over the church institutions and organizations.

Mitch and Janie discussed regularly the multiple evidences of paternalism and the need for change in the missionary approach, and they decided together that their best means of initiating change would be to promote the use of indigenous music in congregational worship. Mitch studied with care the hymnal being used in the churches. It contained, he discovered, almost exclusively European and North American hymn texts and hymn tunes. Even the songs in Shona or Matabele were almost all translations of western hymns or gospel songs. And in the seminary where Mitch and Janie taught as adjunctive professors, the piano was the only musical instrument used in chapel worship services. Moreover, all students, especially the women, were encouraged to study piano and to learn to play at least simple hymn tunes. Students were not prohibited from using indigenous instruments such as drums and the Mbira for parties or occasionally in worship, but their use was not included in the musical training program of the seminary.

---

12. This case was written by Thomas H. Graves and Alan Neely.

When Mitch had the responsibility for leading worship for the seminary chapel, he always included the use of the drums, and he insisted on the use of indigenous melodies and texts. He also established three different teaching centers around the country where he went once a month to train local church leaders in worship planning and the use of music in the church. One of his main goals in establishing the centers was the development of persons who would write and promote their own indigenous music.

The general and often enthusiastic acceptance of his work by seminarians, however, was not matched by national pastors and laypersons. Mitch was not prepared for the resistance he encountered in the local churches. Many were clearly attached to what they called "missionary music" that had been introduced by the Europeans and North Americans. Some of the pastors as well as other church leaders told Mitch they regarded the texts as well as the tunes with a high reverence, and they could not envision abandoning their use.

Seven months passed before the first African, a young man from Bulawayo, wrote a song using an African melody and a text reflecting the local setting. The song required a lot of work before it could be presented by a choir, but two months later Mitch taught it to the seminary choir and used it in a chapel service together with three drums and some other African musical instruments. Some of the students told Mitch they liked the song, but no one from the faculty made any comment. He felt he needed more songs as well as persons skilled in the playing of the instruments. Mitch thus began to look for some trained musicians outside the church community, and he located five who were playing in a nightclub in the capital city of Harare. With their help he produced a vibrant sound track which he was able to use as background music for a performance of the seminary choir.

National and Missionary Responses

Despite these efforts, however, Mitch continued to meet with resistance from some of the pastors and with mostly silence from his missionary colleagues. He was not discouraged by the missionary reaction because he had actually expected some opposition from some of them who he felt were simply not conscious of how culturally out of touch their presentation of the gospel was. What he had not expected were the negative responses from the national pastors and other church leaders who seemed wedded to western forms of worship.

One afternoon Mitch decided to discuss the matter with Richard Farmer, the newly appointed administrator of the mission. He and his wife Martha had been missionaries in Zimbabwe for more than twenty years. They had stayed when many of the whites had fled the country during the wars of liberation. They had remained when blacks espousing a Marxist idealogy gained control of the government, and many of the missionaries asked to be transferred elsewhere. One could not doubt that Richard especially had a deep affection for the people and a strong sense of divine calling to Zimbabwe. Though he could easily justify spending all his time in administrative work, he would frequently go out to the bush to preach and teach in the villages.

Richard was candid with Mitch about introducing indigenous music and instruments into the churches. He said, "I'm not a colonialist, and I'm not interested in making 'little Americans' out of Christian converts. I am concerned, however, about maintaining the distinctiveness of Christian worship. I find nothing wrong with the use of some indigenous songs, or permitting some forms of African dance, and I certainly don't object to the occasional use of drums in worship. But I am very uncomfortable with the extensive use of drums and especially the use of other indigenous instruments because those instruments and the music they produce are tied inextricably to ancestral veneration. To confuse Christian worship with African traditional ceremonies where beer is brewed and offered to the spirits is a serious mistake, I believe.

"Seventy years ago," Richard continued, "five percent of the country's population was Christian. Today it is sixty percent. Such a rapid change has created a unique set of circumstances. Most people in our churches are less than one generation removed, some of them less than five years removed from paganism. Mitch, we should never forget that. Syncretism of the Christian faith and animism would be disastrous."

Whenever he talked about this subject, Richard would always relate two stories. Once in visiting a hospitalized child of one of the more prominent national pastors, Richard said he was astounded by what he found in the room. There hanging on the bed above the child's head were several African charms, and the child himself wore two necklaces and amulets that were used by animists to ward off evil spirits. "I knew then," Richard would say, "that most of our people can easily slip back into paganism. How could one of our finest Christian pastors not see the conflict between the old life and new life in Christ?"

The second story Richard would tell with a wry smile. He said, "Once when talking to a village *N'anga* (a village diviner-healer, erroneously called a 'witch doctor'), the *N'anga* said that one of the potions he recommended was capable of helping Christian pastors preach the finest of sermons.

"In a culture where traditional ways always threaten to pull people back into paganism, the Christian gospel and the Christian way of life must not be compromised. They must always be shown to be absolutely different.

"I hope the time will come," Richard declared to Mitch, "when we can see the gospel more indigenized, when we can use more indigenous instruments and promote more fully the use of traditional African music. But the time is not now. Our task is to make sure the Christian message is in no way confused with the ceremonies of the traditional religions."

Mitch did not argue with Richard. "Richard is not entirely wrong," Mitch said to Janie. "But though he says he does not object to some indigenizing, he shows little enthusiasm for what I am trying to do."

Growing Unrest and Approaching Conflict

Janie and Mitch, nonetheless, continued to teach part-time in the seminary, and Mitch visited monthly the three centers he had established. Additional indigenous songs were written, and the seminary choir would in the future present them. But a week before the annual mission meeting, Richard called and told Mitch that some of the other missionaries were as concerned as he about the danger of syncretism and the implications of the emphasis Mitch was making on indigenous music. "I plan to raise the issue in my annual report, Mitch, and I hope you will speak to the mission about your work and program."

Mitch had hoped Richard would not prejudice the case by appeals to fear and repeating the anecdotes regarding the pastor's child and the *N'anga*, but he tried to anticipate what he should say regardless of Richard's comments. The first day of the mission meeting included time for Richard to report on his activities and the state of the work. In fact, his report was the last item of the morning session. He concluded with a rather lengthy statement about issues the missionaries faced and a specific reference to the problem of syncretism. The illustrations about the pastor's child and the *N'anga* preceded Richard's closing remarks.

"All of you know," he said, "that this is the second mission meeting that Mitch and Janie Hutchison have attended since arriving in Zimbabwe. We all know that they are a very talented couple, and we are grateful to have them here. They are dedicated and diligent in all they do, and they have made a significant contribution to our work. Some of you, however, have raised questions about Mitch's emphasis on indigenous music and have asked that we discuss this issue during our meeting. If you approve, we will consider the question of indigenous music as the first item of business this afternoon. I have alerted Mitch to all this and have asked him to speak to us about his work and his plans for the future. I hope we can hear him before entering into any general discussion.

"If you approve the agenda, Mitch's report will be first this afternoon. Do I hear a motion that the suggested order of business be approved?"

"So move," someone said.

"Second," intoned another.

"Is there any discussion?" Richard asked.

"Then are you ready to vote?"

"All in favor say, 'Aye.' "

"Aye."

"Opposed, 'No.' "

"The vote is unanimous."

By this time Mitch was deep in thought. "How hard should I try to sell them on my program?" he wondered. "Am I the one who is wrong? Should I be more patient? Or am I simply a 'square peg in a round hole'?"

STUDY QUESTIONS

1. What was Mitch Hutchison's missionary philosophy, and how did he attempt to implement it? How would you critique his concepts and actions?

2. What were the various responses? Be specific and summarize the position of each person or group.

3. Why were some people so negative about what Mitch and Janie were trying to do?

4. What were Richard Farmer's two examples of the danger of syncretism? Do you think Richard had a point or not?

5. Can you describe the crisis for Mitch that developed in the meeting of the missionaries?

6. How would you expect and/or hope Mitch would respond to the situation?

SUGGESTED BIBLICAL TEXTS FOR REFLECTION

Psalm 137:1–9. A song of lament supposedly sung during the period of exile in Babylon. "How could we sing the Lord's song in a foreign land?" the Psalmist sighs.

Psalm 149:1–9. A song of praise and triumph in which the worshippers are called upon to "sing a new song to the Lord." (See also Psalm 148, a "cosmic hymn of praise").

Psalm 150:1–6. The last song closing the Psalter, a doxology or hymn of praise in which the worshippers are called upon to praise God with all kinds of musical instruments concludes with the words, "Let everything that breathes praise God! Alleluia!"

Ephesians 5:19–20. An admonition to believers to sing psalms and hymns when they gather together. (A similar text is found in Colossians 3:16–17).

"PHYLLIS CROWDER IS PREGNANT"

A missionary wife has a sexual affair and is pregnant with the child of a national pastor who was her language school teacher. A mission agency executive now is faced with attempting to minister to the missionary wife and her traumatized husband as well as follow the agency's policy regarding missionaries who are guilty of immorality. Then there is the question of the fetus.

CONTEXT
Missionary Morality

Missionaries are human and they struggle with mortal temptations, one of which is sexual temptation. Though a common human experience, dealing with sexual impulses and resisting temptations are particularly difficult for individuals in cross-cultural situations because cultural dissonance intensifies one's emotions, ideas, and vulnerability. Living and working in a milieu different from that in which one has been reared, and being in surroundings in which one feels uprooted creates a sense of anomie, isolation, stress, and even peril. Missionaries are usually separated—often by long distances—from their homes, extended families, networks of friends and acquaintances, and it is almost inevitable for them to feel or conclude that they are in a culture lacking or totally without normative standards of belief and behavior.[1] One result of this sensation of anomie is the diminishing of inner, as well as external pressures to act and respond in customary ways. One who is experiencing these feelings—often without being aware—is in a precarious situation. Little attention has been given to preparing missionaries to deal with such feelings in terms of their own sexuality.

Conversely, for generations missionary writings and publications have been filled with detailed, often lurid descriptions of the depraved lives of the "natives." Early in the twentieth century, for example, an American Board (Congregational) missionary to the Philippines, Robert F. Black, lamented the dissolute state of Filipino morality. "I have been almost in despair," he

---

1. Some would say without biblical or Christian standards. Admittedly, beliefs and behavior that are *different* from those of the missionaries often have been considered and described as being pagan, corrupt, and immoral.

wrote. "Adultery seems to be nothing" to these people.[2] No less dismayed was a Free Methodist who said, "In some places . . . a young man is not considered in society circles" if he does not have several *queridas,* i.e., lovers.[3] Quotations of this kind can be readily found in abundance in missionary reports and publications about Asians, Africans, and Latin Americans. European and North American Christians in turn, particularly Protestants, have read them and responded with a certain degree of moral smugness as they deplored these ethical shortcomings, but assumed the missionaries' exemplary lives would awaken the conscience and alter the moral conduct of the Chinese, the Indians, the Kikuyu, and Shona. Only occasionally does one find any allusion to immoral behavior on the part of missionaries, and then it is usually clothed in adroitly chosen euphemisms, such as, "the poor chap simply went native."[4]

This is not to suggest that mission agencies look lightly on moral lapses. Those who have formalized and published their policies are unambiguous about the penalty for immorality. The following are two examples.

Suspension: If a missionary is found guilty of immorality, gross disobedience, insubordination, serious indiscretion, or some other offense which requires his/her removal from service . . . the offending missionary shall be required to immediately surrender his/her credentials as an [Christian and Missionary] Alliance worker to the field director.[5]

The policy of the Southern Baptist Convention's Foreign Mission Board is no less stringent. While emphasis is given to the Board's being "a Christian organization," and, therefore, relating to its missionaries "in loving, fair, and humane ways," certain "conditions" are specified as "career threatening," meaning they will "preclude continued employment." Among the twelve "career threatening" transgressions listed are: "Failure to exhibit [a] Christian lifestyle in keeping with the missionary calling and responsibility"; "dishonesty in the handling of money or other resources"; "immoral sexual activities"; and "homosexuality."[6]

---

2. Quoted by Kenton J. Clymer, *Protestant Missionaries in the Philippines, 1898–1916* (Urbana: University of Illinois Press, 1986), 78.

3. Ibid.

4. The underlying assumption, of course, is that had the hapless fellow remained European or North American, he would never have succumbed to the downward pull of "native" life. Even the distinguished mission historian Stephen Neill employs this expression when referring to one of the first Protestant missionaries to Tahiti. Neill's comment, however, needs to be considered in its entirety. "Of a party of ten," he says, "three were brutally murdered, one went native—a much commoner happening than is generally reflected in the edifying accounts of these early missions which are current—and the remaining six were picked up by a passing vessel and carried back to Australia. *A History of Christian Missions* (1986), 252.

5. *Missionary Handbook for Overseas Ministries,* (Nyack, NY: Division of Overseas Ministries, The Christian and Missionary Alliance, 1987), 85.

6. Policy No: M0P-221. Effective Date: 1/1/91. In the past, the Board when

Statements such as these are found in virtually every Protestant missionary policy manual, and agencies generally abide by them. Yet, as already noted, little information is available and even less preparation is given to the matter of sexuality in missionary orientation or literature. J. Herbert Kane in his *Life and Work on the Mission Field*[7] devotes whole chapters to being a missionary wife, making a home, and being a single—and supposedly celibate—missionary.[8] But he manages to avoid altogether the matter of sexual relations, except to acknowledge that it "is not uncommon for missionary families to have four or five children," and that pregnancy and childbirth pose formidable problems in some locales.[9]

It would be a mistake to conclude that immorality among missionaries has been widespread or even a frequent problem, for this does not appear to be the case.[10] Instances of missionary immortality, however, have occurred and mission executives currently concede that they appear to be increasing.

---

terminating a missionary, even for immorality, allowed the person to resign, in effect protecting him or her as well as the entire family from public scandal. In October of 1994, however, any missionary judged guilty of immorality, misuse of funds, "the persistent advocating of doctrinal opinion inconsistent" with those of the SBC, or other such serious indiscretions, will not have the option to resign. Those persons will be dismissed with "negative references," meaning that a notation will be added that "the individual failed to meet the standards of performance expected of missionaries of the Foreign Mission Board." Some see this as harsh and punitive, but the FMB trustees insist that they have the responsibility to protect churches and others from former missionaries who failed to maintain Christian standards.

7. Grand Rapids, MI: Baker, 1980.

8. In his chapter on "adjusting to missionary life," Kane warns about showing "too much attention to members of the opposite sex," even in "the most progressive countries." Ibid., 98. Harold Lindsell offers most of his warnings to unmarried women missionaries. "A single woman cannot touch a man," he says, "and, of course, there is equal reason to assert positively that no man, and particularly no married man, should touch a single woman." Lindsell's elaboration is not entirely clear, and it reflects to some extent a questionable point of view toward nationals and the national church. "Faced with never-ending situations involving sex in the national churches," he continues, "the foreign missionaries cannot exercise too much care and caution in this regard. No single woman should ever be alone with either an unmarried or a married man, and at all times the social amenities must be observed. The change for the single woman is more difficult than for a married couple, and she [the single missionary] must develop a rich insight into the customs of the people she wishes to serve. There will be many activities and actions she will be forced to forego because of the sensitivities of the nationals to them. In America it would be different, but the place of her service forces upon her a framework of reference which is unique and she becomes as it were a slave to conventions in a variant culture." *Missionary Principles and Practice* (Westwood, NJ: Fleming H. Revell, 1955), 187.

9. Ibid., 109.

10. For several years it was a part of my assignment to travel throughout Latin America researching and analyzing missionary work. At that time, there were approximately nine hundred missionaries serving in thirteen Latin American countries under

Sexual misconduct in the form of exploitation of positions of power and influence, such as a pastor who takes advantage of a person who seeks counsel and help, cannot be excused nor should it be concealed. Anyone—pastor, missionary, physician, teacher, or otherwise—who preys on individuals susceptible to sexual advances and manipulation are guilty of the worst form of exploitation.

In some respects, however, missionaries can be exposed to temptations and be vulnerable themselves in ways distinct from pastors functioning in their own cultures and in familiar settings. When missionaries fail to recognize the danger signals and fail to adhere to realistic guidelines in relating to others, they can find themselves either exploiter, exploited, or both.

Some doubtless would raise a question here about whether clergypersons and missionaries required by their church to take a vow of celibacy are not more inclined to sexual transgression. On this subject there is a wide range of opinions. The matter of mandatory celibacy, however, while germane to the broader discussion of ministerial and missionary sexual behavior, is not directly related to the issues in the case study, "Phyllis Crowder is Pregnant."[11] Neither of the persons who became sexually involved was celibate.

Two things do appear to be clear. First, more is now being revealed, said, and written about sexual misbehavior among clergypersons than at any time in modern history.[12] Second, it is apparent that neither missionaries nor ministers are above temptation. Further, it would seem that sexual fascination

---

the Foreign Missionary Board of the SBC. I know of only six, perhaps eight cases of moral lapses by missionaries over a period of more than a decade. My information was not necessarily the full picture nor would I consider it evidence that all other missionaries were living a moral life. I do believe, nonetheless, that missionaries who became involved in illicit affairs were few. Missionary agencies, understandably, are reluctant to release information regarding cases of immorality among their personnel, but a comprehensive study is, I believe, needed.

11. I have, therefore, included several respected and widely used studies that deal with the history of celibacy in the Christian church as well as some others addressing the current debate regarding compulsory celibacy. See "For Further Study."

12. This is the major thrust of several of the works cited below, only a few of those available are included. Most of these cited deal with indiscretions by Protestant clergy. In the United States during the past decade, people have become so accustomed to hearing and reading about sexual misconduct by Roman Catholic priests, that many have assumed that there is a correlation between mandatory celibacy and immoral behavior. That assumption can be questioned for several reasons, not the least of which is the "rising incidence" of misconduct by married clergypersons. See, for example, "Affair Leads to $575,000 Settlement," *The Christian Century* 110 (January 20, 1993): 50; Donald C. Clark, Jr., "Sexual Abuse in the Church: The Law Steps In," Ibid. (April 14, 1993): 396–398; G. Lloyd Rediger, *Ministry and Sexuality* (Minneapolis: Fortress, 1990). Also, Gustav Niebuhr, "Episcopal Church Reveals Sexual Misconduct by Bishop," *The New York Times* (January 27, 1995), A13. Niebuhr's story deals with the tragic case of Bishop David E. Johnson of Massachusetts who committed suicide in January 1995.

and seduction are greater problems for some than for others. That there has been a kind of embargo, a general reluctance to recognize openly that sexual lapses occur not only among pastors and other ministers in North America and Europe, but also among missionaries, can hardly be denied. To admit this and move forthrightly and systematically to prevent it therefore appears crucial. The policies of missionary sending agencies are clear and longstanding; condemnation of those who stray is swift; and the penalty for immorality is—almost without exception—inexorable. Prevention, therefore, rather than policies and warnings, seems to be needed.

Finally, for those who fall and have to suffer the consequences, as well as for those who transgress but are never discovered and never exposed, there is also needed a clear declaration that somewhere in the church one can find compassion, experience forgiveness, and move toward reclamation and transformation. Is tendering the hope of grace not also a part of the Christian mission?

FOR FURTHER STUDY

Clark, Donald C. Jr. "Sexual Abuse in the Church: The Law Steps In." *Christian Century* 110 (April 14, 1993): 396–398.

   The author, an attorney and member of a Chicago law firm that represents religious institutions, says that sexual misconduct and accusations of sexual misconduct by clergy represent possibly the most formidable legal threat to religious institutions, but more significant, the danger is far more than legal.

Cochini, Christian. *Apostolic Origins of Priestly Celibacy*. Translated by Nelly Marani. San Francisco: Ignatius Press, 1981.

   Traces the history of celibacy in the priesthood from the Council of Carthage in 390 to the end of the seventh century. Also deals with specific issues, such as, were the apostles of Jesus married, and what kind of life did they lead?

Fortune, Marie. *Is Nothing Sacred? When Sex Invades the Pastoral Relationship*. San Francisco: Harper & Row, 1989.

   A landmark book that begins with the nineteenth century celebrated case of Henry Ward Beecher's affair with his parishioner, Mrs. Elizabeth Tilton, and then moves to a contemporary example of a prominent clergyman whose multiple affairs become known. The author not only deals with the matter of public scandal, but more important, she analyzes the deeper question of professional ethics, how the congregation responds, the role of power and the resulting justice or injustice. The Appendix, "Sexual Misconduct by Clergy within Pastoral Relationships," is a 1987 document prepared by a committee of the American Lutheran Church.

Fortune, Marie M. and James N. Poling. *Sexual Abuse by Clergy*. Decatur, GA: Journal of Pastoral Care Publishers, 1994.

   Fortune, the executive director of a center for the prevention of sexual abuse, and Poling, a professor of pastoral theology and counseling, discuss sex and sexual relationships in the lives of ministers, especially in cases where ministers exploit individuals who come to them for help.

Houts, Donald C. *Clergy Sexual Ethics: A Worship Guide*. Decatur, GA: Journal of Pastoral Care Publications, 1981.

A brief twenty-two page guide or agenda for planning and conducting a one-day workshop on sex and ethics in ministry. Includes suggested format, worship ideas, a code of sexual ethics, and extensive bibliography.

Hunt, Harley D. *The Stained Glass Fishbowl*. Valley Forge, PA: The Ministers Council, 1990.

A symposium addressing the dynamics of Christian marriage, particularly the marriages of clergypersons, and how to nurture and strengthen those relationships.

Lea, Henry Charles. *History of Sacerdotal Celibacy in the Christian Church*. 2 vols. New York: Macmillan, 1957.

A thorough, comprehensive, balanced treatment of the history of celibacy in the Christian ministry.

Mahoney, Donna Tiernan. *Touching the Face of God. Intimacy and Celibacy in Priestly Life*. Boca Raton, FL: Jeremiah Press, 1991.

Discusses intimacy and celibacy in the setting of specific instances of priests today. Also asks the hard questions in light of current realities and implications.

Muck, Terry, ed. *Sins of the Body. Ministry in a Sexual Society*. "The Leadership Library," 19. Carol Stream, IL: Word, 1989.

Particularly relevant to this case because the writers are persons involved themselves or with ministers who have experienced moral failures. Includes chapters on the perils facing individuals in Christian ministry, on treatment for infidelity, and restoring those who have fallen.

Murphy, Sheila A. *A Delicate Dance*. New York: Crossroads, 1992.

An analysis of sexuality, celibacy, and relationships among celibate (Roman Catholic) clergy today.

Piper, Otto A. *The Christian Interpretation of Sex*. New York: Charles Scribner's Sons, 1955.

A study of sexuality and sexual ethics based on a scholarly, holistic approach to the Bible. A classic.

Rediger, Lloyd. *Ministry and Sexuality*. Minneapolis: Fortress, 1990.

A comprehensive analysis of sexuality and the clergy. The author, a professor of pastoral theology, deals with "the star factor" in ministers' lives, sexual affairs and addiction among ministers, intimacy, celibacy, and other related issues.

THE CASE
"Phyllis Crowder is Pregnant"

John Cooper, for fifteen years the Associate Missions Director for the Near East and North Africa, has only twice faced a problem of ethical indiscretion on the part of a missionary. Today, however, a young missionary couple whom he admires is returning to the United States because of moral failure. Cooper is heartsick and unsure about what should be done.

Bad News from Lebanon

Cooper had become aware of the problem the previous Wednesday after receiving a telephone call from Lebanon. Though overseas calls were not unusual, almost always they were in regard to some matter of urgency. Fax and air mail were the ordinary means of communication.

"John, this is David Barker. We have a bad situation here." David Barker was a missionary physician, specialist in gynecology and obstetrics, who had served as director of the mission hospital in Beirut for ten years. Praised by nationals and missionaries alike as a competent physician, many people in Lebanon told Cooper when he visited Beirut how much they appreciated Barker's dedication to the hospital and to mission work. He did his work, in Cooper's judgment, without fanfare, and he rarely asked Cooper for special help. The last time Dave called, Cooper remembered, was during the Jewish invasion of Lebanon in 1982 when the hospital staff was desperate for emergency medical supplies.

"What's the problem, Dave?"

"It's grim, John. To put it briefly: Phyllis Crowder is pregnant. You probably did not know it, but before they were appointed, Mike had a vasectomy."

"I guess I did not know that."

"Well, Mike had a vasectomy a few months before the family came to Beirut for language study," David continued.

"I understand that, Dave, but why is it a problem?"

"The problem is, Mike did not make Phyllis pregnant!"

"How can you be sure?"

"The only certain way would be to do a sperm count on Mike, but Phyllis resisted the idea. When I pressed her yesterday to talk to Mike about it, she broke down and told me that after they came to Lebanon, she got involved with another man.

"Let me go back a little bit. Phyllis came in Monday and told me she had missed two menstrual periods. I examined her and was satisfied she was pregnant. But we ran a lab test to be sure. She was very anxious, and frankly I wondered why. They have four children, but another child should not present an impossible burden. Did her anxiety, I asked myself, stem from reasons other than an unexpected pregnancy?

"Well, she came back yesterday to inquire about the results of the lab test. I told her she was pregnant. She began to wring her hands. Finally she said, 'Mike had a vasectomy before we left the States.' I said, 'Yes, I believe he told me that shortly after you arrived.' I then suggested we do a sperm count on Mike. She resisted the idea. I asked her why.

"That did it, John. She burst into tears and was unable to talk for several minutes. I gave her a glass of water and a mild sedative to calm her down. By that time I anticipated what she finally told me. I thought she had probably gotten mixed up with another language student. But it wasn't a student. She got involved with one of the teachers."

"What? Did she tell you who it was?"

"Yes. She said it was Paul Hadad."

"Oh, no!" Cooper responded. Cooper knew Hadad well because he had studied in the denomination's seminary in the United States and was serving as pastor of a small congregation outside of Beirut. He was also a teacher in the language school for missionaries.

"What do we do now, John? Mike has to know. I certainly don't relish being the one to break this kind of news."

Bad News from St. Louis

"Dave, there's only one thing we can do as far as the Crowders are concerned. Mike has to be told, and they have to return to the States immediately. I'll talk with Dr. Williams, but the policy is clear when it comes to immorality. They'll have to come home."

Dr. Harold Williams to whom John Cooper referred was a former missionary to India, associate director for Pakistan, India, Bangladesh, and Sri Lanka for ten years, and seventeen years ago he became Director for International Missions. Cooper admired Williams for his dedication, his leadership skills, and his oratorical gifts. During the time he had been director, the number of new missionaries appointed and new countries where they worked had grown steadily, and there had been dramatic increases in mission giving by the denomination's churches.

Some new policies had been adopted during Williams' tenure, but the mission agency had a long-standing policy regarding immorality and the misappropriation of agency funds. It was stated in the missionary handbook but rarely discussed because so few times was it necessary to apply it. The handbook was more than 60 pages, and consequently during orientation some policies were discussed in detail, such as those related to language study, children's schooling, furloughs, and missionary assignments. Also, new missionaries were directed to read the handbook and raise any questions they might have. In John Cooper's memory, no one had ever asked about the policy on immorality and mishandling of mission funds. The policy was clearly stated: a missionary guilty of moral turpitude or of misusing mission funds was subject to immediate dismissal from missionary service.

Cooper's Counsel and Instructions

"Dave," Cooper continued, "Sandy White is the mission chair, is he not?"
"Yes, he is."

"I suggest you talk with him as quickly as possible, and then the two of you should probably meet with Phyllis first, and then with her and Mike together. As you said, she has to tell Mike, but it will be better if she does so in your presence. Can you arrange to do this tomorrow?"

"I think so," responded David.

"Well, as soon as you've met with them and can get things arranged, put them on a flight to New York. Call me or send a fax, and I will have someone meet them when they clear immigration and customs. They can spend the night in New York if necessary and come on to St Louis the next morning. I do need a full report as soon as you can get it to me. We'll take it from there. I will have to brief Dr. Williams as soon as he returns to the office. That will be Monday, and I'll need all the details you can supply."

"John, I'll do the best I can. If Sandy is 'out of pocket,' I'll try to get Frank King to meet with us. I'll let you know what happens."

Cooper liked the idea of calling King. Not only was he the oldest active missionary in the country, but he was, as far as Cooper was concerned, a kind of "father figure" for the whole Mission.

"That's fine," replied Cooper, "but once you meet with them, get them out of Lebanon and on their way. They'll probably resist because of the children's being in school, the furniture's needing to be packed, et cetera. Just tell them you can take care of the house and furniture, and that I've said for them to come to the States immediately."

"I understand," said David. "I will send you a fax as soon as they are on the plane, and a full report will follow."

"Thanks, Dave. We will surely be in prayer for all of you. Good-bye."

Cooper's Memories of and Review of the Crowders

Cooper hung up the phone and looked at his watch. It was Wednesday, January 14, 4:45 P.M. He stood and turned to look out the window. The weather appeared to be turning colder, and a light rain was falling. He wondered if it would turn to sleet or snow. He thought about his meeting there in his office with Phyllis and Michael Crowder before their appointment as missionaries. Mike was a clean-cut, medium height, handsome, budding theologian, Cooper thought. "He'll make a good missionary," he said to himself.

Michael Crowder had graduated from Southern Illinois University with a Master's in Near Eastern history, and from the denomination's oldest and most prestigious seminary with a Ph.D. in Church History. Phyllis was a striking woman, not beautiful, Cooper thought, but vivacious, outgoing, and attractive in many ways. They told Cooper they had married at the end of Mike's first year in Seminary.

"I can understand how Hadad would be attracted to Phyllis," Cooper thought, "but I never thought something like this could happen. What's going on that led her to get involved? . . . If there was a problem in the marriage, why didn't Personnel uncover it . . . or the psychiatrist? Should we have anticipated something like this?" He sighed, "Oh me! Those guys don't seem to be any better at predicting than we are!"

Cooper dictated a memo on the conversation with David Barker, closed his desk, and moved toward the door. He turned back to write a note to his secretary:

> Please request personnel files on Phyllis and Michael Crowder, Lebanon.
> I will need them first thing tomorrow morning.

He laid the note on her desk and headed for the parking lot.

The following morning John Cooper had hardly sat down at his desk when the secretary entered with the Crowder files.

"Please take my calls and if possible postpone my appointments until the afternoon. I've got to work on this matter this morning."

For more than an hour Cooper read and reread everything in the folder: the Crowders' personal statements of faith and calling, their school and work records, the recommendations of them for missionary appointment, and the medical and psychiatric reports. He studied the notes and memos written by the agency's personnel representatives—those who had worked with Michael and Phyllis up through the final stages before their appointment.

The Crowders' friends, former professors, church members, and employers were all very positive in their evaluations. John Cooper could not find a single indication that he felt should have signaled that the Crowders were risky or questionable missionary appointees. In fact, their personnel profiles indicated them to be a well-above-average couple. The only thing that now stood out was a memo written by one of the personnel representatives noting that Michael and Phyllis had agreed after having four children in five years—two of these during Mike's graduate work at the Seminary—that their family had reached the limit. This decision, according to the memo, led Mike to have the vasectomy. Had the psychiatrist known about their decision and the vasectomy?

Cooper looked again at the medical record. "Yes, here it is. Surely he read this and talked with them about it." But there was nothing in the psychiatric report to indicate the matter had been explored.

Further News from Lebanon

Thursday passed without a message of any kind from David Barker. Cooper decided to wait until the following day, Friday, and call Beirut if a fax or other message did not arrive. When he walked into his office that morning, a message from David Barker was on his desk. Dated the same day, Friday, 8:00 A.M. Beirut, it read:

"We met with Phyllis and Mike Crowder yesterday. Mike was devastated, but the situation is under control.

"They are scheduled to arrive in New York Monday on KLM 702, 8:40 A.M., and should be on United Flight 505 arriving in St. Louis 3:50 P.M. I will send you a full report by tomorrow noon."

Cooper heard nothing further until Monday. When he arrived at his office on Monday morning, his secretary had already laid out the morning mail. On top of a large stack was another fax from David Barker. Cooper read it hurriedly. It was a detailed account of Barker's meeting with the Crowders and their reaction.

Barker said he had not been able to reach Sanford White until late Wednesday night, and he had requested that White come to the hospital by 10:00 the next morning. White arrived shortly before 10:00 A.M.

"I spent the remainder of the morning briefing Sandy on the background, and together we decided how we would approach the Crowders. I called Phyllis and asked her if Sandy and I could see her early in the afternoon. She was obviously very uncomfortable but agreed that we should come soon after 2:00. She said she expected Mike to return around 2:30 or 3:00. I told her we needed some time to talk with her alone and suggested that we come at least by 2:00. Sandy and I arrived a couple of minutes before 2:00. We found Phyllis understandably self-conscious and manifesting a great deal of anxiety.

"First I told her of my conversation with you and of your instructions for me to call Sandy to meet with her and Mike. I reviewed the situation and asked her if I had all the facts correctly. She indicated I did, but she wanted to know what would happen to them. When I told her Mike would have to know, and you had indicated they would have to return to the States immediately, Phyllis broke down. Mike came in about that time. It was a tense, very tense time. Mike could not understand why we were there, nor why Phyllis was so upset.

"I indicated Phyllis had something she needed to tell him. She began hesitantly at first, but as she reviewed her feelings regarding having four children in such a short time, her sense of loneliness and frustration, of being trapped at home and Mike's always studying and doing church work, some of her pent-up feelings began to come out pretty forcefully. She described the feeling of exhilaration in coming to Beirut, of having a nanny to help with the children, and how she had felt free for the first time in six years. She told of how she had come to admire Hadad and how they had become involved.

"She did not mention the fact that she excelled in language school, and that Mike for the first time in his academic life had to struggle from the first day until now with Arabic. Hadad tutored Phyllis (as he did several language school students), and I believe their liaisons began sometime near the end of the Crowders' second term of study.

"Mike was clearly stunned by the whole story. Rather, I should say he was crushed. He cried some but did not manifest any anger, just deep hurt and bewilderment.

"The second blow came when we told him they would have to return to the U.S. immediately. We did not enter into the matter of their relationship with the Board, but I did discuss with them the decision they faced in whether Phyllis would carry the baby the full term of the pregnancy. It may have been more an impulse than a rational decision, but she indicated she wanted an abortion.

"The earliest we could secure reservations was for Sunday evening. They are scheduled to arrive in St. Louis at 3:50 P.M. Monday.

"I know you will have to make some tough decisions, but I feel I must in good conscience make some recommendations as a doctor and as a friend of the Crowders. You may share these with Dr. Williams, the medical consultants, and anyone else who has a responsibility in making a decision about this case.

"A decision regarding Phyllis' pregnancy will have to be faced soon, but I hope without undue pressure. If an abortion is decided upon, Phyllis and Mike both need to see the long-term effects of this upon them. Further, the time for inducing an abortion with minimum hazard to the mother is limited. In the last analysis, either alternative will be costly in ways other than money.

"Someone, I believe, should confront Paul Hadad with his responsibility in this tragic situation. Should I talk with the language school administrator about this?

"We will be praying for all of you there during these days.

Sincerely yours,
(Signed) David Barker."

Cooper's Emerging Plan

Cooper put the letter into the Crowders' folder and began to outline what he would say and propose to Dr. Williams. He was to see him at 11:00 A.M.

STUDY QUESTIONS

1. How did you feel when you learned the circumstances of Phyllis Crowder's pregnancy?

2. What can you recount about the principal characters in this case? What is important to know about each of them before one can understand and discuss this case?

3. What do you believe is the central issue in this case?

4. One cannot re-write the past, but are there steps that could have been taken which perhaps would have prevented such a tragic series of events?

5. Imagine yourself to be John Cooper. What would you say and recommend to Dr. Williams? How would you deal with Michael and Phyllis Crowder? There is also the matter of the fetus Phyllis is carrying. What would be your approach to this concern?

SUGGESTED BIBLICAL TEXTS FOR REFLECTION

Exodus 20:1–17. The Ten Commandments. The prohibition against adultery is one of ten prohibitions. Is it significant to note that adultery is not singled out as being more iniquitous than idolatry, profaning God's name, breaking the Sabbath, dishonoring parents, stealing, or bearing false witness?

Leviticus 20:1–27. A comprehensive list of behaviors prohibited in Israel and the penalties for disobedience. Several were capital offenses punishable by death.

Hosea 2:2–23. An unfaithful people is compared by the prophet to an unfaithful spouse. Punishment and God's love for both are forcefully declared, as well as a restoration of the relationship.

John 8:1–11. A woman caught in adultery is brought to Jesus. Readers should know that the earliest New Testament manuscripts do not include this passage. In others it is found as an addendum to Luke 21:38 or to John 21:24. Is this an indication that it is a spurious passage, or that the early church was uncertain about how to deal with it?

"COME, HOLY SPIRIT(S)"

A Pentecostal seminary professor attending the Seventh Assembly of the World Council of Churches in Canberra hopes that the theme of the Assembly—"Come, Holy Spirit"—signals that the WCC is reaching out to charismatics and Pentecostals. After the second of the two key-note addresses, however, he was unsure.

CONTEXT
Ecumenism and the Gospel

The formal organization of the World Council of Churches took place in Amsterdam, August 23, 1948, the culmination of more than a decade of preparation. Nearly one hundred fifty churches were represented by three hundred fifty-one delegates from forty-four countries. From this first assembly through the seventh, however, it has been evident that theological and other differences were multiple and some were profound. The text of the Final Message of Amsterdam, nonetheless, clearly affirmed the Trinitarian basis of the relationship and the churches' strong determination to continue the search together for Christian unity.

> We bless God our Father, and our Lord Jesus Christ Who gathers together in one the children of God that are scattered abroad. He has brought us here together at Amsterdam. We are one in acknowledging Him as our God and Saviour. We are divided from one another not only in matters of faith, order and tradition, but also by pride of nation, class and race. But Christ has made us His own, and He is not divided. In seeking Him we find one another. Here at Amsterdam we have committed ourselves afresh to Him, and have covenanted with one another in constituting this World Council of Churches. We intend to stay together.[1]

But staying together has not been easy. As the Council grew in numbers and influence, it became—as several have noted—like a ship on a stormy

---

1. "Messages," *Men's Disorder and God's Design. The Amsterdam Assembly Series* 4 (New York: Harper, 1949), 231.

sea with more than twice the number of passengers it had when it first embarked, passengers representing more churches and manifesting more diversity than ever in the vessel's history. Most of the new passengers boarded from Eastern Europe and from Africa, Asia, Latin America, the Caribbean, and Oceania. Their cultures, traditions, languages, histories, and theologies have threatened, while adding to the variety, to turn an otherwise harmonious voyage into a Tower of Babel, if not open combat. Unity, however, has somehow prevailed.

In Amsterdam it was the East-West conflict that surfaced, a conflict resulting from the intensifying Cold War. The East-West, communism-capitalism debate could have wrecked the fledgling structure anywhere along the way had it not been for a commitment that transcended nationalisms and ideologies. Other tensions, notwithstanding, also emerged over such issues as the Council's relations with the Roman Catholic Church and with peoples of other faiths, the struggles for liberation in former European and American colonies, budgetary appropriations, the role of women in the church, and environmental issues—just to mention a few.[2] Yet, despite radical differences, deep divisions, and intense and sometimes acrimonious debate in the various working groups as well as in the assemblies, the World Council has managed to remain together. As in any organization, there have been a few losses along the way, but far more additions. Thus, when the eight hundred forty-two delegates gathered in Canberra in 1991, they represented three hundred seventeen churches, more than twice the number at Amsterdam.

It has been common knowledge, nonetheless, that the fastest-growing churches are no longer those aligned with the historic Protestant or Catholic communions, but rather with conservative evangelical and Pentecostal movements. Few denominations associated with evangelicalism or Pentecostalism have become members of the World Council, but some have, and a few others are engaged in dialogue with the WCC. It seems evident that by choosing the theme for the Canberra Assembly, "Come, Holy Spirit—Renew the Whole Creation," the Council was making an overt, tangible attempt to appeal to those who identify themselves as Pentecostals. Repeatedly during the Assembly, the Holy Spirit was asked to free the churches from their theological captivities. Yet, never was the intimation made that by importuning the Spirit to liberate the churches was the commitment to the poor and oppressed of the world being lessened or shelved in a desire for broader appeal. General Secretary Emilio Castro in his opening address declared "that

---

2. See Leon Howell, *Acting in Faith. The World Council of Churches Since 1975.* (Geneva: World Council of Churches, 1982); Ans J. van der Bent, *What in the World is the World Council of Churches?* (Geneva: World Council of Churches, 1978); "WCC Assemblies," *Dictionary of the Ecumenical Movement,* ed. Nicholas Lossky, et al. (Geneva: World Council of Churches, 1991), 1090–1096; and Thomas Stransky, "World Council of Churches," Ibid., 1083–1090. These are four brief summaries of the history and functioning of the WCC.

the Spirit's agenda is always anchored in the conflict of history, contrary to the popular stereotypes of the Spirit being abstract and other-worldly, a private and individual experience."[3] It was the African-American preacher, the Reverend Jacquelyn Grant, however, who eloquently and forcefully spelled out the risks and the rewards of the Spirit's presence when she asked who could control or contain the Holy Spirit. The Spirit "defies every attempt at human limitation," she said. Theologians—"intellectuals" she called them—have for centuries decided upon and thereby determined "the doctrines of God and of Jesus Christ, but the Holy Spirit, by its very name, is uncontrollable."[4]

What emerged in Canberra, however, was anything but a unity of spirit. Rather it was an uneasiness with the mixing of expressions of aboriginal spirituality, invocations to various spirits, and the Holy Spirit. The disquiet escalated into a full-blown debate between Orthodox and evangelical spokespersons on one side and Asian and African contextual theologians on the other. The initial flash-point, few if any would question, was the Korean theology professor, Hyun Kyung Chung's keynote address, "Come Holy Spirit, Renew the Whole Creation."[5]

FOR FURTHER STUDY

Other than the works listed below, readers are encouraged to consult the sources related to the issue of syncretism (pp. 144–146, 149–151).

Abraham, K. C. "Syncretism is Not the Issue: A Response to Professor Chung Hyun Kyung." *International Review of Mission* 80 (July–October 1991): 339–346.

Abraham, Director of the South Asia Theological Research Institute and Vice President of the Ecumenical Association of Third World Theologians (EATWOT), challenges those who reject Professor Chung's presentation as "another example of syncretism." The issue, he contends, is the role of culture in inter-faith dialogue.

Balasuriya, Tissa. "Liberation of the Holy Spirit." *The Ecumenical Review* 43 (April 1991): 200–205.

Balasuriya, director of the Centre for Society and Religion in Sri Lanka, contends that by making the Holy Spirit the central theme of the assembly meeting, no one could nor should have sought to control what took place. He states the position of the Orthodox Patriarch of Alexandria who objected vehemently to Chung's address as well as Chung's response. He concludes that the experience should stimulate a fruitful

---

3. John Bluck, *Canberra Take-Aways. What the Assembly Offers a Local Congregation.* (Geneva: WCC Publications, 1991), 15.

4. Ibid., 14.

5. In the literature on the Canberra Assembly, Professor Chung's name is variously written, e.g., as Hyun Kyung Chung, Chung Hyun Kyung, and Chung Hyun-Kyung. All are correct. The Korean form puts the family name first, in this case Chung, and the given names follow. In English, the form is reversed. Again, given names in Korean are often hyphenated as an indication that they are not the family name.

dialogue between the Orthodox churches and the emerging feminist theology, especially in Asia.

Chung, Hyun-Kyung. "Welcome the Spirit; Hear Her Cries." *Christianity and Crisis* 51 (July 15, 1991): 220–223.

An edited text of address that provoked the debate referred to in the case study "Come, Holy Spirit(s)." Much of this edition of the journal is devoted to the Canberra Assembly, and particularly to Chung's presentation. The essays by Kwok Pui-Lan, "Gospel and Culture" (223–224); Jae-Won Lee, "Spirit and Practice: A Radical Understanding" (226–227); Roy Sano, " 'Holy Moments' at Canberra" (227–228); and John Deschner, "Legitimating, Limiting, Pluralism" (230–232) are basically positive. Those by Samuel Solivan and Leonid Kishkovsky are negative. (See annotations below).

Fortune, Marie. "At Canberra, Profound Sexism." *Christianity and Crisis* 51 (July 15, 1991): 219–220.

Author assesses the experience of women at the WCC Assembly in Canberra with the position of the WCC earlier when it inaugurated the Ecumenical Decade of the Churches in Solidarity with Women.

Gros, Jeffrey. "Christian Confession in a Pluralistic World." *The Christian Century* 108 (June 26–July 3, 1991): 644–646.

The problem with Professor Chung's speech, according to Gros, was her identification of "a Korean Buddhist bhodisattva with the Third Person of the Trinity," thereby challenging the WCC's trinitarian cornerstone and the basis of the churches' struggle for unity.

Kishkovsky, Leonid. "Ecumenical Journey: Authentic Dialogue." *Christianity and Crisis* 51 (July 15, 1991): 228–229.

A penetrating analysis of Chung's presentation in which the author, President of the National Council of Churches of Christ, USA, and ecumenical officer of the Orthodox Church in America, muses on why her words provoked "passionate applause" as well as "passionate silence."

"Korean Theologian Shocks Some Delegates." *Ecumenical Trends* 20 (March 1991): 35–37.

A news article about the negative reaction of some delegates who charged Chung with syncretism, paganism, and apostasy.

Lossky, Nicolas and Carl A. Volz. "Reflections on Canberra," and "Reply to Lossky (and Canberra)." *Dialog* 32 (Spring 1993):140–142.

Lossky, an Orthodox theology professor who is also a member of the WCC Faith and Order Commission and was a delegate of the Russian Orthodox Church to the Canberra Assembly, explains why he was disturbed by Chung's discourse. His brief comments are followed by those of Carl A. Volz, a Lutheran church history professor who agrees with Lossky and asserts that the real issue is defining the limits of legitimate theological diversity.

Man-King, Tso. "Theological Controversy in Canberra: A Reflection." *International Review of Mission* 80 (July–October 1991): 355–360.

Defines syncretism and differentiates between a "chop suey" theology, anything and everything thrown together approach, and that of a salad composed of complementary edibles. Man-King, the General Secretary of the Hong Kong Christian Council, suggests that Chung's address was an example of the latter.

McClean, Robert. "Beware: The Holy Spirit." *Christian Social Action* 4 (April 1991): 4–11 (with photographs).

A summary of the controversy arising from Professor Chung's presentation. Concentrates particularly on the relationship of the event to worldwide social concerns.

Pui-Lan, Kwok. "Gospel and Culture," *Christianity and Crisis* 51 (July 15, 1991): 223–224.

A young Asian theologian who teaches religion and culture at the Chinese University in Hong Kong reflects on the question of how Asians should understand the Gospel anew in their own context.

Raiser, Konrad. "Beyond Tradition and Context: In Search of An Ecumenical Framework of Hermeneutics." *International Review of Mission* 80 (July–October 1991): 347–354.

A former theological professor and now General Secretary of the World Council of Churches faces the question regarding whether Professor Chung was fostering syncretism. He examines her address from a hermeneutical perspective, pointing out that it was not simply one more example of syncretism, but rather a sign of a growing theological self-confidence among those who are actually engaged in the process of contextualization.

Solivan, Samuel. "Which Spirit? What Creation?" *Christianity and Crisis* 51 (July 15, 1991): 224–226.

The author, a Venezuelan, ordained Assemblies of God minister, and U.S. seminary professor, maintains that Chung's position "is similar to that held by the Stoics," and that she failed to distinguish between the human ego and the Third Person of the Trinity.

"Survival—Syncretist." *Christian Century* 109 (March 11, 1992):272.

A news article summarizing the repercussions of Professor Chung's address, including her disclosure that following the Canberra experience her telephone was tapped, she received death threats, and was obliged to give up her housing at Ewha Women's University in Seoul.

Tucker, Mary Evelyn. "Expanding Contexts, Breaking Boundaries: the Challenge of Chung Hyun-Kyung." *Cross Currents* 42 (Summer 1992): 236–243.

Tucker, a professor of religion at Bucknell University and author of a recent book on moral and spiritual development in Japanese neo-Confucianism, regards the significance of Chung's address as raising a question concerning whether seminaries are preparing future pastors, priests, and laypersons to understand and appreciate the history, beliefs, and practices of other religions on their terms.

Note: A video of Chung Hyun-Kyung's entire presentation, including the aboriginal entry and dancing, is available from Ecufilm, 810 12th Avenue, South, Nashville, TN 37203. If time is available, viewing the video before discussing the case is strongly recommended.

THE CASE
"Come, Holy Spirit(s)"

Art Elliott left the Canberra National Convention Center the last day of the meeting and walked briskly along the pedestrian route marked with blue kangaroo footprints. Though he was one of hundreds leaving the session, he felt troubled and unusually alone. What he had witnessed and experienced during the past days was profoundly moving, but it was also disconcerting. Public and private discussions of the theme of the meeting, the Holy Spirit, had several times erupted into a heated and divisive debate.

Elliott, a U.S. Pentecostal in background and a seminary professor, was one of four thousand people attending the Seventh Assembly of the World Council of Churches. Though he was in Canberra only as an accredited observer, he knew that when he returned to the United States he would be asked to report on the meeting to his seminary community and also to a number of congregations.

A New Theme and an Old Argument

Prior to Canberra, the themes of the six previous assemblies of the World Council of Churches had focused on Jesus Christ. But for this seventh assembly, the theme was an invocation to the third person of the Trinity, "Come, Holy Spirit—Renew the Whole Creation." At last, Elliott thought as he flew to Australia, the WCC is moving openly and decisively toward charismatics and Pentecostals, as well as emphasizing a theme dear to those in Orthodox communions. "Maybe," he said to himself, "this will open the door to Pentecostals who have remained aloof from the ecumenical movement, and they will begin to see the WCC in a new light." After the second of the key-note addresses and the volatile response, however, Elliott began to wonder.

Addresses and Theme Interpretation

The key-note addresses were given the afternoon of the second day of the meeting. The first, written by Orthodox Patriarch Parthenios who because of the war in the Gulf had remained in Egypt, was read to the assembly by an Orthodox colleague. He was followed by a 34-year-old Presbyterian professor and feminist theologian, Chung Hyun Kyung of the Ewha Women's University in Seoul, Korea, whose appearance and demeanor immediately enlivened the session. Chung was accompanied by a troupe of sixteen white-clad Korean and two Australian aboriginal dancers—the latter dressed in the traditional aboriginal loincloths and body paint—who entered the assembly hall from the rear and danced their way to the platform to the sound of bells, drums, clap-sticks, and gongs.

Professor Chung, dressed in a plain white Korean robe, stepped to the podium and instantly stirred the audience, Elliott thought, by saying: "My dear sisters and brothers, welcome to this land of the Spirit." In Australia, she said, aboriginal people remove their shoes when they sense they are on holy ground. In respect for the aboriginal people of Australia, Chung continued, "I want to take off my shoes," and she invited her listeners to do the same. Taking off one's shoes for Asian and Pacific peoples, she explained, is a gesture of humility and a means of preparing to encounter the Spirit of God.

Then, unrolling a rice-paper scroll, Chung Hyun Kyung began to invoke various spirits.

• "Come. The spirit of Hagar, Egyptian, black slave woman exploited and abandoned by Abraham and Sarah, the ancestors of our faith."

• "Come. The spirit of Jephthah's daughter, victim of her father's faith, burned to death for her father's promise to God if he were to win the war."

• "Come. The spirit of Joan of Arc, and of the many other women burned to death as witches."

• "Come. The spirit of indigenous people of the earth, victims of genocide during the time of colonialism and the period of the great Christian mission to the pagan world."

• "Come. The spirit of people killed in Hiroshima and Nagasaki by atomic bombs."

• "Come. The spirit of Korean women in the Japanese 'prostitution army' during World War Two."

• "Come. The spirit of Gandhi, Steve Biko, Martin Luther King, Malcolm X, Victor Jara, and Oscar Romero."

• "Come. The spirit of the Amazon rain forest now being murdered every day."

• "Come. The spirit of Earth, Air, and Water, raped, tortured, and exploited by human greed for money"; and

• "Come. The spirit of the Liberator, our brother Jesus, tortured and killed on the cross."

Pausing momentarily, Chung Hyun Kyung, trained in Korea as well as in the United States in Clairemont and Union Theological Seminary, then rolled up the scroll, set it afire and held it in her fingers as the ashes and smoke curled toward the ceiling, and the final fragment was consumed by the flame. This was for Arthur Elliott one of the most dramatic scenes he had ever witnessed.

Chung Hyun Kyung continued referring to her own land: "I come from Korea, the land of spirits full of *Han*." *Han,* she explained, is anger, resentment, bitterness, grief, broken-heartedness, and *han* is "the raw energy for struggle for liberation." In Korea, she said, anyone killed or who dies unjustly becomes a "wandering spirit," a *Han*-filled spirit. These spirits are everywhere, and they are searching for ways to right the wrongs that have been committed. It has been through these *han*-filled spirits that the Holy Spirit has spoken to us in Korea of justice and right. Unless we hear "the cries of these spirits we cannot hear the voice of the Holy Spirit."

She then called upon her listeners to repent as "the first step in any truthful prayer." Elliott did not miss the allusion. The theme of the assembly was a prayer. Professor Chung summoned the assembly to repent of their persistent devotion to mammon and of their hidden desire to build another Babel tower. She challenged her hearers to practice a "voluntary poverty" so that "forced poverty" can be eliminated. Of necessity, this involves re-reading the Bible from the perspectives of the poor, the oppressed, women, indigenous, and the Dalits (the untouchables of India). But it also involves, she said, re-reading "the Bible from the perspective of birds, water, air, trees, and mountains." It involves moving from a traditional "anthropocentrism to life-centrism." Only by learning "to think like a mountain, changing our centre from human beings to all living beings," can we "survive," Chung declared.

Her conclusion was a variation of the theme. She prayed, "Wild wind of the Holy Spirit, blow to us. Let us welcome her, letting ourselves go in her wild rhythm of life. Come, Holy Spirit. Renew the Whole Creation. Amen!"

It was an electrifying moment, unlike anything Arthur Elliott had ever witnessed. But it was also troubling because he perceived Chung Hyun Kyung to be fusing Asian animism with Christian faith. He did not have to wait long to learn that others shared his misgivings.

Reactions to Chung Hyun Kyung

Delegates were not given an opportunity in that session to respond to the key-note addresses. Reactions, however, were immediate as people left the hall, conversed in the hotels and restaurants, and debated Chung Hyun Kyung's presentation in the sub-section meetings. Many of them, including the WCC General Secretary Emilio Castro, defended what she had said. Chung, Castro observed, was simply invoking the "saints of popular suffering," not unlike the biblical "cloud of witnesses." Moreover, she was contextualizing the gospel in the soil of Korea. Others, however, especially the Orthodox and members of her own Korean church, accused her of flagrant syncretism.

When asked to respond, Chung challenged her critics to discuss the issue in a formal setting, and word quickly spread that she would debate the Syrian Orthodox leader, Metropolitan Paulos Gregorios, who was also one of the WCC's seven presidents. Instead, a special plenary session was called on "the gospel and inculturation." The ninety minutes set aside for the discussion were exhausted by a stream of speakers who asked to be heard. Each was allowed only three minutes. The Holy Spirit must be distinguished from other spirits, many of them argued. Others insisted that Chung was merely doing what was necessary if the gospel is to be contextualized. Professor Chung was given "the final word." She dismissed the accusation of syncretism, saying in effect that it was a "red herring." The real issue, she contended, was power. White males, primarily white western males, have defined the Holy Spirit and established the boundaries of the Holy Spirit's work. "We have been listening to your intellectualism for 2,000 years," she declared. Now,"please listen to us." Third-world theology is new, she admitted. It is "new wine that can't be put in your [old] wineskins." Third-world theology is dangerous, and we third-world theologians "are dangerous," she concluded, "but it is through such danger that the Holy Spirit can renew the church."

The Orthodox and evangelical delegates, visitors, and observers, however, were not satisfied with her rationale, and they made this clear. In their official responses and reflections on the assembly, the Orthodox said they would await the final texts of the meeting. But they wanted to go on record by reminding the delegates "that some people tend to affirm with very great ease the presence of the Holy Spirit in many movements and developments," but they do so "without discernment." Any "tendency to substitute a 'private' spirit, the spirit of the world or other spirits for the Holy Spirit that proceeds from the Father and rests in the Son" is "sin and error." Orthodox tradition, they added, places great emphasis on the work of the Holy Spirit and at the same time respects "local and national churches." Nonetheless, they said, they found it impossible to invoke the spirits of " 'earth, air, water and sea creatures.' Pneumatology," they declared "is inseparable from Christology."

The evangelicals were a bit more delicate. "As the assembly discussed the process of listening to the Spirit at work in every culture," they said, "we cautioned, with others, that discernment is required to identify the Spirit as the Spirit of Jesus Christ and thus to develop criteria for and limits to theological diversity. We argued for a high Christology to serve as the only authentic Christian basis for dialogue with persons of other living faiths." Chung had abandoned a high Christology, they insisted. They then gently chided the Council for its apparent "reluctance to use straightforward biblical language," and at the same time expressed appreciation for the opportunity accorded evangelicals to participate in the meeting and contribute their insights to the official reports. Theological deficiency and the "imbalance within the WCC," they noted, stem from "insufficient commitment to ecumenical activity by evangelicals in member churches of the WCC and in churches in the wider Christian communion." Elliott agreed with these observations.

Arthur Elliott's Personal Response

He had been present in the special plenary session when Chung's address was debated, and he was in the caucus of evangelicals when they drafted their official letter of reflections to the Assembly. He had made copious notes during both meetings. Now sitting in his hotel room, Elliott looked over his notes and a copy of Professor Chung's address. He wanted to summarize his impressions in his journal because his journal would be the primary source he would use when making presentations in the United States. He would of course talk about the entire meeting, but he knew that much of what he would say would center on his response to the provocative address by Chung Hyun Kyung.

STUDY QUESTIONS

1. Briefly recount the history of the World Council of Churches, its beginnings, theological foundation, development, and divisions.

2. What was the theme of the Canberra Assembly and in what way was it different?

3. Who is Chung Hyun Kyung, and what was the essence of her address to the Assembly?

4. There were at least three different responses to her presentation. What were these and whom do they represent?

5. If you were Arthur Elliott, what notes would you write in your journal about the debate of Chung's keynote address? Be concise.

6. Do you agree with the accusations that her presentation was an example of syncretism, paganism, and apostasy? Explain and be prepared to defend your response.

SUGGESTED BIBLICAL TEXTS FOR REFLECTION

Genesis 1:1–4. The Spirit and the story of creation. The Hebrew word *ruach,* translated Spirit, can be rendered "the power of God," "an awesome wind," "the wind of God," or "the spirit of God."

1 Samuel 16:14–23. Young David summoned by Saul to be a court musician. By playing his harp, David is supposed to free the king from evil spirits.

Psalm 51:1–19. The psalmist prays for forgiveness, a pure heart, and a new spirit. ". . . Do not take your holy spirit away from me."

Matthew 12:22–32. Jesus defends his power as being that of God's Spirit, not the spirit of evil. He warns against those who cannot distinguish between the two.

Mark 5:1–20. Jesus heals a man possessed by evil spirits.

Galatians 5:16–26. The produce of human nature and the fruit of the Spirit.

ASIA RESOURCES, INC.

A former missionary, now member of a new Methodist mission sending agency and committee, hears a presentation by an enthusiastic and charismatic entrepreneur who challenges the group to initiate a "new approach" to the sending of missionaries, namely, send them as business people who can gain entry to countries such as China. Members of the committee are excited and positive, but Doug Murphy is troubled by the proposal.

THE CONTEXT
Entrepreneurism and Mission

Since China began opening to the West in the 1960s and the subsequent collapse of the Soviet Union in the late 1980s, growing numbers of Protestant evangelicals have seen these and other areas of the world as "fields ripe for harvest." These dramatic changes, however, were accompanied by the realization that most Christian missionaries are still sent to regions of the world where the church has long since been planted, while vast numbers of people have no opportunity whatever to hear the gospel, attend a church, or even read a Bible. Who these "unreached" people are and where they live has become a major concern and frequent theme of evangelical discussions and mission planning. A quick review of the articles and books published on this subject in the past decade will give an idea of the intensity with which this issue is approached. Twelve "unevangelized population complexes," brief histories and other ethnographic information, their approximate numbers, and their locations can be found, for example, in the book by V. David Garrison, *The Nonresident Missionary* (1990) mentioned below.

China, however, represents a different, if not unique situation. Though now open to diplomatic relations and trade with the West, missionaries are still prohibited entry into this vast and most populous country. Many "missionaries" are there, nonetheless, working as teachers, scientists, technologists, and business people. Chinese Christian leaders, such as Bishop K. H. Ting, Principal of the Nanjing Theological Seminary and President of the China Christian Council, are less than comfortable with some recent developments, for they do not want a return to the past and the presence of foreign missionaries. He says, for example:

We do not approve of those people overseas who try to mold public opinion into thinking that they should send missionaries back to China. No matter how large the population of China is and how small our Church is, the responsibility for spreading the gospel and building up the Church in China is the mission of Chinese Christians. We will not invite missionaries to China from overseas. We wish to declare that no group or individual overseas should engage in evangelical activity in China without the expressed consent of Chinese Church authorities, who retain responsibility and jurisdiction in this area.[1]

To understand Ting's position, one needs to know the history of Christian missions in China, especially beginning with the shameful Opium Wars (1842–1844), followed by the "unequal treaties" forced upon the defeated Chinese, and the opening of five ports to trade and Western residence for business people and others, including missionaries. Then in 1860 the Western colonial governments, backed by gun-boat diplomacy, compelled China to permit foreigners to reside in inland cities and to guarantee their safety and security. The safety and security requirement was also extended to the converts of the missionaries.[2] More than one historian has observed that the missionaries, for the most part, not only supported the "unequal treaties that had the effect of reducing China to a semi-colonial status," some of them had participated in drawing up and translating the treaties. In 1924 J. Leighton Stuart, missionary president of the New University in Peking, conceded that missionaries were still in control of the Chinese Christian institutions, including the churches, solely because they had behind them "the military power to maintain unequal treaties" and the Chinese government was powerless to do anything about it.[3]

Evangelical Christians in the West, however, either do not know this history or choose to disregard it in their desire to carry out the Great Commission and see the church prosper in China. Meanwhile, with the kaleidoscopic changes taking place in Eastern Europe, especially in the republics of the former Soviet Union, "missionaries" of every kind have been cascading

---

1. "A Call for Clarity: Fourteen Points from Christians in the People's Republic of China to Christians Abroad," trans. Philip Wickeri. Robert A. Evans and Alice Frazer Evans, *Human Rights* (Maryknoll, NY: Orbis, 1983), 223. See also Raymond L. Whitehead, ed., *No Longer Strangers. Selected Writings of K. H. Ting* (Maryknoll, NY: Orbis, 1989) in which Ting comments extensively on China's long experience with the imperialism of the West and the role of the missionaries.

2. The details of these developments can be found in any good history of Christian missions, and they are summarized by F. W. Price in his article, "China," *Concise Dictionary of the Christian World Mission,* ed. Stephen Neill, Gerald H. Anderson, and John Goodwin (New York: Abingdon, 1971), 100–106.

3. Philip L. Wickeri, *Seeking the Common Ground. Protestant Christianity, the Three-Self Movement, and China's United Front* (Maryknoll, NY: Orbis, 1988), 34.

into Russia, Lithuania, and Romania, and also into such areas as Ukraine, Kyrgyzstan, Uzbekistan, Turkmenistan, Tajikistan, and even Albania.

In the Spring of 1992 a major United States missionary agency issued a news release with the headline, "U.S. Christian Businessmen See Turkmenistan Opportunities." The opportunities described were both commercial and evangelistic. The people of Turkmenistan, long isolated from the technological and economic developments in the West, need and desire outside resources, according to the statement. Thus, enterprising evangelical business people, such as the two college teachers described in the story, established what they called a Center for Free Enterprise and Economics, "a nonprofit organization that aims to bring together Christian business people, educators and students with an interest in free enterprise economics."[4] Ostensibly, the Center was to operate as a partnership between the Turkmenistan business people and certain enterprising evangelicals from the United States. The purpose of the endeavor was to help the people of this predominantly Muslim land while promoting free enterprise development.

A third approach to getting missionaries into countries otherwise closed to evangelistic ventures is that of one of the principals in the following case study, "Asia Resources, Inc." The tactic may be described as sending in Christian evangelicals as entrepreneurs who go to do business, make a profit, and thereby support themselves economically by the business enterprise in which they are engaged—apparently making as much money as possible— while doing whatever evangelistic and missionary work they can.

The wisdom, validity, and appropriateness of any or all of these strategies is the crux of the following case study. Discussants should know that the governments of these countries to which the entrepreneurial missionaries are going—ostensibly as business people, technicians, or teachers—are not ignorant of what is taking place. But even though the Chinese, Russian, and Turkmenistan authorities are fully aware of the intent of these new "missionaries," the governments' desperate need to push political change, monetary reform, and obtain hard currency as quickly as possible induces them to close their eyes to the legal implication.

As far as many Christians in the West are concerned, not to seize this present opportunity to evangelize these lands by whatever way possible or to refuse to take the gospel to peoples who have for more than a half-century been prevented from hearing it would be senseless and irresponsible. More seriously, they believe, it would be a betrayal of the church's mission to the world.

FOR FURTHER STUDY

Barrett, David and James Reapsome. *700 Plans to Evangelize the World*. Birmingham, AL: New Hope, 1988.

---

4. "Foreign Mission News," Foreign Mission Board of the Southern Baptist Convention (April 13, 1992), 2.

A fascinating catalogue and brief descriptions of seven hundred plans that did not work. Why they failed is spelled out by the authors.

Barrett, David and Todd Johnson. *Our Globe and How to Reach It.* Birmingham, AL: New Hope, 1990.

A follow-up on the seven hundred plans. Readers need to be critical in the use of the data. See Robert T. Coote's article below.

Coote, Robert T. "Good News, Bad News: North American Protestant Overseas Personnel Statistics in Twenty-Five-Year Perspective." *International Bulletin of Missionary Research* 19 (January 1995): 6–13.

Coote advises that reliable statistics about missions are both difficult to obtain and sometimes perplexing to interpret. Educated (or not so educated) projections or guesses are not uncommon, nor are substantial revisions when new information surfaces, as it often does.

Dyrness, William A. "A Unique Opportunity." *Mission Handbook,* ed. W. Dayton Roberts and John A Siewert, 9–22. Monrovia, CA: MARC, 1989.

A concise and informative appraisal of the state of Christianity and Christian mission in the world today. The author sees the increasing number of "tentmakers" as one of several positive trends.

Garrison, V. David. *The Nonresidential Missionary.* Monrovia, CA: MARC [Missions Advanced Research Center], 1990.

Outlines what is called "a new strategy" for sending missionaries to countries where legally a missionary cannot gain entry. Provides lists and descriptions of significant "unevangelized peoples," why sending "nonresidential" missionaries is crucial, and how to do it. Includes useful and reproducible tables and maps.

Octavianus, Petrus. "Divine Resources for Frontier Missions." In *New Frontiers in Missions,* ed. Patrick Sookhdeo, 136–145. Grand Rapids: Baker, 1987.

Among other resources, a leader in the Indonesian Missionary Fellowship urges the use of laypersons in the planting of churches.

Starling, Allan. *Peoplesfile Index.* Pasadena, CA: Global Mapping International, 1986. [Global Mapping is now located in Colorado Springs, CO.]

Author describes and demonstrates how a great deal of basic and introductory research on unevangelized people groups can be done in most seminary and Christian college or university libraries.

Verkuyl, Johannes. "Challenges and Hindrances to the Unfinished Task." In *Mission in the Nineteen 90s,* ed. Gerald H. Anderson, James M. Phillips, and Robert T. Coote, 17–19. Grand Rapids, MI: William B. Eerdmans, 1991.

A distinguished Dutch missiologist asks, among other things, why evangelicals and "ecumencials" do not cooperate more to reach the unreached.

Wilson, J. Christy, Jr. "Tentmakers Today, an Update." In *Mission Handbook,* ed. W. Dayton Roberts and John A Siewert, 31–32. Monrovia, CA: MARC, 1989.

Wilson contends that the upsurge of self-supporting Christians going as missionaries to other places and lands is following the example of the Apostle Paul, "who made tents for a living while preaching the gospel throughout the Roman world."

Winter, Ralph D. "Unreached Peoples; What, Where, and Why?" In *New Frontiers in Missions,* ed. Patrick Sookhdeo, 146–159. Grand Rapids: Baker, 1987.

An essay re-stating what Winter has emphasized for more than a decade, namely, the need to communicate the gospel to the unreached, what constitutes "an unreached people group," and some limited suggestions about how it can be done.

THE CASE
Asia Resources, Inc.

The missions committee meeting adjourned for the afternoon, and Doug Murphy was moving toward the door when someone called him. "Doug, could I talk with you a moment?" He turned and saw it was Timothy Lindstrom. Doug had not met Lindstrom personally, but he knew who he was.

"Doug," Lindstrom said, "could we have dinner together tonight? I haven't had the opportunity to know you, and I would like to talk with you about what I am planning to say tomorrow morning." Lindstrom had been introduced that afternoon as the President of Asia Resources, Inc., an agency based in Chicago. ARI, it was said, was organized to get evangelical Christians into China and other countries, especially the republics emerging from the former Soviet Union, to work as bivocational missionaries.

"Uh, yes. I would be glad to eat with you," Doug replied, but he wondered why Tim had singled him out. "Could I ask Lois to join us? She is a former missionary to Tanzania, and we tend to ask many of the same questions."

"Of course," Tim responded. "I'm interested in talking with any former missionary. You were a missionary to Korea, were you not?"

"That's correct," Doug replied. "In fact, we are the two on the committee who have had missionary experience.

"Where would you like to eat, and what time?" Doug asked.

"Could we eat here in the hotel dining room, say at 6:00?"

"Sure, that'll be fine," Doug responded. "Lois may already have plans, but if she can't make it, I'll see you here at six o'clock." Doug turned and walked toward the elevator. He glanced at his watch and noted that it was nearly five o'clock.

The Missions Committee

A year earlier, a number of individuals and churches in Doug's denomination, all Evangelical Methodists, decided to begin a new missions program. Their reasons were several and resulted from a growing dissatisfaction with the church's bureaucracy and particularly with the board of mission. Doug and fourteen others had been asked to be a working committee to bring recommendations regarding what the congregations could do to chart a new course in missions.

The committee had met three months earlier to organize itself, but all the members could not be present. This was their first full meeting, and the announced purpose was to finalize their mission statement and discuss the direction they would move. Doug was somewhat surprised that Frank Crawford, the chairperson, had invited two non-members of the committee to attend this meeting as consultants. One, David Lucas, was a well known and respected former administrator in the denomination's mission board who had recently accepted a position in a university. The second was Timothy Lindstrom, introduced by Lucas as the President of Asia Resources, Inc. "Tim is one of the most exciting individuals I have ever met," Lucas declared. "He knows more about getting missionaries into World A than anyone else I know."

Doug understood the reference to World A, but he wondered if others sitting around the table did. Lucas then explained what he meant.

"Let me start with World C. World C represents the part of the world's population that has heard and responded to the gospel, and where there are (and have been for centuries) strong and vibrant churches.

"World B refers to the people who have had opportunities to hear the gospel, but they have not responded. Not only do they have churches planted among them, but missionaries are still there.

"World A, on the other hand, is composed of the 1.2 billion people divided into at least 12,000 people groups where there are no Christian believers and no Christian churches. These 1.2 billion are not exposed to the gospel because for the most part they have no Christians living among them.

"We know there are approximately 150,000 Protestant missionaries working in the world today, and we also know that ninety percent of these missionaries are working in World C and World B where the church is already planted. Less than ten percent of the 150,000 missionaries are working in World A, and less than two percent of this ten percent are working with the 12,000 people groups who have not heard the gospel. These unreached peoples are not going to be reached unless they are targeted and unless a new kind of missionary moves in, lives with them, learns their language, becomes a part of their culture, and begins to understand their values and how these people think.

"If you are going to recommend something new to your churches, then why not concentrate on World A? It is a field ready for harvesting. And if you are going to consider targeting World A, then you need to hear what Tim Lindstrom has to say."

Lucas spoke with passion, and Doug sensed that the members of the committee were impressed.

Frank Crawford thanked Lucas for his comments, announced they would hear Lindstrom the next morning, and turned to some routine items that the committee needed to consider. This took about fifteen minutes after which Crawford declared that the committee would reconvene at eight o'clock that evening. Someone led in a closing prayer and the meeting adjourned. It was then that Tim Lindstrom approached Doug about having dinner together that evening.

Call to Lois Harrison

When Doug got to his room, he picked up the phone and called the hotel operator. "Could you connect me with Lois Harrison's room, please?"

The phone rang twice and Lois answered.

"Lois, this is Doug. As I was leaving the meeting just now, Tim Lindstrom stopped me and asked if I could have dinner with him tonight. He said he would like to brief me on what he is going to say in the morning. I told him I could, but that I would like to ask you to join us. He said that would be fine. Do you have plans?"

"No," Lois said. "I was hoping to find someone to eat with when I go down in a little while."

"Well, why don't you join us?"

"I'll be glad to. What do you think Lindstrom wants?" Lois asked.

"I'm not sure. I was surprised he asked me. I suppose when Frank introduced me as a former missionary and said I had experience in Asia, Tim thought it would be good to talk. He may be wanting support for what he is going to say tomorrow."

"Do you have any idea what he is going to say?" Lois asked.

"No. I only know what we heard this afternoon when he was introduced. You know as much as I do."

"What time are you going to meet?" Lois inquired.

"At six."

"I'll meet you in the lobby," she said.

"Fine. See you there."

Dinner with Timothy Lindstrom

Shortly after six o'clock Lois, Tim, and Doug were shown to a table in a quiet corner of the dining room. After they had eaten, Tim began to talk about his ideas and his work. He repeated some of the remarks David Lucas had made that afternoon about World A, and then Tim said, "You are aware, Doug, that only one percent of the $1.2 billion dollars given annually by U.S. churches for missions is spent in World A."

"I did not know the precise figure," Doug responded, "but I am not surprised. Most denominations are like us, I think. They tend to keep sending missionaries to countries where we have had work a long time."

"Exactly," Tim said. "But I see your group in a unique and very enviable position. You are not locked into a long tradition or an established program. You can begin something absolutely new by focusing on World A. This will galvanize the churches. Moreover, your young people will respond. They are looking for strategic opportunities to get involved in missions. They're asking, 'How can we be a part of God's long-term plan for the world?' "

Tim went on to say that by selecting four or five projects, targeting four or five unreached people groups, the churches would be challenged, and young people would step forward to do something different.

"Pick four cities, for example, and four people groups who live in those cities. Enlist four couples, or even four singles who will commit themselves to study the language of those people groups. Set aside $125,000 for the four couples on the condition that they will learn the language, go live in those cities, and begin to work with the designated unreached people group."

"You mentioned one hundred twenty-five thousand dollars." Doug asked, "Do you mean per couple or what?"

"No," Tim responded. "That would be for the four couples to do language study."

"What languages are you talking about?" Lois inquired.

"It depends on what people groups you target. But I am talking about languages such as Russian, Arabic, Mandarin, Cantonese, or Hindi. These languages would open the door to a large number of unreached people groups. Fund the language learning for the couples on the condition that they covenant to work long-term with the people group selected. You can give them all the training they need for one hundred twenty-five thousand."

"What countries are you are referring to where these four couples would go?" Doug queried.

"China, India, or one of the republics of the former Soviet Union such as Kyrgyzstan, Uzbekistan, or Azerbaijan," Tim answered.

"How would you get them into these countries as missionaries?" Lois asked.

"We don't send them in as missionaries," Tim replied. "They go in as business people."

This last statement was unexpected and somewhat unsettling to Doug, but he was not sure why. He made no comment. It was almost time for the committee to reconvene, and he knew that Tim would be making a more complete presentation the next morning.

The meeting that evening was devoted to working on the committee's mission statement, but Doug found it difficult to concentrate on that task. His mind kept going back to what Tim Lindstrom had said at dinner.

When they adjourned about ten o'clock, Doug asked Lois to go with him to get something to drink. They sat down in the coffee shop and began to discuss what Timothy Lindstrom had said to them that evening. They agreed that he was an energetic, persuasive individual. "What he said," Lois added, "was certainly challenging. But what do you think he meant when he said, 'We won't send them in as missionaries. We'll send them in as business people?' "

"I'm not sure," Doug answered. "Nor am I sure why it is troubling to me."

"Me either," Lois whispered. "I guess we will know more in the morning."

The Presentation: Asia Resources, Inc.

When David Lucas presented Tim Lindstrom the next morning, he told the group more about Tim's background. He said Lindstrom was born and reared in Wisconsin, had gone to the University of Illinois on a football scholarship in the early 1960s, and while in Urbana had been converted and baptized into an evangelical church. David went on to say that Tim had pursued a career in business, later earning a Masters in Business Administration, and had worked for the U.S. Electric Corporation for nearly twenty years. When China began to open, Tim was sent there by U.S. Electric as their chief sales representative. He and his wife lived in Nanjing for five years. "Incidentally," David added, "Tim's wife is Taiwanese." He paused momentarily and then concluded,

> "Four years ago Tim resigned from U.S. Electric and founded his own company, Asia Resources, Inc. It is a company specifically dedicated to the development of business opportunities in China—and now in the republics of the former Soviet Union as well—and to the placement of international personnel, evangelical Christians, in these countries. Officially they go as business people, but really they are bivocational missionaries. You are going to be surprised and excited by what he says."

Tim's presentation that morning was virtually the same that he had made the previous evening to Lois and Doug, but he added two or three things. First, he handed out photocopies of several pages from a recently published book,[5] a list of "the thirty least evangelized countries," and a second list of "the fifty least evangelized cities." As the committee studied the lists, Tim said they could pick almost any of the cities and know that there are people groups there who have never heard the gospel.

"Once the couples you choose are committed to learning the language of the people," he said, "and once they are prepared to go live there among them, we can send them as business people and they can be completely self-supporting. There will be no need for you to have to continue to provide support for them."

"How is that?" someone asked.

"Because they can make enough money to support themselves. For example," Tim continued, "last year my company did over $8 million worth of business in one single Chinese city.

"How did we do it? We sold them compact fluorescent lamps, and these new lights have saved them so many kilowatts, so much electrical energy that they have canceled plans to build a new power plant."

---

5. V. David Garrison, *The Nonresidential Missionary* (Monrovia, CA: MARC, 1990).

Tim then began to talk about a particular congregation in Denver and how he was working directly with them to send one of their couples to "a restricted-access nation." Also, he said, "some wealthy individuals in this congregation along with some other interested parties are helping us establish a capital venture fund for financing entrepreneurial businesses in various restricted-access nations." As he spoke he handed a stack of booklets to Frank Crawford to distribute to the committee. When Doug received a copy he saw that it was a corporate prospectus dated June 15, 1991. The name of the corporation was "Empowerment International Venture Capital Fund, Inc."

Tim said little more about the Fund and began to respond to various questions. Doug glanced through the prospectus. He felt that the opening statement was clear:

Empowerment International Venture Capital Fund, Inc. (the Company) is proposed to be formed as an Illinois corporation. The objective of the Company as defined by the Organizers is as follows:

We shall be an international venture capital fund which seeks to capitalize business among "unreached people groups," with the goal of achieving both financial returns and strategic Kingdom impact.

The prospectus stated that the initial amount of capital needed was to be raised in subscriptions of $300,000 to $500,000. Minimum individual investments were $25,000. "Each business started will require approximately $50,000 in financial assistance." As required by law, the prospectus clearly spelled out the risk factors in such investments.

As Tim continued to respond to questions, Doug suddenly realized why the idea of sending people into China as business representatives was bothering him. He remembered a book he had read several years earlier. He could not remember the name of the book, just the idea.[6] He could not recall any specifics, but he did remember the author's emphasis on how, especially in China and Japan, American missionary and business interests—antithetical, one would have thought—early in the twentieth century became interdependent and mutually beneficial, and how often the fate of the two were linked by those who were doing business in Asia. He also remembered what he had heard when he and his wife were in language school, how Chinese Christians were accused of being lackeys of the "foreign devils" and the general resentment of the people toward western businesses prior to the Communist revolution.

As he was reflecting on this he became aware of and was startled by the committee's response to what Tim had said. One member, a woman who had retired after working for many years in the personnel office of the

---

6. After he returned home he found the book. It was James Reed's *The Missionary Mind and American East Asia Policy, 1911–1915* (Cambridge: Harvard University Press, 1983).

denomination's mission board, said, "I think this is one of the most exciting things that is happening in missions today."

Another, a medical doctor from Ohio, addressed the chairperson. "I want to thank you, Frank, for having the foresight to bring Tim here today."

Ken Anderson, the son of missionaries working in Indonesia, added, "I like this. I think we would have a tremendous response. Young people are looking for new models."

Because of where he was seated Doug could not see Lois. He wondered what she was thinking and if she was going to say something.

At that moment Frank Crawford said, "Doug, you've been a missionary. What do you think about Tim's proposal?"

STUDY QUESTIONS

1. There is a large number of individuals involved in this case. Who are the principal characters about whom you can give some important facts and make some judgments?

2. Explain the background of the new mission program and the committee of which Doug Murphy is a member.

3. Timothy Lindstrom makes a presentation to the committee based on his description of World A, B, and C. What does Lindstrom mean, and how is this depiction related to the work of the committee?

3. How do various members of the committee respond when Tim makes his presentation?

4. Doug is obviously troubled by what he has heard. Why? Should he speak up? If so, what should he say?

5. What is your response to Tim's proposal?

SUGGESTED BIBLICAL TEXTS FOR REFLECTION

Matthew 6:19–21. Jesus, in his "sermon on the mount," warns about accumulation of wealth, concluding, "For where your treasure is, there your heart will be also."

Mark 6:6–12. Jesus sends out the twelve with specific instructions, including the prohibition not to take anything with them, "no bread, no beggar's bag, no money in your pockets." (See also Luke 10:1–12, the sending out of the seventy-two.)

Luke 16:1–13. The parable of the astute and calculating trustee. This is one of the more difficult of Jesus' stories to interpret. Note especially verse 13.

Acts 20:32–35. Paul speaks to the church leaders of the church in Ephesus and recounts his ministry among them concluding with an otherwise "lost beatitude" attributed to Jesus, "It is more blessed to give than to receive."

1 Corinthians 9:1–27. The rights and responsibilities of an apostle or missionary. Though some N.T. scholars question the Pauline authorship of the pastoral epistles (1 & 2 Timothy and Titus), Paul or whoever wrote the letter employs several provocative metaphors of a loyal solider, an athlete, and a farmer. Of the soldier, the writer says, "A soldier on active duty wants to please his commanding officer and so does not get mixed up in the affairs of civilian life" (v. 4).

1 Thessalonians 2:7–9 and 2 Thessalonians 3:7–10. The Apostle Paul reminds the church at Thessalonica that while he was with them, he supported himself by his own labor.

"I WAS IN PRISON . . ."

Osamu and Hisoka Endo, Japanese Christian missionaries living and working in Irian Jaya, feel they should visit two Irian Jayan friends who have been arrested and imprisoned by Indonesian military authorities for subversive activities. Though the missionaries believe that as a part of their Christian duty they should go openly to the prison and visit their imprisoned friends, they are aware that to identify themselves as acquaintances of the incarcerated couple would not only be construed as a political act but, because Osamu and Hisoka are foreigners, they would be suspected of complicity and perhaps be arrested too. At the very least, their future in the country would be jeopardized.

CONTEXT
Gospel and Politics in Irian Jaya

This case study, one of several I have written in the past twenty years on missionaries and politics, deals with a complex set of circumstances involving not a European or North American missionary couple, but rather a Japanese Christian family who have come to Irian Jaya under a Korean missionary agency. To deal in any sense adequately with the issues involved, one must know something about the history of Irian Jaya and its people.

Missionaries and Politics

Though overt political involvement of missionaries working in lands not their own may strike some observers as questionable, inappropriate, or even hazardous, from the fourth until the middle of the twentieth century, engagement in activity that was political or at least quasi-political was commonplace. The reason was two-fold. First, missionaries routinely thought of themselves as representatives both of their church and of their country. Second, it was difficult for some and impossible for others to remain silent in the face of what was patently unjust and unconscionable. Sometimes missionaries spoke out against the policies of their own governments, as did Bartolomé de Las Casas (1484–1566) who assailed verbally and in writing the so-called Laws of the Indies and the Spanish colonial oppression of the Amerindians. Other missionaries, meanwhile, condemned customs and traditional practices of the

225

people they had come to evangelize, practices the missionaries believed should be prohibited by law. William Carey (1761–1834), for example, became a leading voice in the campaign to abolish *Sati* or suttee, the burning alive of Hindu widows on their husbands' pyres. The intrepid founder of the Society of Missionaries of Africa, better known as the White Fathers, Charles M. A. Cardinal Lavigerie (1825–1892), without hesitating, sided with or against his government, depending on the issue. But his charge to those going out as missionaries under his Society is memorable. Not only were the White Fathers to work for the Kingdom of God, Lavigerie declared, "*Nous travaillons aussi pour la France*," that is, they would also be working for France—a spirit and attitude, incidentally, not limited to the White Fathers or to Roman Catholics.[1]

The freedom for missionaries to take political positions in host countries became largely a thing of the past with the demise of Western colonialism. Likewise, patronage and protection of Christian missionaries by their home governments—once a given—is no longer practical or in most cases possible. In fact, for a missionary to speak out in favor of or be identified with any individual, group, movement, or position that a host government disapproves is likely to result in the missionary's deportation, detention, or worse. Since the 1960s, therefore, many mission sending agencies have established policies designed to assure "political neutrality" by all of their missionary personnel. The following is an example.

> The "To All the World" Mission Board maintains a stance of political neutrality in nations where its representatives serve and is concerned for persons regardless of their political conviction or involvements. Its personnel are committed to work for the spiritual and humanitarian welfare of persons on all sides during times of crisis and war.
>
> Missionaries of this Board are to maintain political neutrality in foreign political matters and refrain from actions or statements which might endanger other missionaries or national Christians or jeopardize the witness of Christ in any part of the world.

Few would disagree with the purpose of this regulation, but several questions immediately come to mind. Is authentic political neutrality possible in our kind of world? Should a missionary remain silent and refuse to protest obvious instances of injustice, particularly when an oppressive government interprets silence as de facto approval? Should maintaining a missionary presence in a country, regardless of what is taking place, be the determining factor or ultimate objective? Who is in the best position to decide on what a missionary should or should not do in ambiguous situations? Finally, can and does a policy of "neutrality" become an excuse for doing nothing? These

---

1. David J. Bosch gives a number of examples of Protestants as well as Roman Catholics who assumed that their mission was supposed to benefit the church and their respective homelands. *Transforming Mission* (Maryknoll, NY: Orbis, 1991), 302–313.

are tough questions, and sincere people will disagree about how to respond. Anyone who has ever lived and worked as a missionary will testify that it is not unusual for colleagues to disagree among themselves concerning the proper response. Furthermore, most missionaries have learned that it is less than prudent and it can be precarious to take sides when one is not thoroughly informed about the issues and individuals involved in a political conflict. Having said these things, a few times in life one is confronted with crises when "hunkering down" and saying nothing is simply not a viable option for a disciple of Jesus Christ.

A Brief History of Irian Jaya

The island of New Guinea is a part of the Southeast Asian Archipelago and is located along the Equator less than two hundred miles north of Australia. Politically, it is divided into two areas, the Eastern region known as Papua-New Guinea, and the Western half known as West Irian or Irian Jaya. The people, however, in both areas are mainly Papuan. The western half of the islands, long designated as Netherlands New Guinea, was a former Dutch colony. But the administration of the territory was first turned over to the United Nations, and then on May 1, 1963, to Indonesia. Since that time, Irian Jaya has been—despite intense complaints by the people of oppression at the hands of the Indonesian government forces and a desire for independence—a province of Indonesia.

Hindu and Buddhist influences, almost certainly from India and the Malay peninsula, were apparent in what is now Indonesia at least 2,000 years ago, but today adherents to these faiths are found primarily in Java. Islam was brought to the islands by traders in the fifteenth century, and within a hundred years, it became the principal faith of most of the major island peoples.

Portugal and Spain were the first Western powers to try to gain an economic foothold in the area, but their presence gave way to the Dutch who began colonizing the principal islands in the seventeenth century. By the middle of the eighteenth century, Dutch hegemony was assured, but they were unable to extend their control to the more remote and smaller of the 17,000 islands until the early decades of the present century.

During World War II the Japanese drove the Dutch out of the East Indies, occupying and dominating the area from 1942 to the end of the War in 1945. As soon as it was clear than the Japanese would have to give up control of the countries they had overrun, the Netherlands moved swiftly to regain their mastery over the islands. They encountered, however, a people unwilling to submit again to the yoke of colonialism, and despite repressive measures, Indonesian resistance intensified and the Dutch were forced to capitulate. Lacking international support, the Netherlands yielded and formally recognized Indonesia as an independent republic on December 27, 1949. The Dutch, however, refused to cede their control over West Irian whose people ethnically, culturally, and religiously were unlike the rest of Indonesia. Though geographically close, the history of Western New Guinea had taken a different course.

Portuguese explorers first sighted the western tip of the island of New Guinea in 1511, but a decade and a half passed before one of them, Jorge de Meneses, landed. Then a Spaniard, Inigo Ortiz de Retez, claimed the island for the King of Spain in 1546, and called it Novo Guine because the people reminded him of those he had seen on the West African coast of Guinea.

A British naval officer, Lt. James Hayes, attempted to establish a colony in 1793 but was unsuccessful, making it possible for the Dutch to lay claim to the western half of the island in 1828. European and Australian Protestant missionaries began arriving in the area later in the century, and the peoples—in contrast to the Indonesians—became for the most part Christians. For these and other reasons, the Dutch justified their refusal to relinquish West New Guinea, but—as is described in the case study below—internal unrest among the western New Guinean people and growing international pressure eventually resulted in the Dutch turning control of the area over to the United Nations. In 1963, however, the U.N. withdrew, conveying West Irian to Indonesia on the condition that a plebiscite would soon be held to allow the Irian Jayanese to decide for themselves whether they would continue as a part of Indonesia or be a completely independent nation.

Irian Jaya is comprised of 159,375 square miles (412,781 square kilometers). From West to East it measures some 3,200 miles (5,150 kilometers), and 1,100 miles (1,800 kilometers) from North to South. The population is relatively small and unevenly distributed, averaging less than ten people per square mile. Until the twentieth century, the interior, especially the mountain areas, was virtually unknown to the outside world, and the people were unaware of the rapid technological and scientific changes taking place. In many respects, much of the region remained in a kind of stone age.

Roman Catholic missionaries first arrived in New Guinea in 1547, but their presence was sporadic, their numbers never large, and their influence insignificant. Not until 1881, when the Sacred Heart missionaries began arriving, did the Church commence its remarkable growth and expansion. Still, in the western part of the island, the Church is relatively small.

Protestant missionaries representing four different denominations began coming to New Guinea during the final decades of the nineteenth century— first, the British Congregationalists sent out by the London Missionary Society in 1871, then Australian Methodists four years later, German Lutherans in 1886, and finally Australian Anglicans in 1891. Other missionary groups followed somewhat later, including the Assemblies of God, Baptists, Plymouth Brethren, and Seventh Day Adventists. The earliest interdenominational faith missionaries to begin work in the area were the Unevangelized Fields Missions in 1931. Not until after World War II did increasing numbers of other faith missions take interest in New Guinea. Missionaries representing the Australian South Seas Evangelical Mission arrived in 1948, and the New Tribes Mission came the following year.

The first Protestant mission to send representatives to what is now West Irian was the Utrecht Missionary Union (Netherlands) whose missionaries arrived in 1861.[2] After twenty-five years of arduous effort but discouraging results, they had succeeded in baptizing no more than twenty converts. Missionaries of the German Neuendettelsau Mission who began evangelizing in the eastern regions of the island, in contrast, were much more successful, largely due to the ideas and methods of Christian Keysser who lived and worked in New Guinea from 1899 until 1921. Charles W. Forman recounts the history of Keysser's efforts.

Keysser's method was based on a recognition of the integrity of the village or tribal community. The community should act as a whole, not seriatim in its individuals, when accepting Christianity. Its unity should be maintained and its culture, while purified at points, should be essentially preserved. The leaders of the congregation would be those who are leaders in the community, not trained and ordained ministers brought in from the outside. There would, in fact, be no ordained ministry. A consciousness of missionary responsibility should develop within the congregation so that it would send out its most dedicated members to carry the Christian faith to other peoples and villages.[3]

Rejecting the traditional missionary practice, Keysser insisted that these Papuan missionaries be responsible to the local congregations which had sent them out, not to himself nor to any other European. As Forman notes, conversion of whole villages was not unusual in Oceania, but "Keysser carried through the implications of this communal solidarity more fully and effectively than anyone else."[4] Though his innovative approach was criticized and resisted by his own colleagues for a while, eventually they could not ignore the effectiveness of what was happening. Thousands of indigenous missionaries were being sent out by the local congregations, and tens of thousands of converts were being made.

According to a leader in the Evangelical Christian Church in West Irian in 1974, this denomination's congregations then numbered 876 with approximately 300,000 members. Moreover, he claimed, eighty percent of the area's two million population were professing Christians.[5]

---

2. In an interview with a writer for the *International Review of Mission,* a Protestant church leader from West Irian said that the first missionaries to arrive in the area were "two Germans, Heldring and Grossner," who came from Berlin in 1855, having been sent by the Berlin Missionary Society. But, he added, they came not as missionaries, but as workers. "From Stone Age to Jet Age," 63 (July 1974): 366. F. U. Kamma said the same earlier. "Messianic Movements in Western New Guinea." *International Review of Missions* 41 (1952): 148.

3. *The Island Churches of the South Pacific* (Maryknoll, NY: Orbis, 1982), 59–60.

4. Ibid., 60.

5. "From Stone Age to Jet Age," 367, 368.

FOR FURTHER STUDY

Mission history of New Guinea

Barrett, David B., ed. *World Christian Encyclopedia.* New York: Oxford University Press, 1982.

Contains recent data on the number of denominations, their relative strength, and the multiple endeavors in which they are engaged (381–388 for references to West Irian, and 552-555 for Papua).

Ellenberger, John D. "Evangelistic Outreach in Irian Jaya." In *Church Growth in the Third World,* ed. R. E. Hedlund, 279–282. Bombay: Gospel Literature Services, 1977.

Terse comments on the growth of tribal churches and what a particular group should do when nearly all their people are professing Christians.

Forman, Charles W. *The Island Churches of the South Pacific.* Maryknoll, NY: Orbis, 1982.

Primarily helpful in the account of the work with the Papuans, especially the contribution of Christian Keysser.

Kamma, F. U. "Messianic Movements in Western New Guinea." *International Review of Missions* 41 (1952):148–160.

Though dated, the author summarizes the history of Christian missions in Western New Guinea, the role of myth and ritual, the impact of the Japanese invasion and occupation, and the various messianic movements and their significance. Concludes with a brief discussion of outside influences, both mission and government.

Latourette, Kenneth Scott. *The Great Century.* Vol. 5 of "A History of the Expansion of Christianity." New York: Harper, 1943.

Provides the background for understanding the history of the multiple missionary societies that sent representatives to the "Dutch East Indies" as well as the notable missionaries who labored to bring the gospel and plant the church (e.g., 240–246).

Mumper, Sharon E. "Resettlement Program Could Pave the Way for Outreach Among Indonesian Muslims." *Christianity Today* 29 (March 15, 1985): 37–39.

Describes the plans of missionaries and national Christian leaders to "take advantage of ministry opportunities" among the Muslims who are being moved into Irian Jaya by the Indonesian government. Author recognizes that the Irianese who are struggling for political independence do not welcome these transmigrants.

Neill, Stephen. *A History of Christian Missions.* New York: Penguin Books, 1986.

A concise description of the early Protestant missionary efforts in New Guinea (299–300).

Niklaus, Robert. "Irian Jaya: Resettlement Evangelism." *Evangelical Missions Quarterly* 21 (July 1985): 308–309.

A brief news report about the efforts to evangelize Indonesians being resettled in Irian Jaya.

Sunda, James. *Church Growth in the Central Highlands of West New Guinea.* Lucknow: Lucknow Publishing House, 1963.

A brief (51p.) description of the growth of Christian churches in a region almost unknown to Westerners until after World War II.

Wick, Robert S. *God's Invasion. The Story of Fifty Years of Christian and Missionary Alliance Missionary Work in Irian Jaya.* Camp Hill, PA: Christian Publications, 1990.

Though captivating reading and helpful in terms of early mission history, maps, and photographs, the overall military imagery, such as, "field of battle," "scouting reports," "God's commandos," and the "battles" described are disconcerting.

Winburn, Thomas T. "Trusteeship for Irian." *The Christian Century* 79 (January 24, 1962): 102.

Winburn says that Sukarno's threat to extend Indonesia's control over West New Guinea is a power ploy, and that the two countries have little in common. Besides, the people of West New Guinea (Irian Jaya) have the right to self-rule.

———. "The Irian Settlement." *The Christian Century* 79 (September 5, 1962): 1059.

The agreement of 1962, the writer notes, may be a means of frustrating communist purposes, but President Sukarno is using the Irian question to "divert attention from his own internal problems." The agreement, furthermore, is not in West New Guinea's best interest.

Yost, Jim. "Development Work Can Hinder Church Growth." *Evangelical Missions Quarterly* 20 (October 1984): 352–360.

A Regions Beyond Missionary Union representative who has lived in Irian Jaya for seven years says the tribal churches are "falling into a trap" of trying to meet physical needs. Community development, he insists, that is out of proportion to meeting spiritual needs is inhibiting church growth. Donald A. McGavran's research on this matter is confirmed, the author declares.

Political conflict in Irian Jaya

Materials describing the struggle of the Western New Guinea people for independence is extensive, but much of it is not readily available except in major libraries. Listed below are some of the sources utilized for the writing of this case study.

Banks, Arthur S., ed. *Political Handbook of the World: 1988*. Binghamton, NY: CSA Publications, 1988.

Contains a useful one-page (272) analysis of the history of the Indonesian "annexed territories," including Irian Jaya and East Timor.

"Cry of Distress from West New Guinea. Most Urgent Appeal II to H.E. Secretary-General of the United Nations." September 19, 1967.

A succession of appeals with documentation to various governments, the United Nations, and the International Court of Justice in The Hague to investigate the killings of Papuan people by the Indonesian military (37 pages).

Henderson, William. *West New Guinea. The Dispute and Its Settlement*. West Orange, NJ: American-Educational Exchange, Seton Hall University Press, 1973.

A history and analysis of the struggle, including the complete text of the agreement between the Republic of Indonesia and the Netherlands concerning West New Guinea (West Irian). August 15, 1962.

"A People's Preparation for Its Freedom Brought to Nought by Indonesia's Blackmail Policy." New York, NY: The Freedom Committee of West Papua/West Nieuw-Guinea, June 20, 1968.

A chronological description of events leading up to the declaration of independence by the West Irianese in 1971.

Provisional Constitution of the Republic of West Papua.

A twenty-page document of one hundred twenty-nine articles, but without date or place of publication. The constitution is stated to take effect on the "Day of the Proclamation," that is, July 1, 1971.

Recent Situation of West Irian. Inquiry into New Guinean Problem. Asiatic Problem Research Society, August 5, 1963.

A thirty-four page document without place of publication, but evidently written by Japanese and favorable to the West Irian position. The last two pages contain comments particularly relevant to this case study. President Sukarno is said to have given a talk to "the high Japanese officials and powerful civilians during the East Asia War," and he told them, "Borneo is large enough to involve whole Japan [sic.] and is ready to welcome 1,000,000 to 2,000,000 Japanese at any time." The writer of "Recent Situation" doubts the authenticity of this statement, but then concludes: "It is true that there are pro-Indonesian agitators among the Japanese who make irresponsible remarks. [But] Sukarno does not open West Irian to Japan as the Dutch Government did. West Irian is going to be turned into a large prison and Papuans are imprisoned by Indonesians" (34, 35).

Rivas, M. P., ed. *International Review of Mission* 63 (July 1974).

A special issue on Indonesia with several articles related to the religious and political situation in Irian Jaya. "From Stone Age to Jet Age: A Visit to Irian Jaya, four Conversations," is a series of interviews with a Protestant church leader (362–370), a German layman working as a missionary in Irian Jaya (370–377), a member of the provincial parliament of Irian Jaya (383–385), and with the Roman Catholic bishop of Jayapura (377–382). A valuable resource.

Shenon, Philip. "In Isolation, Papua New Guinea Falls Prey to Foreign Bulldozers." *The New York Times* (June 5, 1994): A1, 14.

A searing description of the economic exploitation of what has been described as "the last rain forest," and the clash of cultures, false promises, and corruption that follow.

Vatikiotis, Michael. "The Centre Takes All." *Far Eastern Economic Review* (30 November 1989): 32–34.

A news article states that while the economic development of Irian Jaya has been remarkable since it was "integrated" with Indonesia, the Irian Jayans have hardly benefitted at all. Included also are comments about why the Free Papua Movement (OPM) continues.

———. "Resettlement Squeeze." *Far Eastern Economic Review* (30 November 1989): 34–35.

Vatikiotis verifies the claims of the Irian Jayan rebels that settlers, especially Javanese, are being brought in by the Indonesian government discriminating against and displacing the indigenous Irianese. Includes comments by some Christian missionaries.

"West New Guinea—One of the World's Last Strongholds of Colonialism." Press release of the Provisional Government of the Republic of West-Papua, New Guinea, n.d. Available through the Buro Informasi R.P.B., P.O. Box 625, Dakar, Senegal.

Though clearly a presentation of the conflict between the Indonesian government and the rebel movement in Irian Jaya written from the perspective of the West-Papuans, this is a concise review of the political history of Irian Jaya from the arrival of the Western colonial powers, through independence from the Dutch in 1949, the intervention of the U.S. and the United Nations in 1962, until the declaration of independence on the part of the Western New Guineans in 1971.

THE CASE
"I was in Prison . . ."

Almost a week had passed since Osamu and Hisoka Endo first learned that Matthew and Keiko had been arrested. Osamu was now saying to Hisoka that he felt strongly that he should visit them. Irian Jaya, however, was not the Endos' country. In fact, though they were working there as missionaries, they had entered Irian Jaya on visitors' visas. Thus to visit political prisoners would not only jeopardize their work, Hisoka replied, but such an act would likely have an adverse effect on their attempt to secure a long-term visa.

The Making of Missionaries

The Endos, Osamu and Hisoka, had been in Irian Jaya only fourteen months. Before coming they had tried for more than four years to get permission for a visa as agricultural missionaries. Though the wait had been long, it was brief in comparison with the preparation they felt they had before deciding to come to Indonesia.

Hisoka was originally from Okinawa and had been a Christian since her early teens. Though reared in a home where both parents were ancestor worshipers, she had attended the Okinawa Christian College, an institution sponsored by the United Church of Christ in Japan, and had graduated in 1972. Soon thereafter she secured employment with a company in Osaka as a lingerie designer and moved there to work. It was in Osaka that she met Osamu who worked for her company in the evenings as a security guard. The two of them became acquainted at a company party, and they began seeing each other shortly thereafter. Hisoka learned that Osamu had a degree in agriculture from the National University, and his principal job was with the Japanese ministry of agriculture.

There was little doubt in Hisoka's mind that Osamu's interest in her was more than mere friendship, but dissatisfaction with her job and homesickness led her to resign and return to Okinawa only three months after meeting Osamu and less than two years after coming to Osaka.

A month after her return, Osamu came to Okinawa to see her. He stayed five days and attended church with her for the first time. She knew, given the fact that his father was a Buddhist priest, that it was no small thing for

---

This case was written by Ryoko Taki of the Pan Pacific Mission Fellowship and Alan Neely.

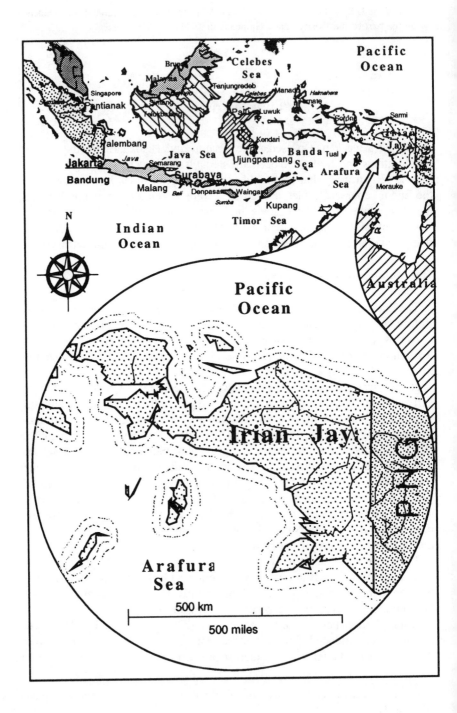

Osamu to enter a Christian church. But before he left the following Wednesday he made two dramatic announcements. First, he told Hisoka he wanted to marry her, and also he would begin attending a Christian church as soon as he arrived in Osaka again. Everything had developed so quickly, Hisoka said, that she was unsure about her feelings. But she agreed to continue writing to him without making any further commitments. Osamu's letters nonetheless reiterated his love for her and indicated he was preparing to become a Christian.

In July 1974, three months after his first visit to Okinawa, Osamu came again, this time to press Hisoka for an answer. They talked for many hours about the differences in their cultures, their understanding of Christianity, and the difficulties they would likely encounter with their parents. Finally, the day before Osamu was scheduled to return to Japan, Hisoka agreed to marriage. As they anticipated, Hisoka's parents strenuously objected. But during the next several months, both sets of parents reluctantly accepted the fact that Osamu and Hisoka would marry.

In the fall of the same year Osamu was baptized. Shortly thereafter, in January 1975, he resigned his post with the ministry of agriculture and moved to Okinawa. He quickly secured work in an orphanage sponsored by the Christian Children's Fund, and he and Hisoka were married the following October.

Their lives were fairly routine, except for the birth of three children, until 1982 when Dr. Manabu Sato came to Okinawa and spoke in the Endos' church. Sato was pastor of an evangelical congregation in Tokyo, one that was part of the Church of Christ in Japan, and he was also head of the Japanese branch of the Pan Pacific Mission Fellowship, a mission agency based in Korea. Dr. Sato related his life story and how he had been a Japanese sailor during World War II, and since that time he struggled with the fact that the Japanese had killed many Asian people during the war. He concluded saying he had pledged to do what he could as an individual to make restitution for the harm the Japanese had done. Restitution for him, he explained, included sending Christian missionaries to other Asian nations.

"In 1980 I was in Indonesia," Sato said, "specifically in the eastern-most territory of Irian Jaya. The Evangelical Church there begged me to find someone who is an expert in agriculture and send that person to help them." Sato explained that the Church, the *Gereja Kristen Injili Irian Jaya,* had an experimental farm located near the border with Papua New Guinea, but they had no one who could administer the project.

Sato's visit proved to be a pivotal experience for Osamu and Hisoka. "There is no question," she says, "that Dr. Sato's words made a profound impression on both Osamu and me. Yet, we talked little about it. We already had three children, and becoming missionaries seemed out of the question. Six months later, however, Osamu read a small article in an Okinawa newspaper about a terrible flood in Irian Jaya and how many people were starving to death. We talked a great deal after that about whether we should volunteer to go to Indonesia. One day Osamu said he was going to write to Dr. Sato saying that we would be willing to go if the Pan Pacific Mission would send us. The reply we received from Dr. Sato was very encouraging, and we began the paper work to prepare to go."

The Endos learned, however, that it would be far more difficult to go as missionaries than they anticipated. Two years passed and they were unable to get a visa from the Indonesian government. Then in 1984 Osamu and Dr. Sato visited Irian Jaya, and later Osamu and Hisoka went to Tokyo in an attempt to secure a visa. Two more years passed, and they made two additional trips to the Indonesian embassy in Tokyo. The response was always the same: "We cannot issue you a visa without the approval of the minister of immigration in Jakarta. He has not given us that approval."

Finally in 1988 the Endos proposed to Dr. Sato that they be allowed to go to Irian Jaya on visitors' visas. "Surely we can get long-term visas when the government sees the kind of work we are doing." After several weeks of conferring with the mission office in Korea, Dr. Sato told the Endos to proceed.

The Irian Jayan Independence Movement

The Indonesian embassy never mentioned any specific reason for not granting the Endos a visa, but soon after their arrival in Irian Jaya in August 1988 they began to discern what they thought was the reason. They learned of the tension between many Irian Jayans and the government of Indonesia. Most of the information about the problem they received from Matthew and Keiko Yapem whom they had met on the plane from Japan. Matthew was Irian Jayan and Keiko was Japanese, and their home was only thirty kilometers from the farm where Osamu, Hisoka, and their children lived and worked.

During the fall of 1988 the Endos and the Yapems visited each other's homes regularly, and Keiko began to tell them of Matthew's involvement in the Irian Jayan independence movement. According to an international agreement, Keiko explained, Western New Guinea was relinquished by the Dutch to United Nations trusteeship in 1962. The following year the territory was placed under Indonesian control pending an "act of free choice" before the end of 1969 by the "West Irian" people, as Indonesia began to refer to the area. The West Irians, however, were to learn later that this "act of free choice" was not interpreted by the Jakarta government as a popular plebiscite. Rather it meant, according to President Sukarno, a convening of leaders from eight regional areas who would vote on whether the territory was to become a part of Indonesia.

As the time for the "act of free choice" neared, the Free Papua Organization or OPM (*Organisasai Papua Merdeka*) began to agitate for West Irian independence, and their representatives were harassed and suppressed, sometimes brutally, by Indonesian army factions stationed in West Irian. Then following the "act of free choice" in which about 1,000 tribal chiefs and urban residents in a *musjawarah*—a Javanese word for group discussion aimed at reaching a consensus—agreed to continue as a part of Indonesia, acts of violence protesting the decision were instigated by the OPM. By 1971 their forces were in control of approximately 15% of the territory, principally in the eastern sector adjacent to Papua New Guinea, and the OPM declared themselves to be the "Provisional Revolutionary Government of West Papua New Guinea."

Since that time, according to Keiko, there have been sporadic clashes between the "terrorists," as the OPM are called by the Indonesian government, and the Indonesian army. In February 1984 the army launched a broad offensive against the OPM resulting in the flight of hundreds of Irian villagers into Papua New Guinea. Also, the arrest and killing of the Irian intellectual and patriot Arnold Ap in the capital city prison in Jayapura provoked widespread resentment and criticism. "More than 500,000 Irians have been killed by the Indonesian military since they began to govern the territory. The people know only oppression, discrimination, and death," Keiko declared.

Hisoka said to Osamu shortly after this conversation that it was obvious that Matthew as well as Keiko were sympathetic with and possibly involved in OPM activities. Later Keiko would tell them that Matthew was not a member of the OPM. "He advocates non-violence," she insisted. "His only weapon is the Bible."

The Endos were soon to learn from two of the workers on the farm that there was another cause for deep resentment against Indonesia. "Look around you," the two young men said. "See how many people are being brought here from Java as immigrants and how the government is giving them the good land that is being expropriated from us! All the government has to do is accuse a farmer of being a part of the OPM, and he is imprisoned or killed and his land is confiscated and given to some Javanese."

The Flag Raising Incident

Four months later about a hundred Irians gathered at a public playground in Jayapura and staged an independence ceremony that included raising the Irian Jayan flag. They sang their national anthem, declared their independence from Indonesia, and called themselves "citizens of the Republic of West Melanesia." Within hours all the participants were arrested by the military authorities. The Endos also learned from the two young farm workers that Matthew had led the ceremony, he and Keiko had been arrested, and both were put in the military prison at Waena, a town located halfway between the farm and the capital city.

Pondering the Words of Jesus

That night Osamu said to Hisoka, "I feel I should go to the prison and see if there is anything I can do to help Matthew and Keiko." Hisoka understood for she had the same feeling. But she also knew that neither of them could go to the prison and ask to see the Yapems without the Indonesian intelligence being aware of their action. Their missionary agricultural work was just beginning, and the children appeared to be adjusting well to their school and environment. To show friendship to persons identified with the OPM would surely be seen by the Indonesian government as a political act, one that would likely prevent the Endos from being allowed to remain in Irian Jaya. Prudence would dictate that Osamu and Hisoka not try to see their friends, at least not now. But Hisoka could not erase from her mind the words of Jesus, "I was in prison and you visited me."

STUDY QUESTIONS

1. Can you summarize the political developments in West New Guinea or Irian Jaya, particularly as they relate to the events described in this case?

2. What can you recall of the mission history of Irian Jaya? In what important way are the Irian Jayans (Irianese) distinct from most Indonesians?

3. Who are Osamu and Hisoka Endo? Why are they in Irian Jaya and how did they get there?

4. Describe the Endos' relationship with the people in this case who were arrested and imprisoned for political activity.

5. What are the reasons you would offer concerning why Osamu and Hisoka should go to the prison? What are the reasons you feel they should not?

6. Given the circumstances, were you in their place, what would you do? Why?

SUGGESTED BIBLICAL TEXTS FOR REFLECTION

Isaiah 42:1–17. The first Servant Song. Note vs. 6–7, "I have given you as a covenant to the people, a light to the nations, to open the eyes that are blind, to bring out the prisoners from the dungeon, from the prison those who sit in darkness" (NRSV). Compare Luke 4:18–19.

Jeremiah 37:37–21. The prophet Jeremiah is accused of sedition and imprisoned.

Matthew 25:31–46. Jesus describes the final judgment. Note vs. 36 and 43: "I . . . was in prison and you visited me."

Acts 12:1–19. The church experiences increased persecution, but the apostle Peter is freed from jail.

Acts 16:16–34. The experience of the apostles Paul and Silas in the Philippian prison. Significant is the reason for their arrest and incarceration.

APPENDIXES

APPENDIXES

APPENDIX A

Case Studies: What They Are and How to Study Them

The use of the "case method"—as distinguished from case histories commonly used in the medical field—is a means of teaching and learning by the analysis of actual events. It originated in the Harvard Law School in 1870, and was later adopted by virtually all of the law schools in the United States. Rather than memorizing legal principles and theorizing about hypothetical situations, law students were thrust into the analysis of real cases as they were recorded. From the student's analysis of the case, he/she was expected to make well-founded generalizations and to anticipate legal decisions based on sound rules of law.

In 1908 the Harvard Business School began to utilize cases from the business world as the central feature of its educational approach. The study of these business cases was framed so as to prepare the student for managerial positions by developing the skills needed for analyzing a situation and making tough decisions. Again, authentic events and situations were the data used in the writing of the cases. At times it was necessary to disguise the people or companies involved, but the facts were not altered in any way.

It was not until the 1960s that the first systematic attempts were made to employ the case method for the teaching of theology, and then it was only by a very limited number of professors. In 1971, the Association of Theological Schools (ATS) with the financial support of the Sealantic Fund began the Case Study Institute in Cambridge, Massachusetts. Since that time hundreds of cases have been written and used in multiple theological institutions in the United States as well as in other countries. More than three hundred theological professors have been trained in the writing and teaching of cases, and a training program has been expanded to include pastors and lay-leaders for the use of cases at the parish level. The history of the case method in theological education is still being written.

I. What is a Case?

A case is a carefully written description of an actual situation. It may be contemporary or the recounting of an event in history. All of the data which one needs "to enter vicariously into the problem" is provided. According to the Harvard Business School model, a case is seen through the eyes of the one person who must make a crucial decision. Usually the case is left open-ended, that is, the reader is not told what decision was made nor informed as to "how it all ended." The student is expected to study the case and to enter into the experience or dilemma as if he or she were the person making the decision. The basic question becomes therefore: What should I do?

Paul Lawrence put it this way:

> A good case is the vehicle by which a chunk of reality is brought into the classroom to be worked over by the class and the instructor. A good case keeps the class discussion grounded upon some of the stubborn facts that must be faced up to in real-life situations. It is the anchor on academic flights of speculation. It is the record of complex situations that must be literally pulled apart and put together again before the situations can be understood. It is the target for the expression of attitudes and ways of thinking brought into the classroom. To be all these things, a case must essentially represent a good job of reporting ("Preparation of Case Material," *The Case Method of Teaching Human Relations and Administration,* ed. Kenneth R. Andrews, 215. Cambridge, MA: Harvard University Press, 1951).

II. How can a Case Best be Studied?

1. Immerse yourself into the situation described in the case study knowing the details of what happened or is happening.

Ways to do this:

—Write out the cast of persons involved (names, characteristics, statements attributed to them, attitudes revealed, inter-relations, responsibilities, and other facts that aid you in knowing the individuals involved in the case).
—Clarify from whose perspective the case has been written.
—Chart with care the chronology or sequence of events in the case.

2. Analyze the case.

—Identify the basic issues.
—Attempt to anticipate the various possible alternatives available to the decision-maker(s) assuming that each is adequately informed and rational. If only one option is possible, or if everyone agrees as to what decision should be made, the case is flawed. The goal of the case teacher, however, is not to list all of the decisions possible and then let the matter rest. Rather, it is to lead the discussants to take a position as to which decision is best, and then defend their choice(s).
—Ask yourself: What will be the likely results of this or that decision? The likely results should help you decide on the proper course of action.

3. Let the facts of the case and the possibilities suggested begin to ferment in your mind.

—Some people do this by taking a walk or engaging in another kind of physical activity.

—Try to get a feel for what is happening by mulling the case over in your mind.

—You may at this point say to yourself, "But I don't have all the facts. I need more information than the case writer has provided." But the fact is, we never have all the facts nor all the information needed. Furthermore, we will never have all the data. Only God is omniscient. No decision we ever make is based on having full and complete information.

4. Research any materials, factual or theoretical, which can help you to clarify or resolve the issues at stake.

—Let us assume, for example, that the primary issue in a particular case study is interpersonal conflict in a church. A conscientious student will go to the library and read as much as possible about church conflicts. Many excellent resources are available such as: Speed Leas and Paul Kittlaus, *Church Fights* (Westminster, 1973); David Augsburger, *When Caring is Not Enough* (Herald Press, 1983); G. Douglas Lewis, *Resolving Church Conflicts* (Harper & Row, 1981); and John Miller, *The Contentious Community* (Westminster, 1978).

5. Decide on what course of action you would take, i.e., what decision you would make given the information you have available. Sometimes, however, during the discussion of the case you will get new insights and change your view. This is not unusual. Discussion and debate should shed new light on a case. It is a mistake, therefore, for one to cling stubbornly to a position simply because this was her or his initial opinion.

—Be prepared, however, to substantiate and defend your points of view.

—Remember, no decision is free from risk, and there is no single correct solution to a dilemma.

6. Participate in the group discussion by sharing your understanding and insights and by listening carefully to what others see in the case.

—You will have a unique perspective and can make a needed contribution to the discussion. "Don't hide your candle under a basket," and do not be afraid to take a position that is different from that of the majority.

—Think about what you are going to say before speaking; as someone has said, "Get on board before you begin to paddle." Express yourself clearly and concisely, and when possible, document what you say.

—Participating in a group discussion involves more listening than speaking, so listen with care and evaluate what is said objectively and honestly.

—Do not be afraid to express your point of view. The goal of a case study is not consensus but insight and understanding. A good case study provokes divergent points of view.

—Be constructive, not mischievous nor prejudicial in your comments. Help the group to clarify the issues.

—Encourage others to talk by passing the ball and allowing them to score.
—Stay on track. If the group begins to wander or bogs down, try to get them back on the subject.

The goal of a good case study discussion is not to win a debate, but to understand the nature of the problem and make a decision about a course of action that is possible, reasonable, and ethical.

III. What is the Role of the Case Teacher?

1. To write or select a case which is applicable to the course of study.
2. To be prepared and thoroughly familiar with the background and details of the case.
3. To act as a catalyst by probing, recording, and facilitating the class discussion.
4. To supply any data or insight which will stimulate the group thinking rather than creating the kind of relationship whereby the students look to the teacher for "the answers."

As you become familiar with the case study method you will note that learning depends much more on the interchange between students, guided and facilitated by the teacher, than it does upon individual study or information provided by the professor.

Case studies, if they are done well, are a *participatory* method of teaching and learning wherein both the students and the teacher are equally responsible to everyone in the class to prepare well and share openly and honestly their insights and points of view. Conscientious preparation for the class experience and participation in the class discussion are not primarily to assure receiving a good grade, but rather to learn and to facilitate learning for others. When case studies are well prepared and discussed, students will quickly note that case learning like case teaching can be an enlightening and exhilarating experience.

APPENDIX B

The Selection and Teaching of a Case

"O.K., I want to use a case study, but which one do I use?" Deciding on which case to select depends, of course, on the objective a teacher has for a particular class session, how much time is available, who the participants or class members are, and what cases are available. In Appendix E, I have listed all case studies in mission(s) that have been written and submitted to the Association for Case Teaching (ACT) through 1994, and how to obtain copies. Other cases are also available, such as Paul G. and Frances Hiebert's *Case Studies in Missions.*[1] One could write a new case, of course, but this presupposes some experience and acquired skill. If you want to write a case study, I suggest you begin by reviewing Appendix D. Be forewarned, however, that case writing is not easy, and it requires patient and careful research, several drafts or revisions, a trial-run or two, and a willingness to have your work criticized.

Sources for case studies are varied, but usually they come from one's own personal experience and/or knowledge of an event, interviews with other persons who have first-hand knowledge of an incident, news stories, biographies, archives and other records, and published or oral histories.

The complexity and length of the case study chosen should be in keeping with the interest and level of preparation of those who will be discussing it, and it should be about a theme that is important to them, as well as to the case teacher.

Unless the case study deals with a bona fide dilemma and raises substantive questions and issues about which there will likely be different points of view, the class session can be prosaic and uneventful. Discussing an interesting happening may pass the time, but it is not doing a case study. A good case study involves serious preparation, centers on a dilemma, and will provoke varying and often conflicting perspectives and conclusions.

If there is anything more exacting and challenging than writing a case study, it is trying to teach one and do it well. In Chapter 2, I made some limited comments about the role of the case teacher. Much more needs to said.

- An effective case teacher is as concerned about the dynamics of the classroom experience, what is happening to the students, as he or she is

---

1. Grand Rapids, MI: Baker Book House, 1987. Consists of more than sixty case studies, but all are brief, two to three pages, and they are without any description of the historical background or cultural context.

about the content of the case. In fact, the focus should be on the students as much as, if not more than on the theme or issue.

- An effective case study teacher has a clear objective for the classroom or discussion period, and chooses a case that is relevant and one that will enhance the learning experience.
- An effective case study teacher will know the case, even the trivia, thoroughly. I make it a point not to refer to the case study itself while teaching, and I urge my students to master the case sufficiently so they do not have to be turning the pages and checking details. If one is prepared, one knows the details—names, times, places, statements made, and the sequence of events.
- An effective case study teacher will be thoroughly prepared both in terms of skill and experience, and will have a good teaching note or plan. (See Appendix C.) The teaching note ordinarily will include an opening, the principal characters, the issue(s) in the case, general ideas the teacher would like to develop, and an appropriate conclusion.
- An effective case study teacher will not, however, be locked into a previously decided plan, but will be flexible and move with the discussion and the direction the participants want to go.
- An effective case study teacher will elicit participation from all the group, teasing out their insights and knowledge and not assume the role of a guru with all the answers or the final solution(s). Above all, no participant will be "put down" or ridiculed for his or her opinion or saying the wrong thing. On the other hand, participants will be challenged, gently but firmly, to defend positions they take.
- An effective case study teacher will make use of a "black board," if one is available, and will write down such things as the names of the key individuals in the case, something about them, why they are important, the time sequence, the key issues, and alternative solutions. One must be especially careful to avoid putting the ideas or responses of some of the participants on the board while overlooking others. In the same way, a sensitive and scrupulous case study teacher will check with the participants to be certain that what is written on the board is what the person said and/or meant.
- An effective case study teacher will be willing to risk innovating by employing different teaching techniques, such as role playing, dividing into small groups for brief discussions of particular points, simulating a debate, and voting on what is the preferred solution.
- An effective case study teacher will stimulate and facilitate discussion, not dominate or control it. Seeing oneself as a prober, an enabler, a clarifier, and sometimes even a referee to keep the game moving and see that everyone plays by the rules, is the principal role of the teacher.
- An effective case study teacher knows when and how to move the group to closure by summarizing what has been said, options available,

decisions which have been made, and what the group has learned from the experience.

How can one develop this range of skills? The easiest and quickest way is to get training which includes observing experienced case teachers, teaching and having one's technique analyzed, and learning from experience. Second, of course, is by doing it. If a trained case teacher is a colleague or friend, invite her or him to observe you teaching a case. Then be open to her or his observations and critique.

Case teaching is demanding, far more demanding than writing and reading a lecture. But every case teacher will tell you, though it is frightening, arduous, and exhausting, it can be exhilarating and fulfilling—unless one has a need to be always "the star."

If you are interested in attending a case study learning event, contact the Association for Case Teaching. ACT is not a closed society or an elitist club. Membership is open to anyone who has an interest in the case study approach. Most of the members have attended and participated in one or more workshops or institutes on case teaching and have sought to develop an expertise in the writing and teaching of case studies. Other than the annual eight-day institutes, one-day workshops are often held for interested groups, including—but not limited to—theological and college faculties. Information about these events may be obtained by writing to the Association for Case Teaching, PO Box 243, Simsbury, CT 06070. Telephone (203) 651-4304 or FAX (203) 651-4305.

APPENDIX C

The Teaching Note

A teaching note is nothing more than a plan used to teach the case. During the first seven or eight years that case studies were being written, cases were often published without teaching notes. The Association for Case Teaching, however, decided in the early 1980s to require TNs if a case was to be accepted for publication and distribution. Personally, I much prefer to prepare my own teaching note, and though the basic structure of all my plans is similar, I often prepare a note for a specific group.

What should be included in a teaching note? Assuming the teacher and the participants have studied the case carefully—and this requires hours of preparation for the teacher—I always ask myself, and sometimes write these down, what are my objectives for this teaching and learning moment? In certain instances, the objectives can be a group decision, and would be a way to begin the case study discussion. After deciding on the objectives, I plan for the following:

- How will I open the case discussion?
- Who are the key characters in the case study and what are the significant facts about each of them? Do I know their names and how to spell and pronounce them?
- Do I know the chronology of events or the "time line"?
- What do I think are the paramount issues in the case? There is rarely *one* issue. What is the dilemma?
- What are the various options for action? Here, one must often distinguish between the ideal and the possible.
- How I will bring the case discussion to a conclusion?

As demonstrated below, I make careful and frequently copious notes. Depending on the time available—ninety minutes are ideal—I include an approximate time flow for each component of the case: the opening (5 to 10 minutes, for example), identification of characters (15 to 20 minutes), issues (15 to 25 minutes), options for action (15 to 25 minutes), and closure (5 to 10 minutes)—and I make a conscious effort not to refer frequently to my teaching note. I always have a copy of the case with me, but I try never to look at it. I want to be so thoroughly familiar with the case study that I do not need to depend on the printed text.

I encourage every case study teacher to make her or his own teaching note, but this does not mean necessarily creating a note de novo. For this reason, I have included four sample teaching notes, two rather lengthy and two briefer.

Even if you choose to use a teaching note that is written by someone else, I would strongly encourage you to adapt it to your own situation. No teaching note should be followed slavishly. It should never be regarded as a pedagogical straightjacket, but rather a general design to get you where you want to go and achieve the objectives you have for the class or group.

A LETTER FROM CLAIRE
Teaching Note

One of the most difficult issues facing Christians today is the challenge of religious pluralism. Whereas a generation or two ago, people in the West, especially in North America, rarely encountered peoples of other faiths (other than a limited number of Jewish acquaintances and even fewer Native Americans), this is not the case today. Hindus, Muslims, Buddhists, and followers of numerous other lesser known religions have migrated to the West and represent a tangible challenge to our traditional Christian assumptions. Nowhere is that challenge more frequent and intense than on college and university campuses.

This case study regarding a young university student's encounter with Hindu and Muslim students, and how she began to question the oft-heard assertion that Christianity is the only way of salvation, is an experience shared by thousands of young people during recent years.

A serious discussion of the issues in the case will surface very deep and long-held convictions of almost every group of professing Christians in the world. How a pastor, teacher, parent, or friend responds will often determine whether the individual—like Claire in the case—discloses his or her most guarded thoughts or denies and represses them.

As in all cases, there are numerous ways to begin the class discussion. One way is to ask the question, "Have you ever asked yourself some of the questions Claire poses in her letter?"

I. Characters in the Case

1. *Jim Forsythe*—a native of Louisville, KY, whose mother still has a home in the city. He is a graduate of Vanderbilt and Louisville Presbyterian Seminary with B.A. and M.Div. degrees, and he also received his doctorate. He is married with at least two children, the oldest who will soon be twelve. He is 33 years old and, together with his wife Katie, has long been interested in international missionary work. He lived in his mother's home in Louisville while in the Seminary, and continued to live there after he married and until

he finished his residency for his last degree. He is now pastor of the University Congregational Church in Bowling Green, Ohio, a growing and stimulating congregation.

2. *Katie Forsythe*—Jim's wife whom he met and married while studying at the Louisville Presbyterian Seminary. After she finished her degree, she worked to help him complete his Th.D. She too has had a longtime interest in overseas mission work.

3. *Claire Evans*—a fourth-year university student in Bowling Green State University in Ohio. She grew up in a fundamentalist church in Ashland, KY, and though she appears not to share the fundamentalist world view, when she goes home to visit her parents, she accompanies them to the church in which she was reared. She is a winsome, beautiful young woman who has been, until recently, an active participant in University Congregational Church. She spent her second college year in France and is now fluent in French and Spanish. She manifests a genuine concern for world issues. Besides her church activities, she has participated in the InterVarsity Christian Fellowship. She has had more contact and been a friend to more international students than anyone else Jim has known with the exception of Bill Taylor.

Claire has recently been much less active in the church and by her letter is questioning the exclusive claims of many Christians.

4. *Bill Taylor*—another university student who spent part of his childhood in the Philippines and in India where his father worked with the U.S. Agency for International Development (AID). He is the only student Jim knows who has more friends than Claire among the international students.

II. Time Line

1. The Forsythes have been in Bowling Green for eighteen months. Both are 33 years old and have been married for nearly thirteen years. They contacted the board of international mission of their denomination two years before coming to Bowling Green. Their oldest daughter will be twelve years old in December.

2. Claire's letter was evidently written in June after she returned home for the summer. Her church attendance became spasmodic after Christmas, and she was in worship only once after Easter.

3. Jim saw Claire the week she was taking her final examinations at the university, and he received her letter some three weeks later.

III. Claire's Letter

A crucial component in understanding this case. Students should know the basic content and also be able to isolate the issues Claire raises.

She says she began to question the exclusiveness of Christian claims after hearing [repeatedly?] that "Jesus is the only way." Did she hear this in her church and/or in IVF? Did she also hear this from Jim? We do not know, but apparently she is assuming at least that this is Jim's position.

If Jesus is the only way, she says, why has God's revelation been limited only to a segment of the world's population?

If the founders and followers of other religions are wrong, why did God not "straighten them out?"

When Jesus said, "I am the only way," could he have meant, Claire inquires, that his manner of life is the way to salvation, not necessarily knowing him personally?

IV. Issues in the Case

1. The exclusive claims of Christians that Jesus Christ is the only way of salvation.

2. The nature of the New Testament witness, especially those texts which have become the cornerstone of traditional conservative Christian theology, such as John 3:18; 14:6; Acts 4:12; Phil 2:9–11, as well as some less frequently used texts such as John 6:68; 8:24; and 1 Cor 3:11.

3. The struggle many people endure who have been reared in conservative and fundamentalist Christian homes and churches when they encounter serious challenges to what they have been accustomed to believe.

Claire may be at a crucial juncture in her life, a time when she can no longer accept Christian exclusivism and thus is avoiding dealing with her doubts and questions by dropping out of church.

4. Jim's and Katie's interest in international missions evidently was one of the stimuli that helped them decide to come to Bowling Green and the First Congregational Church. What is he thinking about Christ as the only way of salvation? Is Katie privy to his deepest reflections and questions? How will responding to Claire's letter help prepare them to work with peoples of other faiths, assuming they do become international missioners?

5. Jim condenses Claire's questions raised in her letter to a single issue, namely, why is one religion not as good as another? Is he correct? Is reducing her struggle to a single issue wise and fair?

6. How should Jim respond, assuming he will respond in some way? Having taught this case several times, the following answers have been most common:

(1) He should recognize that Claire is going through a needed and healthy transition.
(2) He should affirm the legitimacy of her questions, and if he has the same doubts, tell her.
(3) He should seek Katie's counsel for several reasons, not the least of which is to make her aware of Claire's feelings and letter. This could be a growing experience for Jim and Katie as well as for Claire.
(4) He should call or write to Claire and deal with her queries honestly. Whatever his personal position, he could recognize that Christians do

not agree salvation depends on accepting the historical Jesus as one's Lord and Savior. "Some insist that Jesus is the only way because . . ." He should deal with the New Testament witness and not trivialize or ignore it. He should include his personal belief or witness.

(5) He may consider it wise for him and Katie to drive to Ashland, KY, to see and talk with Claire. This may mean more to her at this time than a telephone call or letter.

V. Closure

Assume you are Jim. What would you do?
Assume you are Claire. What kind of response would you prefer from Jim?

ROBERTO DE NOBILI
Teaching Note

This is a case about a young Roman Catholic missionary who went to India via Portugal in the early seventeenth century, and after a period of less than three years attempted to introduce a radically new way of evangelizing Indians of caste. His approach was considered by some of his missionary colleagues to be antithetical to the gospel and threatening to the mission work that had been done for nearly a century. Was de Nobili right or wrong in his approach?

I. A Word about Hinduism

1. It is a religious tradition older than Judaism and Christianity. It boasts more than 5,000 years of history and development.

2. "Hinduism" is from a Persian word meaning "Indian" and dates from c. C.E. 1200.

It may have been given to the Hindu adherents by Moslems in order to distinguish their religion, Islam, from that of the people whose land they were invading.

Hindus prefer to refer to their religion as "the *sanatana dharma*," or "the eternal teaching" or "eternal law."

3. There is no known founder of Hinduism, nor does it boast any creed or prophets.

It has no particular institutional structures. It is an emphasis on a way of living rather than on a way of thinking. In a sense, then, it is more of a cultural expression than doctrinal or creedal expression, though there are common beliefs, such as the reverence for life.

4. Hinduism stresses a reverence for Mother India, for the land, its culture, and its social system. All of nature is living and therefore sacred. Rivers, such as the Ganges (the most sacred), are especially revered.

5. Hinduism is in a sense one faith and many faiths. There is a wide diversity. Most Indians are theists. Some, however, are vegetarians because of their reverence for life, while others offer animal sacrifices. Some worship Shiva, others Vishnu, or an incarnation (avatar), e.g., Krishna or Rama. Some reverence many gods or no god. It is said that Hindus believe in one god with many manifestations.

6. In summary, Hinduism is a religious-cultural umbrella under which a family of values and religious beliefs gathers/assembles. Central is a belief in reincarnation including the doctrine of Karma and Samsara (flow of life).

II. The People of India

The people of India are not homogeneous. There are three major ethnic groups (Indo-Aryan, 72%; Dravidians, 26%; Mongoloids, 3%). There are at least 16 languages with some 700 dialects. Hindi and English are today the official languages of India.

Each of the 700 groups of people has its own customs, language (dialect), and religious practices.

The estimated population of 866,000,000 (1993) is divided among four major religious groups: 718 million Hindus (83%); 95 million Muslims (11%); 25.9 million Christians (3%); and 17.3 million Sikhs (2%).

III. Teaching Objectives

1. To introduce the students to the difficulties in cross-cultural mission endeavors.

2. To introduce the students to the principle of accommodation.

3. To raise the missiological questions regarding accommodation, identification, indigenization, contextualization, strategy, and salvation.

4. To encourage the students to do background reading on Hinduism and deal with the theological issues that Christians face when attempting to relate to Hindus.

5. To acquaint the students with one of the classic figures in mission history.

IV. Possible Openings

1. Read the excerpt from Gregory the Great's letter to the missionary Augustine of Canterbury. (See above, p. 5.)

2. Inquire what the students have learned about Hinduism from this case. What are the major differences between Hinduism and Christianity?

3. "John or Jane Doe, open this case for us." If the group is accustomed to discussing cases, such a statement will quickly move the group into the core issues.

4. Or you may begin, "What do you see as the real issues in this case?" (See below.)

V. Characters

1. *Roberto de Nobili*—Italian Jesuit born in 1577, died in 1656. Some say he was born in Rome, others in Tuscany. Father was a general in the papal army, mother was from a noble family. The family tree included Otto III and Pope Julian II.

His family was very opposed to his becoming a Jesuit (though not necessarily opposed to his entering the priesthood). Roberto's response: "When God calls, no human consideration should stop us." He entered the Jesuit order in 1596.

2. *Alberto Laerzio*—de Nobili's superior (Provincial). He lived in Cochin on the western coast of South India. He consistently supported de Nobili.

3. *The Paravas*—a large tribe of outcasts (untouchables) who lived by fishing and pearl diving along the Fishery Coast. They had become Christians in the 1530s in order to gain Portuguese protection from Muslim raiders. As far as customs were concerned, they had been turned into Portuguese. Their language was Tamil.

4. *Gonçalo Fernández*—a sixty-five-year-old Portuguese Jesuit who had worked for eleven years in Madura. He lived in the mission compound and ministered to Paravas and Portuguese. He had tried to interest the *Nayak* (the regional king) in Christianity, but had been spurned.

5. *Hindu Schoolmaster*—introduced de Nobili to the intricacies of Hindu culture and became Roberto's first convert to Christianity. Roberto christened him "Alberto" in honor of his superior. Albert was a Sudra. He told Roberto that "Parangi" did not mean "Portuguese," but it meant "dirty." Four castes: Brahman, Ksatriya/Raja, Vaisya, and Sudra.

6. *Sivadarma*—a Brahman Sanskrit scholar who converted to Christianity in 1609. Roberto then faced two crucial questions: Should he begin a caste church, and what about the thread and the *kudumi?*

7. *Nicolau Pimenta*—Papal Visitor to Goa and Malabar. In 1611 he condemned de Nobili's approach as excessive, superstitious, and schismatic.

8. *Pero Francisco*—de Nobili's new Superior who replaced Alberto Laerzio.

VI. Time Line

1577—Roberto de Nobili was born in Rome (or Tuscany).
1595—Jesuit mission established in Madurai by Gonçalo Fernández.
1596—Roberto, age 19, entered the Jesuit order.

1604—Embarked for India last week in April (age 27) from Lisbon.

1605—de Nobili arrived in Goa in May. Met his Superior, Alberto Laerzio. Roberto became sick, but was able to move to Cochin toward the end of that year.

1606—de Nobili sent by Laerzio to Fishery Coast where the young missionary lived among the Paravas who in the 1530s had become "Christians." Later, de Nobili was assigned to Madurai by Laerzio.

1608—de Nobili had baptized 10 young men of caste including Alberto the schoolmaster.

1609—Sanskrit scholar Sivadarma was baptized, which provoked a crisis. Should de Nobili have a separate church for higher castes? Should he insist that Sivadarma discard the triple thread and shave the *kudumi?*

Roberto had 60 converts by the end of 1609. Fernández, however, became openly critical. He traveled to the coast and shared misgivings with other priests. He also sent a denunciation to the Archbishop. The entire Jesuit mission was soon divided.

1611—Official censure by Nicolau Pimenta, the Papal Visitor to Goa and Malabar. Said de Nobili's methods were excessive, superstitious, and schismatic.

Roberto responded by writing the Jesuit General.

1613—Reply arrives from Jesuit General, but meanwhile twenty of de Nobili's converts had lapsed. Also, Pero Francisco replaced Alberto Laerzio as Roberto's superior.

Francisco's interpretation of the General's letter was that de Nobili was wrong on three counts:

(1) His dress and name (denial that he was *Parangi*);
(2) Adoption of Hindu ceremonies: baths; and
(3) Separation from Fernández.

Roberto was forbidden to baptize any new converts unless he was willing to change and submit to Francisco's authority. Roberto, however, grasped one phrase in the General's letter and said that to submit would be to "compromise the existence of the mission."

1617—Pope orders a conference for Goa in February 1618.

1618—Conference held in February.

VII. Issues in the Case

1. To what degree can a missionary adopt/adapt to a new culture before blurring the force of the gospel for that culture?

2. What is cultural and what is religious (ethical) in a society? Can we distinguish?

3. What is salvation, and does it involve repudiation of certain aspects of one's culture? If so, which aspects?

4. What is the essence of Christianity above and beyond culture? Can Christianity ever transcend culture?

5. How important is it to understand a culture? Did de Nobili understand the culture? Did Fernández?

6. Was de Nobili's methodology a sound one? What about his philosophy, theology, strategy, and implementation?

7. Are inter-personal relations more important than evangelistic results? When do you "go it alone"?

8. What was de Nobili's concept of authority? Was he willing to be a part of a church that was hierarchical?

9. What about the question of caste? Are there contemporary caste divisions, de facto caste systems today?

10. How can you define genuine, authentic missionary identification?

11. What about the question of syncretism?

12. How would you describe and evaluate de Nobili's sense of calling? ("When God calls, no human consideration should stop us.")

VIII. Missionary Identification

1. Regarding the question of identification, note the following:

- de Nobili's dress, eating, language, bathing, and housing.
- Separation from co-worker(s).
- Acceptance and use of symbols: three-stranded thread, *kudumi,* sandalwood paste mark on the forehead, saffron robe, called himself a "sanyasi," a guru or holy man. He also refused to condemn the caste system or even *suttee.* He organized a separate church for high caste converts.

2. Did de Nobili over-identify?

IX. Concluding the Case

The affair dragged on for years during which time de Nobili was enjoined or suspended from baptizing any converts. Pope Paul V had ordered a conference at Goa for February 1618 at which time de Nobili was obliged to defend his missionary method. At this point, I often ask the class to role play this conference, giving students an opportunity to speak for or against Roberto's missionary approach.

Then I ask the class to vote.[1]

---

1. Inquiring students can, of course, go to the history books or encyclopedias and learn what happened at the Goa conference. Even if every student were to do this, a role play and a final vote can be a stimulating and an effective way to close the case.

After Roberto presented his case, the first Papal Visitor (Inquisitor) voted against the Italian innovator, but the second voted to sustain him. Unfortunately, only four (including the one Papal Visitor and de Nobili himself) voted to sustain the innovative approach.

In 1623, however, when the report was received in Rome, Pope Gregory XV, in

I WANT TO BE A PRIEST!
Teaching Note

I. Teaching Goals

1. To understand and appreciate contemporary questions in mission and ministry.
2. To assist in reflection on ministry in a given context.
3. To provide greater awareness of questions in ministry and church among religious traditions.
4. To present some key theological issues for discussion related to church structures and the goals of mission.

II. Possible Class Format

Role Play: Father Dawson and members of the team take various positions in relation to whether Mario should study for the priesthood. Implications should be clearly indicated for mission policy and continuing questions for church and ministry.

III. Central Issues in the Case

1. Church structures and ministry.
2. Role of the laity.
3. Role of priest and type of training.
4. Context of ministry and image of the priest.
5. Leadership in a given society.
6. Mission and change.
7. Missionaries' facing dilemma of what advice to offer for the benefit of the person and the community.
8. Establishment of the local church.

IV. Resource

A broad theological discussion might bring in the Lima Document, *Baptism, Eucharist, and Ministry,* WCC, 1982.

---

his constitution *Romanae Sedis Antistes* of January 31, 1623, approved de Nobili's method and directed that Brahman converts be allowed to retain the thread and the *kudumi.*

When de Nobili arrived in South India in 1605, there was not a single convert in the hinterland. When he returned to Mylamgore in 1654, it is said that there were 4,183.

Roberto de Nobili died in 1656, virtually blind, at the age of 79.

V. Opening

In a situation such as this the frustrations, joys, hopes, and challenges facing the missionary can be brought out in discussion. "Father Dawson is with us today. What questions and suggestions do you have for him? Let's begin with your questions."

VI. Closing the Case

Possibilities of strategies of action for the future may be the way to bring the case discussion to closure.

"SHOULD I ACCEPT?"
Teaching Note

A young Roman Catholic high school girl in Taiwan is suddenly faced with a decision regarding the eating of food offered to idols. She has accompanied her Buddhist friend to the temple and observed the ceremony of offering food to deceased ancestors. Now she is being invited to return to her friend's home and have lunch. She knows that some of the food is what the family is bringing back from the temple.

I. Characters

   1. *Meijung*—Roman Catholic, 17 years old.
   2. *Shuching*—Baptist, 17 years old.
   3. *Reyhei*—Roman Catholic, 17 years old.
   4. *Shuo*—Buddhist, 17 years old.
These young women met when they were 9 years old (3rd grade) in primary school. "They shared everything." They were inseparable. Often they discussed their faith. They disagreed, but they did not cease being friends.

II. Chronology

   1. They had been friends for nearly eight years. Today is a Buddhist holiday. They arrived at *Shuo's* home about 10:00–10:30 A.M. on a Saturday.
   (1) They engage in "girl-talk" for about 30 minutes.
   (2) Then *Shuo* explains the meaning of the day and the nature of the ceremony.
   (3) *Shuching* asks a question about the food.
   (4) *Meijung* draws a parallel.
   (5) Parents and brothers enter the room.

(6) The walk to the Buddhist temple takes about 10 minutes.

(7) Ceremony/ritual takes about 30 minutes.

III. Crisis—Issue(s)

1. Danger of parallels.
2. Eating food used in pagan worship: compromise, syncretism?
3. Refusal by *Shuching* and acceptance by *Reyhei*. Is *Shuo* offended?
4. Should she have gone to the temple in the first place?
5. Biblical passages: 1 Cor. 8:1–13; Acts 10:28–29.
6. Honesty.
7. Freedom to witness.
8. Friendships—relationships.

IV. Reaching a Decision

1. Ask the group if they are ready to reach a decision. If not, give them a time when they must decide.

2. Be certain that the various alternatives are written on the board.

3. Once the group has agreed to make a decision, ask for a show of hands (or to make it more interesting, have each write his or her decision on a slip of paper which you have prepared and now give to each participant).

4. Announce the results.

Appendix D

Writing Your First Case

Prior to your attempting to write a draft of a case, you will need to reflect on your own experience and knowledge and *begin to gather materials for the writing.* Most people choose to write their first cases regarding some personal experiences. This is not obligatory, however, and excellent cases may be found in current events, within your denomination or church, newspapers, magazines, church history, and through interviews with friends or acquaintances.

1. *Remember that a case describes a difficult problem, a dilemma for which there is no single obvious solution.* If the solution is obvious, or if the courses of possible action would not produce a difference of opinion, then you do not have the material for a good case. (Students or discussants are expected to study a case, develop their own individual solutions, and be prepared to defend their choices. Their study of a case may require them to do research beyond the case material itself and to propose and defend plans of action which they believe will lead to a satisfactory solution.)

2. *A case must describe an actual, not a hypothetical situation.* Nothing will draw the student into the discussion of a case more quickly and intensely than the assurance that "this really happened" or is happening. You may find it necessary at times to disguise a case by changing names and places, but avoid "doctoring" it by exaggerations, embellishments, or alterations which could prompt the discussants to doubt the accuracy or truthfulness of the case itself.

3. *A case should be a question or problem with which many people can identify and in which they will have a genuine interest.* Kierkegaard once said, "There is truth that matters, and there is truth that does not matter." A case needs to be about truth that matters, not about secondary, provincial, or incidental occurrences which are unimportant to the life of the Church.

4. *A case is written from one person's perspective.* In the writing of a case, you will want to be as objective as possible in gathering and recounting the facts, but you will avoid trying to see it through the eyes of everyone who is involved. Do *not* attribute feelings or motives to anyone in the case unless these are verbalized by the persons involved. To write a case from one person's perspective may appear to be too narrow and exclusive. Yet, this is the way all of us perceive reality, and we must make decisions on the basis of the limited facts and data available to us individually. You should, of

course, attempt to include all the pertinent facts available to you, but recognize that you can never, when writing a case, have all the facts gathered and neatly arranged.

The following steps should help you begin to write your first case.

Step 1—Choose an event or situation which poses a question and requires a decision fraught with difficulty and ambiguity.

Step 2—Select a case about an incident in which you were personally involved or in which the participant(s) would be willing to provide you with the information you need to describe the background, the individuals involved, the situation or dilemma itself, and the possible courses of action. (It is not necessary that the decision be already made or the course of action decided. The matter still may be unresolved.) If you are the participant, you are the source of information.

Step 3—If the writing and publication of the case could prove to be embarrassing to individuals or institutions, you will need to secure permission from the people involved and/or disguise the case before releasing it.

Step 4—Choose a situation that will be of interest to your audience (students, church school class, etc.). Ask yourself, "Will the discussion of this case be beneficial to those I will ask to study and discuss it?" If not, look for something else.

Be prepared to work hard and accept criticism. You are trying to learn as well as to teach.

Worksheet for Case Writing

1. *Audience*—For whom are you writing the case?

2. *Teaching objectives*—What do you want to accomplish?

3. *Perspective*—Through whose eyes is the case presented?

4. *Outline*—Give a brief outline.

5. *Decision point*—What is it?

APPENDIX E

Index of Case Studies in Christian Mission

A large number and a wide variety of cases are available to those interested in discussing missiological issues by utilizing the case study approach. This index includes all mission cases in the case study collection through 1994.

Differentiating between international and domestic mission issues has become increasingly difficult and sometimes impossible. For this reason I have included in this list all cases which I believe deal with basic missiological questions.

Since the Fall of 1989 a number of cases have been published annually in the *Journal for Case Teaching* by the Association for Case Teaching, P.O. Box 243, Simsbury, CT 06070. One may order copies of the *Journal* by writing directly to the Association for Case Teaching at the above address. Those who are members of the Association automatically receive volumes as they are published. An annual membership in ACT is twenty-five dollars ($25.00 U.S.) for individuals and institutions.

Copies of individual cases, including those listed below, may be ordered by mail or FAX from the

> ACT Case Clearing House
> Yale Divinity School Library
> 409 Prospect Street
> New Haven, CT 06511
> FAX (203) 432-3906.

You will be billed five dollars ($5.00 U.S.) for each case you order, but for this one-time payment, you will receive not only a "copy-ready" text, but also the right to reproduce as many copies as you need of that particular case.

When ordering cases, be certain to specify the case title, the year of publication, and the author(s). Also, if you desire a copy of the teaching note—provided one is available—please indicate this. (Unfortunately during the early years, cases were accepted by the Case Study Institute without requiring the authors to provide teaching notes. For this reason, teaching notes are not available for some of the earlier published cases.)

The date included in the annotations is the year the case was received and indexed, not the time in which the case incident occurred.

Please note also that a few of the cases have been published in books and journals. I have sought to include that bibliographical information.

A CHURCH FOR ALL PEOPLE
Author: Garnett E. Foster
Setting: Suburb of a major east coast city
Date: 1993
Length: 2 pages
Topics: Multiculturalism, grief, anger, disappointment, and the clash of cultures, values, and expectations in the church.
Abstract: A suburban congregation, located in an area where people have settled from all parts of the world, advertises itself as "A Church for All People" and attracts a variety of non-North American parishioners. The presence of people with different backgrounds, values, customs, and ideas, however, results in numerous frictions and problems. The pastor attempts to involve as many people with different backgrounds as possible in the ministry and administration of the church, but he is suddenly confronted by a disappointed and angry member from Africa who represents the radical differences in expectations and norms. Being a church for all people, the pastor sees, is much easier described than realized. Should his hope for a multi-ethnic, multi-cultural church be abandoned for a "homogeneous" congregation that church growth people promote?
Teaching Note: 2 pages.

This case and teaching note are found in the *Journal for Case Teaching* 5 (Fall 1993): 95–97.

AFFIRMATION OF LIFE
Author: Alice Frazer Evans
Setting: Panama
Date: 1993
Length: 7 pages
Topics: Theological education (by extension), Central America, mission and ministry, justice, pastoral models, liberation, "deculturalization," contextualization, capitalism, and the International Monetary Fund.
Abstract: An evangelical seminary in Panama reevaluates the implications of its investment policies in light of its revised approach to theological education based on "biblical and contextual analyses."
Teaching Note: 2 pages.

APART FROM HIS PEOPLE
Author: Robert A. and Alice F. Evans
Setting: Jamaica
Date: 1977, 1985
Length: 3 pages
Topics: Cross-cultural conflict, theological education outside one's country, church and society, poverty, apathy, social justice, mission of the church, and the clash of values and expectations.

Abstract: Protestant church leaders in Jamaica debate the value and the costs of sending their young people outside the country—especially to the U.S. or Europe—for theological education, especially in light of the conflict that has arisen in a church with a young pastor who has recently returned.
Teaching Note: 2 pages.

This case is found in Alice Frazer Evans, Robert A. Evans, and David A. Roozen, *The Globalization of Theological Education* (Maryknoll, NY: Orbis Books, 1993): 351–355. An earlier version was published in 1978 entitled "A Matter of Pride."

ASIA RESOURCES, INC.
Author: Alan Neely
Setting: USA
Date: 1995
Length: 8 pages
Topics: "Unreached peoples," short-term or bi-vocational missionaries, capitalism, "World A, B, and C," para-church missions, missionaries as entrepreneurs
Abstract: A former missionary, now a member of a new Methodist mission sending agency and committee, hears a presentation by an enthusiastic and charismatic entrepreneur who challenges the group to initiate a "new approach" to the sending of missionaries, namely, sending them as business people who can gain entry to countries such as China. Members of the committee are excited and positive, but Doug Murphy is troubled by the proposal.
Teaching Note: 3 pages.

This case is included in this book.

AYUDA? HELP!
Author: Carl Siegenthaler
Setting: Phoenix, Arizona
Date: 1976
Length: 6 pages + 3 pages of exhibits
Topics: Church and mission, ecumenism, intra- and inter-cultural conflict, and the role of the church in issues of social justice
Abstract: A four-month-old interdenominational coalition for social ministries is threatened with irreparable division when faced with conflicting proposals from two Hispanic American groups regarding what the coalition should do.
Teaching Note not available.

BELGIAN AUTHORITY V. MORRISON AND SHEPPARD
Author: Louis Weeks
Setting: Belgian Congo 1899

Date: 1979

Length: 3 pages

Topics: Church and mission, ethical issues, Africa, Church and society, Presbyterian missions

Abstract: Missionaries from the American Presbyterian Congo Mission discover atrocities being inflicted on tribal people with whom they are working. If they confront the Belgian authorities, they may be forced to leave the country. To ignore the oppression would represent tacit complicity in the demise of the tribes to which they came.

Teaching Note not available.

BILLY GRAHAM AND WORLDWIDE EVANGELISM

Author: Garth M. Rosell

Setting: Amsterdam, Netherlands

Date: 1987

Length: 3 pages + bibliography and exhibits

Topics: Mission of the church, evangelism, Billy Graham, Third World church(es), revivalism

Abstract: In July 1983 the Billy Graham Evangelistic Association sponsored a gathering in Amsterdam, the Netherlands. It was known as the International Conference of Itinerant Evangelists and was attended by 4,000 delegates from 132 countries. Though the case writer skillfully summarizes the life and career of Graham as a world evangelist, no clear dilemma is evident, making the case difficult to use. If one studies the case with care, however, one can conclude that Billy Graham is convinced that the goal of Christian encounters with peoples of other faiths is their personal conversion. Though evangelical Christians generally share this view, not all Christians agree. This difference in perspectives, therefore, may serve well as the basis of a class discussion.

Teaching Note not available.

This case study is also available in *American Christianity,* ed. Ronald C. White, Jr., Louis B. Weeks, and Garth Rosell, 179–183. Grand Rapids: Eerdmans, 1986.

BIRDS OVER ZIMBABWE

Author: Norman N. Bonner

Setting: Zimbabwe

Date: 1980

Length: 4 pages

Topics: Church and mission, nationalism, inter-ethnic struggles, church and state, apartheid, future of missions in Africa, guerilla violence

Abstract: A Zimbabwe national whom a missionary woman has reared from the time he was an infant left on her doorstep is asked by him to bless his involvement in an African guerrilla operation that is preparing to invade

South Africa. He insists that he like other African leaders can be a Christian and participate in the armed struggle against injustice. The pain, oppression, conflict, and contradictions of the situation center on her relations with this young man, her adopted African son. She feels powerless to stop him, but should she as a Christian missionary give her blessing to one involved in a violent revolutionary movement, even though she loves him and deplores the long-standing injustices he and his people have suffered?
Teaching Note: 4 pages.

BREAD FOR THE WORLD
Authors: Jane K. Vella and Candice Fair
Setting: North Carolina
Date: 1987
Length: 6 pages + 2-page appendix
Topics: Church and hunger, Bread for the World, the effectiveness of a small group in influencing public policy, and ways and means to maintain interest and commitment on the part of the group
Abstract: Participants in a local chapter of Bread for the World have lost some of their leaders and are finding it difficult to maintain the needed level of interest and commitment. After a member of the group contacts the national office in Washington, D.C., they learn it is possible for them to have a summer intern who could help rejuvenate the group, provided they are willing and able to assume responsibility for the proposed intern's housing, office space, local transportation, and supervision. Such a step appears to some of the members as overly ambitious and an excessive burden requiring an even greater investment by the group. To refuse to take this or some other step, however, may mean the demise of the group and the end of their effort.
Teaching Note: 1 page.

BUILD YOUR CHURCH HERE
Author: Alan Neely
Setting: Madagascar
Date: 1986
Length: 4 pages
Topics: Mission, African traditional religion, syncretism, missionary strategy, paternalism
Abstract: A Lutheran national missionary wants to secure permission from a local chief who is also the village shaman to conduct Christian worship and lead Bible studies in the village. After initially rebuffing the missionary and even threatening his life, the shaman not only gives permission, but he offers a piece of land for the constructing of a church building. The missionary and his colleagues are unsure about what they should say or do.
Teaching Note: 4 pages.

This case is included in this book.

THE CALL
Author: Alan Neely
Setting: USA
Date: 1995
Length: 7 pages
Topics: Missionary recruitment, missionary calling, candidates for mission-
ary appointment
Abstract: The Recruitment Secretary for the American Reformed Church
Mission has worked with a young couple seeking missionary appointment.
Their records, recommendations, and motives appear good, but the Secre-
tary has a lingering doubt. Should he recommend them to the administrative
board for appointment?
Teaching Note: 4 pages.

This case is included in this book.

CAN MRS. ROSE C. TEACH THE JUNIOR GIRLS SUNDAY SCHOOL
CLASS?
Author: Donald Hohensee
Setting: Kenya
Date: 1989
Length: 3 pages
Topics: Church and mission, clash of cultures, Kenya
Abstract: A faith missionary couple working in western Kenya encounter the
cultural practice in which two women in the Kalenjin tribe marry each
other. One of the women assumes the male role. These unions are an
indigenous solution to a persistent problem. A woman, Mrs. Rose C., is
the wife in one of these "marriages" and has become a faithful Christian.
She volunteers to teach a children's Sunday School class. The elders of
the church object on the basis of her irregular union, and the missionary
wonders what he should say and do.
Teaching Note: 1 page.

This case and the teaching note are found in the *Journal for Case Teaching*
1 (Fall 1989): 62–65.

CHANGING THE FACE OF THE PARISH
Author: Ronald C. White, Jr.
Setting: San Antonio, Texas
Date: 1993
Length: 4 pages
Topics: Multi-culturalism, ethnic diversity, worship and the sacraments, min-
istry in a pluralistic setting, immigration/immigrants, dealing with change
Abstract: A young parish priest, only recently graduated from the seminary
and the first pastor in the congregation's history who can speak Spanish,
is confronted with the growing division as to whether the church should

offer a Mass in Spanish to attract the growing number of Hispanics. Many in the congregation of more than two thousand families object to this possible change and insist that the church should be the one institution that continues tradition. Father Peter, the young priest, however, is asked directly in a meeting what he thinks should be done.
Teaching Note: 2 pages.

This case and teaching note are found in the *Journal for Case Teaching* 5 (Fall 1993): 79–94, and in Alice Frazer Evans, Robert A. Evans and David A. Roozen, 78–83. *The Globalization of Theological Education.* Maryknoll, NY: Orbis Books, 1993.

CHINA AND THE CHURCH
Authors: Robert A. and Alice F. Evans
Setting: China
Date: 1983
Length: 19 pages + 11-page appendix
Topics: Mission, Christians in China, persecution, church and state, reopening of the church in the "New China," the "Three-Self Movement"
Abstract: A Chinese Christian, persecuted during the Cultural Revolution, learns of the recent rebuilding of the Christian church in China and struggles to understand the correct relationship between church and state in the "New China."
Teaching Note: 2 pages.

This case together with the appendix and the teaching note may also be found in Robert A. and Alice F. Evans, *Human Rights: A Dialogue Between the First and Third Worlds,* 198–240. Maryknoll, NY: Orbis Books, 1993.

CITY OF GOLD
Author: Norman N. Bonner
Setting: Swaziland, South Africa
Date: 1978
Length: 4 pages
Topics: Church and mission, discrimination, family relations, church and society, vocational choice, South Africa
Abstract: Samson Sigwane, a young Swazi Christian, is under pressure from his father's cousin, the paramount chief of Swaziland, to become headman at the Royal Kraal. Samson's father, an animist, wants Samson to go to Johannesburg (sometimes called in Swazi language, "Goldie," or the "City of Gold") to earn money which would enable Samson to purchase a wife. The young man is caught between conflicting pressures and must make a decision.
Teaching Note not available.

"COME, HOLY SPIRIT(S)"
Author: Alan Neely
Setting: Australia
Date: 1995
Length: 5 pages
Topics: World Council of Churches Assembly in Canberra (1991), Holy
    Spirit, Pentecostalism, Orthodox churches, feminist theology, Chung Hyun
    Kyung, Korea, integration of creation, syncretism
Abstract: A Pentecostal seminary professor attending the Seventh Assembly
    of the World Council of Churches in Canberra hopes the theme of the
    Assembly—"Come, Holy Spirit"—signals that the WCC is reaching out
    to charismatics and Pentecostals. After the second of the two key-note
    addresses, however, he was unsure.
Teaching Note: 4 pages.

This case is included in this book.

DAILY, DAILY SING THE PRAISES
Author: Douglas H. Gregg
Setting: Uganda 1978
Date: 1978
Length: 8 pages
Topics: Church and mission, Christian ethics, church and state, nature of the
    church, Uganda
Abstract: In 1977 Christians were suffering severe persecution in Uganda.
    The Anglican Archbishop, Janani Luwum, along with many others, was
    martyred. Festo Kivengere, Anglican bishop of the Kigezi province, sees
    his own life in danger. His parishioners urge him to flee the country, but
    he feels he should stay with his suffering community. The case includes
    a brief review of the one hundred years of Christian history in Uganda
    and a summary of events leading up to Luwum's death.
Teaching Note not available.

"DON'T COME OVER AND HELP US"
Author: Alan Neely
Setting: Thailand and Myanmar (Burma)
Date: 1995
Length: 5 pages
Topics: Syncretism, Thailand, Myanmar, Karen, evangelization, Buddhism,
    myth, drama, missionary-national relations
Abstract: Serious objections are voiced by Thai Karen church members when
    a group of Karen students from Myanmar come and utilize ancient myths
    in dramas designed to present the Christian message. The church is divided,
    as are the missionaries, regarding whether the gospel is being compromised.
Teaching Note: 3 pages.

This case is included in this book.

EL SALVADOR AND THE COST OF CHRISTIAN WITNESS Parts A & B
Author: Alan Neely
Setting: El Salvador and the U.S.A. 1983
Date: 1983
Length: Part A is 10 pages; Part B is 6 pages
Topics: Role of missionaries in Central America, U.S. foreign policy, human rights, missionaries and armed insurgency
Abstract: Four Roman Catholic women missioners are killed in El Salvador, December 1980. Government officials in El Salvador and the U.S.A. issue statements implying that the women were killed because they were involved with anti-government guerrillas. Melinda Roper, head of the Maryknoll Sisters, must decide what to do and say in regard to these charges.
Teaching Note is 14 pages and includes detailed background information.

ENSHRINED
Authors: Robert A. and Alice F. Evans
Setting: Japan
Date: 1981
Length: 13 pages + 2-page appendix
Topics: Syncretism, the "Confession of Responsibility in World War II" issued by the United Church of Christ in Japan (the Kyodan), role of women in Japanese society, church and state, militarism, and Japanese economic expansion in Asia
Abstract: A Christian lay leader is faced with a decision of whether to support a Japanese Christian woman in her effort to prevent the enshrinement of her deceased husband in the Yasukuni National Shinto Shrine. The case is complicated, but it opens for discussion crucial issues that are widely debated, especially in Asia.
Teaching Note: 2 pages.

This case together with a teaching note and commentaries is also available in Robert A. and Alice F. Evans, *Human Rights: Dialogue Between the First and Third Worlds* (Maryknoll, NY: Orbis Books, 1983), 53–79.

EVANGELICALS IN A NEW KEY
Author: Robert Stivers
Setting: USA
Date: 1992
Topics: Theological education, Latin America, New Testament exegesis, evangelism, Third-world students in U.S. seminaries, relevance of the theological curriculum to issues in the world, fundamentalism-liberalism polarity, understanding calling, and initiating change.
Abstract: A young Latin American student attending a U.S. evangelical seminary becomes increasingly dubious about the program of study he

and others are being required to do. The courses appear largely unrelated to the issues of poverty, oppression, and injustice he knows first-hand. He is also beginning to question his understanding of his vocational calling. Seeking counsel from his pastor does not resolve the problem, but rather intensifies it. What options does he have and what should he do?
Teaching Note: 3 pages.

This case and the teaching note are found in the *Journal for Case Teaching* 4 (Fall 1992): 11–20, and in Alice Frazer Evans, Robert A. Evans, and David Roozen, 172–177. *The Globalization of Theological Education.* Maryknoll, NY: Orbis Books, 1993.

EVANGELISM EXPLOSION ON TRIAL
Author: Norman E. Thomas
Setting: Ohio
Date: 1986
Length: 7 pages
Topics: Mission of the church, evangelism, Christian witness
Abstract: A local church task force must decide whether to continue in the Evangelism Explosion training program. "Evangelism Explosion" is an evangelistic methodology developed by James Kennedy, pastor of the Coral Ridge Presbyterian Church in Fort Lauderdale, Florida, in 1963. Because of its propositional approach to personal evangelism, some are not convinced this is the best, much less the only way to do evangelism.
Teaching Note: 4 pages.

EYE OF THE NEEDLE
Authors: Robert A. and Alice F. Evans
Setting: A city in New England, U.S.A.
Date: 1983
Length: 17 pages
Topics: Civil rights, mission of the church, housing, racial discrimination
Abstract: A predominantly African-American and Hispanic inner-city community confronts the municipal government and business interests on the issue of adequate housing and urban gentrification.
Teaching Note: 2 pages.

This case together with a teaching note and commentaries is also available in Robert A. and Alice F. Evans, 123–154. *Human Rights: Dialogue Between the First and Third Worlds.* Maryknoll, NY: Orbis Books, 1983.

FAMILYHOOD OF GOD
Authors: Robert A. and Alice F. Evans
Setting: Tanzania 1972
Date: 1977
Length: 3 pages

Topics: Church and mission, health services, value conflict, socialism, Tanzania

Abstract: A German missionary nurse is pressured by a government official to use her influence to persuade the nomadic Masai people to settle in a permanent place. The missionary has sought for twenty years to serve the Masai, but she fears that government policy of forced settlement may ultimately destroy them as a people. She likewise knows that her work could be threatened if she resists doing what the government demands.

Teaching Note not available.

FARM WORKERS OF RHODESIA

Authors: R. A. Couture and S. Schmitz

Setting: Rhodesia 1976

Date: 1979

Length: 15 pages

Topics: Mission of the church, racial discrimination, rural and agricultural questions, unionization, and working conditions

Abstract: A community of American teaching nuns who staff a private high school in eastern Rhodesia (now Zimbabwe) is trying to decide whether to engage the school in a well-publicized, all-day teach-in to draw attention to the deplorable working conditions and inadequate wages of Rhodesia's farm workers.

Teaching Note not available.

FIRST BAPTIST CHURCH OF MIDDLETOWN

Author: G. L. Marshall

Setting: U.S.A.

Date: 1974

Length: 5 pages

Topics: Church and mission, social responsibility to unwed mothers, congregational controversy

Abstract: A pastor struggles with his desire to gain support for a potentially controversial project of opening a home for unwed mothers. Though the congregation is socially progressive and has accepted the pastor's leadership in beginning other programs, he fears this proposal will incite intense debate, divide the congregation, and possibly jeopardize all that has been accomplished thus far.

Teaching Note not available.

FOR ALL PEOPLE

Author: Leland Elhard

Setting: San Antonio, Texas

Date: 1987

Length: 8 pages

Topics: Church and mission, church in transitional neighborhood, cultural and ethnic tensions

Abstract: Seven months into his year-long internship, a young seminarian delivers a sermon to an old Lutheran congregation composed of white and upper middle class members. Only two in the church are non-Anglos. The church building is located in a neighborhood in transition from predominantly white and middle-class to Hispanic. Though the church has a food pantry open to all, there is fear and resentment toward Hispanics because of incidents in the past. In his sermon the intern addresses the need for the church to be inclusive and seize the opportunity to minister to all people in the neighborhood. Some react negatively and then ignore the issue. The intern wonders if his approach made any difference.

Teaching Note: 3 pages.

FUNERAL FOR NORIKO-SAN Parts A & B
Author: Alan Neely
Setting: Japan
Date: 1991
Length: Part A is 8 pages; Part B is 2 pages
Topics: Christian mission, Buddhism, cross-cultural communication of Christian faith, Japanese burial practices, question of syncretism
Abstract: An evangelical missionary woman has enjoyed a close friendship for many years with a Japanese business woman who just died of cancer. The missionary is invited by her friend's family to speak at the deceased woman's Buddhist funeral. If the missionary accepts the invitation, she will be accused of compromising the Christian faith. If she refuses, she risks offending the family of her friend.
Teaching Note: 5 pages.

This case and the teaching note are found in the *Journal for Case Teaching* 3 (Fall 1991): 43–50 (Part A), 51–52 (Part B), and 53–57 (Teaching Note). The case is also included in this book.

GOD BIGGIE BIGGIE
Author: Arthur G. Holder
Setting: Nigeria
Date: 1992
Length: 5 pages
Topics: Cross-cultural experience, globalization of theological education, ordination of women, conflicting expectations, women in ministry, clash of customs and values, New Testament exegesis (1 Cor 14:35 and Gal 3:28), and question of accommodation
Abstract: A husband and wife, both Episcopal ordinands, are studying in a Nigerian Anglican theological school as a part of a globalization program. He is recognized as a student moving toward ordination while she is

always presented as his wife. He is invited to preach repeatedly while she is ignored. They want to be sensitive to the culture, but they—he particularly—objects to the discrimination his wife is experiencing. A letter from the Nigerian bishop forces them to make a decision.
Teaching Note: 2 pages.

This case and the teaching note are found in the *Journal for Case Teaching* 3 (Fall 1992): 27–33.

GOSPEL AGENDA IN A GLOBAL CONTEXT
Author: Marie Augusta Neal
Setting: Boston
Date: 1987
Length: 10 pages + 3-page appendix
Topics: Poverty and the poor, Christian response to the poor, pedagogy for the non-poor, conscientization
Abstract: A Roman Catholic sister, teaching in a short-term institute, confronts a group of non-poor attending the institute with the question, "When the poor reach out to take what is rightfully theirs, what does the gospel mandate the non-poor to do?" The case traces the history of the Brazilian base Christian communities, the conscientization work that began with Paulo Freire, and subsequent efforts of various leaders including the teacher herself and others to develop useful pedagogies for working with the poor as well as the non-poor. A significant issue raised by the case is how their approach can be modified to make it more effective for educating the non-poor.
Teaching Note: 2 pages.

HAS THE CHURCH ANYTHING TO SAY?
Author: Alan Neely
Setting: Namibia and Southern Africa
Date: 1986
Length: 3 pages
Topics: Church and mission, role of missionaries in liberation, biblical authority and interpretation, liberation theology, apartheid, authority of international government bodies
Abstract: Black seminarians in Namibia decide to boycott classes to protest what a missionary teacher is saying about Christians obeying the government, but who claims he has no idea what the church's position should be in regard to the occupation of Namibia by South Africa, an occupation declared illegal by the World Court and the United Nations. Another missionary teacher is challenged to respond to the students' boycott and complaints.
Teaching Note: 3 pages.

HOW CAN WE ANSWER THIS LETTER?

Authors: Sister Bernice Kita and Alan Neely
Setting: Guatemala, Indian highlands
Date: 1987
Length: 4 pages
Topics: Church and mission, church and state, political and religious persecution, human rights, justice, Guatemala, and oppression in Central America
Abstract: Two Roman Catholic missionaries living and working in a Mayan Indian village in the highlands of Guatemala must balance their concern for the safety of church workers and a village elder, and the meaning of truth. The case highlights the tensions for those working with an oppressed indigenous people in a country known for its repressive and violent government.
Teaching Note: 4 pages.

I CAN KEEP QUIET NO LONGER Parts A & B

Author: Alan Neely
Setting: Nicaragua and U.S.A.
Date: 1986
Length: Part A is 6 pages. Part B is 5 pages
Topics: Church and mission, U.S. foreign policy, political neutrality for missionaries, Nicaragua, Central America
Abstract: A Protestant lay missioner in Nicaragua decides to write an open letter criticizing U.S. policy in Central America, even though he had made an earlier commitment to remain neutral. The mission agency's area director has to respond.
Teaching Note: 2 pages.

INITIATION

Authors: Robert A. and Alice F. Evans
Setting: Uganda
Date: 1977
Length: 3 pages
Topics: Church and mission, cross-cultural communication, Eucharist, Uganda
Abstract: A U.S. mission fraternal worker with many years of experience in East Africa is assigned the task of being a co-worker with a Ugandan, recently graduated from seminary, to establish a mission church. The Ugandan is asked by the village elders to serve the eucharist in connection with the traditional rite of Imbalu (circumcision of tribal youth as a sign of induction into adulthood). He expresses a profound reluctance to mix the two rites, the second of which he regards as non-Christian. The fraternal worker, committed to the indigenization of Christianity in East Africa, struggles with whether to express his disagreement with his young associate

and thereby jeopardize the partnership, or remain silent and thereby forfeit an opportunity for integrating the gospel and the culture.
Teaching Note not available.

This case is included in this book.

THE INTERCHURCH WORLD MOVEMENT
Author: David L. Townsley
Setting: USA following World War I
Date: 1982
Length: 8 pages + notes
Topics: Ecumenicism, church and mission, interdenominational cooperation in mission
Abstract: Following World War I, many Protestant leaders in the U.S.A. believed that American Protestantism was providentially indicated as the leader to fulfill the Christian mission in the world. The case outlines the formation of the Interchurch World Movement and provides a setting for discussing the prevailing idealism versus the socio-religious ambiguities of the era, the dynamics of the movement, its eventual collapse, and the feasibility of ecumenical cooperation.
Teaching Note: 2 pages.

I WANT TO BE A PRIEST
Author: Sister Marcella Hoesl
Setting: Guatemala
Date: 1986
Length: 5 pages
Topics: Church and mission, contextualization, ordination qualifications
Abstract: An American missionary priest struggles with the request of one of the lay leaders who wishes to become a priest. Mario has little formal education, but there is a critical shortage of priests. What is the best way a man of his age can serve the people in the highlands of Guatemala? The case confronts questions such as the role of the priest, the role of the laity, and the traditions of the church in the changing context.
Teaching Note: 2 pages.

This case is included in this book.

I WANT TO COME HOME
Author: Alan Neely
Setting: Peru
Date: 1979
Length: 4 pages
Topics: Short-term missioners, preparation and administration, Peru
Abstract: A young college graduate decides to volunteer for a two-year assignment as a Baptist missioner to Peru. Following six weeks of prepara-

tion, she is sent to Lima to work in the Mission office, only to discover that her job expectations do not conform to the reality of the situation. Deciding after the first week that she has made a mistake, she informs the missionaries and the Mission Board that she wants to return to the United States. Attempts are made to persuade her to remain in Peru, and she weighs the consequences of staying or returning to her homeland.
Teaching Note: 3 pages.

I WAS A STRANGER
Authors: Robert A. and Alice F. Evans
Setting: Switzerland
Date: 1983
Length: 10 pages
Topics: Mission of the church, migrant workers
Abstract: A Swiss pastor struggles with the role of the church in relation to issues dealing with migrant workers. Though the setting is in Switzerland, the issues are germane to the North American situation.
Teaching Note: 2 pages.

This case together with the appendix and the teaching note may also be found in Robert A. and Alice F. Evans, 155–166. *Human Rights: A Dialogue Between the First and Third Worlds.* Maryknoll, NY: Orbis Books, 1993.

I WAS A STRANGER AND YOU WELCOMED ME
Authors: Brian Banwell and Alice F. Evans
Setting: South Africa
Date: 1991
Length: 4 pages + 2-page appendix
Topics: Homelessness, apartheid, church and state, racism, mission of the church
Abstract: A white South African pastor is confronted by a black homeless couple seeking shelter. His response is complicated by legal restrictions, church authorities, and possible reaction by his congregation. The study offers ready entry into the issues of homelessness in North America.
Teaching Note: 4 pages.

This case together with the appendix and teaching note may also be found in the *Journal for Case Teaching* 3 (Fall 1991): 59–68.

I WAS IN PRISON
Authors: Ryoko Taki and Alan Neely
Setting: Irian Jaya
Date: 1991
Length: 5 pages
Topics: Church and mission, political involvement by missionaries, nationalism, government oppression of minority groups, human rights

Abstract: A Japanese missionary couple, whose work in agricultural development has just begun, consider jeopardizing their tenuous visa status in
Irian Jaya, Indonesia, by visiting friends whom the missionaries believe
have been wrongly imprisoned by the Indonesian government for "ter-
rorism."

Teaching Note: 6 pages.

This case and the teaching note are found in the *Journal for Case Teaching*
3 (Fall 1991): 69–79. It is also included in this book.

JOHN HOWARD YODER AND THE HOMOGENEOUS UNIT PRINCIPLE

Author: E. A. Martens

Setting: U.S.A.

Date: 1980

Length: 11 pages + bibliography

Topics: Church and mission, Christian ethics, church history, church growth,
homogeneous unit principle

Abstract: A well-known Mennonite theologian is asked to write and present
a response to C. Peter Wagner's paper, "How Ethical is the Homogeneous
Unit Principle?" Yoder's response is to be given to a colloquium sponsored
by the Lausanne Continuation Committee of the International Congress
on World Evangelism. His dilemma is how to critique the Church Growth
theory in order to get a hearing.

Teaching Note: 2 pages.

KIMBANGUIST MEMBERSHIP IN THE WORLD COUNCIL OF CHURCHES

Author: Louis Weeks

Setting: Congo and Canterbury, England, 1969

Date: 1975

Length: 5 pages

Topics: Church and mission, African independent churches, ecumenism, theological orthodoxy

Abstract: The Church of Jesus Christ on Earth Through the Prophet Simon
Kimbangu applies for membership in the World Council of Churches.
Representatives of the Kimbanguist Church indicate their motive for
requesting admission to the WCC is that their participation would fulfill
a prophecy of Simon Kimbangu. Members of the WCC Central Committee
are faced with three options: refuse to accept them, request a *pro forma*
investigation, or, given some of their theological views, ask for a full
investigation of the Church. If accepted for membership, the Church would
be the first Two-Thirds World indigenous body received into the WCC
without historic ties to a western parent denomination. The case includes
the historical background of the Kimbanguists and provides readers with

sufficient information to understand why some would question whether the church was sufficiently Christian to justify admission to the WCC. Teaching Note not available.

LAUSANNE CONGRESS, 1974
Authors: Jack Rogers, M. Gallion, G. Hess, and D. Price
Setting: Switzerland 1974
Date: 1976
Length: 9 pages + 11 pages of exhibits
Topics: Church and mission, church membership, evangelism, and social responsibility
Abstract: Some four thousand evangelicals from around the world meet in Lausanne, Switzerland, for an International Congress on World Evangelism initiated by the Billy Graham Evangelistic Association. Tensions develop between the proponents of the "church growth" strategy of cross-cultural evangelism and Two-Thirds World critics of what they call "cultural Christianity" in Europe and the United States. Also, disciples of Francis Schaeffer demand a more exclusive doctrinal statement about the Bible. The exhibits include a copy of "The Lausanne Covenant" as well as other doctrinal statements.
Teaching Note not available.

This case is also available under the title, "The International Congress on World Evangelization (A.D. 1974)" in *Case Studies in Christ and Salvation,* ed. Jack Rogers, Ross Mackenzie, and Louis Weeks, 151–160. Philadelphia: Westminster Press, 1974.

A LETTER FROM CLAIRE
Author: Alan Neely
Setting: USA
Date: 1988
Length: 5 pages
Topics: Religious pluralism, inter-religious encounter, exclusive claims of Christianity, New Testament witness and exegesis, Christian fundamentalism, the nature of mission
Abstract: The pastor of a university church is troubled because a student who has been active in the church has almost ceased to participate. He receives a letter from her in which she discloses the reason for her behavior, namely, she has begun to question the Christian assertion that Jesus is the only way to God and to salvation.
Teaching Note: 4 pages.

This case is included in this book.

MARTYR
Author: Robert A. Evans

Setting: Uganda and Kenya
Date: 1977
Length: 5 pages
Topics: Church and state, mission, religious persecution, role of pastor
Abstract: A well-known Ugandan Anglican priest who is also a church history professor wonders if he should return to Uganda and almost certain persecution by the government's secret police. He is torn by his sense of responsibility for his parishioners and students, and the possibility that, if he returns, he will be arrested and perhaps killed. Conflicting advice from colleagues heightens his dilemma. Though the individuals in the case and the situation described are dated, the issues are perennial.
Teaching Note not available.

MISSION ENTERPRISE LOAN AND INVESTMENT COMMITTEE
Authors: J. B. Silvers and E. M. Graham
Setting: New York, the United Methodist Church, 1970
Date: 1973
Length: 22 pages
Topics: Mission of the church, investing church funds in minority business ventures, social responsibility
Abstract: The Mission Enterprise Loan and Investment Committee of the United Methodist Church's Board of Missions encounters serious difficulties when in its efforts to remedy economic injustice a high rate of failures of minority businesses result because of their inability to repay the loans. Students are asked to assess the actions of the Committee and make recommendations about future strategies.
Teaching Note not available.

MORE QUESTIONS THAN ANSWERS
Author: Anne Reissner
Setting: Southern Africa and USA
Date: 1992
Length: 8 pages
Topics: Globalization in theological education, poverty, injustice, vocational calling, and Third World immersion experience
Abstract: Responsible for teaching a basic moral theology course, a young theological teacher who has traveled little outside the United States wonders how he can incorporate the impact of the recent wrenching and profound learning he had gained from an immersion seminar in Zimbabwe and in South Africa to motivate his students to grapple with global ethical issues. Though he has taught the course several times before, he decides on a different approach. Is this wise and will students conclude the course with questions and no answers?
Teaching Note: 2 pages.

This case study and teaching note are found in the *Journal for Case Teaching* 4 (Fall 1992): 1–10, and in Alice Frazer Evans, Robert A. Evans, and David A. Roozen, 288–294. *The Globalization of Theological Education.* Maryknoll, NY: Orbis Books, 1993.

MOZAMBIQUE MISSION
Author: H. M. Goodpasture
Setting: Mozambique 1971
Date: 1975
Length: 5 pages + 7 pages of appendices
Topics: Church and mission, colonialism, White Fathers, guerilla activity, concordats, the Vatican, Mozambique
Abstract: A group of White Fathers must make a decision about whether to remain in Mozambique during the morally ambiguous guerilla struggle against the Portuguese colonial government, or go elsewhere. Complicating the matter is the fact that Portugal and the Vatican have signed a concordat giving privileges to the Roman Catholic missioners on the condition that they support Portuguese rule. The missioners find themselves having to choose between abiding by the treaty and thus favoring in effect what they perceive to be an unjust colonial system, or heeding their collective conscience, announcing their support of the liberation movement and abandoning the country. In short the missioners can stay by remaining silent, or side with the people and be forced to leave.
Teaching Note not available.

NEVER SAY DIE Parts A & B
Author: Marjorie Hall Davis
Setting: Massachusetts
Date: 1982
Length: Part A is 8 pages + 3 pages of appendices; Part B is 3 pages
Topics: Church and mission, church planting
Abstract: A pastor of a new Protestant congregation in a highly mobile suburban community disagrees with the church's decision regarding its future. The church had decreased from its high of 75 members to less than 25. Though attendance under the present pastor has increased from an average of 18 to 24, the total number of active members is still only 20. Moreover, despite the pastor's vigorous visitation work, his emphasis on church growth, and his efforts to involve the members of the congregation in the church's ministry of witness, the future to him appears bleak. The congregation initially votes to close and then reverses its decision. The climax of the case comes when the church's steering committee meets to consider their options.
Teaching Note: 2 pages.

NO ROOM AT THE INN
Author: R. S. Anderson
Setting: Pacific coastal city, U.S.A.
Date: 1977
Length: 6 pages
Topics: Urban mission, church conflict, leadership, social responsibility
Abstract: The senior pastor of a large church along with the church staff
   have initiated a ministry of housing street people, some of whom are
   teenage runaways. Two of the three church trustees object and then resign
   over the issue of using church property for this ministry to the homeless.
   Also, there is the threat from law enforcement agencies to take legal action
   against the church for what is described as "harboring fugitives from the
   law." The pastor is caught between the need for the ministry and those
   who are conservative elements in the church.
Teaching Note not available.

NOWHERE TO LAY HIS HEAD
Author: Philip E. Devenish
Setting: Maine
Date: 1989
Length: 2 pages
Topics: Church and mission, poverty, homelessness, Tourette's syndrome,
   neurological disease, and church support for people with psycho-physi-
   cal disabilities
Abstract: A pastor receives a telephone call from a person he does not know.
   The time is early January. The individual who calls says he has no food
   and no heat in the cabin where he is staying. He also says he is suffering
   from Tourette's syndrome. The pastor visits the man that day and learns
   he is a musical genius who because of his disability has been rejected by
   his family and friends and victimized by the medical system. The pastor's
   question is whether he should involve the church in the man's plight, and
   if so, how.
Teaching Note: 2 pages.

   This case and the teaching note are found in the *Journal for Case Teaching*
1 (Fall 1989): 51–54.

OPERATION REACH OUT
Author: Robert A. Evans
Setting: U.S.A.
Date: 1974
Length: 12 pages
Topics: Mission of the church, evangelism, social action, role of the pastor
   and other church leaders, conflict
Abstract: A Presbyterian church with a strong tradition of social action is
   plunged into conflict over a church-approved program of evangelism.

Initially, individuals in the congregation resist involvement. The pastor and the evangelism committee are upset because of the small number participating. The climax comes when on a Sunday morning the pastor attempts to pressure congregants to remain for lunch and then make an evangelistic call that afternoon. The conflict escalates when subsequently the motion is made to eliminate the evangelistic program.
Teaching Note not available.

For a shorter version of this case, see "Proclaim the Good News."

PEACE CHILD
Author: Jack Rogers
Setting: Irian Jaya
Date: 1977
Length: 4 pages
Topics: Church and mission, cross-cultural communication of Christianity, ethics, rites and symbols.
Abstract: Based on the book by the same title, the case centers on the difficulty in communicating the Christian faith to an indigenous people whose highest values are treachery, deception, and violence, but who have a ritual (with remarkable parallels to Christian rites and symbols) whereby peace, mutual trust, and forgiveness are possible. Teachers are strongly advised to read *Peace Child* by Don Richardson (Glendale, CA: Regal Books, 1974) and note other parallels not included in the case study.
Teaching Note not available.

This case is also available with commentaries in *Christian Theology: A Case Study Approach*, ed. Robert A. Evans and Thomas D. Parker, 108–132. New York: Harper & Row, 1976.

"PHYLLIS CROWDER IS PREGNANT!" Parts A, B, and C
Author: Alan Neely
Setting: Lebanon and USA
Date: 1995
Length: 8 pages + Parts B (1 page) and C (1 page)
Topics: Sexuality, immorality, Lebanon, missionary and mission agency policy, abortion
Abstract: A missionary wife has a sexual affair and is pregnant with the child of a national pastor who was her language school teacher. A mission agency executive now is faced with attempting to minister to the missionary wife and her traumatized husband, as well as follow the agency's policy regarding missionaries who are guilty of immorality. Then there is the question of the fetus.
Teaching Note: 3 pages.

Part A of this case is included in this book.

PROCLAIM THE GOOD NEWS
Authors: Robert A. Evans and Alice F. Evans
Setting: U.S.A.
Date: 1977
Length: 3 pages
Topics: Mission of the church, evangelism, social action, role of the pastor and other church leaders, conflict
Abstract: A condensed version of Case "Operation Reach Out" (see p. 283 above).
Teaching Note not available.

This case is also available with commentaries in *Christian Theology: A Case Study Approach,* ed. Robert A. Evans and Thomas D. Parker, 192–211. New York: Harper & Row, 1976.

PROPHET OR PROVOCATEUR
Author: Robert A. Evans
Setting: Brazil
Date: 1980
Length: 8 pages
Topics: Mission of the church, human rights, economic justice, liberation theology, Brazil, multinational corporations
Abstract: A General Electric executive who is also a church officer returns from a trip to Brazil. He struggles with the questions regarding whether he should recommend that his company expand in Brazil and whether he should urge his 1500-member-church in Stamford, CT, to make Brazil a mission priority. A U.S. Methodist missionary to Brazil is arrested, imprisoned, and tortured by the Brazilian government police, thus occasioning an analysis by four Brazilian church leaders with radically differing opinions about how the U.S. church should respond to the Brazilian situation. Their positions range from avoiding political involvement for the sake of evangelism to being in solidarity with those struggling for economic and political justice. The case, though dated, raises significant issues for those involved in multinational businesses as well as the role of the U.S. church in the struggle for human rights and justice.
Teaching Note: 3 pages.

This case together with a teaching note and commentaries is also available in Robert A. and Alice F. Evans, 177–197. *Human Rights: Dialogue Between the First and Third Worlds.* Maryknoll, NY: Orbis Books, 1983.

RED JACKET AND THE MISSIONARY
Author: Garth M. Rosell
Setting: New England in late eighteenth century
Date: 1979
Length: 4 pages

Topics: Church and mission, theology, relations with Native Americans, and the role of the church

Abstract: A young Protestant missionary from Boston encounters "Red Jacket," the principal spokesperson for the chiefs and warriors of six Native American nations. The missionary is confronted by the injustices suffered by the indigenous peoples at the hand of the North American colonists and government, U.S. policy regarding Native Americans, and the role of the church.

Teaching Note not available.

This case is also available in *American Christianity,* ed. Ronald C. White, Jr., Louis B. Weeks, and Garth M. Rosell, 70–74. Grand Rapids, MI: Eerdmans, 1986. The title, however, has been changed to "Red Jacket and the Missionary Impulse."

RETURNING HOME

Authors: Alice F. and Robert A. Evans

Setting: Kenya and Uganda

Date: 1981

Length: 9 pages

Topics: Church in mission, value conflict, responsibility to family and church responsibilities

Abstract: A self-exiled Christian Ugandan university professor tries to decide if he should return to his war-torn homeland and leave a safe position in Kenya. His internal conflict stems from his commitment to the Church, his anguish over the suffering masses in his home country, and the security of his family, both his wife and children who are with him, and his extended family in Uganda. The case also deals with the question of the Church's role in rebuilding a nation following a war.

Teaching Note: 2 pages.

This case together with a teaching note and commentaries is also available in Robert A. and Alice F. Evans, 80–96. *Human Rights: Dialogue Between the First and Third Worlds.* Maryknoll, NY: Orbis Books, 1983.

ROBERTO DE NOBILI: AN EXAMPLE OF MISSIONARY IDENTIFICATION

Author: Alan Neely

Setting: India, seventeenth century

Date: 1979

Length: 7 pages

Topics: Church and mission, cross-cultural communication of Christianity, indigenization, evangelization, Hinduism

Abstract: In 1606 a young Italian Jesuit, Roberto de Nobili, was sent to an inland town in Southeast India. Within two years he developed a new approach for the evangelization of high caste Hindus. His methods, how-

ever, incited a storm of protest which impeded his work for more than two decades. Though ostensibly the controversy was resolved by a papal decree, the missiological issues raised by the de Nobili case remain unsettled and provoke widely differing opinions today.
Teaching Note: 5 pages.

This case is included in this book.

SACRED SITES
Author: Gordon S. Dicker
Setting: Australia
Date: 1981
Length: 8 pages
Topics: Mission of the church, land rights for aboriginal peoples, the indigenous belief in the sacredness of the land, church and state
Abstract: A church's National Board of Social Responsibility meets to decide whether to support an Australian aboriginal protest of proposed oil drilling on sacred sites. The case examines the struggle of the aboriginal peoples to protect their land from multinational exploitation, and the broader issue of the sacredness of land for many minority indigenous peoples in the world. The case is written from the perspective of a theologically conservative but socially sensitive minster who is a member of the church board.
Teaching Note: 1 page.

This case together with a teaching note and commentaries is also available in Robert A. and Alice F. Evans, 97–123. *Human Rights: Dialogue Between the First and Third Worlds.* Maryknoll, NY: Orbis Books, 1983; and in Alice Frazer Evans, Robert A. Evans, and David Roozen, ed., 104–113. *The Globalization of Theological Education.* Maryknoll, NY: Orbis Books, 1993.

SANCTUARY
Author: Norman E. Thomas
Setting: U.S.A.
Date: 1986
Length: 8 pages + 3 pages of appendices
Topics: Church and mission, human rights, church and state, refugees, Central America
Abstract: A Protestant congregation faces the controversial decision concerning whether they should declare their church a sanctuary for refugees fleeing the violence in their Central America homelands. The historical, ethical, political, and legal issues as well as the ambiguities posed by the sanctuary movement are surfaced.
Teaching Note: 3 pages.

A SECONDARY MANIFESTATION
Author: Alice Frazer Evans
Setting: Brazil
Date: 1980
Length: 5 pages
Topics: Mission of the church, charismatic movement, Brazil, Baptist denomination in Brazil, Holy Spirit
Abstract: José Silva, a prominent Brazilian Baptist lawyer, has been selected to represent his church in the annual meeting of the Brazilian Baptist Convention. An *ad hoc* committee appointed to study the sweep of the charismatic movement through the Baptist churches has announced that the committee will recommend "disfellowshipping," i.e., excluding churches engaged in or permitting "healing and speaking in tongues." Though Silva had openly supported the position of the committee, a recent personal experience now causes him to question his previous conviction. He now is struggling with what he should say and do.
Teaching Note: 2 pages.

"SHOULD I ACCEPT?"
Author: Alan Neely
Setting: Taiwan
Date: 1995
Length: 3 pages
Topics: Ancestor veneration, Buddhism, Confucianism, inter-faith relations, Taiwan
Abstract: A young Roman Catholic girl, Meijung, accepts an invitation to celebrate a Buddhist holiday with three of her friends, one a Roman Catholic, another a Baptist, and the third a Buddhist in whose home they meet. After going together to the temple with her Buddhist friend's family and seeing and learning the significance of the rite, her Buddhist friend's mother invites Meijung and the others to return to the home and share the food that had been used in the Buddhist ceremony. One of the girls accepts immediately, but the second declines, saying she could not eat food that had been used in a Buddhist rite. It is an awkward moment, and Meijung does not know what she should do.
Teaching Note: 3 pages.

This case is included in this book.

SHOULD I BAPTIZE THEM NOW?
Author: Alan Neely
Setting: Kenya
Date: 1983
Length: 4 pages

Topics: Mission of the church, polygamy, Christian marriage, cross-cultural communication, church in Africa

Abstract: A group of Masai women request Christian baptism from a Baptist missionary couple who have been teaching the women the Bible for many months. The women, however, are wives of polygynous husbands, and Baptists in Kenya have thus far refused to baptize such persons, husbands or wives. The missionary does not necessarily agree with the policy, but should he take the risk of trying to change it now?

Teaching Note: 7 pages.

This case is included in this book.

SHOULD I BURN INCENSE AT GRANDPA'S GRAVE?

Author: Henry N. Smith

Setting: Hong Kong

Date: 1992

Length: 5 pages

Topics: Contextualization, ancestor veneration, Ching Ming festival, Christianity and culture, disillusionment with traditional religion, and the ensuing family conflict.

Abstract: A young Chinese woman who has recently become a Christian tells her father that she can no longer participate in the veneration ceremonies. He is incensed and accuses her of disrespect and turning her back on her Chinese heritage. She must participate without reservation, he insists, or he will forbid her from studying or practicing her "new religion." She goes to her pastor, tells him her dilemma, and asks his counsel.

Teaching Note: 3 pages.

SINGING THE LORD'S SONG

Authors: Thomas H. Graves and Alan Neely

Setting: Zimbabwe

Date: 1991

Length: 6 pages

Topics: Church and mission, contextualization, indigenous music, mission strategy, conflict, syncretism

Abstract: A Methodist missionary couple appointed as music missionaries attempt to introduce indigenous instruments and hymn tunes in the seminary and churches. The national pastors appear satisfied with Western hymns and instruments, and missionary colleagues voice their concern about the syncretism of Christianity and animism. The issue is discussed at a meeting of the missionaries, and the couple is given the opportunity to respond to their critics in a less than ideal setting.

Teaching Note: 4 pages.

This case and the teaching note are found in the *Journal for Case Teaching* 3 (Fall 1991): 125–134. It is also included in this book.

SLAVES, OBEY YOUR MASTERS
Author: Henry N. Smith
Setting: Jamaica and London
Date: 1992
Length: 5 pages
Topics: Slavery, biblical teaching and interpretation, violence, official mission
  policy of non-involvement in political and social issues, liberation theology
Abstract: A missionary in early nineteenth century Jamaica faces the agonizing dilemma of conforming to the officially stated policy of his mission
  society, namely, to refrain from any involvement in political issues, and
  the worsening conditions and sufferings of the slaves. The missionary's
  situation is complicated by his growing conviction that the institution of
  slavery is evil and should be abolished. Furthermore, suppression of a
  recent slave revolt is threatening the missionary's work with the slaves.
  What is he to do in view of the missionary society's prohibition and the
  teaching of the New Testament that slaves should obey their masters?
Teaching Note: 4 pages

This case and the teaching note are found in the *Journal for Case Teaching*
4 (Fall 1992): 93–101.

THOMAS PERKINS, SHORT-TERM MISSIONARY
Author: Calvin H. Reber, Jr.
Setting: Hong Kong
Date: 1976
Length: 6 pages
Topics: Church and mission, role of short-term missionaries, mission and
  political questions, value conflict, church and state, Hong Kong
Abstract: A short-term missionary tries to decide if he should attempt to
  renew his visa, remain in Hong Kong, and continue his social ministry
  activities which are disapproved by the government and church authorities.
  He sees what he believes is a critical need for social change, but he is
  convinced that it is being blocked by religious and political leaders.
Teaching Note: 2 pages.

TOAST FOR BOB ALLISON
Author: B. E. Adams
Setting: Argentina
Date: 1979
Length: 3 pages
Topics: National church and missionaries, ethical issue of beverage alcohol,
  conflict in personal and collective values, Argentina
Abstract: A North American missionary is faced with having to agree with
  most of his missionary colleagues who frown on drinking wine at any
  time—a position supported by the missionary's denomination—or follow-

ing his conscience and agreeing openly with Argentine church leaders and members, including the pastors, who customarily serve and drink wine with meals as well as using wine in the sacrament of the Lord's Supper. Teaching Note: 1 page.

TO EAT OR NOT TO EAT
Author: Terrance Tiessen
Setting: Philippines
Date: 1991
Length: 4 pages
Topics: Church and mission, cross-cultural application of Christian principles, biblical exegesis of Acts 15
Abstract: An evangelical Protestant missionary is faced with the possibility of offending neighbors whom he is trying to evangelize and the local church members who believe that Acts 15 prohibits consuming blood.
Teaching Note: 2 pages.

This case and the teaching note are found in the *Journal for Case Teaching* 3 (Fall 1991): 143–148.

TO GO HOME AGAIN
Author: Erskine Clarke
Setting: Central America and USA
Date: 1992
Length: 4 pages
Topics: Central America, cross-cultural immersion, US foreign policy, poverty and wealth, "liberal guilt," and calling.
Abstract: Inner conflict and confusion as to her calling to ministry are the results of a required immersion experience in Central America for a middle-aged married and prosperous woman seminarian. Can requiring such a course be justified? If so, what is she to do now?
Teaching Note: 2 pages.

This case and the teaching note are found in the *Journal for Case Teaching* 4 (Fall 1992): 21–26, and in Alice Frazer Evans, Robert A. Evans, and David A. Roozen, 200–203. *The Globalization of Theological Education.* Maryknoll, NY: Orbis Books, 1993.

TROUBLE IN TOGOLAND
Author: Alan Neely
Setting: W. Africa
Date: 1981
Length: 5 pages
Topics: Church and mission, missionary imperialism, liberation theology, role of short-term missioners

Abstract: A short-term Baptist missioner returns to the United States after two years in W. Africa. His experiences were basically positive, but he is anxious about the future of the work. A letter from a short-term colleague still in Togo reminds the returnee of the continued missionary domination of the church and the efforts on the part of a young Togolese pastor for liberation from missionary control. The letter writer describes recent events and asks for advice, thereby posing a serious dilemma for the returnee.
Teaching Note: 2 pages.

THE UNITED PARISH IN BROOKLINE
Author: Ann D. Myers
Setting: Boston
Date: 1973
Length: 24 pages + 15 pages of exhibits
Topics: Church and ministry to homosexuals
Abstract: The Homophile Community Health Service, providing psychiatric counseling and referral assistance to homosexuals of the greater Boston area, requests the use of several rooms for individual and group counseling sessions in the facilities of the United Parish Church. The congregation has already made a financial donation to the Service, but now they must decide whether to grant this second request. Crucial issues about how the church should structure its mission effort are raised. Though the case was written in the 1970s, the problems are painfully contemporary.
Teaching Note not available.

This case may be found also in *Case-Book on Church and Society,* ed. Keith R. Bridston, Fred K. Foulkes, Ann D. Myers, and Louis Weeks, 55–94. Nashville: Abingdon, 1974. Also included is a 5-page appendix on the practice of homosexuality and the ethics of the Holy Scripture.

WALNUT AVENUE CHURCH
Author: R. W. Ackerman
Setting: Philadelphia
Date: 1972
Length: 4 pages + 1 page exhibit
Topics: Mission of the church, conflict, congregational polity, and the role of the pastor and other leaders.
Abstract: The steeple of an inner city church is badly damaged by lightning forcing the congregation to face the issue of their purpose and ministry. The membership has been declining, but those who remain are committed to a ministry to their neighborhood. To repair the steeple would cost some $40,000, and the committee in charge recommends proceeding with the repairs. Members of the Mission and Community Committee object saying the poverty and problems of the city are such that to spend money repairing a steeple is poor stewardship. The individual from whose perspective the

case is written ponders the nature of the church's mission and what should be done.

Teaching Note not available.

This case may be found also in *Case-Book on Church and Society,* ed. Keith R. Bridston, Fred K. Foulkes, Ann D. Myers, and Louis Weeks, 15–20. Nashville: Abingdon Press, 1974. And in the *Journal for Case Teaching* 1 (Fall 1989): 107–112.

WHAT KIND OF GOD WOULD LET THIS HAPPEN? Parts A & B
Author: Alan Neely
Setting: U.S.A.
Date: 1991
Length: Part A is 3 pages; Part B is 2 pages
Topics: Jewish-Christian encounter, problem of premature death, communication of Christian faith, theodicy
Abstract: A theology professor meets an elderly Jewish couple in a restaurant. When the couple learns the professor's vocation, they tell him their son has just died of a heart attack, leaving his wife and children. The question is the title of the case. The case includes a Part B, 2 pages, which describes the professor's subsequent action and the response of the couple.
Teaching Note: 4 pages.

This case and the teaching note are found in the *Journal for Case Teaching* 3 (Fall 1991):149–158. It is also included in this book.

"WHAT'S THE MATTER, ABDARAMAN?" Parts A & B
Author: Alan Neely
Setting: Algeria, North Africa
Date: 1983
Length: Part A is 4 pages; Part B is 1 page
Topics: Mission of the church, Christian-Muslim encounter, cross-cultural communication, evangelism, Islam
Abstract: Carlo Carretto, a member of the community of the Little Brothers of Jesus, has become a close friend of a little Muslim boy named Abdaraman. One evening Abdaraman cannot talk, and he begins to cry. When Carlo asks him why he is crying, he learns the lad is distressed because Carlo is not a Muslim. Carlo is pressed to respond to the boy's anxiety.
Teaching Note: 2 pages.

This case is included in this book.

WHEN ECUMENICAL RELATIONS COOL
Authors: R. Gordon Nodwell
Setting: Atlantic costal city of 200,000, U.S.A.
Date: 1976

Length: 5 pages

Topics: Church and mission, ecumenism, Roman Catholic-Protestant cooperation and relations

Abstract: Recent acceptance of Roman Catholic representatives in the local
council of churches and their participation in what is called a "School for
Marriage," an on-going program of pre-marriage counseling established
earlier by the council, leads to complications. The future of the School,
the non-Roman Catholics say, is threatened by what appears to be a move
by the Roman Catholic Archdiocese to take over the program.

Teaching Note not available.

WORLD COUNCIL OF CHURCHES, FIFTH ASSEMBLY, NAIROBI 1975

Authors: Roberta Hestenes, Kirk Kestler, Jim Reeve, et al. Written under the
supervision of Jack Rogers

Setting: Nairobi, Kenya, 1975

Date: 1976

Length: 13 pages + 3 pages of exhibits

Topics: Church and mission, ecumenism, contextualization, evangelism and
social action, inter-religious dialogue

Abstract: Written from the perspective of the General Secretary of the WCC,
the case raises the issues implicit and debated at the fifth assembly, issues
such as the tensions over evangelism versus social action, contextualization
of the Christian message, inter-religious dialogue, and the need for broader
participation and support of member churches. The role of the General
Secretary in facing these issues is also a significant question.

Teaching Note not available.

This case is also available in *Case Studies in Christ and Salvation,* ed.
Jack Rogers, Ross Mackenzie, and Louis Weeks, 161–176. Philadelphia:
Westminster Press, 1974.

WORLD HUNGER, THE FIRST BAPTIST CHURCH, AND THE SAND-
INISTAS

Author: Alan Neely

Setting: Kentucky and Nicaragua

Date: 1985

Length: 8 pages

Topics: World hunger, poverty, church and mission, U.S. foreign policy,
Marxism

Abstract: A Baptist seminary professor and former missionary to Latin
America becomes interim pastor of the First Baptist Church. He is invited
to speak at a church dinner designed to raise money for world hunger,
and he tells about what the Nicaraguan government has done to combat
hunger in that country since 1979. One person attending the dinner takes
strong exception with the professor's "soft attitude on communism" and

says so in a strongly critical letter. The professor wonders how he should respond.
Teaching Note: 2 pages.

"YOU MUST PURIFY THIS HOUSE"
Author: Alan Neely
Setting: Nigeria
Date: 1995
Length: 4 pages
Topics: The Fulani, Nigeria, West Africa, purification rites, evangelization, reverence for life (insects), inculturation, clash of world views, Islam
Abstract: A British Wesleyan Methodist couple have returned to Nigeria from a year of leave in England. The second day after their arrival they discover a colony of bees in the wall of their house, and they proceed to exterminate the insects. When their Fulani Muslim neighbors discover what has happened, they are shocked that the missionaries would recklessly kill the bees that God had beneficently sent. Later, several Fulani elders come and declare that the house must be purified by the shaman, or else the missionaries will suffer the wrath of God. Unsure about how they should respond, the missionaries seek counsel.
Teaching Note: 3 pages.

This case is included in this book.